The GDL Cookbook 2

Teach yourself GDL by the cookbook method
• and •
'ArchiCAD Tips and Tricks'

by David Nicholson-Cole

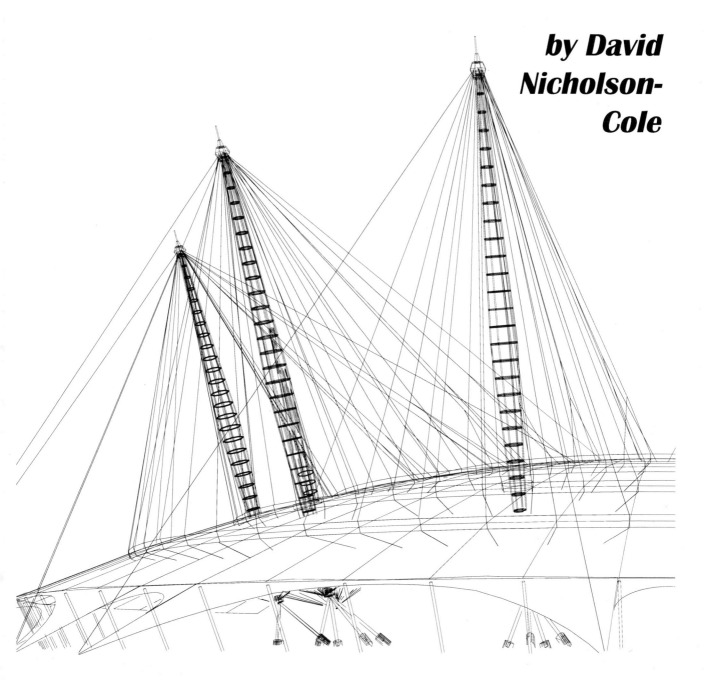

The GDL Cookbook2 is published by
Marmalade Graphics, Nottingham ©1998, 1999, 2000
Marmalade Graphics, 15 Elmtree Ave, West Bridgford, Nottingham
NG2 7JU, England
International Tel +44-115-945-5077 : Fax +44-115-945-5121:
UK Tel 0115-945-5077 : Fax 0115-945-5121:
email: davidnc@innotts.co.uk / david@the-object-factory.com

Cookbook Website> http://www.nottingham.ac.uk/sbe/cookbook/
The GDL Cookbook is distributed through the Internet,
ArchiCAD dealers and by word of mouth
• ISBN 0 9535216 0 5 •
First published March 98; This edition: Cookbook 2.10 March 2000
Text printed by Alpha Graphics, Angel Row, Nottingham, England, covers by Adlard Print.
Set in Britannica, Garamond and Frutiger, using Adobe Pagemaker on a G3 Powerbook

The Cookbook2 is to be extended as a series of web based supplements, on a subscription basis. Please look at **www.the-object-factory.com** for further information. The Object Factory offers my-object creation, object sales, and a subscription based GDL support service for ArchiCAD users throughout the world.

the-object-factory.com

Key to Illustrations:

Interleaves bottom left: Model of Wellington Circus for landscaping proposals by Marsh Grokowski and Sculpture by Anish Kapoor, model by DNC.

Inset back cover and interleaves: Staircase at 9 Sloane St by Eva Jiricna, model by Cathy Wood (University of Nottingham 1998), one of DNC's students.

Back cover: The Tower crane, David N-C's second GDL object (yeah, those were the crazy days, my friends.) (DNC's first was the 'Bad Chair', in the Discovery course.)

Cover and Frontispiece: Millennium Dome (Richard Rogers Partnership), model by Steve Brown (University of Nottingham 1998), one of DNC's students.

What is GDL?

GEOMETRIC Description Language (GDL) is ArchiCAD's built in scripting language.

GDL scripting in a nutshell...

GDL uses a variety of written commands like EXTRUDE, BLOCK and TUBE. Combining these in GDL, you can built up **2D and 3D objects** which can be used in ArchiCAD as Library Parts.

• Because GDL includes Cylinder, Cones, Tubes, Surfaces and much more, you can make **Objects** that cannot be made with wall+slab tools.

• Because you can use variables like X and Y, you can make the objects change their parameters – they can be **Parametric**.

• Because you can write IF statements, you can make the objects obey rules – they can be **Smart**.

• Because you can build in repetitive loops, you can go beyond object making – and make **Tools**.

• Because you can rotate and move elements, you can make **Mechanisms**.

What can you do with GDL?

WITH GDL, you can build **structural elements** that look right for their purpose, **elements of detail** that make a building model look authentic, **furniture** that is smart and elegant, **lights** that let you turn them on and tune their luminance, **windows** that can open or swivel, **doors** that can change their panel styles, **stairs** that offer a choice of landing and handrail styles, **picture objects** on which you can plaster building elevations and thus build whole street scenes, **2D drawing tools** that can enhance our productivity – and much more besides.

• **Let's learn something of this power!**

Who is GDL really useful for?

THE normal **ArchiCAD user** can use GDL to enhance the quality of their models, improve their productivity, and to further their personal skills base.

The **component manufacturer** can see GDL as a way of providing components and tools that will encourage ArchiCAD users to specify their products. The **engineer** can see GDL as a means of providing building components that can display levels of intelligence and adaptability. The would-be **GDL developer** can find enough in GDL to grasp career enhancing opportunities. The **university student** can find a way to extend all that maths learnt at college and add value to their architectural portfolio. The **ArchiCAD reseller** has the means to prove to potential customers that ArchiCAD carries a significant power advantage.

Could you learn GDL?

ALL major CAD packages have an internal scripting language. It is most fortunate for ArchiCAD users that GDL grew out of BASIC, the most popular and widely taught programming language of the eighties, thus making it accessible to all users, not just to people with a degree in Computer Science. With a few hours of exploration into GDL, the total beginner can make something surprisingly useful, indeed powerful. For the more experienced user, GDL has a depth that never ceases to turn up interesting new techniques and possibilities.

• **Now you have this book you have the key!**

Who supports the GDL user?

THE worldwide culture of GDL is assisted by **Graphisoft** itself by providing a reliable product in the stable and growing environment of ArchiCAD; by the efforts of organisations like the **Object Factory** (online GDL support, shopping, and my-object service); the **GDL Alliance** (a network of GDL developers supporting the culture); **Objects on Line** (on line GDL shopping mall); a number of enlightened **ArchiCAD dealers** who are willing to foster the wider use of ArchiCAD; the users of **ArchiCAD-Talk** (Internet conference on all ArchiCAD matters); and finally by the **GDL Cookbook** (a book which teaches a whole project based approach to design with GDL, from beginner to expert).

The GDL Cookbook 2.10

Teach yourself GDL by the Cookbook method!

THE GDL Cookbook is a collection of models which have been produced to help teach GDL. Each one is accompanied by explanatory text and images. The models are sequenced to give a 'Cookbook' style of progressive learning.

The Cookbook Idea

THE original GDL manual is good but it has too few examples and explanations. This 'Cookbook' approach to learning is designed to change what seems like a daunting task into something enjoyable and useful.

This book is not intended to rewrite the manual, nor to repeat the GDL textbook from Graphisoft, published in 1997. All of these have their place and are useful. Please have the GDL manual handy while you work, and please use the 'Helpmenus' when in ArchiCAD.

The metaphor of 'Cookbook' suggests that you will learn some GDL in a few days. This is quite true if you work through the starting exercises. This is also true the first time you pick up a guitar and have a few basic lessons. However, you will require much longer than that, and need to try some real projects, to acquire proficiency to the level of a Voyager.

The design environment is constantly changing – no sooner had this book settled down to a level of completion in 1998 than I was having to adjust to ArchiCAD 6.0 at the end of 1998, and at the end of 1999, ArchiCAD 6.5 has appeared! As each fresh release of ArchiCAD is expected, the Cookbook has to adapt. This is why I operate a generous upgrade policy. Whenever you feel that ArchiCAD has moved on a step or two, you can have a replacement Cookbook for half the original price.

Smart Parametric Models

YOU are truly privileged. You are the only members of the CAD community who have the ability to build PARAMETRIC objects without needing a degree in Computer Science. Quite simply, 'Parametric' means that you can change the parameters of an object. With GDL, it also means that the object can be 'smart' – change its own parameters according to rules or calculations. Thus it can display a level of 'artificial intelligence'. This is the power of GDL!

In other CAD software, if you stretch an object, it will stretch, but the elements of the object will be distorted proportionally. Whereas, with a parametrically built window, handrail, stair or structural truss tool, it can be written to recalculate the spacing of members, to resize members if necessary, correct user's errors, offer the user intelligent choices through pop-down menus in the object, and change the way it looks at different scales or distances. All these techniques are covered in the GDL Cookbook.

Tips and Tricks

THE Tips and Tricks sections of this book are not just about GDL. They are designed to make your whole use of ArchiCAD more fulfilling and productive. Many of them are contributed by experts from around the world. **Please Enjoy!**

Reasons why you need not learn GDL

- You can already make library objects using the Wall, Slab and Roof tools.
- You are contented with the existing ArchiCAD library.
- You can purchase CDs of more objects.
- You can pay a bureau to make 3-D objects when the need arises.
- A lot of the work you do is 2-D and doesn't need 3D modelling.
- It looks difficult – the GDL manual makes you shudder, just looking at it.
- You can't remember trigonometry or circle geometry, and cannot program.
- None of the objects you make need to be 'smart' or elegant, or get repeated (surely not?)

Reasons why you should learn GDL

- You can make insanely great things that, for interest and complexity, go far beyond library objects made with wall, roof and slab tools.
- You can make 'tools' – such as a joist tool, louvre tool or a handrail tool – that increase your productivity.
- You can make parametric models – i.e. an object that offers you a dialog box with the means of changing its height, diameter, colour, frequency, style, etc.
- It is very economical in disk space – GDL models only occupy the disk size of a script plus a small header and footer.
- You speed up rendering time; objects can be written with clean coding, unlike the dirty code produced by DXF or library objects made with wall, roof and slab, which needlessly calculate forms to a millionth of a metre accuracy.
- You can have really cool features like modestly intelligent objects which complain if you enter wrong parameters; which offer you options in the language of your choice; offer you popdown menus to assist you with choosing parameters; which dynamically turn to face the camera; which can change colour or shape as their position in the model, storey, or camera location changes. They can even consider whether to bother drawing themselves or not.
- You can do a useful cleaning up job on objects created with wall, roof and slab tools, if you know a bit of GDL.
- You can increase the level of detail in a model by being firmly in control of the number of polygons.
- It's fun, and easy once you get the hang. It is enjoyable to use simple mathematics and programming skills to see 3D forms popping out of the screen in front of your eyes!
- With GDL, you have the opportunity to develop a niche skill that will put you ahead of others in your field, and could open the way to new career opportunities now that Graphisoft have 'liberated' GDL by making GDL objects usable in other CAD environments.

Clearly, the reasons to use GDL far outnumber the reasons not to(:-)

About the Author

David Nicholson-Cole teaches Architecture at the University of Nottingham Institute of Architecture, but this involves a lot of ArchiCAD and GDL. David is the founder of ExMicro Ltd, Apple Resellers. Through the CAD & DTP side of ExMicro, 'Marmalade', he is available as a consultant to architects who want to use ArchiCAD as more than just a drawing tool.

With the support of Graphisoft, David has been running the ArchiCAD Lift Off courses, which include GDL Discovery, and GDL Voyager. In September of each year, David's and friends put on the 'ArchiCAD University' event at Nottingham, a 2-day learning festival of ArchiCAD.

When not using ArchiCAD, David likes being on his BMW Motorbike, or sailing on his yacht-share off the Suffolk coast.

David says,

Now that you have started with the Cookbook, I do request you to leave me with emails to say how you are getting on. This will be most encouraging, and will repay the many hours spent preparing GDL examples, Pagemilling and Pagemaking, bookbinding, packing and posting, all to provide you with this 'doorway' into a higher level of skill. The Cookbook improves with encouragement, and constructive criticism. I am always willing to dispense advice to email correspondents.

email: davidnc@innotts.co.uk

You've read the book, now tell me what you think:

• I found the GDL Cookbook an excellent support for GDL object generation in ArchiCAD. The style of your book is really refreshing and informative. Its personal touch helps in learning GDL in an entertaining way. I fully recommend the GDL Cookbook to any ArchiCAD user who wants to access the full power of object parametrics in their designs. *Andras Haidekker, CEO Graphisoft UK, Dec'98*

• The more I write, the more I'm addicted to it – GDL is so great! Again, I cannot thankyou enough for teaching us GDL. *Chee Horng Chang, architect, Leeds*

• Today I actually created an object with embedded text scaling related to drawing scale for a client. Paid off the Cookbook in just one exercise. Thankyou. Also, gratitude for the squiffle line idea. Fabulous! *Dwight Atkinson, Canada*

• I LOVE THE COOKBOOK!!!! I think you've done a great job! *Greg Richmond, Dallas*

• Great book, v. exciting because it at least gets you doing things! So far, can't put it down – has made me keen to learn more – *Kevin Hayes, Brisbane, Australia*

• I'm wading through the Cookbook and am (oh-so) slowly getting it for the first time in ten years of using ArchiCAD. *Jack Suben, California, USA.*

• I am the no. 1 fan of your Cookbook and your organisation. *Majid Ahari, structural engineer*

• I have had a much better chance to study the Cookbook... its a wonderful work. I regret not having the book in 94 when I started teaching myself ArchiCAD it would saved me a lot of headaches and money. Even though I have done a lot of GDL development, you have clearly done a lot more; there is very little you haven't covered. I have tended to favour a smaller subset of the 2d and 3d GDL statements and not delved too deeply into the full range of GDL possibilities. *Mike Carbone - Australia*

• The best thing I've done apart from buying AC has been your CB's and the establishment of "My_Library". *Rod Jurich & Associates, Australia*

• Thank you, thank you! Your GDL Cookbook is wonderful. Too many ArchiCAD users deprive themselves of the rich rewards available through the use of this script. On the average, end users find the GDL manuals too daunting and never progress further then perhaps using objects made in the 3D-view window if even that. Your rational, clear and abundantly documented examples help the neophyte and others in demystifying this very powerful language. *Jacques Couture, ASYM technologies, the first reseller of ArchiCAD in the United States*

• I got your book last month. Congratulations, it is great. I never had time to update my book, but you do a much better job of evangelising GDL. *Pal Szabo, author of The Introductory Guide to GDL*

• I am reading your book and cannot express my feeling. Everything in this book is so interesting, innovating and intelligent. This book is more than GDL. This book is more than a book. It's a way of thinking, it's a way of life! *Dusko Maksimovich, Aalto Skola Racnara*

• The cookbook is one of the best purchases this year. It's a real eye-opener: it gives me the anwers to most of my questions about Archicad and GDL and it also provides me some solutions for problems I didn't even know existed before. I hope I find the time to go through it all. Thank you for your excellent work and helping making GDL easier. *Christian Cerliani, Zurich*

• Without a doubt, the GDL Cookbook is the best manual I've seen written on GDL. The Cookbook is so thoroughly indexed and documented that I'm finding it has not been difficult to quickly find answers to my questions. The Cookbook, in combination with the GDL training I received, has also made Graphisoft's GDL Reference Manual much easier to understand. You have successfully demonstrated that there are no limits to what can be done in ArchiCAD if one applies the skills & techniques that you teach in your training and in the Cookbook. *Chris Stringer USA*

• You very effectively got me over the hump of GDL and I am very appreciative of your efforts. *Robert Davis, Houston, Texas*

The GDL Cookbook 2.10

Discovery course

Voyager course

INDEX

Tips and Tricks

Note to readers

The Cookbook started off as a set of web pages, and was authored entirely in an HTML editor (Adobe Pagemill). It has now been converted over to full DTP using Pagemaker.

In December 98, the GDL Cookbook became **ArchiCAD 6.0** compatible. The **GDL Cookbook 2** of June '99 was a major rewrite with many exercises modified or added, with the Primer dissolved amongst the exercises to form a more progressive delivery of the information required to get you going with GDL. This is **GDL Cookbook 2.06**; the difference between this and Cookbook 2 is a number of small misprints corrected, tidier graphics, more tips and tricks, many exercises updated, some 6.5 information, and the 6.5 User Interface explained. **ArchiCAD 6.5** is now with us, and offers many improved opportunities for the GDL writer.

The book is available in Acrobat format on the enclosed CD. With AC 6.x, if put into your Documentation folder, it will appear in your 'Help' menu.

Acknowledgements

I should like to thank: Howard Gill, my partner in LiftOff courses; Richard Swann for the idea of writing the sections on Theory; Dick Morgan for the idea of holding a Voyager course, and Chris Phillips for the idea of making it into a book; Alfred Man for keeping the GDL enthusiasm flowing when I am tired of it; Sally NicholsonCole for keeping the office going while I do anything except working for ExMicro; my students for challenging me with difficult tasks which sharpen my skills; all the participants of the ArchiCAD-Talk conference who display unfailing patience in putting up with my many emails; John Stebbins, Djordje Grujic and others for their ceaseless support for the Cookbook and the GDL culture; Sanjay Patel and Andras Haidekker of Graphisoft UK for their unfailing support and encouragement; Apple for providing me with G3 technology! The University of Nottingham for paying half of my salary so that I can be paid for what I enjoy doing most - teaching ArchiCAD! Finally, Graphisoft in Budapest for ArchiCAD itself.

The GDL Cookbook

**Teach yourself GDL
by the cookbook method
& 'ArchiCAD Tips and Tricks'**

**Version 2.1
for ArchiCAD users**

Vol 1 - GDL Discovery

Marmalade

Introducing GDL
(Geometric Description Language)

IN the early days of ArchiCAD, the prototype of ArchiCAD (RaDar) was on a Hewlett Packard as a 3D Piping design solution. Not having a mouse or windows, ArchiCAD *was* GDL – a scripting language to produce 3D form. The arrival of the Apple Lisa followed by the Macintosh enabled programmers to put the building plan into one window, the building tools into another (to form a pallette of clickable buttons), coordinates in another, and so on. ArchiCAD as we now know it became visible. Designers could drop walls and other building elements into a plan window, stretch them to fit and change their properties; view the 3-D results in another window. GDL survived as a speciality, evolving in its own way as a means of building library objects.

G DL commands – produce 3D entities – like BLOCK, SPHERE, CONE, TUBE.

3 D organisation of the object – look at it analytically and understand what 3D shapes it contains.

P ROGRAMMING – the organisation of the script in a structured way, observing rules of syntax.

I NTERFACING with ArchiCAD – to enable the object to respond to conditions in the main project.

Working with GDL consists of four main areas of knowledge:

G DL commands – in their raw state are avail able to you in the GDL manual. It is difficult to understand their use and syntax until you have to apply them for real. Therefore, the cookbook approach in this book gives you an easier way of learning them by doing small projects, a bit at a time. The cookbook method – being based on small projects, growing in complexity, is analogous to the process of architectural education. The GDL explanations in this cookbook runs systematically through all the 2D and 3D commands with small examples of the commands at work.

3 D Organisation – You may not be able to build something in every detail, but you look at it, and decide what parts of it need to be included. You also decide how the object behaves if is to be stretched or hinged, and what 3D primitive shapes would best produce the object.

P rogramming – A program is just a sequence of instructions. You can read instructions to someone over the telephone, you can struggle through the instructions for setting the controls on your new video, you can explain a cookery recipe to a friend, or plan the most efficient way of mowing the lawn. There is even a program in making a cup of tea! In all these cases you use a program, even if you didn't think of it as a program. Suppose you write down the sequence of

tasks, you would be sure to get them into the right order, to avoid doing tasks you had just done, or doing tasks that would undo ones you had done. You can write the sequence as a series of pictures, or as written commands. That's all there is to it!

Which language would you use? For cookery, you would speak in English, or French or Spanish, but you would use similar food ingredients. For GDL, you use the language of BASIC, and your ingredients are commands like BLOCK and CONE and TUBE. BASIC is the easiest of the major programming languages, devised in the seventies, and predominant on micros during the eighties. BASIC is easy to learn.

Graphisoft must be thanked for choosing BASIC as the model for their programming language. We can all write a few lines of code, and see 3-D objects springing up into existence. It is fun! One's capabilities are vastly increased – in the 'old days' of programming, BASIC could build menu driven programs for dull things like accounts and calculations, many of which were far easier to do in spreadsheets. Now, with GDL, towers, chairs, bridges, space structures, buildings and trees can all grow from your keyboard.

I nterfacing – GDL objects can behave slightly intelligently in that they can know current wall thicknesses, storey, scale, frame number, location, current pen and so forth, and behave accordingly.

So, What is Structured Programming?

IN the context of GDL, it means taking a very disciplined approach to model building, in particular these three rules

Analyse the model to understand all aspects of its symmetry, repetition and essential geometry.	**O**rganise the script into a number of subroutines that reflect the 3D organisation of the object.	**M**aintain strict control over the location of the 3D cursor.

Why use Structured Programming?

FOR SMALL MODELS, you can write BLOCK this, CYLINDer that, CONE the other and finish up with simple models – the scripting may not be elegant, but it works. However, if you make the model bigger, you will produce a script of spaghetti-like complexity. If you structure your 3D script with more discipline, you can build models of great complexity without losing track of what you are doing – and you are able to repair it or amend it without despair. Professional programmers despise BASIC because they associate it with amateurishly written, unstructured code, that only just works, that cannot produce merchantable applications, that can only be debugged by the original writer, and so on. The virtue of systems like PASCAL, LISP and 'C' is that programs are 'object oriented', modular, structured, and so on. Perhaps this is why AutoCAD uses Lisp, and why MiniCAD uses PASCAL for their equivalents of GDL.

But listen! BASIC, as used in GDL, does everything that is needed to produce 3D objects, and is perfectly capable of being written in an 'object oriented', modular, structured way, that can be debugged by other people and which can produce library objects that are of merchantable quality. It's just the way you do it!!

3-D Model Analysis

SCRIPTING is easier if you understand the 3-D nature of the object. All that really matters is that you analyse the object accurately, which you must do regardless of the language you are using or thinking in. For architects and designers who are in the business of 3-D, this should be the easiest part.

The universal language of 3D is the 3D primitive – the Block, Cylinder, Cone, Sphere, Extrusion etc. Slab shapes are flat blocks, and wall shapes are tall thin blocks.

At the next level of 3D interpretation, you have slabs which curve, holes drilled, surfaces rounded or chamfered, extrusions taken through curved or angular pathways, saddle shapes, lathed objects, elements repeated around axes, and many such variations.

At yet another level, you must identify elements which might change, like lights which come on, elements that must be able to slide or rotate, or to disappear if they are too detailed, which might need random numbers, or do something special.

Think these out on paper: if you cannot draw the object freehand in pencil, then you probably cannot script it.

Origin and 3D Cursor

GDL gives you a **3D Cursor** – a bit like the blinking cursor in Word or Excel. Whatever you type will appear where the cursor is blinking. In GDL, if you move the cursor 2 metres upwards, and rotate it by 45 degrees, then the next thing you type will occur there, at that angle.

Every model has an **Origin** – it's like the 'top of page' in a word processing document. As a result of your ADD, MUL or ROTate commands, the 3-D cursor departs from that origin; you can then draw an object, and then either goes on to draw something else, or you return it to the origin. If you want to keep control of the model, you need to return to the origin before you tackle the next part of the model.

Look at the scripts in the GDL Cookbook, and you will see a constant re-iteration of the value of Structure in programming

This needs thinking about...

• **What investment value does your object really have?** Will it be used once, for your eyes only, or could it be used dozens of times in coming years by many people? Imagine someone else using the library object, and ask yourself, which aspects of the model really need to be parametric? What happens if the user enters negative quantities or angles? How many choices should the user be offered?

• **Where should the model origin be?** This is the point that usually defines the object's height and location in the project model. It would help if it was at a centre of symmetry or rotation. Can you take advantage of symmetry? – you could build half or quarter the model only, and then multiply or mirror the rest.

• **Can your object be subdivided into 'tasks' or elements?** Take a swivel chair: this has axes of symmetry, elements which repeat themselves, elements which are clearly lathed round an axis, elements which curve or twist, elements which hinge or bend. If you modify parameters such as length and height, do elements which elongate also have to thicken? Will they then become larger than the element they join on to, or punch through it? Is there a logical sequence to the assembly? Do the elements have 'sub-elements'? For example,with the Swivel chair, you have: multi-toed foot (with coned floorpads), central shaft (with adjusting handle), swivelling upholstered seat (nice and curvy), upholstered backrest (also curvy), and support for the back rest (metallic with adjusting handle.)

• **Are there hinging or sliding elements?** In how many planes do they hinge or slide? Is there a succession of moving elements, such as in the human arm? (in which, you get rotation as well as hinging!)

• **What elements are repetitious and can be done with loops?** Are some quantities unknown? Perhaps they will be generated after the user has entered a parameter – e.g., the number of rungs of a ladder depends on the height and slope of the ladder, assuming a regular spacing.

• **Which commands (in GDL) would best achieve the result?** If you analyse the model into primitives, are the elements formed from cylinders, cones, prisms, tubes, extrusions, cut objects, blocks or spheres? There are frequently more ways than one to 'cook your fish'.

• **What maths or circle geometry problems are involved?** How may arcs or circles are there, and can you locate their centres, and calculate their radii? Are curved shapes circular, elliptical or parabolic?

• **Can you estimate the required 'level of detail' accurately?** Do you really need to show planar glazing fittings, or handles on the doors? Could you get away with using 2D elements in the 3D model? Is your level of detail (LOD) likely to generate too many polygons?

• **Are you planning to animate the model at some stage?** If so, is it worth considering writing objects that hide themselves or reduce their level of detail when the camera is a long way away??

Tips and Tricks for ArchiCAD users

Introduction

THESE are spread through the GDL Cookbook like nuggets of gold and are about ArchiCAD in all its forms, not just GDL. In this edition, they are grouped somewhat more heavily in the Voyager section. I have used them to fill space at the bottom of pages. When I want to expand on a topic in a later edition, I move the tip to another page to free up space.

The best place to find Tips and Tricks at their place of origin is to be a member of the **ArchiCAD-Talk** list server conference, on the Internet. Although I have tested out all my own tricks here, many of the ideas for them started from questions and answers on that conference. **Try it!**

Clean machine

IF you are reading this, it is probably because ArchiCAD is quite an important part of your living. So avoid using the computer with ArchiCAD for games, testing shareware, or installing fancy desktop backgrounds, or funny things which put animated eyeballs on your menu bar, or check spelling as you type text. **Keep a clean machine.** ArchiCAD itself requires quite a lot of background software to be loaded, such as Quicktime, its own scratchpad files, background print spooling etc. The computer has enough work to do. If you keep a clean machine, you can avoid the need for a constant virus checker (which takes up CPU time.) Run a virus check periodically, especially after inserting disks from outside sources.

So, you think you can't program...

Theory

WELL you can! Squirrels can program, birds can program, spiders do it, small children do it – in that they plan a series of actions, they try to get them in the right order, they correct their own mistakes when they make them, and they achieve a result – perhaps a hoard of nuts, a nest full of eggs, a web, or a Lego model.

The British Standards Institute recently (Sept '99) received the 'Ig Nobel' Prize for Literature in that they wrote BS.6008: *Method for Preparation of a Liquor of Tea*, and took 5000 words to do it, going into the minutest detail! We will not go quite so far, but let's use tea making as an example of human programming. Let's write down a series of 'Operations' involved in making Tea. Without going into too much detail, list the sequence of operations to someone who knows the obvious things like how to turn on taps. Anybody reading this (above the age of 10) should be able to recite the following list in the right order.

```
1.  Fill Kettle with water
2.  Boil water
3.  Get teapot
4.  Fill teapot with bags
5.  Fill with water
6.  Get cups
7.  Wait until ready
8.  Pour out
9.  Add Milk
10. Serve Tea
```

1

Now because we are going to teach a computer how to make tea, you need to rewrite the list giving each Operation a number(with a colon), and use an exclamation mark to make each Operation name into a Label. For a human, you might number each task 1, 2, 3, etc, but for computers its easier to use larger numbers (because later, you could insert extra things you hadn't thought of.)

```
100:  !Fill Kettle with water
200:  !Boil water
300:  !Get teapot
400:  !Fill teapot with bags
500:  !Fill with water
600:  !Get cups
700:  !Wait until ready
800:  !Pour out
900:  !Add Milk
1000: !Serve Tea
```

2

NEXT, you look at each Operation and realise that none of them are single Actions. Each Operation consists of a number of Actions which might include Error Checking. For example, if the teapot contains last night's teabags, then Wash Teapot. This might require quite a lot of IF statements, followed by the Actions taken as a result of the IF statements. Depending on the level of knowledge or stupidity of the machine, you instruct it appropriately. For example we assume here that the machine knows how to turn a tap or a kettle on. In the same way, GDL knows that Cylinders are round and that Cones are tapered *and* round without us having to define 'roundness' mathematically.

The final program for making tea

Goes round until kettle filled: 2 IF statements

A single line way of writing two IF statements

People are 'integer' quantities; but this makes doubly sure that you can make tea for 2.

For the 'parameter' of tea, you could let the user select from a list of choices.

In the event of a major problem you might have to jump back to the start.

```
100:!Fill Kettle with water
IF kettle (empty) THEN (Fill kettle with water)
IF kettle (filled) THEN GOTO 200:!Boil water

200:!Boil water
IF water (boiling) THEN (turn kettle off) ELSE (boil water)

300:!Get teapot
IF (number of people) less than 2.01 GET smallteapot
IF (number of people) greater than 2 GET largeteapot
IF teapot (dirty) THEN (wash out teapot) UNTIL (clean)
IF teapot (clean) THEN (swirl hot water) UNTIL (warm)
IF teapot (warm)  THEN (Fill teapot with bags)  !continue

400:!Fill teapot with bags
LET teatype=USERCHOOSE(EarlGrey,Lapsang,Camomile,Tetleys)
IF teapot (large) THEN add 2 teabag USING teatype
IF teapot (small) THEN add 1 teabag USING teatype

500:!Fill with water
POUR water INTO teapot UNTIL (full)
IF (not enough water) THEN GOTO 100:
PLACE teacosy UPON teapot
START timeclock USING seconds
```

3

Continued next page

Continued from last page

4

This was going on while you were getting the cups.

Another repeating 'Loop'

Another example of getting the parameter from the user's choice.

```
700:!Wait until ready
IF TIMECLOCK less than 120 seconds THEN WAIT

800:!Pour out
REPEAT (on the teatray)
  IF fullness=0 THEN POUR (a cup) UNTIL fullness=7/8
    UNTIL (enough cups for everybody)

900:!Add Milk
LET milkcondition=USERCHOOSE(with milk,without milk)
  REPEAT (for each cup on the teatray)
    IF milkcondition=(with milk) THEN (add milk to cup)
      UNTIL (each cup tested)

1000:!Serve Tea
```

Now this isn't written in BASIC, and it isn't written in GDL, but it's close to both of those two, and shows that programming can be like writing in English in a slightly mathematical style.

OK, we can't all be perfect. The British Standard says put the milk in the cup first, and of course, I haven't tested to see if the users have chosen sugar, or want spoons, saucers or biscuits. And what happens if there isn't enough tea for everyone? Then you have to loop back and top up the teapot, or even reboil the kettle. This could be built into the program. That level of detail and error correction would make the program more professional and user friendly.

I hope this shows the sort of thing you can do, and has persuaded you that you can indeed write a program.

Working in 3D space – the 3D Cursor

JUST HOW do you write in GDL in 3D? Well, when you are word processing, you move your cursor to a location and start typing. Move the cursor, and type again, and the new words appear at the new position.

With GDL, you have a 3D cursor; you can move the curcor; when you issue a 3D GDL command like BLOCK or CONE, you will get a 3D object wherever the 3D cursor happens to be. Move the 3D cursor to a new position and issue the same command and now it appears in the new position.

Thus to make a chair, you can move to each corner, plant a chair leg, then raise the cursor up to plant the seat and finally, move the cursor to plant the back of the chair.

When you have achieved a group of things (like a bunch of chair legs), you have completed a task. So now return the cursor to the global origin. Now you can depart and do another task, for example the seat of the chair.

When you have finished, you can do a small 2D script so that a 2D symbol will appear in the project plan, save the file, and you are done.

FIRST GET **acquainted with the idea of the X, Y, Z universe that you have to work in.** All locations are defined in these coordinates. If you want to move sideways, you move in the X direction. If you move forward, you move in a Y direction. If you move up or down, you move in a Z direction. You can Rotate the cursor and the XYZ world gets rotated too.

- The 'G' (global) coordinates remain fixed at the **Origin** of the model. When you bring an object into the project plan, this origin is what decides the height of the object in the project. The origin should be planned carefully – preferably at the base of the object, and at the axis of any symmetry or rotational axis that you perceive.

- The 'L' (local) coordinates are like the moving cursor in your word processor – they travel with you, wherever you are drawing an component. Always try to return the GDL cursor to the origin before you start out with another element of the model.

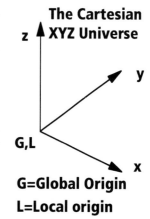

The Cartesian XYZ Universe

G=Global Origin
L=Local origin

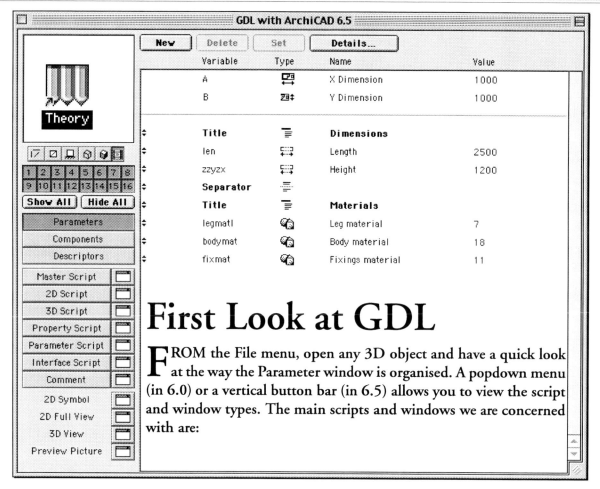

First Look at GDL

FROM the File menu, open any 3D object and have a quick look at the way the Parameter window is organised. A popdown menu (in 6.0) or a vertical button bar (in 6.5) allows you to view the script and window types. The main scripts and windows we are concerned with are:

Master Script:– there are many housekeeping tasks such as reading in Value lists, setting up Parameters, checking user Errors, defining Materials, setting Flags and so on. These are read by the 3D Script, the 2D Script and the Properties Script. If you didn't use a Master Script, you would have to write all these things time and time again.

2D Symbol:– is a window into which you could paste a 2D image, or draw using 2D tools, but it will only be displayed if there is no 2D script. With GDL knowlege, you are better to write 2D script.

2D Script:– this can be used simply to tell GDL to draw in 2D whatever it finds in 3D (Project2), or whatever is in the 2D Symbol window (Fragment2). You can (and should) use it for writing a parametrically organised script to draw what the object will look like. By designating Hotspots, the 2D script can also govern how stretchy the object can be. By leaving this script blank, the GDL object will display what ever is drawn into the 2D Symbol window. If you leave both blank, the object will not show in the project.

2D Full View:– is generated by the 2D Script. This will not show what is in the Symbol window (unless commanded to.)

3D Script:– the primary means of building parametric 3D objects. If the object is simple, almost all the work can done in the 3D Script.

3D View:– is generated by the 3D Script – not to be confused with the 3D window of the main project.

Properties Script:– in which you can write Compo nents and Descriptor commands if the object is to be in a schedule.

The Parameter Script (a.k.a. **Value List**):– this is the means of creating Pop-Down menu selections in the main parameters box. It is read first, even before the Master Script.

Comment:– is a small text field in which you can write a small set of instructions to your user on how to use the object, or could record a log of the development of the object.

Preview Picture:- is a window containing a pasted in bitmap image of a view of the object. It tells the user what the object will look like in its setting, and could come from Artlantis Render or an ArchiCAD photorendering. This becomes the Icon of the object in the settings box finder.

Parameter table:– we also fill out the table of param eters by hitting the New button, and filling in the small details. A, B and ZZYZX are 'obligatory parameters' – they already exist – but we can make many more.

User Interface Script:- This enables you to build a Custom dialog box with your own text fields and im- ages, with buttons and input fields for the user to enter pa- rameters. It is great for complex objects where the user might need more explanation of the purpose of parameters. (AC- 6.5 only)

Your first object... **very simple Chair**

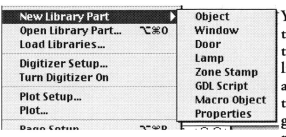

You want to do something practical? Well try this VERY simple little kitchen chair for a starter. Turn over the page for some guidance on cursor movement.

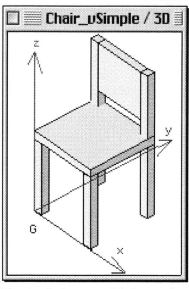

From the **File Menu**, Select **New Library Part->Object**, and you will get a new **Library Part** opened, and from this, you will be able to pull up the **3D Script window**.

This simple chair is entirely composed of the **BLOCK** command. Move the 3-D cursor from place to place, drawing a Block in each place, and then move on. The syntax of Block is very simple, just BLOCK x,y,z. You define the X, Y, and Z dimensions of the block and it always grows outwards from the bottom left corner of the block.

Notice that the stages of the script are marked with labels (or 'comments') which all start with an exclamation mark. When you look at the script later, you will know what's what if you have labelled frequently.

As you build each Block, you use the ADDx, ADDy, ADDz or ADD commands to move the cursor to the next location, then build the next Block. After a group of commands is completed, get the cursor back to the start before doing the next group, using the DEL command – this 'undos' the number of ADDs that you have made. Make sure that at the very end, you have moved the cursor back to the origin of the model.

If you do not specify a material, your objects will turn out all one colour, which can be disconcerting. So the PEN and MATERIAL command is one of the first ones you learn.

If you work in Imperial dimensions, one of the first things I suggest is to work entirely in decimal Inches, as this avoids spurious punctuation marks and maths operators such as in 1'-2 3/4".

This simple chair starts life from its front right leg. It is valuable to do each part in stages, and to move the cursor back to its origin at the end.

```
!Simple chair
!3D Script
MATERIAL "Whitewash"
PEN 1
!Legs
BLOCK 2",2",18"
   ADDx 16"
BLOCK 2",2",18"
   ADDy 16"
BLOCK 2",2",30"
   ADDx -16"
BLOCK 2",2",30"
   DEL 3
!Seat
   ADDz 18"
BLOCK 18",18",2"
   DEL 1
!Back
   ADD 2",16.5",24"
BLOCK 14",1.5",12"
   DEL 1 !Back to origin
```

2D Symbol: The ArchiCAD objects that are autoscripted from the Wall/Floor/Roof tools always have their own 2-D symbol or script.

When you write a script yourself, you need to create the 2D symbol. You can write a tiny script. Open the 2D-Script Window and write as follows: **PROJECT2 3,270,2**. It is explained later in this book – it draws a Plan view of the 3D object, with a camera angle of 270° and it is in hidden line.

Throughout the book, I encourage you to write 2D scripts properly, so make a start here.

This example is done in imperial. All GDL metric scripting has to be done in Metres, and if in Imperial must be clearly signified with Foot and Inch symbols.

```
!Chair - 2D-Script

! PROJECT2 3,270,2
HOTSPOT2 0,0

!Seat
RECT2 0,0, 18",18"

!Legs
RECT2 0,16", 2",18"
RECT2 16",16",18",18"

!Back
LINE2 0,16", 18",16"
```

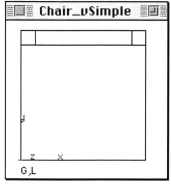

You can build the whole chair from rectangles and a line. **RECT2** defines a rectangle from the X,Y location of the bottom left to the X,Y location of the tip right. **LINE2** is similar, joining two X,Y locations together.

Cursor Movement

ADD dx,dy,dz, ADDx dx, ADDy dy and ADDz dz are the way to move the 3D cursor from location to location. You can then issue a 3D command. Most frequently, you add in one direction, but when you want to move in two directions or more it's more economical to use the ADD x,y,z command to do 3 in one go. The best way to get the hang of these movements is to launch into typing in some of the exercises.

ADD2 dx,dy is the 2D equivalent of ADD, but is is not as often used, because many of the 2D commands can be issued without moving from the origin.

For example in 3D, you might go:
ADD 1,1.5,0: CIRCLE 0.5: DEL 1

but in 2D it is:
ADD2 1,1.5: CIRCLE2 0,0,0.5: DEL 1

but this can be shortened to:
CIRCLE2 1,1.5,0.5

MUL means **Multiply** – along the axis stated. So **MULz -1** converts all references to Z to negative, **MULx** does this to X and so on.

You can use a MUL x,y,z command and do three multiplications at once .

What MUL means in reality is that you can use it to change the scale of entire objects or parts of objects – all ArchiCAD Autoscripted objects use MUL to enable objects to be resized, or to be stretchy.

All objects can easily be mirrored by **MUL**tiplying by -1 around the mirroring axis. Symmetrical objects are labour saving, as you build just half, then mirror around X or Y.

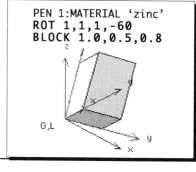

```
!MUL Demonstration
ELLIPS 1,1
```

```
!MUL Demonstration
 MULx 0.5
ELLIPSE 1,1
 DEL 1
```

```
!MUL Demonstration
 MULz -1
ELLIPSE 1,1
 DEL 1
```

Starting with a plain ELLIPS... which starts life as half a sphere, you can make it shrink to an elliptical plan shape by MULx or can flip it vertically with a MULz.

ROT means **Rotate the Cursor** around an axis. You use it in the form of **ROTx, ROTy or ROTz**. You use them one at a time. You use them in the order that logic tells you – the order is vital.

There is a combined **ROT** command, but it is not used in the way that you use the combined ADD and MUL commands. The **ROT** command rotates the object around a vector – defined as the line connecting 0,0,0 to a point defined by an X,Y,Z definition. It is unexplained and unillustrated in the GDL manual, so here is a simple example! It is very effective if the circumstance arises where it is needed: when it is, you will recognise its usefulness.

ROT2 is the equivalent in 2D of the ROTz command. One of the problems of 2D scripting is that you don't have a visible cursor, so if you do a lot of ADD2 and ROT2 and MUL2, you need to imagine the cursor's location.

```
PEN 1:MATERIAL 'zinc'
ROT 1,1,1,-60
BLOCK 1.0,0.5,0.8
```

DEL means **Delete the most recent Cursor Movement command** – ADD, MUL or ROT. DEL 2 means delete the last two. DEL is the most important command of this page. If you don't control the cursor, your model will be unmanageable after a page of script. Use DEL to return to the Origin as often as possible. DEL is to GDL what the brakes are to your car. They are just as important to safe, purposeful motion as the engine and gearbox (the 3D commands)

One way to get back to the origin is to repeat all your moves backwards. For every ROTy 45, you do a ROTy -45, and so on. This is not good! It is much easier to use the DEL command. The ROT, MUL and ADD commands are stored in a stack, and if you

DEL 1, it knocks one off the stack. If you DEL 4, it knocks the previous 4 off the stack – in reverse order. You can also DEL using a variable like *num*.

If you use subroutines, DEL must match the number of Cursor movements within a subroutine. Look at the small number of commands on this and the next page to see how DEL is used.

The DEL command cannot run past the stack. If you DEL 2 when there is only one item to DEL, you will get an error message.

DEL TOP removes all the Cursor commands – returns you to the Origin of the model by brute force.

DEL TOP is useful because GDL does not declare an error when you use it, even if there is nothing to DEL. However, it is far better to control the model by using DEL intelligently – with every subroutine – so that you never need to use the DEL TOP command until the END statement. DEL TOP is dangerous – apart from encouraging you to program in a sloppy fashion, it can wipe out global commands (like 'ROTx 90') that exist at the beginning of the program.

Your first 3D Elements

Theory

U NTIL you feel ready to progress to PRISM and other more powerful commands, get used to building 3D GDL objects using the items on this page. These are the essential primitives of 3D building. It is amazing how much you can do with these.

BLOCK is the primary building block of GDL, and with X,Y,Z dimensions for the parameters, you can't get much simpler.

In GDL projects it is actually rather limited to use; you have to get the cursor to the lower left corner of a block, and you have no control over corners, lines etc.

```
!Block Demonstration
!Syntax:- BLOCK x,y,z
BLOCK 0.3,0.2,0.25
  ADD 0.1,0.1,0.25
BLOCK 0.1,0.1,0.2
  DEL 1
```

*Some existing Graphisoft library objects use **BRICK** – but it works to the same syntax.*

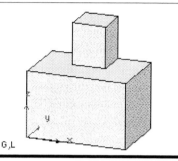

CYLIND drives a cylinder up the Z axis. If you want a cylinder at an angle, you first have to rotate the cursor with a ROT command so that the Z-axis points in the desired direction.

Note that RESOL 6 or 8 can change Cylinders into hexagons or octagons.

```
!Cylind demonstration
!Syntax:- CYLIND height,radius
 CYLIND 0.2,0.05
  ADDx 0.2
 RESOL 6
  CYLIND 0.2,0.05
 RESOL 8
  ADDz 0.15
  ROTy 45
  CYLIND 0.1,0.03
```

By the way, if you want the cursor to return to the origin, you would have to finish this script with a DEL 3.

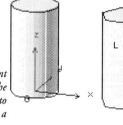

SPHERE is the easiest one of all – but the one most likely to cause you to have so many polygons that ArchiCAD will have trouble rendering it. Use strict control of the surface resolution with RESOL commands. If you do not specify resol, the resol value is assumed to be 36, which means that the sphere will have 648 faces! RESOL 10 is the smallest that still looks spherical.

```
!SPHERE demonstration
!Syntax:- SPHERE radius
!RESOL sets the number of faces
 SPHERE 0.1
  ADDx 0.2
 RESOL 12
  SPHERE 0.05
  DEL 1
```

By the way, the single sphere on the left, if saved as a DXF 3D file would require 21,000 lines of code to describe it.

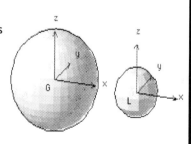

ELLIPS produces a hemisphere, but by changing the height, it can be distorted into a bullet shape. RESOL can be used to make it look polygonal. ELLIPS is always solid.

If you want a hollow dome, you need to use REVOLVE.

```
!ELLIPS demonstration
!Syntax:- ELLIPS height,radius
ELLIPS 0.2,0.06
  ADDx 0.15
RESOL 12
ELLIPS 0.16,0.04
```

When you use any curved surface, always set the lowest resolution that will look acceptable – to speed up rendering.

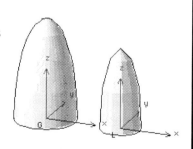

CONE is like a cylinder in which the radius can be varied at the top and bottom.

It also includes a cutting command, to decide if the top should be cut square (90,90 degree cuts) or cut like a ship's funnel, at an angle. The angles are always cut along the X-axis, and must be positive.

```
!CONE demonstration
!Syntax:- CONE height,radius1,
!        radius2,cut1,cut2
 CONE 0.2,0.06,0.03,90,90
  ADDx 0.15
 CONE 0.2,0.06,0.03,40,140
```

The number of faces on a Cone can also be controlled with the RESOL command

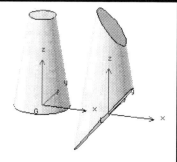

Your First 2D Elements

Theory

UNLESS you have a 2D Symbol or a 2D Script, your object will not appear on the Project Plan! If you been using ArchiCAD's conventional tools to make library objects, you have been used to it making automatically generated scripts, and automatically drawn 2D symbols generated from the view of the object.

HOTSPOT2 x, y places a Hotspot at the point x,y in the 2D symbol of the object. It lights up when you select the object.

The purpose of HOTSPOTs are 4-fold: To enable you to see objects when touched or marqueed, to pick up the object, to make objects stretchy, and to provide 'gravity' for snapping objects to line or to other hotspots.

LINE2   draws a line from one XY location to another XY location – relative to your current cursor position.

RECT2   draws a rectangle from one XY location to another XY location diagonally opposite – relative to your current cursor position and angle. RECT2 is always wireline (you can see through it).

PROJECT2 is a command that you MUST learn, even with your first scripted Object!

Until you learn parametric 2-D scripting, the easiest thing is to write a short 2-D script containing **PROJECT2 3,270,2**. This reads the 3D Script and draws whatever it can see, faithfully, in wireline or hidden line view. Be warned – it could slow down the time it takes to draw the symbol.

PROJECT2 should be learnt almost parrot fashion, or at least should be written into your NotePad for copying and pasting into the 2D script.

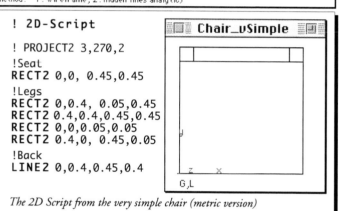

The 2D Script from the very simple chair (metric version)

PROJECT2 has interesting possibilities. For example, it can be told to display the object in the Project Plan in elevation or axonometric form. Together with HOTSPOTs in the right places, you can make things stretchy in the vertical direction. Or you can use it for a quick view of the elevation of the object to make sure that you have set it up correctly.

```
!Typical short 2D Script for any 3D object
HOTSPOT2 0,0
PROJECT2 3,270,2
```

Perhaps by now, you have noticed that every command in 2D scripting ends with the character '2'

Starting GDL Syntax

GDL Syntax is the way you organise commands together into a program.

END is one of the first things I write, after I have written a Title of the object, the Date and my Name. It is because everything in front of **END** is the 'executive script' and everything after **END** is going to be a useful Subroutine that needs to be stored until used. Even the most complex of objects need be no more verbose than the example here. It is immensely easier to detect errors or make changes if the script is written as subroutines. Put a line of dashes after the END statement.

```
!Swivel Chair
!3D Script

!Main 3D Script
PEN 1
GOSUB  50:!Error Checking
GOSUB 300:!Foot of Chair
GOSUB 400:!Vertical Shaft
GOSUB 500:!Seat
GOSUB 600:!Back

END:!--------------

50:!Error Checking
IF height>0.9 THEN height=0.9
RETURN
```

Line Numbers

LINE numbers are always written with a colon (e.g. '250:'), and should be followed by a text comment label (e.g. '!Chair legs'). They do not have to be in sequence, but it helps you if they are.

Early forms of BASIC required a number on EVERY line, which is why numbers were large – enabling you to insert extra ones later. Now you have freedom to write without numbers.

Curvature Control

MOST of the workload of the processor during rendering is working out the values of light and shade on each surface (polygon) in the model. If it is trying to work out Shadows, it's also working out the outline of the object and what the shadow will do when falling on each polygon. **Fewer polygons means faster rendering.** Sometimes, the object you are doing may not be visible (such as a nut or bolt) so why give it 36 or more polygons, especially when there could be thousands of nuts and bolts in the model? So control the curvature!

RESOL is used extensively throughout this Cookbook as a way of controlling the resolution of curvature of curved surfaces such as Spheres, Cones and Cylinders. RESOL is highly important; an excess of Polygons will lead to excessive rendering times, or if you haven't got a lot of RAM, to ArchiCAD giving up altogether.

The default resolution is 36, so a single sphere will have 648 surfaces right from the start. Get it down to the lowest practical quantity – or even lower. If you are Photorendering the resolution can be set even lower. It is a good tip to set resolution to an odd number – 5, 7 or 9 look more cylindrical than the patently hexagonal look of RESOL 6. RESOL cannot be less than 3.

RESOL can be controlled by a variable, for example RESOL 6+10/dd will make the resolution higher as the distance to camera 'dd' reduces. If the resolution is stated as a real number – eg 6.35, it is always rounded down.

RADIUS is even more useful than RESOL because it gives you 3 RESOL commands in a single line. Some models, such as a curved handrail, has two curves to resolve, the curve of the handrail and the curve of the tubing. Some curves are so small (such as holes drilled into a steel plate, or thin cables) that even if they were RESOL 3 they would look good.

With RADIUS, you state it in the form:

```
RADIUS rmin, rmax
```
Any curve equal to or less than 'rmin' will render with 6 faces. Any curve equal to or more than rmax will render with 36 faces. Any curve between the two will render with a variable number of faces, on a sliding scale between 6 and 36 – similar to my example of the sliding scale RESOL command above.

Because RADIUS cannot be higher than 36 faces, there are rare occasions when you are forced to use RESOL, if you need 80 or 120 faces. But the 'Long Handrail' exercise in Voyager shows you how to get very large smooth curves without increasing the polygon count excessively. Or you can use TOLER.

TOLER is another interesting way of setting Resolution of curvature. TOLER is the distance from the actual arc of the curve, and the distance you are willing to allow the chord of the curve to exist away from the curve. GDL will recalculate the resolution to match the object. For example, a large curve like stadium roofing could work out its own RESOL if you told to to curve with a TOLER (tolerance) of 0.1 metres. TOLER could be set using variables or IF statements, just like RESOL or RADIUS.

Note of Warning – RESOL, TOLER and RADIUS cancel each other out if used, so decide which one you want to use for a model, or for a component of a model.

ELBOW is for a curved tubular bend object. It always grows up the Z-Axis, following the course of the X-Axis. The alpha angle can be anything from 0 to 360.

RESOL is an important issue – if you have a low resol, the curvature of the tube looks unfortunately angular. However, if you set a high resol, you have too many surfaces on the elbow, and it will take too long to render. The best solution to the resolution problem with the ELBOW is to use the RADIUS command – in which you separate the resolution of the surface of the tube itself from the resolution of the curve that it follows.

If you cannot reconcile these two considerations, then TUBE is a good alternative to ELBOW, but requires you to learn the PUT and GET routines, some trigonometry, and the For... Next Loop.

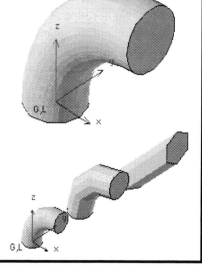

3D GDL Shapes

Other 3D elements

ELBOW r1, alpha, r2 {a segment elbow in the x-y plane; r1 is the arc's radius, alpha is the angle and r2 is the tube segment's radius }

```
!ELBOW Demonstration
!Syntax:- ELBOW rad1,alpha,rad2
ELBOW 0.12,90,0.03
```

'alpha' is the sweep angle of the Elbow.

The illustration of three ELBOWs shows what a clumsy tool is RESOL. The Elbow can become sadly polygonal, or even straight. Use RADIUS.

```
!ELBOW Demonstration
!Syntax:- ELBOW rad1,alpha,rad2
ELBOW 0.12,90,0.03
  RESOL 12
  ADDy 0.1
ELBOW 0.16,90,0.04
  RESOL 6
  ADDy 0.1
ELBOW 0.20,90,0.05
  DEL 2
```

About Subroutines...

THE essence of structured programming is that 3-D models should consist of subroutines which reflect the 3-D nature of the model. The other point of using subroutines is to avoid ever having to type out complex GDL commands more than once.

The example here is what you should be aiming towards. Every **GOSUB** command is telling GDL to **GO** and run the **SUB**routine of that line number.

The 'Executive Script'

THE first part of the script (as far as the END statement) can be called your 'executive script'. This is the main controlling script, that decides on what will be drawn, and in what order. When GDL reaches the END statement, it stops.

After the END statement, you carry a lot of useful baggage, called Subroutines. Each element of the model could be a subroutine. They can only be used if they are called by the executive script, or by another subroutine. The END statement prevents them from being read accidentally.

It is a good idea to keep the executive script short and decisive. When you want to repair, modify or extend the model, you will know exactly which subroutine to go to.

```
!Swivel Chair - 3D executive script

GOSUB 50    !Error Checking
GOSUB 300   !Foot of chair
GOSUB 400   !Shaft of chair
GOSUB 500   !Seat of Chair
GOSUB 600   !Back of Chair
END         !----------    A typical Executive Script
```

The Subroutine

THE subroutine is a short script that performs an action, and then finishes with the command RETURN, which tells GDL to go back to the GOSUB command that it came from; and then to continue with the program. A subroutine starts with a number so that you use that number when you write the GOSUB command – e.g. GOSUB 200.

The subroutine should behave like an **elemental object** in its own right. If you want to move the element sideways, or swivel it, you apply those move or swivel commands to the cursor, and then GOSUB the subroutine.

Here is a typical subroutine, numbered 250: The number must always be followed by a colon and you should add a

Golden Rules for Subroutines!

- Subroutines are always written after the **END** statement. END is essential – you must **never** accidentally run from the executive script into the subroutines.

- Subroutines always start with a **Line Number**, and finish with the statement 'RETURN', otherwise, GDL will accidentally run into the next subroutine.

- **Never** GOSUB the subroutine you are already in, or GDL will go on trying to do this **for ever** (Cmd-period to stop it).

- **Never** use a GOTO command to jump out of a subroutine – you will get quite lost!

- The subroutine must be entirely self contained – the **3D cursor** must finish up exactly where it was at the start of the subroutine. So you DEL all the ADD, ROT and MUL commands within the Subroutine. Never use DEL TOP for this purpose.

- Subroutines can GOSUB other subroutines: For example, in the human body, an Arm is an object written with a subroutine; but the Arm will need another subroutine to draw the object called Hand, and the Hand will need one for each of the objects called Finger.

- The 2D, 3D and Properties scripts can use Subroutines; but do not jump to one in another script from the one you are in! **Note, You cannot use END or Subroutines in a Master Script.**

For further reading on the syntax of BASIC, it is worth considering getting a book on BASIC. Although these are probably more difficult to find in the late nineties than books on C++, there must be some in libraries and well stocked bookshops.

comment line after the number, so that you know what the subroutine is actually doing. In each subroutine, there must be exactly the right number of DELs to ensure that the cursor returns to the same place as it was at the start of the subroutine.

```
250:!Two Spheres subroutine
SPHERE 0.1
  ADDx 0.2
SPHERE 0.05
  DEL 1
RETURN              A typical Subroutine
```

Tips and Tricks
Multiply, don't Divide!

Processors find it much easier to multiply than to divide. To divide once can take perhaps 32 cycles of a processors time, whereas a multiplication can take 1, 2 or 4 cycles, depending on which processor we are talking about, and whether

it is optimised for floating point or integer. So although it may be easier on the eye to write an expression like

'LET len=wid*3/4', it may process faster in the form 'LET len=wid*0.75'. Seriously, the time difference would only matter on extremely long scripts. You are better off writing efficient code, by using polylines and clear structure.

The Good Chair

Making your first chair into a PARAMETRIC object

THE very simple chair was an example of GDL that works, but isn't smart, isn't parametric, and isn't structured. So let's look at ways of improving it in all three ways. In so doing, you will learn the primary techniques in making GDL move from Object-making to Tool-making.

Click on your simple chair, and 'Open Library Object', and you get the main parameter building window (as right for v 6.5). You can make new parameters by clicking the 'New' button. These will give you new parameters of Length, named C, D, E, F and so on. Create parameters and change their **Variable** names to sensible ones like 'fsec' and 'shigt' according to the parameter table here (right). The **Name** here is what the User will see when using the dialog box that you are now creating. Put in nominal **Values** for each parameter. In this example, they are in decimal inches.

You can decide whether a parameter is a dimension, a number, a material, or whatever by holding the mouse down on the small symbol; the selection pallette pops up, and you can select one type. Only use 'Length' for dimensions, because ArchiCAD changes these according to your dimensional system settings. For numbers which remain constant, use 'Real Numbers' or 'Integers'. For materials, use the little cube and sphere logo. The others you will use more as you progress with GDL.

3 D Script: Take the 3D script of the Simple chair, and change all the 2" to 'fsec' (frame section); continue to work through all the dimensions changing them to parameters. As a design improvement, let's make all the legs the same height, and then have the chair-back permitting an inclination angle, so the leg components of the back of the chair gets written when we do the back. Because the seat height is 'shigt', the height of all the legs is 'shigt–fsec'. Do a similar small calculation for the width and depth ADD commands, allowing for the frame thickness.

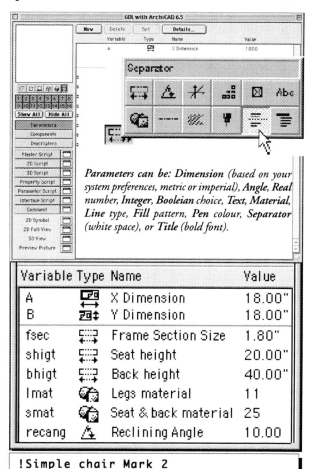

Parameters can be: Dimension (based on your system preferences, metric or imperial), Angle, Real number, Integer, Boolean choice, Text, Material, Line type, Fill pattern, Pen colour, Separator (white space), or Title (bold font).

Variable	Type	Name	Value
A		X Dimension	18.00"
B		Y Dimension	18.00"
fsec		Frame Section Size	1.80"
shigt		Seat height	20.00"
bhigt		Back height	40.00"
lmat		Legs material	11
smat		Seat & back material	25
recang		Reclining Angle	10.00

```
!Simple chair Mark 2
!3D Script
!GDL Discovery Course

wid=A        !Width
dep=B        !Depth
p=1/25" !One pixel

!Legs
MATERIAL lmat
BLOCK fsec,fsec,shigt-fsec
    ADDx wid-fsec
BLOCK fsec,fsec,shigt-fsec
    ADDy dep-fsec
BLOCK fsec,fsec,shigt-fsec
    ADDx -(wid-fsec)
BLOCK fsec,fsec,shigt-fsec
    DEL 3

!Seat
MATERIAL smat
    ADD p,p,shigt-fsec
BLOCK wid-p*2,dep-p*2,fsec
    DEL 1

!Back
    ADD 0,dep-fsec,shigt-fsec
    ROTx -recang
MATERIAL lmat
    BLOCK fsec,fsec,bhigt-shigt
    ADDx wid-fsec
    BLOCK fsec,fsec,bhigt-shigt
    DEL 1
MATERIAL smat
    ADD fsec,0,(bhigt-shigt)/3
BLOCK wid-fsec*2,fsec,(bhigt-shigt)*2/3
    DEL 3
```

Note that the use of 'p' for a pixel of 1 mm saves having to type 0.001 all the time. By shrinking the size of the seat by 1 millimetre (1/25") we avoid a rendering problem between seat and legs.

*We are using A and B here, so convert these to **wid** and **dep** early in the script*

Here, we move into position, rotate the cursor, then do the upper legs and the back as one operation, changing Materials as we go

```
!Simple chair
!Mark 1
!3D Script
MATERIAL "Whitewash"
PEN 1
!Legs
BLOCK 2",2",18"
    ADDx 16"
BLOCK 2",2",18"
    ADDy 16"
BLOCK 2",2",30"
    ADDx -16"
BLOCK 2",2",30"
    DEL 3
!Seat
    ADDz 18"
BLOCK 18",18",2"
    DEL 1
!Back
    ADD 2",16.5",24"
BLOCK 14",1.5",12"
    DEL 1
```

THIS chair is a useful starting exercise in:
- Handling rectangular blocks in 3-D
- Dimensioning the object as Parameters
- Writing Subroutines
- Making an object stretchy

CHANGING the script from the raw (but parametric) script is an easy progressive change. First number the groups. Each one will be a subroutine. Make sure that in each group, the number of DELs is right in that the cursor goes back to the origin each time. Use 100's to increment the numbers of your groups.

Next, put in the END command, clearly marked with a comment marker and a row of dashes. This signifies the end of the main part of the 3D script (the 'executive script'). What follows now is a series of Subroutines which have to be called. Put the word RETURN at the end of each subroutine. Now, in the Executive script, write GOSUB followed by the Line number and a copy of the name of the subroutine – do it as I have done here.

If it doesn't work (you get errors) it's due to forgetting the colon after the line numbers, or forgetting END or RETURN. Perhaps you didn't get the number of DELs right. Go over my example until you get it completely right. Go back to the page on Subroutines, and thoroughly check through the Golden Rules on Subroutines.

```
!Simple chair Mark 2
!3D Script
!GDL Discovery Course

wid=A        !Width
dep=B        !Depth
p=1/25"!One pixel

100:!Legs
MATERIAL lmat
BLOCK fsec,fsec,shigt-fsec
  ADDx wid-fsec
BLOCK fsec,fsec,shigt-fsec
  ADDy dep-fsec
BLOCK fsec,fsec,shigt-fsec
  ADDx -(wid-fsec)
BLOCK fsec,fsec,shigt-fsec
  DEL 3

200:!Seat
MATERIAL smat
  ADD p,p,shigt-fsec
BLOCK wid-p*2,dep-p*2,fsec
  DEL 1

300:!Back
  ADD 0,dep-fsec,shigt-fsec
  ROTx -recang
MATERIAL lmat
  BLOCK fsec,fsec,bhigt-shigt
    ADDx wid-fsec
  BLOCK fsec,fsec,bhigt-shigt
    DEL 1
MATERIAL smat
 ADD fsec,0,(bhigt-shigt)/3
BLOCK wid-fsec*2,fsec,(bhigt-shigt)*2/3
  DEL 3
```

```
!Simple chair Mark 3
!3D Script
!GDL Discovery Course

wid=A        !Width
dep=B        !Depth
p=1/25"!One pixel
GOSUB 100:!Legs
GOSUB 200:!Seat
GOSUB 300:!Back
END:!----------------------

100:!Legs
MATERIAL lmat
BLOCK fsec,fsec,shigt-fsec
  ADDx wid-fsec
BLOCK fsec,fsec,shigt-fsec
  ADDy dep-fsec
BLOCK fsec,fsec,shigt-fsec
  ADDx -(wid-fsec)
BLOCK fsec,fsec,shigt-fsec
  DEL 3
RETURN
200:!Seat
MATERIAL smat
  ADD p,p,shigt-fsec
BLOCK wid-p*2,dep-p*2,fsec
  DEL 1
RETURN
300:!Back
  ADD 0,dep-fsec,shigt-fsec
  ROTx -recang
MATERIAL lmat
  BLOCK fsec,fsec,bhigt-shigt
    ADDx wid-fsec
  BLOCK fsec,fsec,bhigt-shigt
    DEL 1
MATERIAL smat
 ADD fsec,0,(bhigt-shigt)/3
BLOCK wid-fsec*2,fsec,(bhigt-shigt)*2/3
  DEL 3
RETURN
```

2D Script

Because the Chair is able to recline at different angles, it is more difficult to write a script in 2D and may be easier to just use PROJECT2 3,270,2. You would need trigonometry to work out where the back appeared in the 2D plan. Put in A-B Hotspots as shown, and your chair will become S-T-R-E-T-C-H-Y!

```
!Chair - 2D-Script
  HOTSPOT2 0,0:HOTSPOT2 A/2,B/2
  HOTSPOT2 A,0
  HOTSPOT2 A,B
  HOTSPOT2 0,B
  PROJECT2 3,270,2 !The object!
```

The four main ones are for stretching, and the middle one is for picking up

Use the GDL Manual!

Several ArchiCAD 6 commands are covered in various sections in the GDL Cookbook. But please note that it is not the function of the Cookbook to replace the GDL Manual. You need to use both. You will find the GDL Manual a lot easier to read now you have tried the Cookbook. You will also find sections of the Cookbook easier if you dip into the manual.

Congratulations to Graphisoft on making the AC6 GDL manual better than its predecessors.

Help files + Documentation folder

It is most helpful with ArchiCAD 6 that the manuals are now available on line in the Documentation folder, in your ArchiCAD folder. In fact, you can write any document yourself, save as Acrobat file, and put it in that folder. They appear in the HELP menu.

The search command with Acrobat makes it easier to use the GDL manual (easier than the paper version!) So it may be easier to enjoy using your GDL manual. **You can put the GDL Cookbook.pdf into the Help Menu.**

BAD Chair example

IF you are working at home, you may have looked through pages in the GDL Cookbook. Look at the script on this page, and CRITICISE! Come back to it later for another read when you have done more scripting.

IF you have been on the Lift-Off course, the principles of Structured Programming and good typography will have been explained to you by now.

Do not type this script in!!

....it's an example of the untidy kind of scripts you write when you first start writing GDL scripts.

Let's notice the good points first:

- The script results in a chair!
- The script is documented with a few comments

Therefore, it is not all bad!!

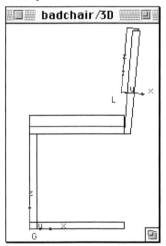

The side elevation shows that it still works, even though it is a bad script!

```
! Tubular Steel chair
! badly written GDL
Pen 1
! Draw Legs
block .03,.03,.45
block .45,.03,.03
addz .45
block .45,.03,.03
addx .45
roty 5
block .03,.03,.45
roty -5
addz -.45: addx -.45
addy .45
block .03,.03,.45
block .45,.03,.03
addz .45
block .45,.03,.03
addx .45
roty 5
block .03,.03,.45
roty -5
addz -.45: addx -.45
addy -.45
Material "Chrome"
!Seat
addz .48
Material "LimeStone"
!Seat
block .45,.48,.05
addx .44
addz .15
!Back
roty 5
addy .03
block .05,.42,.28
```

```
!2D Script
PROJECT2 3,270,2
```

This cookbook is all about learning to used 'structured programming' techniques.

It is easier to learn from mistakes than from successes – so please look at the criticisms on this page when you have tried some scripts yourself.

If you make mistakes with a sequential script like this, you get tangles like the one here – and you find it very difficult to disentangle the distorted framework.

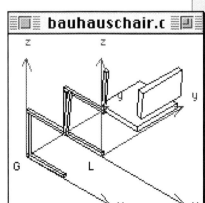

Criticism of Script

- The script is 'sequential' instead of being organised into a modular structure. For example, in this script, the entire leg is written once, and then it is written all over again, nearby. This is wasteful, and difficult to edit later. The legs, being the same, should be repeated in a neater way, either using a LOOP or a SUBROUTINE.

- The PEN colour should also be a parameter in case pen colour 1 is not what the user wants.

- Make even more use of COMMENTS, INDENTS and CARRIAGE RETURNS in the script to make it easier to understand. Indents are used in this example, but there is no logic to them. Indent cursor movements.

- The Model starts from the bottom left corner, although it would be better with a symmetrical object to start from the Centre line.

- The material for the legs is specified after they have been drawn. They will turn out green!

- The entire script is written in lower case. Although lower case is easier to read, it is more difficult to pick out commands from comments and variable, and it is therefore more difficult to edit the script. ALWAYS use •UPPER• case for command words and •lower• case for comments and variables.

- The script makes occasional use of multistatement lines using the colon: – eg addy -.03:roty -5 on one line. This is legal syntax, but is bad because you will have problems debugging the script.

- It is bad to write numbers in the form .03. Always give low numbers a leading zero, e.g. 0.03.

- It is not parametric. The script specifies all materials and dimensions very specifically – whereas you should provide the user with all the parameters they need in the dialog box.

- At the end of the script, no attempt is made to bring the cursor back to a final resting place at the origin.

- Although the author brings the cursor back before beginning the next operation (most commendable!), there are far easier ways to do it; instead of wriggling backwards in reverse, use the DEL command.

- PROJECT2 is quite legal in the 2D script but it is always better to try a real script with RECT2 and LINE2 commands. Also, you should add in some Hotspots.

Tubular Handrail

In this library object we look at:

- Handling cylindrical entities – **CYLIND** and **ELBOW**
- Using **RADIUS** to control curve smoothness
- Using **HOTSPOTs** in 2D

The handrails can be grouped together to form useful structures which would be difficult to do in any other way.

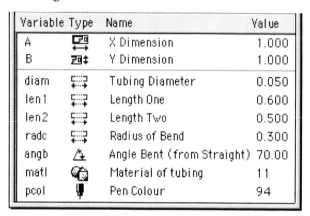

Variable	Type	Name	Value
A		X Dimension	1.000
B		Y Dimension	1.000
diam		Tubing Diameter	0.050
len1		Length One	0.600
len2		Length Two	0.500
radc		Radius of Bend	0.300
angb		Angle Bent (from Straight)	70.00
matl		Material of tubing	11
pcol		Pen Colour	94

Parameters: You want the user to enter small dimensions for tubing, in the form of Diameter, not in Radius. People always think of handrails and other round things in 'diameter'. Your program can easily convert Diameter to Radius. As the handrail dimensions can be altered, A and B are not used in this script or in the parameters box – but they could be.

Angle – You can think of the angle in terms of the angle formed by two lines. But a tube bender, or GDL thinks of the 'sweep angle' formed by the tube, from the straight.

Radius – You want the main curve to be as smooth as possible, but don't want the surface of the tubing to have 36 faces as it will take too long to render. The RADIUS command allows you to control the surfaces of small and large curves, and to relate it to the actual tube radius. (See RADIUS in the explanation of curvature and in the GDL Manual.) It is confusing that GDL uses the word RADIUS for this purpose, but we have to live with that now.

When you only want to control one set of surface curves, such as for cones or cylinders, you can use the simpler command RESOL.

PEN and Material – If you make the material zero, then the PEN colour will make the whole surface to be that colour.

If you want to 'HAND' the finished handrail, i.e. Mirror it, then you can do that in the object settings box, later.

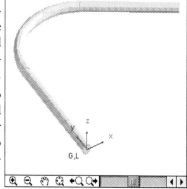

```
!Curved Handrail system
!3D Script Mk2

trad=diam*0.5    !TubeRadius
RADIUS trad*0.5,trad*4

!prelims
MATERIAL matl
PEN pcol

!Make it!
  ROTx -90
CYLIND len1,trad
  ADDz len1
ELBOW radc,angb,trad
  ADDx radc
  ROTy angb
  ADDx -radc
CYLIND len2,trad
  DEL 5

END:!-----------------
```

*The **Origin** for this Handrail starts the drawing the tube from one end, and proceeds to 'worm' its way around the bend, along the tube.*

3D Script: Convert the diameter to Tube radius. Issue the RADIUS command based on *trad.* Set the Material and Pen colours.

Starting from the end of the first tube, use a ROTx -90 to lie the handrail down horizontally (or it will grow upwards). Do the first Rail by pushing out a cylinder horizontally, then move to its end by adding along the Z axis – which is now horizontal. You can push the ELBOW round the corner, as it grows along the Z axis, which is already in the right direction. Then go round the bend – go to the centre of the curve, rotate by the angle, and move to the start of the second tube. Push out the final cylinder.

This script is too short to justify a strict approach to structured programming, but you should still use the DEL command to bring your 3D cursor back to the origin before writing END.

Using the principles of the script for this simple library object, you can assemble handrail and tubing structures of great complexity.

If you used A and B to make it stretchy, you would have to work backwards from the curve radius to decide what the straight tube lengths would be.

Notice how the cursor movement commands are indented. When you have a long run of them, it makes it easier to count them up.

continued next page

IF... THEN... ELSE... ENDIF

WHEN we talk about 'programming' we are often thinking of the ability of our script to tell the computer to follow a path, make decisions, follow courses of action based on those decisions, and thus display a level of 'articifial intelligence'.

The **IF** statement is the essential mechanism by which computers make decisions – whichever language they are working in.

IF statements can stay on one line, or can refer to a long sequence of commands. Examples are given here.

ENDIF means that it has reached the end of the long version of the IF statement.

ELSE Finally, you could have two complicated tasks to do, one if the IF condition is true, and the other if it is false. You use ELSE to help decide whether to do one task or the other. In this case, ELSE must be on a line by itself.

Nested IF Statements

As the GDL parser encounters each IF... THEN, it remembers it, and as it encounters each ENDIF, it signs it off. So you can 'Nest' many IF.. THEN.. ENDIFs inside each other, and the machine keeps count accurately. You may lose count though, so I dont encourage excessively complex nests.

```
IF s=13 THEN GOSUB 250
```

This is the simplest example of an IF statement. If the IF condition is 'false' (i.e. 's' is not equal to 13), then the program continues to the next line.

```
IF p>13 THEN n=1 ELSE n=0
```

This is an extension of the IF statement; if the first IF condition is not 'true' then it will take an alternative course of action. In this example, one is setting a flag called 'n' to values of 1 or zero.

Long IF Statement

```
IF s=13 THEN
    ADDz 1.2
    GOSUB 250
    nq=1
    DEL 1
ELSE
    ADDx 0.3
    GOSUB 150
    DEL 1
ENDIF
```

In this example, there are so many things to do as a result of the IF statement that it can no longer fit on one line. So you leave the first line with a 'THEN' hanging off the end of the line. Everything on every line after that will then work if the IF statement is true. If the IF statement is false, GDL ignores the whole group, until it reaches the ENDIF statement – logically. If there is an alternative action required (in case the first IF statement is false, then you can use the ELSE command to make it do something else.

```
IF s>13 OR s<26 THEN GOSUB 250
IF nq=1 AND s<13 THEN GOSUB 150
```

Elsewhere in the Cookbook, you may find examples of 'Nested' IF... THEN... ENDIF statements – where one entire IF... ENDIF statement is inside another. You may also find examples, as above, where a 'Boolean' choice is to be made, using AND and OR.

```
IF Curr<0 THEN
   IF closd=1 THEN
     PRINT "Holes not allowed"
     END
   ELSE
     closd=1
   ENDIF
ELSE
   IF Curr>=900 AND Curr<1000 THEN
   S900X=CurrX-OrX
   S900Y=CurrY-OrY
   ELSE
IF int(Curr/2)%2 THEN
IF int(Curr/64)%2 THEN
   StatusE=2
ELSE
   StatusE=0
ENDIF

   ELSE
     StatusE=1
   ENDIF
IF int(Curr/4)%2
     StatusP=-1
     ELSE
     StatusP=1
     ENDIF
IF Curr>=4000 AN[
   GOSUB 4000
ELSE
   SHX[PtCount]=Cu
   SHY[PtCount]=Cu
   SHM[1][PtCount]=StatusE
   SHM[2][PtCount]=StatusP
PtCount=PtCount+1
   ENDIF
      ENDIF
        ENDIF
```

This small chunk of a script by one of the worlds most expert GDL artists, Oleg Shmidt reveals how complex you can get with nested IF... ENDIF statements

---

Tubular Handrail: continued

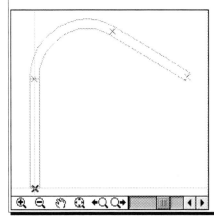

2D Script: As the user can change the handrail details, you cannot use a standard symbol. You need to write a 2-D script. For quick-to-draw objects, issue the PROJECT2 command as here.

Hotspots: This handrail is a slippery object to pick up because the 'Bounding box' hotspots are going to be positioned well away from the actual rail. You need to plant HOTSPOTs in the 2D script. Turn off Bounding boxes. The 2D cursor can be moved about in a similar way to the 3D script, using the ADD2 and ROT2 commands, until you find the end of the tube.

```
!Handrail 2D script
PROJECT2 3,270,2
HOTSPOT2 0,0

!First Tube
  ADD2 0,len1
HOTSPOT2 0,0

!Round the bend
  ADD2 radc,0
  ROT2 -angb
  ADD2 -radc,0
HOTSPOT2 0,0

!Second tube
  ADD2 0,len2
HOTSPOT2 0,0
  DEL 5

!It is often easiest to
!mimic the 3D script
```

FOR... NEXT Loops

FOR k=1 TO n: NEXT k

FOR non-programmers, the FOR... NEXT Loop seems at first perhaps the greatest challenge. It is in reality your strongest friend, because it has tremendous capacity for work. With a few economical lines of script within a FOR... NEXT loop, huge lattices or structures can be created.

When you want to repeat an operation, there will be more than one way in which you can repeat it. For example, you may simply want to repeat it 4 times. So 4 is the parameter.

If you wanted to plant poles in the ground at 10 metre intervals over a distance of 125 metres, you have a choice of parameters – you can either plant 13 poles, or you can use the parameters of 10 and 125 metres.

NEXT: In every case, NEXT must be followed by the name of the variable. You could have some FOR...NEXT loops nested inside each other, and it is important that GDL knows which loop you are referring to.

LOOPS: Some Golden Rules

• Do not change the value of the variable that is being used as the counter while in the loop.

• Once you are in a loop, you must never branch out of it, except to use a Subroutine. GOTO commands are quite forbidden, unless you stay inside the loop.

• If you don't know exactly how long the loop will be, use REPEAT... UNTIL

```
dist=0 !distance travelled
FOR k=1 TO 4
dist=dist+10
CYLIND 2,0.1 !Pole
ADDx 10
NEXT k
DEL 4
PRINT 'you have gone',dist, 'm'
```

Let's Plant 4 poles at a spacing of 10 metres, and calculate distance gone.

IN this script we nominate 'k' to be a counter – the value changes from 1 to 4. Every time that GDL reads through the loop, it increases the value by 1. So the first time, k=1 and it draws the pole, moves sideways 10 metres, then encounters the NEXT k command. At this point GDL asks itself if 'k' has reached 4 yet. If it has not yet reached 4, it goes back to the first line, and runs through the loop again – until it finishes.

As you have moved 4 times, you have to issue a DEL 4 command at the end to get back to the origin for your next action. Meanwhile a little accumulator called 'dist' works out how far you have gone.

As a matter of discipline, always try to use i, j, k, m, or n for loops based on round numbers (integers). Never use these variables for anything else, especially not Real Numbers like dimensions. If your loop is based on real numbers, use p, q, r, s or t, or something like 'dist'. This tradition dates from the days of Fortran, but it is good, in that it reduces the risk of getting in a muddle.

```
pn=0 !number of poles
FOR dist=0 TO 125 STEP 10
pn=pn+1
ADDx dist
CYLIND 2,0.1 !Pole
DEL 1
NEXT dist
PRINT 'you planted',pn,'poles'
```

Let's plant an unknown number of poles at a spacing of 10 metres.

WE don't know how many poles there will be – let GDL work that out for us – until we run out of road. We have 125 metres of road to plant. In this case, 'dist' acts as a distance dimension. Do not use 'k' here. It is best to associate 'k' in your mind with integer counters, not with 'real numbers'. In the first run through the loop, 'dist' is zero, so the cursor moves zero, plants a tree, then returns to the origin – and then does it again with a new value of 'dist'. For this, the loop needs to be told the 'stepping' rate of the loop. If no stepping rate is given, it assumes you mean a value of One. Here, you want to step 10 metres each time.

As you have been using DEL inside the pole planting loop, you do not need to finish with a DEL. Moreover, you do not need to worry about how many poles to plant. When it has planted 13 poles and reached a distance of 120 metres, it realises that if it plants another, it will go to 130 metres, which is too far. Therefore, it stops at 120 metres run.

The little accumulator called 'pn' tells you how many you planted.

REPEAT...UNTIL Other commands related to loops are **REPEAT...UNTIL**, and **DO WHILE**. I have found REPEAT... UNTIL to be the best way of checking user errors in a complex situation where only a trial-and-error approach will work. For example, if the end value of the loop is constantly changing (if it's generated as a random number) or you want to go on doing something until you exceed a certain value, then use REPEAT...UNTIL. On the other hand, DO WHILE occurs while a value remains unchanging, and if something that results from your loop changes that value, then you can escape from the loop.

GOTO is something that I never use, as it the worst thing that you can do if you believe in the structured programming approach. You can issue a command such as: 'GOTO 250', and it will jump to that numbered line. It doesn't care if the number is part of a subroutine, it doesn't check as to whether it is already in a subroutine. It just jumps, even if it is illegal. Chaos can be the result.

Graphisoft library objects are littered with dozens of GOTO's, perhaps to discourage users editing the scripts.

The use of Subroutines, Loops and IF.. THEN.. ELSE commands should give you ways of getting round every possible situation where you might want or need to use GOTO.

Before the FOR... NEXT Loop was invented, one could make something that behaved like a loop, using GOTO. But now, there should be no need for it in clean scripting.

```
p=0                      p=1
if p GOTO 1              if p THEN 1
PRINT "hello'            PRINT "hello'
1:END                    1:END
```

You can even omit the THEN, or omit the GOTO - as long as one of them is present. But why am I telling you this? It's bad form.

Steps in 2D – **Dimension Tool**

Object

11'-9 1/4"

2.872

YOU might think the GDL Cookbook was only about 3D modelling – Not so! 2D scripting can be useful for practical work.

This dimension tool is simply a dimension line with two witness lines, but it is stretchy (or you can type in the dimension) and allows Metric and Imperial, and a choice of tick marks.

Variable	Type	Name	Value
A		X Dimension	1.000
B		Y Dimension	0.100
fsize		Font Plotting size in mm	2
marks	☒	Markers - Circles-ON Ticks-OFF	On
units	☒	Units - Metres-ON Feet-OFF	On

Parameters: The Font size in millimetres is based •absolutely• on the plotting or printing size, and disregards the scale of the drawing. (You can buy a commercial dimension tool from the author which include autosizing fonts.)

Here, we try using Booleian Parameters, which allow a simple binary choice between OFF or ON. These are sent to the GDL script as being 0 or 1.

The IF... ELSE.... ENDIF statements illustrate how alternative actions can be taken. Note also that a line that ends in a comma is assumed to continue on to the next line. (I have to keep scripts narrow so they fit the page!)

Finally, for the TEXT2 display, it is **always** necessary to define the font and style of the text, so this is jumping you ahead a little. Type it in as you find it for now, and have a look ahead at the pages in the manual and here on DEFINE STYLE. This method forces TEXT2 to display a number (signified by the '%' sign) to be in Metres or in Feet+Inches, and the 0.8 forces it to a precision of 1/8".

```
!Dimensioning Tool
!2D script
!Hotspots - Stretch&Pickup
HOTSPOT2 0,0
HOTSPOT2 A,0
HOTSPOT2 A/2,0
HOTSPOT2 0,-B
HOTSPOT2 A,-B

!Dim_Line & Witness Lines
LINE2 0,0,  A,0 !Dim_line
LINE2 0,-B, 0,B*0.2
LINE2 A,-B, A,B*0.2

!Dimension markers
IF marks=1 THEN
  LINE2 -A/100,-A/100,
         A/100, A/100
  LINE2 A-A/100,-A/100,
         A+A/100, A/100
  ELSE
  CIRCLE2 0,0,A/100
  CIRCLE2 A,0,A/100
  ENDIF

!Text
DEFINE STYLE "diasty" "Geneva",
             fsize,5,0
SET STYLE "diasty"
IF units=1 THEN
  TEXT2 A/2,0,STR('%0.8 ffi',A)
  ELSE
  TEXT2 A/2,0,STR('%m',A)
  ENDIF
```

PEN

PEN sets the pen colour. This can be changed during the execution of the script, so that different parts of the model can be drawn separately.

On PEN, there are some points to note: PEN must have a value. You cannot have PEN zero. PEN 1 gives you Black line. However, people can modify the PEN pallette and the pallete values can be re-assigned. This can have mischievous effects on your model. It is best therefore not to hard code the PEN colours, but to make them items in the dialog box, that the user can select.

PEN can be used as a convenient way to create bright coloured surfaces. If you set MATERIAL to zero, then the PEN colour becomes the surface colour. This is why most of your first efforts at modelling come out as GREEN – because Graphisoft designate PEN 4 as the default, and no material has been specified.

PRINT

Theory

PRINT is a way of getting GDL to tell you or the user something – used in pointing out errors, or in debugging. The warning box only shows when you display in 3D.

My advice is not to use it unless you have a very important object, and a very important message to tell the user. If you do it for commonplace objects like windows, the user could be faced with 20 or 50 identical shouting warning boxes, and would not know which object was wrongly set.

```
slenr=colht/colwid !Slenderness Ratio
IF slenr>24 THEN
  PRINT "Warning, Column Slenderness Ratio is:",slenr
ENDIF
```

Warning, Column Slenderness Ratio is: 36

⚠ [Stop] [Continue]

Using the PRINT Command

PRINT is most useful during the writing and debugging process, for example, to see if the result of a Trigonometrical calculation is giving the right result. Execution of the 3D script is halted at the Print command, so it's a good way to test something even when it isn't fully working.

It's also useful if you lack a pocket calculator capable of Trig or complex functions. Type in a quick expression and get the answer.

Tubular Steel Chair

HERE is a different chair – but rendered in round tubes – like the original Breuer chair.

This chair is a useful starting exercise in

- Handling straight and curved tubular sections
- Keeping track of many 3-D cursor moves
- Structuring the program in the form of subroutines
- Using Symmetry and Mirroring

Parameters: take a copy of the previous chair and let's change it radically – using cylinders and tubes – add some extra parameters for Seat thickness, Pen colour and a Booleian option to change the 2D view of the object.

We are going to make the origin in the centre front of the chair, go out half a width, draw one leg, all in subroutine 100. Then repeat that on the other side (mirroring the first). Then finish off with the seat and back, all in subroutine 200. The steel of this tubular chair meets at the bottom. It could also do at the top, but I am trying to keep this simple!

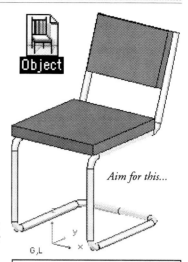

Aim for this...

Variable	Type	Name	Value
A	⟷	X Dimension	450
B	↕	Y Dimension	500
fsec	⟷	Tubing section/Diam	30
shigt	⟷	Seat height	500
bhigt	⟷	Back height	450
lmat	🎨	Leg Material	11
smat	🎨	Seat Material	19
recang	∠	Slope of Back	20.00
sthik	⟷	Seat+Back thickness	50
pcol	✏	Pen colour	1
truvu	☒	Truview ON or OFF?	Off

```
!Tubular steel chair
!Master Script

wid   = A !<-these need to be
dep   = B !<-in Master script
trad  = fsec/2 !Tube radius
crad  = trad*3 !Curv radius
bhit  = bhigt-shigt !back ht.
sinr  = SIN(recang)
```

```
!Tubular steel chair
!3D Script
 PEN pcol
 RADIUS trad,trad*2

GOSUB 100: !Leg
 MULx -1
GOSUB 100: !Leg
 DEL 1
GOSUB 200: !Seat
GOSUB 300: !Back

END!---------------------
```

```
100:!Cylindrical Leg
MATERIAL lmat
 ADD 0,dep,trad
 ROTy 90
CYLIND wid/2-crad-trad,
       trad
 ADDz wid/2-crad-trad
 ROTz -90
ELBOW crad,90,trad
 ADD crad,0,crad
 ROTy 90
CYLIND dep-crad*2,trad
 ADDz dep-crad*2
 ROTz -90
ELBOW crad,90,trad
 ADD crad,0,crad
 ROTy 90
!(Work out cylinder height)
clen=shigt-crad*2-trad*2-sthik
CYLIND clen,trad
 ADDz clen
ELBOW crad,90,trad
 ADD crad,0,crad
 ROTy 90
CYLIND dep-crad*2,trad
 ADDz dep-crad*2
 ROTz 180
ELBOW crad,90-recang,trad
 ADDx crad
 ROTy 90-recang
 ADDx -crad
CYLIND bhit-crad,trad
    DEL 18
RETURN
```

Master Script: Use this now, for the first time. It's for parameters etc. that are needed by both 2D and 3D scripts.

'Crad', 'trad' and 'clen' are examples of 'internal parameters'. This means a parameter that is not changeable by the user in the normal dialog box. The best place for these is in the Master Script. The author of the script can tweak the value of 'crad'. 'clen' is calculated on the fly.

3D Script: To simplify matters, the curved bend radius 'crad' is 3 times the tube radius. We also add the RADIUS command to control the two curvatures of **tube bend** and **tube surface**. It dramatically shortens the time taken to render just one chair – imagine a lecture room or café filled with such chairs!

Axial Symmetry: Because of the symmetry of a round tube chair, you can see the great advantage of starting from the Centre Line, doing only one leg, and then mirroring that whole leg. The MUL command multiplies everything in the direction of the axis. So MULx -1 makes the leg draw itself.

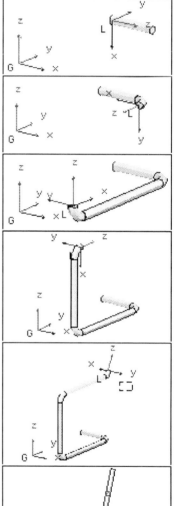

Worm your way round the tube

Tubular Steel Chair 2: continued

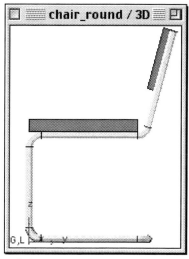

100: Starting from the centre back of the chair, you 'worm' your way round the tubular frame, issuing Cylinder and Elbow commands as you go. Almost always, you have to issue a ROTz to get the next Elbow to grow in the right direction – it always wants to grow over the X-axis.

The way of getting round the final corner is the same as for the Handrail. The height of the vertical leg cylinder is tricky, so it is calculated on a line of its own, then used as 'clen' in the script.

Upholstering the chair

200: and 300: The Seat is easy to place (BLOCK command) but the Back is more difficult. Maneouvring up to the right place for the Back of the chair (which rests *between* them) proves to be a bit tough.

We could move in just three moves, not seven; but I advise you to keep your moves separate when it is this complicated. When you look at the script later, it is easier to see how the figures were arrived at.

All these ROTs and ADDs are necessary to get the cursor to the right position for the chair back.

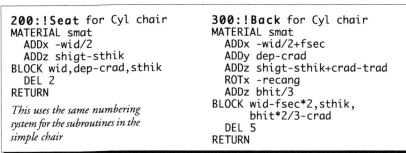

```
200:!Seat for Cyl chair       300:!Back for Cyl chair
MATERIAL smat                 MATERIAL smat
  ADDx -wid/2                    ADDx -wid/2+fsec
  ADDz shigt-sthik                ADDy dep-crad
BLOCK wid,dep-crad,sthik         ADDz shigt-sthik+crad-trad
  DEL 2                          ROTx -recang
RETURN                          ADDz bhit/3
                              BLOCK wid-fsec*2,sthik,
This uses the same numbering        bhit*2/3-crad
system for the subroutines in the   DEL 5
simple chair                    RETURN
```

2 D Script: As the user can change the chair style and size, you cannot use a standard symbol. You need to write a 2-D script. For quick-to-draw objects, just issue the PROJECT2 command as below.

```
!Tubular steel chair
!2D Script
PEN pcol
HOTSPOT2 -A/2,0  !Stretchy
HOTSPOT2  A/2,0  !hotspots
HOTSPOT2 -A/2,B
HOTSPOT2  A/2,B
HOTSPOT2  0,B/2  !Pickup
PROJECT2 3,270,2
```

You need to organise a 'nest' of Hotspots at each corner and one in the middle to make sure the chair will stretch correctly.

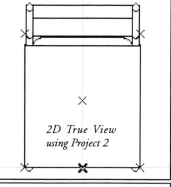

2D True View using Project 2

```
!Tubular steel chair
!2D Script
PEN pcol
HOTSPOT2 -A/2,0  !Stretchy
HOTSPOT2  A/2,0  !hotspots
HOTSPOT2 -A/2,B
HOTSPOT2  A/2,B
HOTSPOT2  0,B/2  !Pickup
!PROJECT2 3,270,2 !Test

IF truvu THEN
    PROJECT2 3,270,2
ELSE
100:!Legs
RECT2 -wid/2,0,-wid/2+fsec,
      dep+bhit*sinr
MUL2 -1,1
RECT2 -wid/2,0,-wid/2+fsec,
      dep+bhit*sinr
DEL 1
200:!Seat
RECT2 -wid/2,0,
      wid/2,dep-crad
300:!Back
RECT2 -wid/2,dep-sthik+bhit*sinr/3,
      wid/2,dep+bhit*sinr
ENDIF
```

Refinement of the 2-D script:

Boolean Choice: If the user decides to have a true plan of the object in the 2D symbol, they can opt for a True View, alternatively, they can have a simplified 2D scripted symbol.

The true view may take too long to form if the plan has many chairs in it.

If the scripted symbol is required, then draw rectangles, for the legs, the seat and one of which is determined as the function of the back height and the SIN of the back slope.

How does one know how to use Trig to determine XY locations? Well the Maths primer in the Voyager volume will tell you!

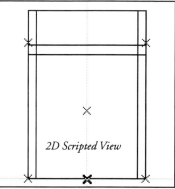

2D Scripted View

2-D Script may take longer to write, but saves masses of time in the redraw process of the project plan – especially important with furniture.

Object Naming

ArchiCAD 6.5 requires that all Library Objects end in the suffix .GSM (even on the Mac), and a similar limit applies to Doors and Windows. This makes them more portable. Beware if you convert a complex 6.0 project to 6.5.

Domino House: Loops

THIS Domino House type frame structure is a practical demonstration of the FOR... NEXT Loop. The resulting object could be used in site models for buildings surrounding your own (much better) scheme.

FOR... NEXT is a way of achieving repetition without having to type in the script for each part. Simply by setting a counter running, and then doing an operation every time that counter is incremented (until the counter reaches its end) you may finish with something very complex.

Doing it without Loops

For example, in this script, you can build a two or three storey building by naming each slab, ADDz-ing to get to the next floor, doing another Block, and so on.

Variable	Type	Name	Value
bwid		Number of Bays Width	2
bdep		Number of Bays Depth	3
snum		Number of Storeys	6
ftfh		Floor to Floor height	3000
bays		Bay Spacing	3600
clsz		Column/Slab size	300
matl		Material	18

Parameters: Looking at this building, you can make every aspect parametric – the total width and depth of the building can be calculated in the script.

Notice that in the parameter box, one takes care to ensure that things which are INTEGERs, such as number of Bays and floors are shown as Integers.

The advantage of a parametric structure is simply that it can be any width, length, height, column size and spacing, floor to floor height. In an Urban Design model, this could be a good way to do surrounding buildings; better than trying to build them fully, or put them into the model as boring solid slab blocks. All one needs is an option to instal Glass to complete this model.

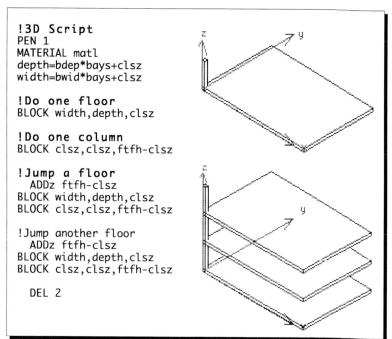

```
!3D Script
PEN 1
MATERIAL matl
depth=bdep*bays+clsz
width=bwid*bays+clsz

!Do one floor
BLOCK width,depth,clsz

!Do one column
BLOCK clsz,clsz,ftfh-clsz

!Jump a floor
    ADDz ftfh-clsz
BLOCK width,depth,clsz
BLOCK clsz,clsz,ftfh-clsz

!Jump another floor
    ADDz ftfh-clsz
BLOCK width,depth,clsz
BLOCK clsz,clsz,ftfh-clsz

    DEL 2
```

3D Script: Reasons to do it with Loops

This doesn't sound too bad, but imagine doing it for all the columns on every floor! An even bigger benefit of the FOR...NEXT loop is that the loop can be parametric – the range of the counter can be parametric, as can the stepping increment. The counter itself can be used as a parameter e.g. an angle can be stepping at 15 degrees with each iteration, and you can do a SIN or COS with each loop, or the distance can be advancing each time.

In a building like this, there is so much repetition, even to do one floor that you really will need to learn to use FOR... NEXT Loops to cope with the number of columns and floors involved.

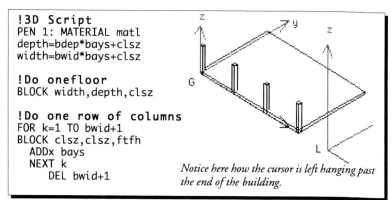

```
!3D Script
PEN 1: MATERIAL matl
depth=bdep*bays+clsz
width=bwid*bays+clsz

!Do onefloor
BLOCK width,depth,clsz

!Do one row of columns
FOR k=1 TO bwid+1
BLOCK clsz,clsz,ftfh
    ADDx bays
    NEXT k
        DEL bwid+1
```

Notice here how the cursor is left hanging past the end of the building.

FOR...NEXT Loops

Look at the above way of doing a loop. If there are three bays in the building, you want to draw four columns.

In this loop, you draw a BLOCK (which is the column); then you move the cursor, draw another block and so on, until they are all drawn. At the end of this process (see illustration), the cursor is hanging off the end of the building and you have to issue a DEL bwid+1 command to get the cursor back to the origin.

LOOP Counter name Why do I use K so often for Loops? Well it is one of the easiest characters to read in a small font, and used to be a favourite letter for counters in Fortran, the predecessor to BASIC.

Domino House: continued

Another, neater way of doing a loop

In the first loop on the previous page, the cursor worked its way from one side of the building to the other, drawing blocks and moving until it reached the end – like a creature laying eggs. I prefer a different method whereby the cursor always stays at the corner of the building, darts out to draw each column one at a time, and then darts back to the start; then darts out to do the next one – a bit like a chameleon's tongue leaping out over increasing distances to catch flies!

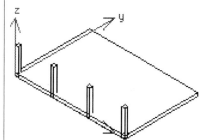

Notice how the cursor stays at the corner except when darting out to do another column.

```
!3D Script

PEN 1: MATERIAL matl
depth=bdep*bays+clsz
width=bwid*bays+clsz

!Do one floor
BLOCK width,depth,clsz

!Do 1 row of columns
FOR k=1 TO bwid+1
  ADDx bays*(k-1)
BLOCK clsz,clsz,ftfh
  DEL 1
NEXT k
```

Therefore, in this Loop, you issue the cursor ADD command BEFORE you draw the BLOCK. Since you want to start with a Block/column, the first ADD command must be equal to zero – which you get by multiplying bays*(k-1). You DEL 1 within the loop, which means your cursor jumps back to the origin for every column. This is far tidier, and there are no DELs to do after the loop is finished.

Nested For.. Next Loops

You will want to repeat that set of columns throughout the floor. Having already done the front row, you can repeat the loop for the middle row and end row. Instead of repeating the loop, you could put another loop around the loop! It is called 'nesting'.

If you do this, be sure to use a different counter name – in this case, I have used 'n' and 'k'. I have used the 'tidy' method of drawing the loop. And you can now see why the tidy method is better. If you use the other method, you risk getting confused as to the best place and number to DEL. This now represents a complete 'Storey' module – which could be looped vertically too – No reason why you cannot have three nested loops!

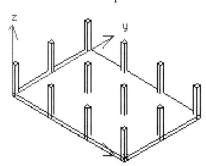

Modify the script you have been working on so that it looks like this – the result should look like a whole floor of the building, with columns.

Add in Titles at the start of the script. When you make the final modifications in the next stage, you will have the whole building.

```
!Domino House demo
!For... Next Loops
!3D Script

PEN 1: MATERIAL matl
depth=bdep*bays+clsz
width=bwid*bays+clsz

!Do one floor
BLOCK width,depth,clsz

!Do all the columns
FOR n=1 TO bdep+1
  ADDy bays*(n-1)

!Do one row of columns
FOR k=1 TO bwid+1
  ADDx bays*(k-1)
!One Column
BLOCK clsz,clsz,ftfh
  DEL 1
  NEXT k

  DEL 1
  NEXT n
```

```
!Domino House demo
!For... Next Loops
!3D Script

PEN 1: MATERIAL matl
depth=bdep*bays+clsz
width=bwid*bays+clsz

!Do all the floors
FOR m=1 TO snum
  ADDz ftfh*(m-1)

!Do one floor
BLOCK width,depth,clsz

!Do all the columns
FOR n=1 TO bdep+1
  ADDy bays*(n-1)

!Do 1 row of columns
FOR k=1 TO bwid+1
  ADDx bays*(k-1)
BLOCK clsz,clsz,ftfh
```

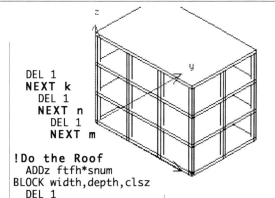

```
    DEL 1
  NEXT k
    DEL 1
  NEXT n
    DEL 1
  NEXT m

!Do the Roof
  ADDz ftfh*snum
BLOCK width,depth,clsz
  DEL 1

!Glass
MATERIAL "Glass"
  ADD clsz/2,clsz/2,0
BLOCK width-clsz,
    depth-clsz,ftfh*snum
  DEL 1
```

2D script: As this is a simple rectangle, with columns, use

PROJECT2 3,270,1

which will show a wireline view of the house, revealing the columns.

Now Loop the Floors...

You can now add in another loop around the first two, using the counter 'm' which will repeat the floors for as many floors as you have in the building.

Finally, you could add a Glass sheath for the building.

More 3D Commands – Prisms

Theory

SOONER or later, you have to produce shapes which cannot be done with the Blocks and Cylinders. I even use Prism in preference to using Block, so that I can get concentric blocks – i.e. ones that grow centrally up the Z-axis like a cylinder... what I call a 'squilinder'.

It is **always** best to **draw the Prism out on paper** before you enter the XY coordinates.

PRISM is for a polygonal shaped object which has the same colour all over, no hollow faces or curved surfaces, and no holes. The local origin can be anywhere, but the prism is always built up the Z-axis, off the X-Y Plane. You may have to declare the MATERIAL property before hand. None of the points have to be at 0,0. PRISMs can have *negative* thickness values and grow *down* instead of *up* the Z-axis.

```
!PRISM Demonstration
!Syntax:- PRISM number,height,
!         x1,y1, x2,y2,...etc
MATERIAL "Sandstone"
PRISM 9, 0.2,
  0.00,0.00,
 -0.10,0.30,
  0.10,0.30,
  0.10,0.40,
  0.20,0.40,
  0.20,0.10,
  0.15,0.10,
  0.15,0.00,
  0.00,0.00
```

PRISM (and its variations) is perhaps the most commonly used 3D command in GDL

PRISM_ (prism underscore) gives you the power to control the faces and to include curves and holes by using masking values. For now, just put 15 after every XY location; later in the Cookbook, the role of *masks* is explained in more detail.

You can finish off the final coordinate with a 15, or if you plan to add holes, you can put a negative number (–1 will do) which tells GDL that you have finished drawing the outline.

```
!PRISM_ Demonstration
!Syntax:- PRISM_ number,height,
!         x1,y1,15,
!         x2,y2,15,...etc
MATERIAL "Sandstone"
PRISM_ 9,0.2,
  0.00,0.00,15,
 -0.10,0.30,15,
  0.10,0.30,15,
  0.10,0.40,15,
  0.20,0.40,15,
  0.20,0.10,1000+15,
  0.15,0.10,15,
  0.15,0.00,15,
  0.00,0.00,-1
```

*Note, that by adding 1000 to the 15, you can create interesting tangential curves. This is your first view of the power of **Polylines***

cPRISM_ (coloured PRISM underscore) is identical to **PRISM_** with the addition of a line to describe the materials of the top surface, bottom surface and side surface. It also uses masking codes for the edges, and supports polylines (curves) and holes.

When you make a library object by the conventional method from the floorslab tool, ArchiCAD always does floor slabs as cPRISM_s in the 3D script.

```
!cPRISM_ Demonstration
!Syntax:-
! cPRISM_ topmat,botmat,sidmat,
!         number,height,
!         x1,y1,15,
!         x2,y2,15,...etc
cPRISM_ "Sandstone","Pine","Zinc",
        9,0.1,
  0.00,0.00,15,
 -0.10,0.30,15,
  0.10,0.30,15,
  0.10,0.40,15,
  0.20,0.40,15-2,
  0.20,0.10,1015-2,
  0.15,0.10,15,
  0.15,0.00,15,
  0.00,0.00,-1
```

Note that by changing 15 to 13 (or write it as 15-2), you can effect subtle changes in the appearance of the curved surface. The vertical lines in the curve can be hidden

Tips and Tricks – Typographical format for all PRISMs

• Indent the numbers – it is much easier to read and repair.

• Express numbers in the 0.00 format, so that all the commas line up. Even if they do not line up, force the commas to line up, using your spacebar.

• When you have a problem with Prism, it is often because you have made an error with the commas. That is where you should first look for errors.

• Prisms close themselves. The Prism above has 8 sides and 8 points, but I advise you to get into the habit of joining the first point to the last, making 9 point XY coordinates in all. This is because when you insert holes or openings, or write out XY lists for other forms such as extrude, you need to return to the starting point.

Modify Library object

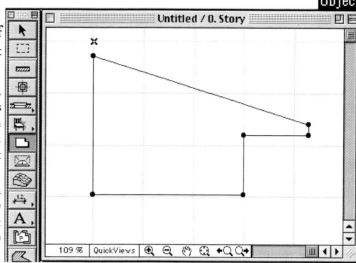

THIS exercise is a demonstration of how to modify a library object autoscripted by ArchiCAD.

First, using slab tool, you knock out a shape, like this. My first recommendation is to build it as CLOSE TO, or ON to the origin of the main model as you can. Better still, use 'snap-to-grid'. That means that one of the points in the slab script will be 0,0.

Procedure for ArchiCAD 5.0 and 5.1 and which can be used for 6.0: Position the camera using 3D Projection Settings so that it views it orthographically in plan with the camera at 270 degrees.

Note that many models, like slab built windows or trussed rafters require you to position the camera as if looking from **north** of the object, in **elevation**. You should get a view like the one below, either in Hidden Line mode or in Shaded mode.

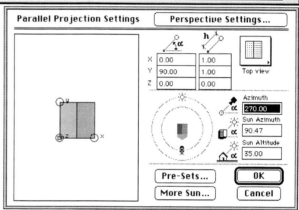

From the File Menu, do a Save As... and save it as a Library Object (.GSM object for PC users). You will see a box asking if it is an Object, a Window or a Door. Why they don't ask you if it is a Lamp, I don't know – if you want to make Lamps, you have another stage to go through to convert it. Tick the 'remove redundant lines' box. If you hide redundant lines, only the visible top lines will be saved.

You are asked if you want to save as editable or as non-editable binary data. Never save as Binary if you want to edit the object. The File will take far more space on disk, and loses all parametric qualities except for size. The script (right) shows you what you will get if you save as Binary – a file that cannot be edited, because it has all been compressed into one lump of data. So I hope you will save this in EDITABLE form.

Whichever method you have used, Save it, and then drop the object into the Project – then Open Library part.

A third method for making Library objects that you can use in ArchiCAD 6 is the one in the Tips and Tricks box on the next page! If you use it, do it with components created near the project origin.

Procedure for ArchiCAD 6: If the object is built flat on its side on the ground, like a window or trussed rafter, use the procedure for AC5. If the object is the right way up, then select the group of elements, then from the File Menu, Save Special... as an 'ArchiCAD object'. You save it to your library, and you can then open it from the File menu and modify it, perhaps convert it to a window or a lamp, or just tweak it.

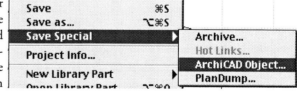

I recommend that you always use the AC6 procedure if the object is seen in plan. It is quicker and easier, and guarantees that the object will be an Editable Object. Even better, the object is fully 2D scripted with POLY2 and HOTSPOTs, whereas the other method draws a 2D Symbol instead. If the object is going to be on its side, then you can still use the AC5 3D-based method.

Tips and Tricks – Join a User Group – or make one!

Graphisoft are always willing to listen to constructive criticism or wishlists. But users' voices are more effective if you are a member of a user group; also, you might find from the more experienced users that many of the things you want are already possible. If there isn't a group around, then form one with friends, locally. Register the group with Graphisoft in your country. In the **UK**, you could call Ian Pamplin +44-(0)1935-840759 or Mike Hohmann +44-(0)181-857-3133 for details.

```
!   Name    : tempbin - BINARY OBJECT
!   Date    : Wednesday, May 5, 1999
!   Version : 6.00
!   Written by ArchiCAD
!
MULX  A/     8.599127
MULY  B/     5.354173
MULZ  ZZYZX/    0.2
ADDX         0.012093
ADDY         5.922268
BINARY 1,1
```

*This is what you get if you save as **Binary**. You can do nothing with it, except to insert a ROT or MUL. It has no parameters apart from A, B and zzyzx (height)*

```
!   Name    : temp
!   Date    : Wednesday,May 5,1999
!   Version : 6.00
!   Written by ArchiCAD
!
MULX  A/   8.599127
MULY  B/   5.354173
MULZ  ZZYZX/    0.2
ADD        0.012093,5.922268,0.2
RESOL      36
GLOB_SCRIPT_TYPE =       3
GLOB_CONTEXT =           3
GLOB_SCALE =           100
GLOB_NORTH_DIR =        90.0
GLOB_FRAME_NR =         -1
GLOB_EYEPOS_X =        299.259
GLOB_EYEPOS_Y =        165.035
GLOB_EYEPOS_Z =          1.7
GLOB_TARGPOS_X =       289.381
GLOB_TARGPOS_Y =       184.934
GLOB_TARGPOS_Z =         1.7
GLOB_HSTORY_HEIGHT =     2.9
!!Slab-001
PEN            1
ADDZ          -0.2
GLOB_LAYER = "Floors"
GLOB_ID = "Slab-001"
GLOB_INTID =       3
BODY      -1
cPRISM_ "Pine","Pine","Pine",
              7,    0.2,
    -0.012093,  -0.568094,  15,
    -0.012093,  -5.922268,  15,
     5.991071,  -5.922268,  15,
     5.991071,  -3.618351,  15,
     8.587034,  -3.618351,  15,
     8.587034,  -3.196507,  15,
    -0.012093,  -0.568094,  -1
BODY      -1
DEL       1
```

This is what your Autoscripted 3D Script looks like

Because the locations are stored in millionths of a metre accuracy, you are causing the ArchiCAD parser must spend longer reading through all that data and building the object.

```
!Name   : temp
ADD20.012093,  5.922268
PEN 1
POLY2_B 7,1,0,0,
  -0.012093, -0.568094,1,
  -0.012093, -5.922268,1,
   5.991071, -5.922268,1,
   5.991071, -3.618351,1,
   8.587034, -3.618351,1,
   8.587034, -3.196507,1,
  -0.012093, -0.568094,  -1
HOTSPOT2 -0.012093, -0.568094
HOTSPOT2 -0.012093, -5.922268
HOTSPOT2  5.991071, -5.922268
HOTSPOT2  5.991071, -3.618351
HOTSPOT2  8.587034, -3.618351
HOTSPOT2  8.587034, -3.196507
HOTSPOT2 -0.012093, -0.568094
```

This is the tidied up 2D script. the original auto script is far to long to print here!

2D Script: Amazingly, this is even more verbose with Global Variables than the 3D script. These can all be cleared out. You are left with a matching ADD command, a POLY2 to outline the PRISM shape, and a nice bunch of Hotspots for each point in the slab.

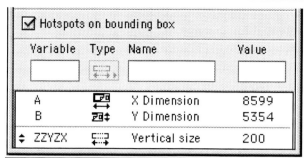

```
! Name :temp - Editable Object
! May 1999

ADD    0.012093,5.922268,zzyzx
PEN   1
ADDZ    -zzyzx
MATERIAL "Pine"
PRISM 7, zzyzx,
   -0.012,  -0.568,
   -0.012,  -5.922,
    5.991,  -5.922,
    5.991,  -3.618,
    8.587,  -3.618,
    8.587,  -3.197,
   -0.012,  -0.568
DEL TOP
```

This is what it can look like after some pruning

Change height of 0.2 to zzyzx

If you are a fanatical pruner, you can even truncate the XY coordinates to 3 decimal places – this speeds up 3D drawing. Make sure the start and end points are the same.

3D Script: These MUL commands allow the object to be stretchy. If your object is fixed in size and not stretchy, delete all the MULs and delete zzyzx from the parameter box. Leave the ADD commands in place, unless you build your object over the Project Origin.

• These long lists of Global Variables are simply a housekeeping record of the conditions prevailing at the time the object was made – current drawing scale, eye position etc. These can all go.

• As the first object is based on a floorslab, there is additional housekeeping in the form of the GVs for the slab – current layers etc. These can all go. BODY commands can go.

• Finally, you should replace the DEL 1 command at the end of the script with a DEL TOP. If not, leave each DEL 1 or DEL 2 in place until you get more used to tinkering with object scripts.

• Finally, if you really want to cut deep with the pruning knife, you can change the CPRISM_ to a PRISM_, thus enabling you to remove the references to materials. You need to place a MATERIAL command before the prism.

• You can cut even deeper by removing all the masking values, and the underscore, to make it a bare PRISM. Do not do this if you want to add holes or polylines, or to retain different coloured surfaces on the prism.

Tips and Tricks: Instant GDL!

Every element in ArchiCAD can be expressed in GDL, which is the underlying language of ArchiCAD. If you want to see what anything looks like in GDL, try this and be amazed.

Arrange your project window so it occupies half the screen. Open a New Library object file and arrange the empty 3D script window so it occupies the other half. Now pick up any part of the Project and Drag'n'Drop it into the 3D script. Instant GDL!! You can do the same with any group of 2D elements, Drag'n'Drop into the 2D script window. It's brilliant!

Analysing and Extending the 3D Script

This is very simple example – you might go a lot further, for example, make the Pen parametric, adding parametric Materials, drilling holes in the prism, or editing the dimensional data outlining the prism, or duplicating the prism into a stack of repeated prisms, in case it is part of a shelving system.

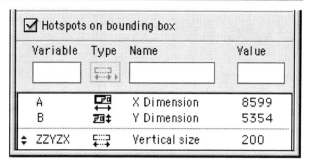

	Variable	Type	Name	Value
	A		X Dimension	8599
	B		Y Dimension	5354
↕	ZZYZX		Vertical size	200

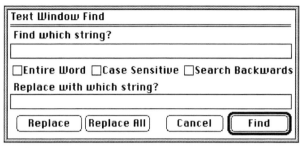

If the script is really very long, then you can use the Find and Replace Feature quite effectively. It must speed up reading of the script if you can remove a lot of the clutter. Search and replace all instances of "!GLOB_" with "!"..... and more besides. You can also insert useful comments above PRISMS to identify what they are.

With AC5, autoscripted objects always have a vertical parameter called V_SCALE, and in AC6, this is called 'zzyzx'. There is no reason why AC5 users cannot rename the height factor 'zzyzx' and thus make their objects more useful when they upgrade.

Leave the ADD commands in place. If you had built the slab literally ON THE ORIGIN, you could delete these too.

• You could add an extra pair of lines:

```
MATERIAL M_
PEN L_
```

to make the object conform to the pen and material selectors in the main settings box. This is making use of Global Variables. However, if your object contains several objects of different materials and pen colours, you are best to include those in the script, and to tick the box to use the 'Object's own Settings'.

Steal this routine....

This procedure is quite convenient even for hardened GDL users. It is good for knocking out complicated shapes, without having to work out the XY locations yourself. If you build the Slabby object right on the origin (with Grid Snap

on), so that its corner has an XY of 0,0, you can erase the ADD commands, then just Copy the PRISM script from the 3D script, and Paste it into the script of the object you are trying to build. Once you have got the hang of this, you can 'steal' the X,Y locations in a Prism to define many other things, such as the pathway of a tube, or the locations of glazing bars.

I have written a routine that parses the XY locations of a Prism, and produces a 3D tubular steel spaceframe.... might be in the Cookbook one day.

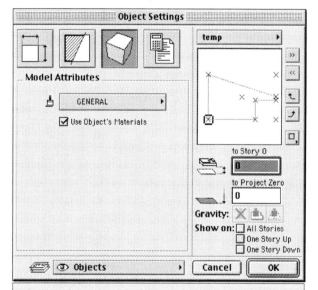

The Golden Rule

One of the most important rules to remember is to try to build the original object ON THE ORIGIN of the Project. Moving the origin somewhere else doesn't work. You have to do it on the original origin. To move a temporary origin back to the original, click once on the temporary origin, hit delete, and it should restore the main origin.

Example of modifying library objects

This S-shaped truss can be made in about 60 seconds, based on an algorithm that parses the outlines of a PRISM (saved as an ArchiCAD object just by clicking out a piece of floorslab). The user just has to copy the Prism's XY locations, and paste them into the 3D script; the remainder of the script just has to read them in. Pre arranged routines decide how to organise the tubular steel framing.

More about GDL 2D Commands

Theory

Advice on 2D Scripting

WHENEVER you can, and if you have the skill, always write a 2D script with a parametric or complex object.

2D scripting is good because...

(1) of the speed of drawing in the project plan. With PROJECT2 AC must do a 3D hidden line projection of the object before drawing it.

(2) a Symbol, which could be the alternative, is not parametric.

(3) the 2D script can itself be highly parametric, error checking, informative, and scale aware.

If it is too complex to script in 2D, and too slow to generate a PROJECT2 image from the 3D script, consider using symbols called by the FRAGMENT2 command.

Modifying Objects

UNDER AC5, autoscripted objects used to be given a symbol, and some code in the 3D script made them stretchy. In AC6, autoscripted objects are fully scripted as a mass of LINE2s and HOTSPOT2s.

This can sometimes be a pain, and I often delete the whole lot and replace them with a PROJECT2 command. This is essential if you alter or rotate the object in the 3D code. If you are willing to, you are best to rescript it in a much simpler, more usable, pasrametric form.

Another method is to place it in the Project Plan window with a Project2 command active, Explode the object, then Copy the 2D symbol thus created and Paste it into the 2D symbol window of the object. Add the command **FRAGMENT2 ALL,1** to the 2D script. Retain Project2 until you get the symbol and drawing aligned. Then delete the Project2. You can add Hotspots manually to the 2D symbol.

Note: **POLY2, POLY2_** and **FRAGMENT2** are covered in more detail eslewhere in the GDL Cookbook.

HOTSPOT2 x,y should be used in every 2D script:

Picking Up: to enable you to pick objects up.

Snapping To: they also give a point that adjoining objects can 'snap-to', which could be useful for objects which need precise location – like lecture theatre chairs, or gutters to walls.

Making Stretchy: if you use A and B as dimensions, the Hotspots at the outer corners may enable you to stretch the object. Stretchy objects are among the most useful and user friendly objects.

Stretchy Objects

```
HOTSPOT2 0,0
HOTSPOT2 A,0
HOTSPOT2 A,B
HOTSPOT2 0,B
```

Stretchy: A typical listing of HOTSPOTs when the Origin of the model is at the bottom left.

```
HOTSPOT2 -A/2,-B/2
HOTSPOT2  A/2,-B/2
HOTSPOT2  A/2, B/2
HOTSPOT2 -A/2, B/2
```

Stretchy: A typical listing of HOTSPOTs when the Origin of the model is at the centre of the model.

TEXT2 is for adding text to an object's symbol. Apart from being able to label the object, the object can use it to display a level of intelligence, e.g. flashing up a text warning if the slenderness ratio of tubes in a structure is exceeded, or displaying the final size of a stretched object – or the pitch of a stretched staircase.

It is only worth using if you are first prepared to learn how to **DEFINE STYLE**; if you do not, you will have no control over the size of the text, or how it plots at different drawing scales. See the 'Fire Extinguisher' exercise for an example of DEFINE STYLE.

If the Hotspots are written as illustrated here, and if A and B are parameters of the 2D and 3D forms of the object, then it will be STRETCHY!

CIRCLE2 Draws a circle which you can control by location and radius.

```
!Syntax: CIRCLE2 x,y,radius
CIRCLE2 0,0,0.5
```

You can send a Hotspot directly to a location, e.g. HOTSPOT2 1.6,0.9 or you can write it the long way as:

```
ADD2 1.6,0.9              !The same result
HOTSPOT2 0,0             HOTSPOT2 1.6,0.9
DEL 1
```

ARC2 draws a circular line, which you can control by location, radius and angles (in degrees). Angles start from the Horizontal and move in an **anticlockwise** direction.

```
!Syntax: ARC2 x,y,radius,startangle,endangle
ARC2 0,0,0.5,90,180
```

Cursor control in 2D scripting

ADD2, ROT2 and MUL2 are the Cursor movement commands in 2D scripting. ADD2 and MUL2 always have to be specified with X <u>and</u> Y in the same command. e.g. ADD2 1.50,0 will do the equivalent of an ADDx in 3D.

Unfortunately, you do not see a visible cursor. One trick is to use the CIRCLE2 0,0,0.01 command as a substitute cursor and keep pushing it along just in front of the cursor movement command. e.g.

```
ADD2 1.50,0
CIRCLE2 0,0,0.01
```

Car Park Barrier

Object

This useful exercise illustrates:

- Using a PRISM to keep a rectangular object axial with a cylinder
- Having articulated elements in the model
- Using the FOR...NEXT Loop to repeat objects
- Using IF... THEN... ELSE... ENDIF
- Using Subroutines to ensure modularity
- Using PEN command to set colour of object

This library object could be used in designing a campus or car park. In a flythrough, the bar could lift as the camera passes.

Variable	Type	Name	Value
A		X Dimension	=1.000
B		Y Dimension	=1.000
‡ rotarm		Angle of Bar (0=up 90=down)	=0.00
‡ blen		Barrier Length	=2.000
‡ bmatl		Material of Barrier	=22
‡ ccol		Colour of Circle & Stripes	=10

Parameters: As the barrier changes its plan shape, you cannot use A and B. Fill in the remainder of the parameters. To avoid excessive complexity, I have not made everything parametric, only the things that matter in this exercise.

```
!Barrier w lifting bar
!3D Script

RESOL 12

GOSUB 100   !Post

   ADD 0,-0.3,0.9
   ROTy rotarm
GOSUB 200   !Arm itself
   DEL 2

END !-----------------

100:!Main Post object
MATERIAL bmatl: PEN 1
PRISM 4,1.0,
   0.15, 0.15,
   -0.15, 0.15,
   -0.15,-0.15,
   0.15,-0.15
   ADDz 0.9
   ROTx 90
CYLIND 0.4,0.05
   DEL 2
RETURN
```

3D Script: The first part of the script (until the END command) could be called the 'executive script'. Always title your scripts. Use RESOL to set a limit to the curvature of the bar.

Because this model has moving elements, set out from the beginning to use subroutines. Remember to write the END statement before you write the subroutines.

100: First the Post is built. You should start by specifying Material and Pen. For this post, we make use of the PRISM – far more useful than BLOCK, although more difficult to write, at first. PRISM allows you to locate points anywhere on the X-Y plane, whereas BLOCK always ties you to the local origin. The hinge is a cylinder.

200: The object which includes the bar is a Cylinder first, and then a colour circle is placed at the halfway point on the bar, and finally, the script includes a counterweight, using a Prism command. Ensure that the right number of DELs is used within the subroutine.

This is an object oriented approach. The arm is wholly contained in a subroutine so that it behaves like an object. Returning to the main script, you just have to raise the cursor to the height of the hinge, issue a rotation command, and then call the subroutine with a GOSUB command. Hey Presto! it appears in the right place.

```
200: !Swinging Arm
MATERIAL bmatl: PEN 1
  CYLIND blen,0.03 !Arm
  ADDz blen/2
  ROTx 90
MATERIAL 0: PEN ccol
  CYLIND 0.01,0.2  !Disk
   DEL 2
  ROTy 180
MATERIAL bmatl: PEN 1
PRISM 4,0.5,     !Weight
   0.1, 0.1,
   -0.1, 0.1,
   -0.1,-0.1,
   0.1,-0.1
   DEL 1
RETURN
```

Material and Pens

To make an item a bright colour, set Material to ZERO and the object's colour will then follow the PEN colour. This is easier than having to create many materials of different colours.

For this reason, it's a good idea not to tinker about with the colour pallette, at least not the top line of the pallette – if you are likely to be using Pen colours to set object colours.

Right: This is what it should look like.

Car Park Barrier: continued

Stripy Arm – using the FOR... NEXT loop

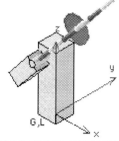

THIS is a good example of the need for a repeating loop – for example where we need alternating colour stripes on the bar. It is also an example of the IF... THEN... ELSE... ENDIF in action. First of all, add a Booleian choice to the parameter box offering the user a plain or stripy arm.

200: Next, take the CYLINDER command out of subroutine 200: and replace it with a GOSUB 250. The GOSUB becomes as much of an object as the CYLIND command was before – another example of the object oriented approach,

250: Assuming that the ideal stripe length is approx 0.3 metres, the script calculates how many stripes could be in the bar length. It rounds that down to an integer number, and works backward from that number to calculate what the exact stripe length should be. Now run a FOR...NEXT loop to draw the stripes. A little 'flag' called *stcol* keeps track of which colour stripe we are drawing. As it draws each stripe, it multiplies *stcol* by (-1), which changes its value from -1 to +1. When *stcol* is negative, the stripe is white, and when positive, it is red.

Variable	Type	Name	Value
rotarm	△	Angle of Bar (0=up 90=down)	=0.00
blen	↔	Barrier Length	=2.000
bmatl	🎨	Material of Barrier	=22
ccol	🖌	Colour of Circle & Stripes	=10
stripy	⊠	Stripy Bar ON or OFF	= ON

```
250:!Stripy Arm
IF stripy=0 THEN
MATERIAL bmatl: PEN 1
  CYLIND blen,0.03
ELSE
MATERIAL 0
  stnum=blen/0.3 !num of stripes
  strsp=blen/INT(stnum)  !length
  stcol=1         !Set a 'flag'
FOR k=1 TO stnum
  stcol=stcol*(-1) !Toggle flag
IF stcol>0 THEN PEN 91 ELSE PEN ccol
  ADDz strsp*(k-1)
    CYLIND strsp,0.03
    DEL 1
  NEXT k
ENDIF
RETURN
```

```
200: !Swinging Arm
MATERIAL bmatl: PEN 1
GOSUB 250:!StripyArm
 ADDz blen/2
 ROTx 90
MATERIAL 0: PEN ccol
  CYLIND 0.01,0.2  !Disk
  DEL 2
  ROTy 180
MATERIAL bmatl: PEN 1
PRISM 4,0.5,    !Weight
  0.1, 0.1,
  -0.1, 0.1,
  -0.1,-0.1,
  0.1,-0.1
  DEL 1
RETURN
```

By using the counter 'k' in the FOR NEXT loop as part of the calculation, it is possible to DEL after drawing each coloured cylinder, before hitting the NEXT k command. In these cases, you usually multiply the distance to be travelled by (k-1), one less than the counter.

2-D Script: As the model articulates, you cannot use a standard symbol, you need to write a 2-D script. Issue the **PROJECT2** command as in the previous examples.

Stretchy Beam Tool

Object

THIS is a useful little object that I use all the time, and it makes 3D modelling in ArchiCAD almost as easy as using good old ModelShop of years gone by. It is simply a stretchy rectangular object that can be dropped into the plan, stretched into shape, set material and height. Put several of them together, save them and you have a new Library object without having to use GDL! It's a great way to knock up pergolas, frames, furniture etc – easier than using Slabs and Walls. Recently I made a glass Elevator car entirely out of BeamTool – with lots of detail – and a group of my students built an entire timber framed house!

Main value of this exercise:

• To make things stretchy – do this whenever possible.

• Using a dual 2D script – If it is difficult (tilted) THEN use PROJECT2, ELSE when it is easy (untilted) use a 2D script.

```
!Beamtool
!2D-Script
    HOTSPOT2 0,0
    HOTSPOT2 A,0
IF tilt THEN
    PROJECT2 3,270,2
ELSE
    RECT2 0,0,A,B
    HOTSPOT2 0,B
    HOTSPOT2 A,B
ENDIF
```

```
!Beamtool
!3D-Script

MATERIAL bmat
PEN bpen

  ROTx tilt
BLOCK A,B,higt
  DEL 1
```

Variable	Type	Name	Value
A	▱	X Dimension	1.000
B	▱	Y Dimension	1.000
higt	↔	Height of beam/slab	0.300
bmat	🎨	Material	18
bpen	🖌	Pen colour	1
tilt	△	Tilt Angle	0.00

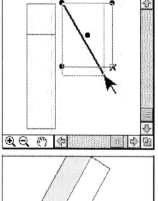

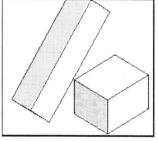

3D Script: Do it with BLOCK. If you wanted to be able to vary the top, side and bottom colours, you would have to do it with a cPRISM command.

2D Script: The HOTSPOT commands give the object stretchiness. When the object tilts, you can no longer use RECT2 so you use an IF...ENDIF statement to generate a PROJECT view of the object.

More 3D

Drilling Holes in Prisms

PRISMs may not be able to have holes through them, but the addition of an Underscore makes **PRISM_** which can have holes and curved lines.

With PRISM_, you end each XY location with a 15. The trick with holes is that you must end the description of the outline with a -1, then begin a new set of XY points, also with 15, and then use a -1 to end that hole. You can have as many holes as you like as long as you follow that sequence.

```
!PRISM_ Demonstration
!    including Hole
!Syntax:- PRISM_ number,height,
!         x1,y1,15,
!         x2,y2,15,...etc
MATERIAL "Sandstone"
PRISM_ 9+7,0.2,
   0.00,0.00, 15,
  -0.10,0.30, 15,
   0.10,0.30, 15,
   0.10,0.40, 15,
   0.20,0.40, 15,
   0.20,0.10, 15,
   0.15,0.10, 15,
   0.15,0.00, 15,
   0.00,0.00, -1,

   0.00,0.05, 15,
  -0.07,0.25, 15,
   0.15,0.25, 15,
   0.15,0.15, 15,
   0.10,0.15, 15,
   0.10,0.05, 15,
   0.00,0.05, -1
RETURN
```

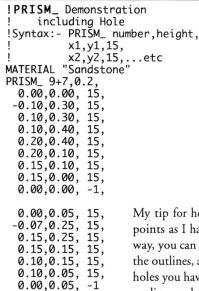

My tip for hole making is to express the number of points as I have done here, e.g. 9+7, not as 16. This way, you can remind yourself how many points make the outlines, and how many the hole – and how many holes you have. Put a linefeed between the list for the outline, and the one for the hole.

More 2D

POLY2

POLY2 is simply to draw a whole sequence of lines – a lot more economical than a series of LINE2 commands.

POLY2_

POLY2_ (underscore) is an enhancement of POLY2 – you can control the line drawing of each part of the polygon; you can use 'polylines' (curved elements). POLY2 and POLY2_ can be filled with a fill pattern. The figure must be *closed* for this to work. For any poly

```
!Syntax POLY2 n, framefill,
!x1,y1, ..... xn,yn

PEN 1
SET FILL 'Earth'
POLY2 9,3,
   0.00,0.00,
  -0.10,0.30,
   0.10,0.30,
   0.10,0.40,
   0.20,0.40,
   0.20,0.10,
   0.15,0.10,
   0.15,0.00,
   0.00,0.00
```

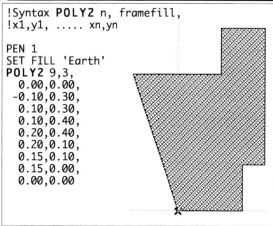

What is Framefill?
0 means draw nothing, 1 draws the line, 2 draws the fill pattern but no line, 4 means close the Polygon (if not already closed).

Any additive combi-nation of these can be used – eg 3 is the sum of 1 and 2 so you get the lines and the fill pattern, 6 [2+4] results in a closed filled polygon with no line!, 7 [1+2+4] gives you everything.

to be filled, you must specify one more than the number of points – the first point is repeated as the last point. The Framefill attribute is normally left as '1' for Poly drawing. However, you can vary this with 7 permutations. If you wish to control Pen Colours of the Fill, then you must use POLY_2A and POLY2_B.

More Syntax

SHADOW

SHADOW – sometimes you must turn off shadow rendering even when the rest of the object is shadowed – for example glazing fittings – which if curvy and casting shadows could prevent ArchiCAD ever finishing a render. In a model of a car, you can speed up rendering by issuing a SHADOW OFF command before drawing hubcaps or door handles.

SHADOW ON and SHADOW OFF could be used in IF statements – for example, if the object is further than 50 metres from the camera location then do not cast shadows.

Example:

```
IF dd>30 THEN SHADOW OFF ELSE SHADOW ON
```

MODEL

MODEL – sets a viewing mode for the model, or parts of the model. Normally, if you want the whole model to be wireline, hidden-line surface, or solid shaded surface, you can change it in the main menus of ArchiCAD. The benefit of the MODEL command is that you can single out parts of the model to draw differently from the rest.

For example, in a tree model, you might want the trunk and branches to have a clearly outlined form, yet make the leaves to be drawn as shaded surfaces only, with no edge lines. Another example could be an atrium roof glazing structure, where, with a Boolean Yes/No command in the dialog box, the glazing could change from shaded to transparent wireline.

Syntax:

MODEL WIRE: MODEL SURFACE: MODEL SOLID

Stretchy Joist Tool

This exercise demonstrates :

- **Making objects stretchy**
- **Using a FOR NEXT Loop to convert stretchy object into a multiple stretchy object**

THE ArchiCAD Toolkit provides floor slabs, but these may appear too 'plastic' in nature. Even though the slab can contain a theoretical content of joists and insulation and boards, this is difficult to see on anything but sections. This joist tool object is for people who want their model to display visible structure. This is a development of the BeamTool that was in an earlier exercise.

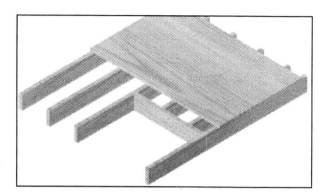

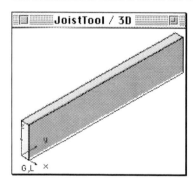

3D Script: At the beginning of a new object, I tend to just knock something out that works before I introduce structure, and typographical formality. So this is a first stab at a script, where you get a single joist working. I recommend that you use quasi english variable names, hence the conversion of 'B' to 'jlen'.

```
MATERIAL jmat
PEN jpen

jlen=B

BLOCK jwid,jlen,jdep
```

Parameters: Think about the parameters that you would want your object to offer to the user. If you want the object to be stretchy, the overall dimension is the primary consideration; the actual number of joists will be worked out by your script.

A and B are used for the plan area.

The joist details are also entered.

As this is a practical tool for building, you can offer an option to provide a final joist if the room is not an exact multiple of the joist spacing.

Variable	Type	Name	Value
A	⊞ X Dimension		= 1.000
B	⊞ Y Dimension		= 1.000
jwid	Joist Width		= 0.050
jdep	Joist Depth		= 0.200
jspa	Joist Spacing		= 0.400
jmat	Joist Material		= 15
jpen	Pen Colour		= 1
finj	Insert Final Joist?=1 No=0		= 1

```
!Joisting/BoardingTool
!Discovery Course

!Settings--------
MATERIAL jmat
PEN jpen

!Parameters------
 jlen=B
 numj=INT(A/jspa)+1
 remj=A-INT(A/jspa)*jspa

!Main Joists-----
FOR k=0 TO A STEP jspa
 ADDx k
 BLOCK jwid,jlen,jdep
 DEL 1
 NEXT k
```

Note that on the first run through the loop it moves a zero distance, but as you have issued an ADD command, you still need the DEL command.

3 D Script: continuing: Now is the time to tidy up and formalise the script. First, put in the title, signature and date. Add some titles for sections of the script.

- Two more "Internal" parameters are now needed. One is the actual number of joists in the object (this would be useful for properties scripting, but not needed for 3D). The other thing is to find out how much space is left after you have put in a 'round' number of joists, in case there is room to put in a final joist. This is simply A minus the number of joist_spacings times the joist_spacing.

Use a FOR... NEXT Loop

The joist we first put in can now be 'wrapped up' in a FOR-NEXT loop which spaces out the joists at the required spacing. Each joist is drawn, and the cursor returns to the origin before drawing the next joist – the Loop is stepping in Distance, not counting the joists one by one.

IF.. THEN.. ENDIF

This is an example of an IF.. THEN.. ENDIF, where there is more than one condition in the IF statement, and more than one line resulting from the IF statement. If the left over space is more than twice the width of a joist, then this routine puts an extra one in. The easiest way to do it with precision is to go to the end – to A – and then step back the thickness of one joist =A-jwid.

```
!Put in last joist
IF finj AND remj>jwid*2 THEN
 ADDx A-jwid
 BLOCK jwid,jlen,jdep
 DEL 1
 ENDIF
```

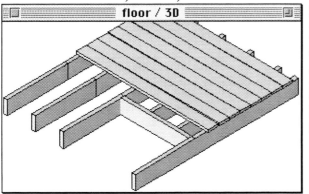

ArchiCAD 6.0 allows an degree of editing in 3D axo view, so it will become easier to use stretchy tools like JoistTool. In ArchiCAD 5.0, you can use the sectional view to get parts of the assembly working perfectly.

3D Assembly

Now you can assemble quite complex groupings, and the JoistTool can also be used for floorboarding – in fact for any parallel, linear assemblies. Single joists, such as the trimmer here can be created simply by squeezing the JoistTool to the thickness of a single joist.

2D Script: You now have a 3D Tool that you can place into the Project Plan, and stretch to fit. But it must have a 2D symbol. Initially, your 2D script could be just PROJECT2 3,270,2 because the model is dynamic.

If you leave it at that, it will work, but the Project Plan will slow down as the model size increases due to the time required to work out hidden line 2D Plan views of the 3D objects. I always script in 2D if it is going to be practical and time saving.

Your object will not be properly stretchy unless you add the HOTSPOT2 script routine. Some objects are stretchy using the 'bounding box' hotspots. However the above script guarantees stretchiness, providing that A and B are used as dimensions.

```
!Stretchy Joist Tool
!2D Script

HOTSPOT2 0,0
HOTSPOT2 A,0
HOTSPOT2 A,B
HOTSPOT2 0,B
PROJECT2 3,270,2
```

```
!Stretchy Joist Tool
!2D Script

!!!!PROJECT2 3,270,2

HOTSPOT2 0,0
HOTSPOT2 A,0
HOTSPOT2 A,B
HOTSPOT2 0,B

jlen=B
numj=INT(A/jspa)+1
remj=A-INT(A/jspa)*jspa

FOR k=0 TO A STEP jspa
 ADD2 k,0
 RECT2 0,0,jwid,jlen
 DEL 1
 NEXT k

IF finj AND remj>jwid*2 THEN
 ADD2 A-jwid,0
 RECT2 0,0, jwid,jlen
 DEL 1
 ENDIF
```

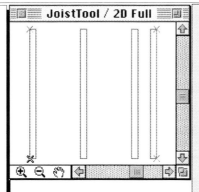

Using this algorithm, you can develop similar tools for timber framed studwork, rafter tools, handrails, trussed rafters, fencing.

Hot Tip for rapid 2D Scripting

Leave PROJECT2 in action until you are sure that your script works perfectly. In fact leave it there permanently, with comment marks preceding. This is in case you need to edit or check the 2D script.

• *In fact, you can copy your 3D script and paste it into the 2D script window.*

Change the ADD x,y,z commands appropriately, to ADD2 x,y. ADDx and ADDy can be changed to ADD2. MUL can be changed to MUL2. Moves in the Z direction can be deleted if they will have no effect on the plan view.

As there is no height in 2D, you can change a BLOCK command to a RECT2 command:- for example, BLOCK jwid,jlen,jdep becomes RECT2 0,0, jwid,jlen.

Loops can use the same counters, and you use DEL to cancel Cursor movements just like you can do in 3D scripts.

More GDL Syntax

Introducing Global Variables

Theory

GDL Syntax

Reserved global variables

A_ drawing scale
B_ elevation of the home story
C_ wall thickness
D_ wall height
E_ pen number of wall contour
F_ pen number of wall fill
G_ wall material index opposite to opening side
H_ wall material index on opening side
I_ material index of wall edge
J_ parapet/door step or object bottom elevation
K_ window/door sill/reveall thickness

L_ pen number of the symbol
M_ material index of the symbol
N_ frame number in animation
O_ first frame index in fly-through
P_ last frame index in fly-through
Q_ height of home story
R_ radius of the bended wall
S_...Z_ free for users

This illustration comes from the Help pages on Syntax and GDL which are available to you in ArchiCAD 5.0 and 5.1. Help in ArchiCAD 6.0 is now provided through Web Pages and Acrobat files.I have retained this image as it presents a very simple route to using Global Variables.

GLOBAL Variables are current conditions and settings of your project. They are known by ArchiCAD. GDL objects can, at any time, interrogate them and make use of the information.Under ArchiCAD 6.0 and 6.5, you have many more Globals available than with AC5, although many of the new ones are not usable for 2D and 3D model building (they are for listing). Meanwhile the following are the GV's you could usefully use. For the rest, check the GDL manual.

GLOB_SCALE Drawing Scale, (formerly known as (f.k.a.) **A_**) Use this to determine how complex a 2D scripted symbol will be. For example, at scales up to 1/20, you show rebates in door jambs, at 1/50 you can show them as rectangles, and beyond that, they are rendered as simple door swings. this can reduce the time of screen redraw and plotting times. The Filestamp/Desktop clock in the Voyager cookbook demonstrates how A_ can be used.

GLOB_HSTORY_ELEV (f.k.a. **B_**) tells the elevation of the storey (the 'home' storey) that the object is currently placed on. This is important if you have a staircase, and want it to show on the home storey as the start of a flight, and on the next as the end of the same flight.

C_, D_, E_ F_, G_, H_, I_,K_, L_, M_, R_ are all vital for windows and doors. They will not fit correctly into walls unless you use these.

WALL_THICKNESS (f.k.a. **C_**) is the most vital GV in window making! **WALL_MAT_A** (f.k.a. **G_**) is the wall material on the side opposite to the opening side. This can vary from opening to opening placed in the same wall. I standardise this to be the internal wall surface (opposite the 'hotline' of the wall). **WALL_MAT_B** (f.k.a. **H_**) material of the wall on the opening (or Hotline) side. **WALL_MAT_EDGE** (f.k.a. **I_**) material of the wall reveals. By lucky coincidence, if you use a **cPRISM_** to build a window surround, you can start with CPRISM_ G_,H_,I_,.... Isn't that easy to remember!

GLOB_FRAME_NR (f.k.a. **N_**) current frame number in animation/flythrough, **GLOB_FIRST_FRAME** (f.k.a.**O_**) first frame index in flythrough, and **GLOB_ LAST_FRAME** (f.k.a.**P_**) last frame index in flythrough are useful for making objects change during an animation. (see the Crane in Voyager cookbook). The object can change angle, position, level of detail or size according to the index number.

S_ to Z_ could be freely used as variables, and were needed in all versions of ArchiCAD before 5.0, because it was easy to run out of simple alphabetic latters for variables. But now, you must NEVER use these. Although GV names are now in a long format, the OLD ones are still valid, and old Global Variable names are still recognised.

SYMB_VIEW_PEN (f.k.a. **L_**) is the default pen of the library part. **SYMB_MAT** (f.k.a. **M_**) is the default material of the library part.

A script like this below will reduce the number of parameters in your dialog box by two, as the user can now click on the pop-up selectors provided by Graphisoft in the normal object settings dialog box.

```
MATERIAL SYMB_MAT  : PEN SYMB_VIEW_PEN
MATERIAL M_        : PEN L_
```

Selected : 1

Whitewash ▶ ○ **Symbol Pens**

◉ ♉ 1 ■

Limitations to Globals: Certain things cannot be found from Globals and may have to be found using the REQ and the REQUEST commands. Of which more anon.

Most globals are numbers; REQUESTs are usually used for returning Strings (of letters). An example of REQUEST is current System Time and Date. Another is the object's own name and label.

RTFM – After you have been through these pages, you may find the manual easier to read! However, it is more likely that after you have tried a few exercises, you will also find these pages easier to read.
Do everything one step at a time.

More Global Variables

A~ to J~ are useful (essential!) in getting windows and doors working in 3D and drawing in 2D correctly. Windows are somewhat of a black art and are the subject of a special exercises in the Discovery and Voyager course.

The following are most useful for Location Aware objects.

GLOB_EYEPOS_X, GLOB_EYEPOS_Y, & GLOB_EYEPOS_Z (f.k.a. K~, L~ & M~) tell the object where the most recent camera is located.

GLOB_TARGPOS_X, GLOB_TARGPOS_Y, & GLOB_TARGPOS_Z (f.k.a. N~, O~, & P~) tell the object what the camera is looking at – the 'target position'.

SYMB_POS_X, SYMB_POS_Y, SYMB_POS_Z (f.k.a. X~, Y~ & Z~) tell the object where the object itself is in the overall project.

These are useful for getting things to face the camera, or change as the camera approaches..

SYMB_ROTANGLE (f.k.a. W~) is the rotational angle of the object. No matter how you rotate the object, it will always face the camera if you use the algorithm illustrated on this page.

GLOB_CSTORY_ELEV, GLOB_CSTORY_HEIGHT, GLOB_CH_STORY_DIST (f.k.a. Q~, R~ & S~) tell you how objects relate to the storey displayed in the Project Floor Plan window.

GDL Syntax

Reserved global variables (continued)

A~ wall pattern
B~ window/door jamb
C~ window sill/door threshold depth
D~ window/door head depth
E~ reveal side opposite to (1)/on (0) opening side
F~ frame thickness of window/door in 2D
G~ (reserved)
H~ position angle of the opening: the rotation angle of the opening's axis relative to the radius α of the wall's starting point
I~ (reserved)
J~ 3D resolution of a bended wall

K~, L~, M~ eye position
N~, O~, P~ target position
Q~ elevation of the current story
R~ height of the current story
S~ position of the current story relative to the home story
T~ usage type
U~ project North direction
V~ symbol mirrored (1) or not (0)
W~ rotation angle of the symbol
X~, Y~, Z~ symbol position

GLOB_SCRIPT_TYPE and GLOB_CONTEXT (f.k.a. T~) returns information on the ArchiCAD window, or view that you are currently using. T~ used to do both. Now, you can know if you object is being executed in a particular Script or in a Window (Elev or Plan or 3D) and modify it accordingly.

GLOB_NORTH_DIR (f.k.a. U~) gives the direction of Project North; you could tell where the Sun is – for solar panels or shading devices. With U~ (and finding from the user the time, date and Latitude, you can write a script to calculate the quantities of sunlight falling on Solar panels, Walls, Windows, etc, and can get sun breaking devices like louvres to change their angle during an animation. It is not yet possible to find out (by Request or Global) the Lat. and Long of a site.

My 'Stardome' (a model of the visible Universe) automatically finds the northpoint and rotates accordingly.

```
!Location Awareness
!with camera global variables
dkx=K~ - X~:IF dkx=0 THEN dkx=1
  dly=L~ -  Y~
  dmz=M~ -  Z~

dr =SQR(dkx^2 + dly^2) !Plan distance
dd =SQR(dkx^2 +dly^2 +dmz^2)!Distance
azi=ATN(dly/dkx)           !Azimuth

IF facecam THEN ROTz 90+azi-W~
```

The classic Location awareness subroutine

SYMB_MIRRORED (f.k.a. V~) is useful if you have a scripted 2D symbol, and want to ensure that Hotspots and text in objects still appear the right way round and in the right place, even when the symbol is mirrored. When you tick the 'mirrored' checkbox in the Object settings dialog, the 2D symbol and the hotspots will be mirrored for you. However, you might want the Properties script to know that the object has been mirrored – for example in specifying right or left handed desking units in interior layouts.

Long or Short Globals?

THE AC6 manual explains GVs a lot better than its predecessors. However, I preferred it when Globals were based on short names. When you use them with long names, you always have to check the manual that you have spelt them correctly!

Globals in Action

As an example of using Globals, here is a tiny 2D Script.

THIS little object is a stretchy pointer/labeller, whereby no matter how much you rotate the entire object, the round box with the line in it remains upright.

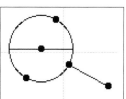

Object

```
!2D Script
!Demonstrates
!control of rotation

!Stretchy Hotspots
 HOTSPOT2 0,0
 HOTSPOT2 A,0
 HOTSPOT2 0, B/2
 HOTSPOT2 0,-B/2

!This one-line routine
!keeps the circle level
IF V~=0 THEN ROT2 -W~
IF V~=1 THEN ROT2  W~
   CIRCLE2 0,0,B/2
   LINE2 -B/2,0,B/2,0
   DEL 1
```

```
!Pointer Line
psiz=B/10
HOTSPOT2 B/2,0
   LINE2 B/2,0,A,0
!Arrow
  POLY2 3,1,
     A-psiz*2,psiz,
     A,0,
     A-psiz*2,-psiz
```

If the object is 'mirrored' then V~ is 1, else V~ is zero. W~ is the angle of rotation of the object. Two simple IF statements enable you to decide which way to rotate the circle. If you want tighter code then you can reduce the IF to one line. For the tightest code, you can use the V~ as a 'Flag' (either 1 or 0); you can then apply a trick which changes 1 and 0 to 1 and -1 (see TIPS:Maths Tricks of the Trade.)

```
!Another way of doing it - shorter
IF V~ THEN ROT2 W~ ELSE ROT2 -W~

!The shortest way of doing it - as a flag
ROT2  W~*(V~*2-1)
```

Attribute Definitions

See the Attribute Definition example in the Fire Extinguisher!

DEFINE

ONLY a Masochist could possibly enjoy **DEFINE FILL** and **DEFINE LINE_TYPE**; but **DEFINE STYLE** and **MATERIAL** are essential parts of your vocabulary. You command GDL to use a Style, Material etc, by the command SET. In fact, you do not need SET; just saying "MATERIAL 'zinc'" or similar will be sufficient.

DEFINE STYLE is essential if

any TEXT2 is to be included in a 2D symbol – followed by the **SET STYLE** (or just '**STYLE**') command for short).

It is even more important if you have more than one line of text, and if you intend to print or plot the plans, because you can control the position of the text, and the font plotting and printing height.

Once you have a correct working statement like this one, you can copy it and paste it to your next 2D Script. In fact, keep it in your Scrapbook or Notepad for frequent use.

Size Most dimensions in GDL are always assumed to be in Metres, but this is one odd case where font height produced by the plotter has to be defined in millimetres (even in the USA) For this reason, when you state the font size in the parameter box, you must use use 'real number', or 'integer', and not use the 'length', because 'length' could be changed by the dimension settings of the project. If font size is not stated, the TEXT will not appear.

GDL Syntax

Theory

Attribute definitions

```
DEFINE FILL  name  pat1, pat2, pat3, pat4, pat5, pat6, pat7, pat8, spacing, angle,
n, freq1, dir1, offsetx1, offsety1, m1, len11, . . . lenm1  ...   freqn, dirn,
offsetxn, offsetyn, mn, lenn1, . . . lennm
```
Any GDL script may include fill definitions prior to the first reference to that fill name.The fill defined this way can be used only in the script where it was defined and its second generation-scripts.

```
DEFINE LINE_TYPE  name  spacing, n, len1, . . . lenn
```
Any GDL script may include line-type definitions prior to the first reference to that line-type name. The line-type defined this way can be used only for 2D elements in the script where it was defined and its second generation-scripts.

```
DEFINE MATERIAL name type, m1, m2, ... mn {type 0 = general definition, type 1 = simple
```
definition, types 2 to 6 = predefined materials, see GDL Reference Manual Chapter 5}

```
DEFINE STYLE   name font_family, size, anchor, facecode
DEFINE STYLE   name PLOTMAKER, size, anchor, slant
DEFINE STYLE   name PLOTTER, size, anchor, slant
```

```
IF shodata THEN
DEFINE STYLE 'display' 'arial',
              fhigt,1,0
  SET STYLE 'display'
  TEXT2 0,w2,'span'
  TEXT2 0,0, tmod*(tnum-1)
ENDIF
RETURN
```

1	2	3
4	5	6
7	8	9

The 'touchtone' keypad symbolises the way that TEXT is located vertically and justified horizontally.

Anchor defines the position where the text starts writing. If you use '1', it will be left justified, and above the point of text entry. If you use 2, it will be centred, and if you use 3 it will be right justified. Larger numbers change the vertical position of the text. It's like the keypad of a touchtone phone.

FaceCode is simply whether the text is plain, italic, bold etc. Codes are:

0=Normal, 1=**Bold**, 2=*Italic*, 4=<u>Underline</u>, 8=Outline, 16=Shadow. You can combine the numbers.

DEFINE MATERIAL is very important if you want to carry materials with your GDL object that, when dropped into someone else's model will still have the correct colour and appearance. People often tweak their materials and material index numbers change. 'Whitewash' and 'Stainless Steel' may have disappeared... Mercy!

In my smart car object, it is vital that red tail lamps and indicators look right, and that the white bodywork of the police car does not look as grey as 'whitewash'. The taillamps change from reflective red in daylight, to brightly emitting red when the lights are turned on.

```
DEFINE MATERIAL "Bright_Metal" 0,
0.84, 0.83, 0.85, !Surface RGB
0.95, 0.10, !ambient, diffuse
0.95, 0.0,!specular,transparent
57,    !shining
4,     !transparency attenuation
1,1,1,!Specular RGB
0.0, 0.0, 0.0, !Emission RGB
0.0   !Emission attenuation
shmat=IND(MATERIAL,"Bright_Metal")
```

This is definitely Voyager stuff so the example is for reference. GDL has predefined surface qualities, like 'metallic'(3) so try this simpler definition:

```
DEFINE MATERIAL "Metalpaint" 3,
0.84, 0.83, 0.85, !Surface RGB
```

This is better than Material 0: PEN ccol

Value Lists

See the Value List example in the Fire Extinguisher!

I HAD WRITTEN in earlier version of the GDL Cookbook how I wished that ArchiCAD could support **Popdown menus** in GDL – but Lo and Behold, in AC6 I find that it does! – but it's in an unexplained part of the manual – called **VALUES**.

Value Lists are one of the most desirable features of GDL in ArchiCAD. You can make objects even smarter by offering the user a list of options in words or numbers, in the same way that you are offered materials and pen colours. There are many examples throughout the Cookbook of Value lists at work. Words or numbers work well in value lists, but

I find that wordy value lists are more helpful to the user in describing the purpose of their choice – from which numbers may be the consequence.

For example, for a smart car model, you can script a pop-up menu saying 'Saloon', 'Coupe', 'Estate', 'Convertible' and your script can interpret that and produce the correct shape of car. The imagination runs riot just thinking of how much friendlier GDL objects can now be.

Value Lists are written in the Parameter Script or Master Script, and in 6.0, they can be written in their own script window.

Status and Masking values

See the Masking example in the Fire Extinguisher!

Theory

S TATUS & Masking values – are one of the reasons why new purchasers of ArchiCAD snap the GDL manual shut again, assuming that they will never cope with GDL.

Status Values apply to things which are 2-dimensional in nature (even if they are 3D objects). All they can do is to say if a Line is to be drawn or missed out. POLY_ and POLY2_ are the prime examples of 2D elements that uses Status Values.

3D Scripts which define a 2D outline for 3D form-making also use Status values – for example, defining a profile in TUBE, SWEEP and REVOLVE.

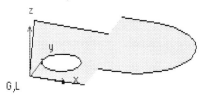

For Planar elements the choice of drawing line edges is either Yes or No

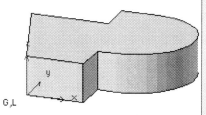

For Prisms, there are 0-15 permutations for the status of edges. This is an example of 13.

Masking Values on Prisms

M ASKING values are used to define how a surface is to be drawn on a 3-D Prism. The Top surface is always drawn. But the definition of the side surface needs to describe the actual face and all the lines surrounding the surface.

On Prisms, there are only 0-15 permutations of lines and surface to each facet of the prism. When you are not sure, just write 15 – that draws everything. If you put an 8 in, it draws the surfaces without the lines. If you want to make one side draw differently from, experiment with the script to make sure that you attach the different value to the correct line.

Masking Values on everything else

W ITH more complex objects, you declare an overall masking value for the whole thing, which is written on the first line. For safety, just start by writing 63 for most objects until you need to change it.

Certain objects also have special considerations:- for example, with REVOLVE, you can have a starting angle surface and an ending surface. The masking values for this will behave differently from a SWEEP. Therefore for Masking values, you need to have handy access to a manual. I usually give everything a value of 63 unless special circumstances decree otherwise.

Let's explain Prism masking better...

Masking values are the numbers that come after each XY location in the listing of a PRISM_ (underscore) and other similar 3D objects. In Autoscripted objects, these are either 15 or 79, or -1.

1 draws the bottom edge line.

2 draws the vertical side line.

4 draws the top edge line.

8 draws the side surface as solid.

You can add these yourself in any combination. The examples adjacent illustrate this point.

15 means draw everything, 13 means draw everything except vertical lines (left). 8 draws the Prism with surface only, but no lines. 0 makes that portion of the Prism look vacant. 79 means that 64 is added to 15, telling GDL that the point is part of a curve – but only in autoscripted objects. –1 means that the object outline is finished.

This is the binary system in action.

Polylines Special mask/status values

See the Polylines example in the Fire Extinguisher!

I T IS DIFFICULT to say which part of the GDL Manual is the worst – I think that if put to a referendum, this section on ••**Polylines**•• would come out a slim nose ahead of the other leading contenders like the PIPG, VERT, BODY sections, the Properties scripting; CWALL and CROOF; OUTPUT & INPUT; PUT & GET; XFORM, or countless other, less guilty offenders.

GDL Voyagers need Polylines: let's make a start. Polylines are best learnt a bit at a time. The exercises in the Voyager and a few in the Discovery make use of Polylines and explain them as you go along.

```
▓▓▓▓▓▓▓▓▓▓▓▓▓▓▓        Polylines        ▓▓▓▓▓▓▓▓▓▓▓▓▓
╔═════════════════════════════════════════════════════╗
 ⚙  Special mask/status values

Special constraints based on additional mask/status codes help you create segments
and arcs in polylines
 mask  for POLY_, PRISM_, CPRISM_, BPRISM_, POLY2_;   0 to 15
 s     for EXTRUDE, PYRAMID, REVOLVE, SWEEP, TUBE     0 to 1

Segment by absolute endpoint – x, y, s – where 0 <= s < 100
Segment by relative endpoint – dx, dy, 100+s – where 0 <= s < 100
Segment, by length and direction – l, a, 200+s – where 0 <= s < 100
Tangential segment by length – l, 0, 300+s – where 0 <= s < 100
Set start point – x1, y1, 600,
Close polyline – 0, 0, 700,
Set tangent – ex, ey, 800,
Set centerpoint – x0, y0, 900,
Tangential arc to endpoint – x, y, 1000+s – where 0 <= s < 100
Tangential arc by radius and angle – r, a, 2000+s – where 0 <= s < 100
Arc using centerpoint and point on the final radius – x, y, 3000+s – where 0 <= s < 100
Arc using centerpoint and angle – 0, a, 4000+s – where 0 <= s < 100
Full circle using centerpoint and radius – r, 360, 4000+s – where 0 <= s < 100
```

PolyLines – why use them?

POLYLINES enable you to make interesting shapes with PRISMs and other functions that you could not achieve with XY coordinates. You can use Polylines with POLY_, PRISM_, CPRISM_, BPRISM_, CROOF, EXTRUDE, PYRAMID, REVOLVE, SWEEP, TUBE, POLY2_, CUTPOLYA, WALLHOLE and more.

Polylines are also more economical – if you look at a curve that has been autoscripted, it turns a circle into 36 polygonal X-Y coordinates, each with 6 figures of decimals, and followed by a 79.

Make a slab with a circular hole into a simple Library part and examine the script for yourself.

All these 79's can be replaced by just two lines, or sometimes just a tweak of an existing line. Polylines are also controllable by the RESOL and RADIUS commands.

Some Polylines have to work together – e.g. if you want to issue a command that involves Radius of rotation, it will return an error unless you have first defined a Centre of rotation.

PolyLines that are USEFUL and USABLE:

900, 1000, 3000, 4000.

Some of these have already been illustrated in earlier pages of the Cookbook.

PolyLines that I do not cover yet with examples, but will do when I get time.

100, 200, 300, 600, 700, 800, 2000.

If you get the idea of the useful ones here, you can tackle these remaining ones in good time.

Try Polylines yourself!

THIS SHAPE on the right is an ordinary PRISM_ with all points defined as XY locations, and 15 used as the mask (15 means draw all lines and surfaces on the edge).

Now try converting it to make use of Polylines. 1000 is the easiest PolyLine to use – starting from one point, it branches off in a graceful round curve and lands on the next point – the one that has the 1000 command written into it. It's a tangential curve, because the existing straight start and straight ending lines define the way that the curve leaves and arrives.

You can write 1015 or you can write it as 1000+15 – this helps you pick it out visually from a long block of script, and displays how the 1015 was derived.

Using PRISM and Polylines to make a Hollow Cylinder

Polyline 900 and 4000 are good companions for making circles.

0,0,900 means that the centre of the Cylinder or circle is at the point of the origin, 0,0.

0.1,360,4000 means draw a circle of Radius 0.1, through a full circle of 360 degrees.

This gets you a solid Cylinder.

Using the same Circle Centre, you can issue the 4000 command again, with a smaller radius, and you will get a hollow tube.

Using 13 instead of 15, you could reduce the number of lines to be drawn on the side surfaces.

```
!PolyLine 1000 Demo
PRISM_ 9,0.2,
    0.00,0.00,15,
   -0.10,0.30,15,
    0.10,0.30,15,
    0.10,0.40,15,
    0.20,0.40,15,
    0.20,0.10,15,
    0.15,0.10,15,
    0.15,0.00,15,
    0.00,0.00,-1
```

```
!PolyLine 1000 Demo
PRISM_ 9,0.2,
    0.00,0.00,15,
   -0.10,0.30,15,
    0.10,0.30,15,
    0.10,0.40,15,
    0.20,0.40,15,
    0.20,0.10,1000+15, !<add
    0.15,0.10,15,
    0.15,0.00,15,
    0.00,0.00,-1
```

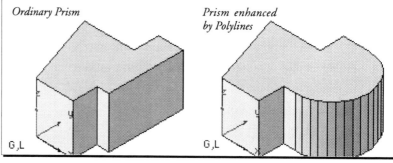

Ordinary Prism

Prism enhanced by Polylines

3D GDL Shapes

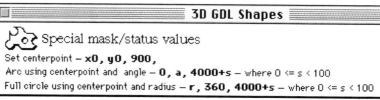

Special mask/status values

Set centerpoint – **x0, y0, 900,**

Arc using centerpoint and angle – **0, a, 4000+s** – where 0 <= s < 100

Full circle using centerpoint and radius – **r, 360, 4000+s** – where 0 <= s < 100

```
!PolyLine 900,4000 Demo
PRISM_ 2,0.2,
    0,0,900+15,
    0.10,360,4000+15

!below
```

```
!PolyLine 900,4000 Demo
PRISM_ 3,0.2,
    0,0,900+15,
    0.10,360,4000+15,
    0.08,360,4000+15

!below
```

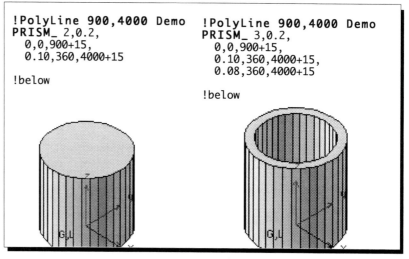

Curvy 3D commands

bPRISM_

bPRISM_ (bent PRISM underscore) is the similar to cPRISM, with the added ability to curve it. It always curves in a downward direction, along the X-axis.

If you want to curve •upwards•, you can issue a MULz -1 (multiply all Z values by -1) command first.

You can also enter a negative value for the depth of the prism, and bring it below the origin (and thus make a tighter curve).

When you do a cursor movement or change, it's wise to DEL as soon as it is possible afterwards.

```
360:!bPRISM_ Demonstration
!Syntax:-
! bPRISM_ topmat,botmat,sidmat,
!         number,height,radius,
!         x1,y1,15,
!         x2,y2,15,...etc
bPRISM_ "Sandstone","Pine","Zinc",
      9,0.05,0.4,
   0.00,0.00,15,
  -0.10,0.30,15,
   0.10,0.30,15,
   0.10,0.40,15,
   0.20,0.40,13,
   0.20,0.10,1013,
   0.15,0.10,15,
   0.15,0.00,15,
   0.00,0.00,-1
```

bPRISM requires every point to have a masking value. Start by giving it 15, then change some to 13 [15-2] to remove vertical lines.

```
    MULZ -1
    GOSUB 360:!bPRISM Demo
    DEL 1
```

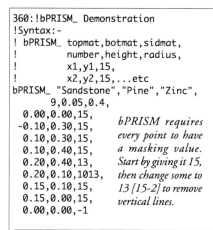

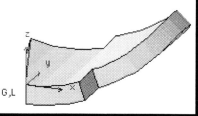

With bPRISM, you can make long helices, and perforated tubular structures.

Most 3D commands require you to enter the **'number'** of **X-Y** coordinates in the object. For example PRISM 4,0.2 means that there are 4 points on the prism, with a height of 0.2. Similar rules apply to REVOLVE, SWEEP and almost all complex 3D forms.

Masking Values: The next command, REVOLVE is the first to use a Masking value for the whole object – usually 63. Each command has a different way of using these. As I have decided that the Cookbook is not intended to be a total replacement for the manual, I have not printed the keys to these values for each and every object. This is a case for delving into the manual, where they are quite well explained.

FPRISM_ and **SPRISM_** are covered in the Voyager Course

REVOLVE!

See the REVOLVE example in the Fire Extinguisher!

REVOLVE takes the outline (that can be 'drawn' in the same way as in POLY_, PYRAMID or EXTRUDE – onto the X-Y plane) and Revolves it around the X axis.

It doesn't allow you to describe any points with a Y value that is zero or negative. i.e. All points must be higher than the X-axis - one millimetre will suffice. You cannot drill a hole in the cross section.

The last number on the first line is the MASK. To get the REVOLVE drawn as totally solid, 63 is the ideal mask. If the object is solid and lathed, then 63 will do. However, a revolving object that is free of the centre (like a torus / doughnut) must have a masking value of 0 to start off with.

REVOLVE can give you an object standing upright if you first apply **ROTy –90** first. A Vase, Baluster, Classical column – in fact, most REVOLVEs are preceded by a ROTy -90.

RESOL is a big issue with REVOLVE. One single revolve can result in hundreds of polygons, especially as the drawn out line can have include curved polylines.

```
!REVOLVE Demonstration
!Syntax:- REVOLVE n,alpha,mask,
!            x1,y1,s1,....xn,yn,sn
REVOLVE 9,90,63,
   0.00,0.01,0,
  -0.10,0.30,0,
   0.10,0.30,0,
   0.10,0.40,0,
   0.20,0.40,0,
   0.20,0.10,1000,
   0.15,0.10,0,
   0.15,0.01,0,
   0.00,0.01,-1
```

Remember, the 'n' after commands like REVOLVE and SWEEP is the number of XY points defining the outline.

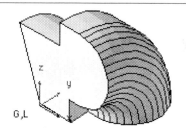

Revolve is one of the must useful commands in GDL – but draw the X-Y outline on paper first to think it out

```
!REVOLVE Demonstration
!Syntax:- REVOLVE n,alpha,mask,
!            x1,y1,s1,....xn,yn,sn
ROTy -90
REVOLVE 9,90,63+64,
   0.00,0.01,0,
  -0.10,0.30,0,
   0.10,0.30,0,
   0.10,0.40,0,
   0.20,0.40,0,
   0.20,0.10,1000,
   0.15,0.10,0,
   0.15,0.01,0,
   0.00,0.01,-1
DEL 1
```

Changing these last values from 0 to 1 will remove the line that follow the surface of the revolve

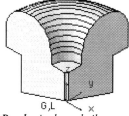

Revolve is always built around the X axis. So if you want it to stand upright, issue a ROTy -90 command before the Revolve command.

Masking: 1=Base surface, 2=Top surface, 4=Side surface Start, 8=Side surface End, 16=Side edges Start, 32=Side edges End, 64=Cross section edges.

With a mask of 127 (or 63+64) you get all the lines drawn, but do you want all these? – your choice!

Fire Extinguisher

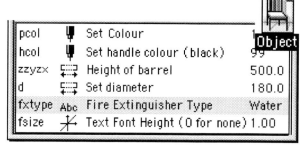

pcol	🔫	Set Colour	1
hcol	🔫	Set handle colour (black)	99
zzyzx	⟷	Height of barrel	500.0
d	⟷	Set diameter	180.0
fxtype	Abc	Fire Extinguisher Type	Water
fsize	⊬	Text Font Height (0 for none)	1.00

THIS LITTLE SCRIPT produces a useful object; it also introduces more techniques in 1 page than any other exercise in the Cookbook! It covers: REVOLVE; PolyLines; Pen to set colour, zzyzx, Value Lists, Defining Material, 2D text.

```
!Fire Extinguisher
!3D Script
!Bottle Body
MATERIAL 'fxmat'
PEN pcol
RESOL 16
  ROTy -90
REVOLVE 4,360,63,
 0       ,d/2,1,
 zzyzx-0.06,d/2,1,
 zzyzx   ,d/6,1001,
 zzyzx   ,0.001,1
DEL 1

!Handle
MATERIAL 0:PEN hcol
RESOL 8
  ADDz zzyzx
CYLIND 0.03,0.03
    ADD -0.03,0,0.06
    ROTy -110
    CYLIND 0.05,0.01
    DEL 2
  ADDz 0.03
  ROTx 90
  ADDz -0.02
PRISM_ 9,0.04,
  -0.03,0,15,
  -0.04,0.05,15,
   0.11,0.10,15-2,
   0.12,0.09,1015,
   0.03,0.05,15,
   0.12,0.01,15,
   0.12,0.00,15,
   0.03,0.03,15,
   0.03,0.00,15
DEL 4
```

Parameters: The colour and type of the extinguisher is determined by the Value List - which also generates a Defined Material and a Text annotation. The height of the barrel is called 'zzyzx' – enabling it to be stretched. You could also have a value list for Litres/Gallons and let the value list work out the best diameter and size from a known range of sizes (you could then delete 'd' and 'zzyzx').

```
Parameters | Components | Descriptors | ▦ | ▥▥  [ New ][ Delete ]
Variable        Type    Name                        Value
[fxtype     ]  [Abc▸]  [Fire Extinguisher Type  ]  [Water  ][▸]
VALUES 'fxtype' 'Water','Halon',
                'Powder','Foam','CO2'
```

If you want the user to have a pop-up menu of options, put this script into the Values List. Click on the button next to the word 'Descriptors' to enable the list. The Master Script parses the result.

3D View

3D Script: Declare Material & Pen. Reduced RESOLution of curvature will speed up rendering.

• **REVOLVE** is done along the X-Axis, so you have to **ROTy -90** for the object to stand upright. Remember to **DEL 1** afterwards. Setting out the X-Y locations for REVOLVE is like laying out a set of points on the X,Y plane – just as you might do for a POLY.

• Material 0 will cause a new material to be made based on the Pen colour - in this case, black.

• You need a sleeve at the top of the bottle, & a squirting spout – done with **CYLIND** and a few cursor movements.

• Finally, you build a PRISMatic handle on top. This requires you to position the X-Y plane sideways, so more cursor commands are required to get the cylindrical top and handle into place. DEL 4 to finish – always return the cursor to the origin.

```
!Master Script
IF fxtype="Water"   THEN
 pred=0.6:pgrn=0.0:pblu=0.0
ENDIF
IF fxtype="Halon"   THEN
 pred=0.0:pgrn=0.6:pblu=0.0
ENDIF
IF fxtype="Powder"  THEN
 pred=0.0:pgrn=0.0:pblu=0.6
ENDIF
IF fxtype="Foam"    THEN
 pred=1.0:pgrn=1.0:pblu=1.0
ENDIF
IF fxtype="CO2"     THEN
 pred=0.0:pgrn=0.0:pblu=0.0
ENDIF
DEFINE MATERIAL 'fxmat' 3,
pred,pgrn,pblu
```

Polylines: In the REVOLVE and PRISM commands, the use of a 1000 poly line command (added to 15 in the PRISM) is required to get a tangential curve between the two points mentioned. Type in the same commands without the 1000; use a 0 or a 15 instead, and then put the 1000 back in – see what happens. This is a good exercise to experiment with Polylines. The last status codes for the Revolve, 1, remove visible lines on the bottle. Try them with 0 instead. You can also remove surplus lines from the handle with a -2.

Master Script: This works out suitable values for the Red, Green and Blue components of the colour of the bottle and defines a new Material based on these colours – using a metallic surface quality.

```
!Fire Extinguisher
!2D Script
PEN pcol
ARC2 0,0,d/2,15,345
CIRCLE2 0,0,0.03
RECT2 -0.04,0.02,
      0.12,-0.02
IF fsize>0 THEN
  DEFINE STYLE "ftext" Arial,
           fsize,2,0
  SET STYLE "ftext"
  TEXT2 0,0,fxtype
ENDIF
```

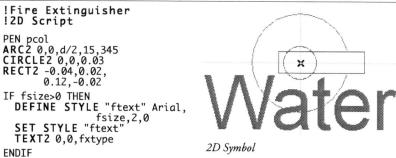

2D Symbol

2D Script: Instead of using PROJECT2 (just too easy), try writing a simple 2D script, which looks just as good, and will guarantee faster drawing in your plan view. Use the ARC2 command to get a hidden line effect. If the user enters a valid Font size, the script can label the Extinguisher. The TEXT2 routine can indicate whether it is Water, CO_2, Foam, or Powder. You could also write a short properties script that will send this information to a Components Listing. **Question:** If you use A_ (drawing scale) can you autosize the text so it is always the same relative to the object?

Simple Sash Window

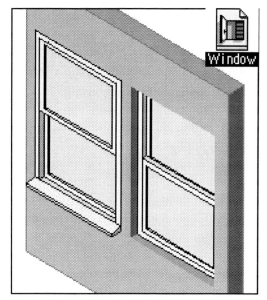

T HIS EXERCISE explains the basics of how to make a simple window, using drilled prisms.

For serious architectural work, authentic looking windows and doors are essential. If you do not find a suitable one in the existing library, you have to make one. It is not well explained in any of the official literature, and too much trust is placed in building windows with the slab tool, and relying on a 3D view saved as a Library object to make the window. These may look OK, but will not be parametric.

The window explained here is so simple that you could easily make it with slabs, but then it wouldnt be parametric. This exercise shows how a window COULD be made with scripting. With the knowledge gained from doing this exercise, you will better understand how ArchiCAD uses windows, and can then attempt windows of a more complex nature that go well beyond what can be done with the slab tool.

Exterior (left) and Interior (right) views

Windows that use soldier courses and sills, or chamfered reveals require a knowledge of **Global Variables**. These tell the GDL object the current thickness and materials of the walls. Windows always cut **rectangular holes** in the wall based on the dimensions A and B. If the window is not rectangular, you have to build chunks of wall around it (to finish as a rectangular shape) or use the new AC6 command, WALLHOLE. Let's stick with a rectangular hole for now.

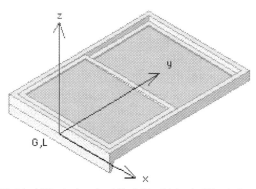

Finished 3D window should look like this in the 3D window – lying face down, bottom face flat on the X-Y Plane.

Golden Rules

...for making Windows (and Doors)

• Build the window with the outside face facing downwards, level with project zero. (Even though you may want to recess the frame into the opening, you should build the GDL model as stated).

• Position the origin on the centre line of the lowest sill of the window.

• PRISMs make better sashes than BLOCK. Use fPRISM for a chamfered look to frames.

• Use POLY instead of PRISM for Glass unless you want it to look thick.

• Repeated items like sashes should be self contained subroutines.

• Create the 2D view by using the PROJECT2 4,90,1 command, with a ROT2 180 command to 'turn the camera upside down'. You could then attempt some 2D scripting, using Project2 as a guide.

• The A dimension is the width of the window, and B is the height. (Autoscripted windows do this too, but go very wrong when you add jamb, sill and head brickwork.) If you use B for height, you will be able to stretch the windows in Section / Elevation.

• When you get more confident, experiment a bit at a time with opening sashes, multiple glazing bars, jamb, head and sill details, reveals, architraves and ironmongery.

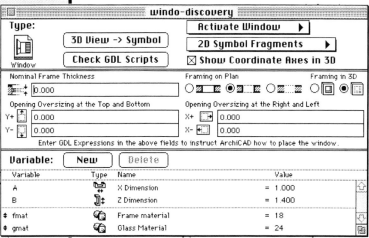

Parameter Box

If you open the new Library object as a Window, you get a parameter box like this. Much of the middle section is not required until you start using jambs and head details. It is possible to start a window as an 'object', and convert it to a window later. It cannot cut holes in walls until it is officially defined as a 'window' in ArchiCAD.

```
!Truly simple window
!GDL Cookbook
!3D Script

p=0.04 !Min. frame dimens'n
PEN 1
!Offset to lower left corner
  ADDx -A/2

!Main Frame
MATERIAL fmat
PRISM_ 5+5,p*2,
  0,0,15,
  A,0,15,
  A,B,15,
  0,B,15,
  0,0,-1,

  p,  p,15,
  A-p,p,15,
  A-p,B-p,15,
  p,  B-p,15,
  p,  p,-1

!Both sashes
  ADD p,p,p
GOSUB 100 !Lower Sash
  DEL 1

  ADD p,B/2-p/2,0
GOSUB 100 !Upper Sash
  DEL 1

!Sill
  ROTy 90
MATERIAL fmat
PRISM 5,A,
  0,0,
  p*2,0,
  p*2,p/2,
  0,p,
  0,0
DEL 1

DEL 1 !Undo offset

END:!---------------------
```

With PRISM_ you have to add a 'status value' of 15 to the end of each coordinate, and -1 to tell it to change from the outer to the inner outlines of the frame.

Complex window shapes

Windows and Doors are made, by default, with Rectangular openings. More complex window shapes can now be made with the WALLHOLE command. See the Curvy Window in the Voyager course, and a simpler curvy window in the Discovery course.

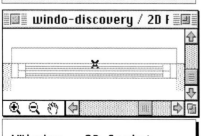

```
!Window - 2D Script
  ROT2 180
PROJECT2 4,90,1
  DEL 1
```

3D Script commentary:

• Use a simple variable to represent the smallest 'pixel' size of your object. Here, 'p' (for defining frame thickness) is much easier to use in the prism commands than real dimensions. It means you can change the frame thickness by changing the value of the one single variable.

• Because you must Centre the origin on the axis of the window, but because it is also easier to build anything from the bottom left corner, apply an ADDx -A/2 off-set. You will see how it works when you try it.

• Material command is essential because sash windows could be wood, PVC, aluminium, or a variety of colours.

• PRISM_ command defines the main frame of the window. By using the main variables of A and B, and a frame thickness of 'p', it is easily defined. Use 15 for all the points, and -1 to denote the end of one surface and the start of another.

• The sashes occur twice, and you need to have the sash frame and the glass act together as a single object, so you should make the sashes as a subroutine.

• The Sill is a simple prism, rotated so as to lie flat in the correct location, facing downwards.

• Make sure you put comments in for each small routine.

• Finally, you DEL the -A/2 offset.

• The routine must finish with an 'END' command so that you can write your subroutines below.

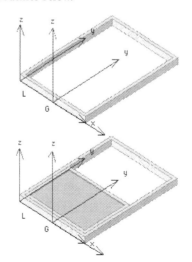

2D Script commentary:

Finally, the 2D window script looks like this. I use a Project2 command, but unlike the 3 you have used for other objects, you use 4. The ROTy 180 turns the camera upside down. If you want superfast 2D redrawing in a large building, this 2D image should be scripted using the Project2 as a guide – and when the scripted one looks correct, you delete the Project2 command.

```
END:!----------------

100:!Sash Subroutine
sh=(B-p*2)/2+p/2 !Sash Ht
sw=A-p*2         !Sash Width

MATERIAL fmat
PRISM_ 5+5,p,
  0, 0,15,
  sw,0,15,
  sw,sh,15,
  0, sh,15,
  0, 0,-1,

  p,    p,15,
  sw-p,p,15,
  sw-p,sh-p,15,
  p,   sh-p,15,
  p,    p,-1

  ADDz p/2
MATERIAL gmat
PRISM_ 5,p/4,
  p,    p,15,
  sw-p,p,15,
  sw-p,sh-p,15,
  p,   sh-p,15,
  p,    p,-1

  DEL 1
RETURN
```

• The sash is created with a subroutine. To keep it simple, work out the height and width of the sash first, and then use the simple variables 'sh' and sw' in the PRISM command. Note that the Glass is exactly the same prism profile as the hole in the sash frame prism – so you can copy and paste the coordinates.

• It is a good idea to enable the user to define the material for Glass in case the user wants to use Ice (for translucency) or Mirror.

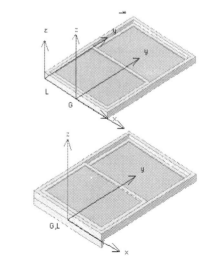

Simple Curvy Window

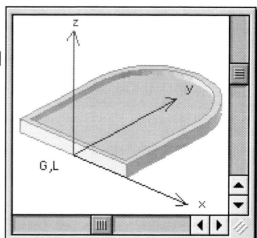

Build it on the X-Y floorplane as usual, with the outside frame face on level zero, and the origin on the centre axis.

T HIS EXERCISE exploits the wonderful new command in ArchiCAD 6 called WALLHOLE.

It quite liberates the GDL user from the complex procedures for making windows that are not rectangular. If you can define the outline of the window shape with the similar set of commands that you would use to draw a POLY, EXTRUDE or PRISM , then you can make a window..... with the limitation that a single WALLHOLE command must be convex in shape. To make concave window shapes (such as an L-Shape, you can make two or more Wallholes together.)

This window is a simple arched window, with fixed glazing and a simple outlined frame, but it is ideal for illustrating the principle. A more complex use of Wallhole is illustrated in the Voyager course.

A		X Dimension	0.914
B		Z Dimension	1.219
gmat		Material for Glass	24
fmat		Material for Frame	14
fdep		Frame Depth	0.100
fwid		Frame Width	0.050

Parameters: A and B define width and height

```
!Very Simple round window       3D Script
!GDL Cookbook

RESOL 36                MATERIAL fmat
WALLHOLE 4,2,           PRISM_ 5+5,fdep,
-A/2,      0,7,         -A/2,      0,15,
-A/2,B-A/2,5,           -A/2,B-A/2,13,
 A/2,B-A/2,1007,         A/2,B-A/2,1015,
 A/2,      0,7           A/2,      0,15,
                        -A/2,      0,-1,

ADDz fdep/2
MATERIAL gmat           -A/2+fwid, fwid,15,
POLY_ 4,                -A/2+fwid,B-A/2,13,
-A/2,      0,7,          A/2-fwid,B-A/2,1015,
-A/2,B-A/2,5,            A/2-fwid, fwid,15,
 A/2,B-A/2,1007,        -A/2+fwid, fwid,-1
 A/2,      0,7
DEL 1
```

The list of X-Y locations can be copied and pasted from the WALLHOLE outline straight into the POLY definition, without change. Although POLY requires only 1 or 0 for the Status setting, any odd number is the same as 1, and even number is equivalent to 0.

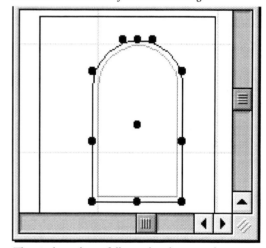

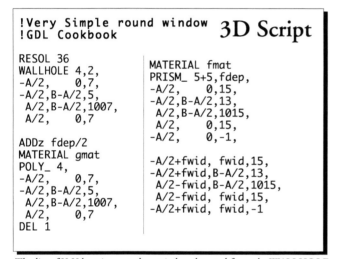

The window is beautifully stretchy when viewed in section. I love WALLHOLE. It's so effective and compact that I managed to fit this whole exercise into one page!

The Wallhole outline has been modified with a 5 instead of the usual 7, to remove the lines around the arch. The same has been done for the Prism, using 13 instead of 15.

The 2D symbol in plan

```
!Simple round window
!2D Script

ROT2 180
PROJECT2 4,270,1
DEL 1
```

2 D Script: Note that for the script in 2D, you follow the trick shown here, to do a Project2 having first done a 180degree rotation. For a building with many windows, you could script the window with the RECT2 command.

Maths Operators

ABS(number) returns the positive value of a number, regardless of whether it is negative or positive. You can prevent the user entering negative parameters into the dialog box with a simple statement like: item=ABS(item).

SGN(number) returns a 1 if the number is positive, or a -1 if the number is negative. Small token numbers like this which signify the status of a number are called 'flags', in programming jargon.

RND(number) returns a random number value between 0.0 and 1.0 and is multiplied by the number in the bracket, e.g. RND(50) is numbers from 0 to 50, RND(0.1) is from 0.0 to 0.1. RND numbers are Real Numbers, so can only be used to generate Dimensions if you are using Metres. Unfortunately, GDL's random number generator is weak, and generates the same sequence each time from a fixed list, with a preponderance of low numbers. The only way to get a more nearly random number is to get the list to start from anywhere but the start. You could do FOR k=0 TO SYMB_POS_X: x=RDN(1): NEXT k (the list is started from the number equal to the object's horizontal distance from the plan origin – different in most cases). In animations, you could use the Frame number as a randomisation seed.

INT(number) returns the integer of the number – an integer is a round number (without decimals). The INT command ALWAYS rounds downwards, so you can do x=INT(number + 0.5) to get it to round up OR downward correctly.

Example: INT(8.56) = 8 (rounds down)

INT(8.56+0.5)=9 (rounds up)

SQR(number) returns the square root of the number. This is useful in matters like the use of Pythagoras Theorem in Triangles, and Circle geometry. If you need Cube and Quad roots, try using the Power symbol – e.g. length**(1/3), width**(1/4)

FRA (number) is the other side of INT(). It returns the fraction remaining when you remove the integers. Unfortunately it behaves always in one direction, so FRA(6.3) returns 0.3, but FRA(-6.3) returns 0.7.

PI is useful in circle geometry – it is exact, and therefore better than trying to put in your own number, such as 3.1416, and incurring errors in a calculation.

MIN( ) and MAX( ) are useful – they simply tell you the highest or lowest of a series of numbers or variables that you print in the brackets.

For example:

ADDz MAX(leftht,rightht)

to raise the cursor to the height of one of the ridge of a monopitch gable wall.

NOT( ) is useful in IF statements. You could write IF thing=0 THEN GOSUB 100, but it is more like english to write IF NOT(thing) THEN GOSUB 100. Also because NOT() either returns a value of 1 or zero, you could use it as a flag, as in:

LET rotation_angle= 30*NOT(thing).

When 'thing' is valid, the angle would be zero and if 'thing' is zero, then the angle will be at 30degrees.

SIN( ), COS( ) and TAN( ) – Trigonometry functions are explained in the diagram below.

ATN(), ASN(), ACS() mean respectively ArcTan, ArcSin and ArcCos. This means that if you know the sides of a right angle triangle, you can easily work out the angles. ArcTan(0.231) will return you the Angle which, if you calculated TAN(angle) would give you a TAN of 0.231. This is essential if you are building lattice trusses.

AND and OR and EXOR are used as arguments in IF statements. For example, you could say: IF item>4 AND item<6 THEN GOSUB 500. This would certainly identify a floating point number in the region of five. IF item<4 OR item>64 THEN GOSUB 500 would activate with all numbers except those between 4.0001 and 63.999. Usually, if you say it to yourself slowly in English, and digest the natural logic of the AND and the OR argument, you will get it right. I have never needed to use EXOR, but it is exclusive whereas OR is inclusive.

EXP, LGT, LOG are 'transcendental' functions, to do with 'e' and logarithms. These would be useful if using curves, but I have not needed them yet.

MOD is a way of finding the remainder after a division. For example 8 MOD 2 equals 0 because 2 divides perfectly into 8. 8 MOD 3 equals 2 because if you divide 8 by 3 it goes twice and leaves a remainder of 2.

<> means Not Equal to
> Greater than, < Smaller than
>= Great than or Equal to
<= Smaller than or Equal to

All numbers in GDL are 'Floating Point', you cannot force a variable to be an integer.

Trigonometry: You need a basic knowledge of the right angle triangle – all you need to know is:

- **Pythagoras** – the Square of the Hypotenuse is the Sum of the Squares of the other two sides.

- **SOH CAH TOA** – You need to remember this motto so that you can always calculate the characteristics of a triangle from minimal information. If you don't know this one already, say it to yourself as a mantra whilst being kept on hold on the phone, or standing under the shower.

- **Irregular triangles** can be analysed by breaking into small right angled ones and using SOH CAH TOA.

- The angles of any triangle add up to 180°.

- Many Circle geometry problems (e.g. converting a known Angle and Radius into X and Y coordinates) are easily solved with SOH CAH TOA.

See more about Circle Geometry and Trig in the Maths Primer in the Voyager Section.

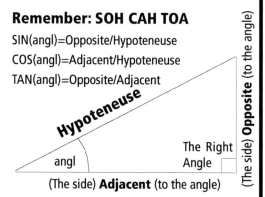

Remember: SOH CAH TOA

SIN(angl)=Opposite/Hypoteneuse
COS(angl)=Adjacent/Hypoteneuse
TAN(angl)=Opposite/Adjacent

Hypoteneuse

angl

The Right Angle

(The side) **Opposite** (to the angle)

(The side) **Adjacent** (to the angle)

Lattice Truss

This model is a useful exercise in:

- Using Trigonometry to determine lengths and angles
- FOR... NEXT loops
- 2-D script writing
- Using 2-D image to display information
- Defining text styles

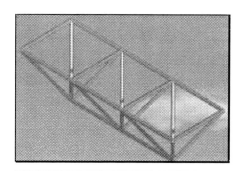

Parameters: The model is not stretchy, as the lattice is built from manufacturer's standard sized modules.

- The Truss is to be done here using only CYLIND to form the tubes.
- The user is offered a choice of width, height and any number of modules, and tubing diameter. This example does not worry about joints, but it would be easy to add balls or cones, which could be a user option.
- The user can ask the truss to 'Show Data' – this could be a print out of its span or weight.
- As the truss could in fact be a vertical structure (column) or could be leaning (over an atrium) the lean angle option is offered.

3 D Script: Even for a small object, a strictly structured approach is adopted from the start. Analyse the model as a series of subroutines, one to solve every element of the model. The executive script is short in the extreme, just calling subroutines.

The technique is to make all the upper elements, in a FOR...NEXT loop, then the bottom tube, and finally, the diagonal tubes. Some trigonometry is required to work out the angles of the diagonal tubes. As this is an important part of the script, a special subroutine 100: is proposed for working out the trigonometry and setting up other parameters.

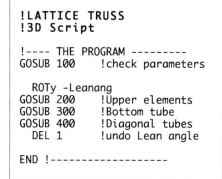

```
!LATTICE TRUSS
!3D Script

!---- THE PROGRAM ---------
GOSUB 100      !check parameters

  ROTy -Leanang
GOSUB 200      !Upper elements
GOSUB 300      !Bottom tube
GOSUB 400      !Diagonal tubes
  DEL 1        !undo Lean angle

END !------------------
```

```
100: !parameter set up
!or put into Master Script

RESOL 8
MATERIAL tmatl
PEN tpen
trad  =tdiam/2   !tube radius
dtang =ATN((tmod*sqr(2)/2)/tdep)
dtlen =tdep/cos(dtang)
RETURN
```

100: First set up the usual things like RESOL, Material and Pen. Then convert diameter to radius.

Now work out the angle of the diagonal tubes. As the truss module as seen in plan is a perfect square, the diagonal across the square is the 'truss module times √2'; the angle of lean of the cylinder will be the ArcTan of half that diagonal and the truss depth.

Finally, the Length of the diagonal tube can be found as the hypoteneuse of the right angle triangle formed by the tube – the depth divided by the COS of the angle. Alternatively, you could work out the tube length by Pythagoras. In later exercises (winged truss) you will see that it is possible almost to dispense with trigonometry and use the TUBE command to go from XYZ point to XYZ point.

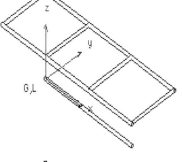

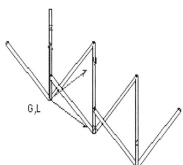

Variable	Type	Name	Value
tmod	⟷	Truss Module plan size	1200
tdep	⟷	Depth of Truss	1000
tdiam	⟷	Diameter of tubing m	60
tnum	⊞	Number of Truss Modules	3
shodata	☒	Show Data Yes=1 No=0	On
fhigt	⊞	Font height mm	2
leanang	△	Leaning Angle (0=horiz)	0.00
tmatl	🎨	Tubing material	11
tpen	✏	Pen Colour	1

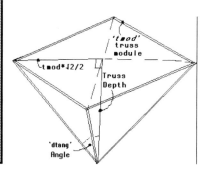

200: The Upper longitudinal tubes are easy enough : a matter of getting to the right position, and pumping out a CYLIND. However, note that one steps backwards by one tube radius, and makes the tube a tiny bit longer to give the impression of a butt end to the tube. The same is done for the bottom member.

The FOR...NEXT Loop is needed to generate the lateral tubes. By using a loop, you can use the number of modules as a counter to decide how many to draw. Notice in this example, that we use K as a counter in the loop and also as a way of calculating how far the cursor travels before generating the cylinder. For the first tube, it moves 'tmod*(k-1)' which is, effectively, zero. When it gets to the 4th tube, it is moving 'tmod*(4-1)' which gets it to the right place. Using this method, you can do the DEL command INSIDE the FOR... NEXT loop, which is much tidier.

300: Bottom member of the truss is very easy. One long Cylinder, slightly elongated to improve the junction detail.

400: The Diagonals – well, the routine to draw the 4 diagonal tubes is a bit complicated, so it uses subroutine 450 for each truss module, so that the main FOR...NEXT loop looks tidier.

450: Rotate 45° then issue 4 leaning-over cylinders rotating 90° each time. At the end, put DEL 4+1 instead of 5. It reminds you not to forget the ROTz 45 with which you started drawing the tubes.

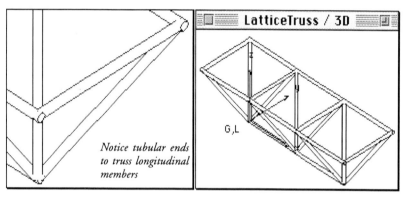

Notice tubular ends to truss longitudinal members

2D Script:
It is important to have a good 2-D script, as the Project2 command will take too long to display, with all those cylinders.

If you wish to tilt the Truss so that it's a leanto or a Column, the 2D script would not work, so you need to use Project2.

The 2D script here takes the same parameters as the 3D script, works out a few locations of the nodes, and draws quick lines and rectangles to draw the truss in plan. It also plants Hotspots in the right places.

Finally, you might like to try getting the 2D symbol to give you information. In this case, the span of the truss. For this, you need to define a text style – the size of the text is parametric. This 2-D display ability could be used to print out structural or weight data. It is also useful in circular objects in displaying Radius or span.

The Truss can also be used as a Walling element Another way to Make the Truss draw extremely quickly in the project plan is to 'encapsulate' your Truss: make your parametrically defined truss a library object AGAIN, so that it has a standard object symbol – providing you have no further intention of changing it. You can use this method to make an entire PORTAL.

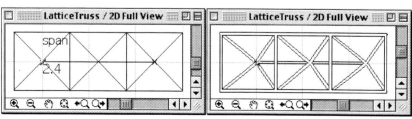

Scripted 2D symbol if the truss is flat

Use PROJECT2 if the truss is tilted

```
200: !Truss upper element
     !Longitudinal
  ADD -tmod/2-trad,-tmod/2,tdep
  ROTy 90
CYLIND tmod*tnum+tdiam,trad
  ADDy tmod
CYLIND tmod*tnum+tdiam,trad
  DEL 3

!Truss upper tube - Lateral
FOR k = 1 TO tnum+1
  ADD -tmod/2,-tmod/2,tdep
  ROTx -90
  ADDx tmod*(k-1)
CYLIND tmod,trad
  DEL 3
  NEXT k
RETURN

300: !Bottom boom
  ROTy 90
  ADDz -trad    !slightly longer
CYLIND tmod*(tnum-1)+tdiam,trad
  DEL 2
RETURN

400: !Diagonal Truss element
FOR k = 1 TO tnum
  ADDx tmod*(k-1)
  GOSUB 450
    DEL 1
    NEXT k
RETURN

450: !Diagonals
  ROTz 45 !first tube angle
FOR n=1 to 4
  ROTx dtang
    CYLIND dtlen,trad
    DEL 1
  ROTz 90
NEXT n
  DEL 4+1
RETURN
```

```
!2-D Script
IF Leanang THEN
        PROJECT2 3,270,2

  ELSE   !if Truss is Flat
LET w2    = tmod/2
!Top and bottom lengths
tenx= tmod*tnum-tmod/2
benx= tmod*(tnum-1)
!------------------------
RECT2 -w2,w2,  tenx,-w2
FOR k=1 to tnum
  ADD2 tmod*(k-1),0
  LINE2 -w2,-w2,w2, w2
  LINE2 -w2, w2,w2,-w2
  LINE2  w2, w2,w2,-w2
  DEL 1
NEXT k
  LINE2  0,0,    benx,0
!-------------------------
HOTSPOT2 0,0
HOTSPOT2 benx,0
!-------------------------
IF shodata THEN
DEFINE STYLE "display"
  "geneva", fhigt,1,0
  STYLE "display"
  TEXT2 0,w2,"span"
  TEXT2 0,0 ,tmod*(tnum-1)
  ENDIF
```

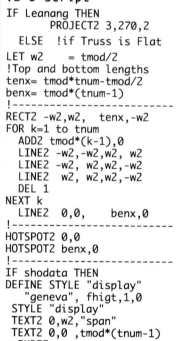

Truss as a wall element

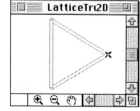

Lattice Portal – using Lattice Truss

This model is an exercise in:

- Finding ways to speed up your plan drawing
- Encapsulating : Making Library objects of library objects
- Using the Elevation/Section window to get the model right

Relax! There is no GDL coding in this exercise.

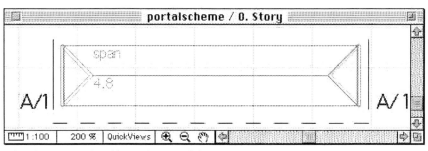

The Plan – Using three library objects, and showing section A/1.

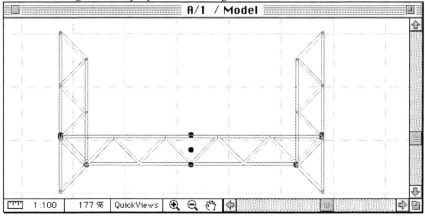

Section A/1 – Lift the truss into position on the columns.

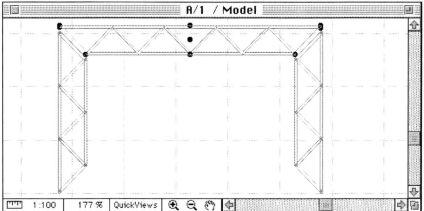

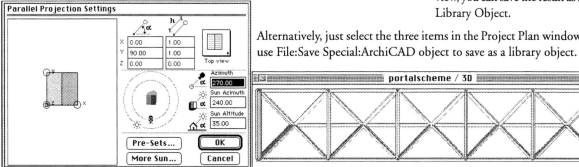

I N THE Lattice Truss exercise, you had a choice of scripting the 2-D as a Project2 command, or as a script. If the Truss is used as a column or a sloping beam, the Project2 command has to be used, which will take a long time to redraw.

A way to make the Truss draw extremely quickly in the project plan is to **encapsulate** your Truss: make your parametrically defined truss a library object AGAIN, so that it has a standard object symbol – providing you have no further intention of changing it. Here is the means of doing this.

Procedure

Here is a single truss with 5 modules of 1.2 metres, supported by two columns of 3 modules each (3.6 metres high) Lay them in the plan, so that they relate correctly in plan.

Plant a section line just in front of the truss to give you a view of the Portal, then view the section.

The columns and the beam elements start off on the floor. Use the section window to lift the beam to the correct height.

Set up a 3D view, with the camera at 270° and the view set to Plan (Top View), When you have a 3D view, you can save the result as a new Library Object.

Alternatively, just select the three items in the Project Plan window, and use File:Save Special:ArchiCAD object to save as a library object.

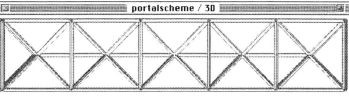

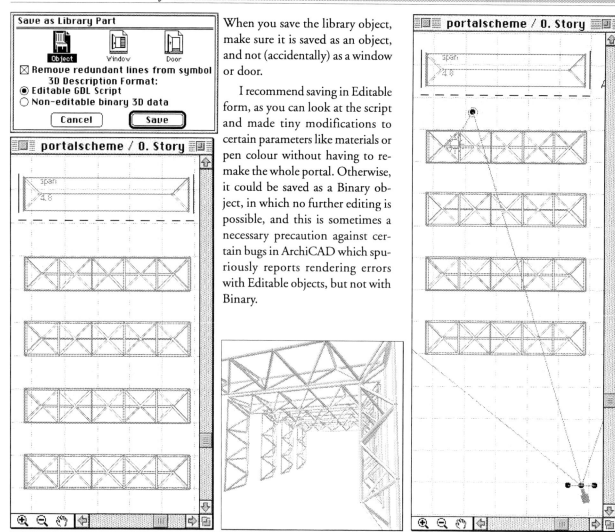

When you save the library object, make sure it is saved as an object, and not (accidentally) as a window or door.

I recommend saving in Editable form, as you can look at the script and made tiny modifications to certain parameters like materials or pen colour without having to re-make the whole portal. Otherwise, it could be saved as a Binary object, in which no further editing is possible, and this is sometimes a necessary precaution against certain bugs in ArchiCAD which spuriously reports rendering errors with Editable objects, but not with Binary.

Raised Computer Flooring Tool

THIS is a classic example of stretchiness resulting in a useful tool. It is done with Nested FOR... NEXT Loops. This object also reminds you of the usefulness of using VALUE scripts and a Master Script.

Raised computer flooring is a genuinely useful object – by arranging small stretchy rectangles of floortool, you can adapt to complex room shapes.

Parameters: For this the only parameters that really matter are the total width and length dimension, the panel size and floor height. However, you can make the object more user friendly by adding in options, such as to leave out the panels. You also control the Materials. When you have more than one material in an object, you need to have them specified in the parameter box. When you have one (such as the pen colour here) there is no need for this, as the user can control it from other parts of the Library part settings box.

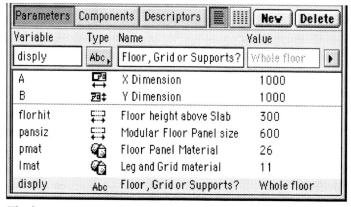

Variable	Type	Name	Value
disply	Abc	Floor, Grid or Supports?	Whole floor
A	↔	X Dimension	1000
B	↕	Y Dimension	1000
florhit		Floor height above Slab	300
pansiz		Modular Floor Panel size	600
pmat		Floor Panel Material	26
lmat		Leg and Grid material	11
disply	Abc	Floor, Grid or Supports?	Whole floor

The dimensioning system here is in millimetres, although, note, that the GDL script is ALWAYS written in Metres, or if you wish to write in imperial, with inch or foot markers (as in 2'-0")

1.48

```
!Raised Flooring System - 3D

!Legs
FOR n=0 TO B+pansiz STEP pansiz
  ADDy n
  FOR k=0 TO A+pansiz STEP pansiz
    ADDx k
    GOSUB 100:!Floor leg
    DEL 1
    NEXT k
    DEL 1
  NEXT n

!Panels
IF d3d=2 THEN
FOR n=0 TO B STEP pansiz
  ADDy n
  FOR k=0 TO A STEP pansiz
    ADDx k
    GOSUB 120:!Panel
    DEL 1
    NEXT k
      DEL 1
      NEXT n
      ENDIF

!Grid
IF d3d AND NOT(simple) THEN
MATERIAL lmat
ADDz florhit-panth
FOR n=0 TO B+pansiz  STEP pansiz
  ADDy n
  BLOCK numpana*pansiz,jonth,panth
  DEL 1
  NEXT n
FOR k=0 TO A+pansiz  STEP pansiz
  ADDx k
  BLOCK jonth,numpanb*pansiz,panth
  DEL 1
  NEXT k
  DEL 1
  ENDIF

END:!--------------------------

100:!Floor leg
MATERIAL lmat
 RESOL 8
 CYLIND 0.01,0.04
 CYLIND florhit-panth,lgrad
 ADDz florhit-panth-0.01
 CYLIND 0.01,0.04
 DEL 1
RETURN

120:!Panel
psiz=pansiz-jonth
MATERIAL pmat
 ADD jonth/2,jonth/2,florhit-0.02
 BLOCK psiz,psiz,0.02
 DEL 1
RETURN
```

3D Script: FOR...

NEXT Loops can be based on distance, angle or number. Here you can do it with distance, although to get it to work usefully, it is best to make the panelling extend beyond the A and B dimensions; hence the final dimension is (A+pansiz), not A. If the panelling stayed within the AB dimensions, the active hotspot that makes it stretchy would get lost in walls or over other areas of floor.

```
!Master Script - feeds parameters
!to both 2D and 3D scripts

IF disply="Whole floor"      THEN d3d=2
IF disply="Panels removed"   THEN d3d=1
IF disply="Supports only"    THEN d3d=0

 numpana=INT(A/pansiz)+1
 numpanb=INT(B/pansiz)+1
 panth=0.02 !Panel thickness
 jonth=0.01 !Joint thickness
 lgrad=0.02 !Leg Radius
```

```
VALUES "disply" "Whole floor",
       "Panels removed",
       "Supports only"
```

Value list: Avoid putting titles or comments into the Value script as they can behave erratically. Value Lists are best used for strings ('abc'), even though numbers are possible. Put Value Lists into **Parameter script** in AC 6.5.

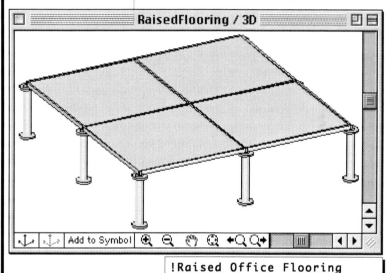

RaisedFlooring / 3D

Master Script: is the

best way to 'parse' a Values list script and convert the results into numbers. Internal parameters such as panel thickness (ones you do not want the user to change) can also be here. Master scripts should not exceed 10k in size or Value Lists do not work correctly (bug).

```
!Raised Office Flooring
!2D Script

!PROJECT2 3,270,2

HOTSPOT2 0,0
HOTSPOT2 A,0
HOTSPOT2 A,B
HOTSPOT2 0,B
!Crosshair
LINE2 A,B+panth,A,B-panth
LINE2 A+panth,B,A-panth,B

!Legs
FOR n=0 TO B+pansiz STEP pansiz
  ADD2 0,n
FOR k=0 TO A+pansiz STEP pansiz
  ADD2 k,0
  CIRCLE2 0,0,0.03:!Floor leg
  DEL 1
  NEXT k
  DEL 1
  NEXT n

!Panels
IF d3d=2 THEN
FOR n=0 TO B STEP pansiz
  ADD2 0,n
  FOR k=0 TO A STEP pansiz
  ADD2 k,0
  RECT2 0,0,pansiz,pansiz
  DEL 1
  NEXT k
    DEL 1
    NEXT n
    ENDIF
```

2D Script: You

could use just a Project 2, and the four primary hotspots (bounding box hotspots will not be stretchy). It is also helpful to write a small 'Crosshair' routine to tell the user where the A,B Hotspot is located. You can mimic the structure of the 3D script.

The fully written 2D script rewards the time you have invested because it speeds up Redraw in the Project plan.

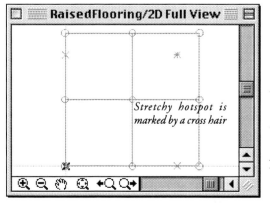

RaisedFlooring/2D Full View

Stretchy hotspot is marked by a cross hair

1.49

Louvre Sunbreaker

THIS IS SIMILAR in some way to the Joist tool or the Computer flooring, in that it is stretchy and uses a FOR... NEXT Loop; but this operates as a mechanism. One can rotate the louvres, tilt the assembly and change the curvature of the blades. The idea is to look at ways of mechanising louvres to follow the sun path.

Parameters: Two of the parameters are based on a Value List, for Louvre shape and for the design of the surround. the shape could be based on asking for a Radius, but it is more user friendly to offer a Value List selection.

3D Script: First the Value Lists are parsed to calculate some internal flags and parameters. Then Tilt and Pen.

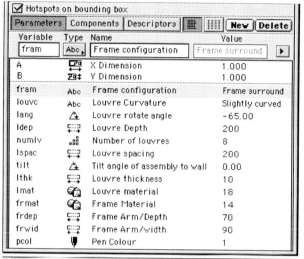

Variable	Type	Name	Value
fram	Abc	Frame configuration	Frame surround
A		X Dimension	1.000
B		Y Dimension	1.000
fram	Abc	Frame configuration	Frame surround
louvc	Abc	Louvre Curvature	Slightly curved
lang		Louvre rotate angle	-65.00
ldep		Louvre Depth	200
numlv		Number of louvres	8
lspac		Louvre spacing	200
tilt		Tilt angle of assembly to wall	0.00
lthk		Louvre thickness	10
lmat		Louvre material	18
frmat		Frame Material	14
frdep		Frame Arm/Depth	70
frwid		Frame Arm/width	90
pcol		Pen Colour	1

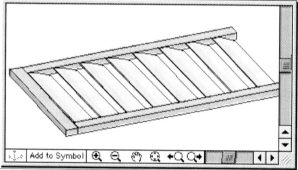

```
!Louvre wizard
!3D Script

IF fram='No Frame'        THEN frm=0
IF fram='Arms only'       THEN frm=1
IF fram='Frame surround' THEN frm=2
IF frm=0 THEN lwid=A
IF frm THEN lwid=A-frwid*2-lthk

IF louvc='Flat'            THEN radc=lspac*100
IF louvc='Slightly curved' THEN radc=lspac*2
IF louvc='Very Curved'     THEN radc=lspac/1.5
```
This varies the curvature of the louvres
```
!tilt if required
ROTx tilt
PEN pcol

!Draw the Louvre Assembly
MATERIAL lmat
ADDy lspac/2
FOR k=1 TO numlv
  ADDy lspac*(k-1)
  GOSUB 100:!Louvre
  DEL 1
  NEXT k
DEL 1
```
This loop is based on distance
```
!Draw the Frame
!first the Arms
IF frm THEN
MATERIAL frmat
  ADDz -frdep/2
BLOCK frwid,lspac*(numlv),frdep
  ADDx A-frwid
BLOCK frwid,lspac*(numlv),frdep
  DEL 2
ENDIF
```
The frame might better be done with a PRISM, but I am trying to keep things simple
```
!Draw frame
IF frm=2 THEN
MATERIAL frmat
  ADDy lspac*numlv
  ADDz -frdep/2
  BLOCK A,frwid,frdep
  DEL 2

ENDIF

DEL 1 !Undo tilt

END!--------------------------------
```

VALUES 'fram' 'No Frame','Arms only', 'Frame surround'
VALUES 'louvc' 'Flat','Slightly curved', 'Very Curved'

The louvres are laid out using a FOR... NEXT Loop, and the hard work is done by a short subroutine 100. By using a bPRISM, and making the radius variable, you can in effect get flat louvres.

Because the RESOL of curvature is 36, a louvre blade with a radius of 100*louvre spacing will be less then 1/36 of a circle, i.e. it will be flat.

```
!------SUBROUTINES -----
100: !Louvre curved
IF frm THEN
  ADDx frwid+lthk/2
  ENDIF
ROTz -90
ROTy 90+lang
ADDz -lthk/2
bPRISM_ lmat,lmat,lmat,
  4,lthk,radc,
  -ldep/2,0,   15,
   ldep/2,0,   15,
   ldep/2,lwid,15,
  -ldep/2,lwid,15
DEL 3
IF frm THEN DEL 1
RETURN
```

2D Script: You could script this if it was always to remain level, but as it might tilt, you can use Project2.

```
!2D Script
HOTSPOT2 0,0
HOTSPOT2 A,0
PROJECT2 3,270,2
```

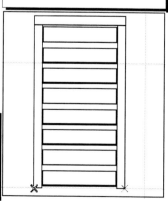

Tips and Tricks
Rendering

Anti Aliasing: For quick on-screen rendering, always turn off shadows and lamps. Both require greater amounts of disk and ram and time. Avoid anti-aliasing, or anything that will slow it down.

However, for quality rendering, first thing to restore is anti-aliasing. This 'softens' the pixels, that that thin or small objects are still drawn, whereas without anti-aliasing, they would judder between being drawn and being omitted. Hence they would look jagged. 'Anti-aliasing' means that it looks at the surrounding pixels and does a controlled blur, in which the colour of surrounding pixels are taken into account to produce a softer image – for example the outline of a roof against a blue sky.

Higher levels of anti aliasing slow it down, but produce better results. For each pixel of the final image, four pixels will be calculated, and the final pixel will be averaged – for example a thin vertical glazing bar that is normally smaller than a single pixel would now show. This results in 4 times as much rendering time.

As a rule of thumb, 'Good' anti-aliasing does not cause serious slowdowns in rendering, but 'Better' and 'Best' can delay rendering quite seriously. So use 'Good' most of the time.

Anti aliasing procedures are improved in AC-6.5, with a slider to control quality (but only if in AC's own rendering engine, and set to Best quality.

Textures versus 3D: Textures are always quicker to paint than geometrically modelled surfaces. For example, a tree model could have thousands of polygons if leaves are geometrically modelled. However, a lollipop shape with a dome or sphere shaped leaf ball, and an alpha-channelled image of leaves mapped onto the ball will look almost as good and reduce the polygon count to less than a hundred.

DPI and Resolution: Computer monitors work at 72dpi (dots per inch), and if you want to see how an image is progressing always use 72dpi – no matter what the final image size will be. If your image is to be printed, do not be tempted to enter any other figure in the Photo-rendering settings box. Stay with 72, but make the number of pixels in the image larger. For example, if you want to print an A3 landscape image, that is 17"x11" (420x297mm) with a final resolution of 200 dpi multiply 17x200=3400 and 11x200=2200. Set the size of the ArchiCAD Render to 3400x2200 at 72 dpi. It doesnt matter that this is bigger than your screen.

When it is done, quit ArchiCAD, open the file with Photoshop, Graphic Converter or PhotoPro, and you can resize the image to 17"x11" with 200dpi. You can also convert it to JPEG at varying levels of quality – always use 'maximum' if the artwork has to be presented. You can also scale the same file down to 340x220 GIF or lower quality jpegs for Web page presentation.

Comment, Preview and Labels

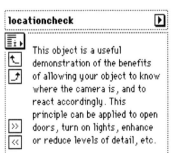

THE **Comment field** is a good way to document your object so that a user has a guide as to its purpose or to how it functions. If you are building investment objects (where you won't be around to explain), the comment box is like a tiny manual – or a copyright notice.

It has a wierd word-wrap mode, so you are best just to write it without carriage returns, and let it work out the wrap itself. It cannot scroll, so you cannot write much.

THE **Preview Picture** – is used to show what the object should look like. Since it would take too long to photorender, you can place a picture from the clipboard straight into the Preview Picture Window – this could be one you made earlier with Artlantis. I try to provide everything I do with Preview images. Preview images can also be used in the User Interface dialogs (with AC_6.5).

LABELS – Every Wall, Roof, Floor and Library Object has a label assigned to it by ArchiCAD. This is difficult to write into (although you can do). It is possible for each object in the plan to be displaying its label.

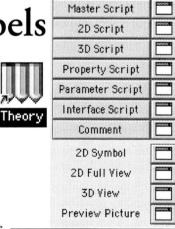

Early editions of the GDL Cookbook for AC_5.0 carried an exercise on Properties scripting. Properties scripting has been extensively reviewed by Graphisoft for AC_6.5, and provides greater opportunities for Properties scripting, but also greater complexity. AC 6.5 carries a new manual on the subject.

Planar 3D Elements

Theory

PLANAR 3D elements are very useful because they only generate one single polygon; when it comes to rendering speed, the 'polygon count' of a model is all important (because AC has to calculate the line outlines and the shading values for each polygon.) CIRCLE, POLY, PLANE and RECT all appear in renderings – but LIN_ disappears. Whenever you would normally use a PRISM or a CYLIND, stop to think whether the same job can be done with a PLANE or a POLY or a CIRCLE.

CIRCLE is simply defined by its radius. Use it instead of thin cylinders.

LIN_ draws a straight line in 3D from one XYZ location to another; but only shows up in 3D views with Best contours.

ARC draws a curved line sector shape. The rotation angle goes in an anti clockwise direction starting from horizontal. Here, the start angle is 45degrees, and it finishes with 100degrees – anti clockwise.

POLY the syntax is identical to that of PRISM, without a thickness. (No holes or curved edges or masking codes permitted.) POLY must always be laid on the X-Y plane, so if you want a poly in an odd place and angle, you have to move the cursor there first.

POLY_ (Poly underscore) is similar to Prism underscore – it supports holes and curved edges. With prisms, masks go from 0 to 15, but with POLY_ you only need to know if the line is to be drawn or omitted – so one or zero is enough. In addition, by adding 1000, you get curved lines. As a bit of adventure, I have shown you an example of a hole drilled in the Poly – this is explained in later pages of the cookbook.

PLANE is most useful, as you can specify XYZ locations of any points and GDL will endeavour to join them up with a surface. With three points, you can do anything. With more than 3, you must ensure that the surface will be planar. If they are not planar, the whole surface may appear as empty.

PLANE_ (Plane underscore) allows you to decide if edge lines are to be drawn or not.

Planar Elements

Planar elements

CIRCLE r {a circle in the x-y plane with its center at the origin and a radius of r}

ARC r, alpha, beta {an arc in the x-y plane with its center at the origin from angle alpha to beta with a radius of r}

LIN_ x1, y1, z1, x2, y2, z2 {a line segment between two points}

RECT a, b {a rectangle in the x-y plane whose sides are a and b}

POLY n, x1, y1, ... xn, yn
POLY_ n, x1, y1, mask1, ... xn, yn, maskn
a polygon with n edges in the x-y plane; with **POLY_**, any edge can be omitted; if mask is 1, edge is shown, if it is 0, edge is omitted, if it is -1, a hole is created inside the polygon

PLANE n, x1, y1, z1, ... xn, yn, zn a polygon with n edges on an arbitrary plane
PLANE_ n, x1, y1, z1, mask1, ... xn, yn, zn, maskn
with **PLANE_**, any edge can be omitted as in **POLY_**

```
!Two-D elements
!Syntax:- CIRCLE radius
!ARC radius, startangl,endangl
!LIN_ x1,y1,z1,  x2,y2,z2
!RECT x,y

CIRCLE 0.2
ARC 0.3,45,100
LIN_ 0.00,0.00,0.00,
  -0.15,-0.15,0.15
  ADDz -0.2
RECT 0.3,0.3
```

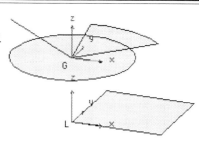

```
!POLY Demo
!Syntax:- POLY number,
!          x1,y1, x2,y2, etc
POLY 9,
  0.00,0.00,
  -0.10,0.30,
  0.10,0.30,
  0.10,0.40,
  0.20,0.40,
  0.20,0.10,
  0.15,0.10,
  0.15,0.00,
  0.00,0.00
```

Example of POLY – a simple outline with straight edges.

Example of POLY_ – an outline with the opportunity for curved & straight edges and drilled holes (round or polygonal).

```
!POLY_ Demo w' hole
!Syntax:- POLY_ number,
!          x1,y1,mask,
!          x2,y2,mask, etc
POLY_ 9+2,
  0.00,0.00,1,
  -0.10,0.30,1,
  0.10,0.30,0,
  0.10,0.40,1,
  0.20,0.40,1,
  0.20,0.10,1001,
  0.15,0.10,0,
  0.15,0.00,1,
  0.00,0.00,-1,
0.05,0.1,900,  !Hole centre
0.05,360,4000  !Hole drawn
```

```
!PLANE Demonstration
!Syntax:- PLANE number,
!          x1,y1,z1,
!          x2,y2,z2,
!          x3,y3,z3, etc..
PLANE 3,
  0.20,-0.4,-0.2,
  -0.20, 0.3, 0.1,
  0.25, 0.4, 0.1

PLANE_ 4,
  -0.3,0.0,-0.20,0,
  0.3,0.0,-0.20,1,
  0.3,0.2,-0.05,1,
  -0.3,0.2,-0.05,1
```

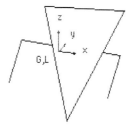

Imported 3D DXF files often get converted to a large number of PLANEs when read in by GDL.

1.52

More 3D Elements

SLAB

SLAB is very similar to PRISM, but far more flexible. You only need to define the XYZ points of the nodes – like PLANE. As with Prism, you define a thickness, but depending on the pitch, this is really a 'height' quantity.

Plain SLAB and SLAB_ are all one colour. The XYZ points are actually the points on the lower surface unless you specify a Negative Height.

One problem with SLAB is that you need to be sure that the surface will be planar – or it may not render properly. It does not check for you. Also, if the pitch gets too steep, the ridge and eaves detail get very distorted.

SLAB retains its sides perpendicular to the ground, or to the current XY plane – making it ideal for ramps, roof slabs etc. It is good because you do not have to move the cursor to its location, or Rotate the XY plane, as you do with a Prism.

SLAB_

SLAB_ is similar, but you can control the edges in 3D drawings. (However, all the edges in the illustration here still get shown in photo render.)

SLAB_ does not appear to support windows – you have to use CROOF, or PRISM_. SLABs do not support PolyLines.

CSLAB_

CSLAB_ is SLAB_ with the ability to set different materials for top, bottom and edge surfaces. CSLABs are what you get when you make an autoscripted Library object using hipped roofs.

CSLAB_ allows you to control the upper, lower and side surface material definitions. The Materials can be defined by name, or by index number, or with variables.

This is analogous to cPRISM. Because of the way it handles the edges, and because you do not have to lift or rotate the cursor into position, the SLAB family can be more useful than Prism.

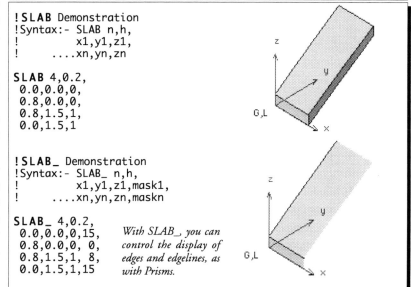

```
3D GDL Shapes
Other 3D elements
SLAB n, h, x1, y1, z1, ... xn, yn, zn
SLAB_ n, h, x1, y1, z1, mask1, ... xn, yn, zn, maskn
CSLAB_ topmat, botmat, sidemat, n, h, x1, y1, z1, mask1, ... xn, yn, zn, maskn
(an oblique prism whose lateral faces are always perpendicular to the x-y plane, its base is a flat
polygon; with SLAB_, any of the horizontal edges and surfaces can be omitted, as in PRISM_; with
CSLAB_, you can add material definitions for the top, bottom and side surfaces.
```

```
!SLAB Demonstration
!Syntax:- SLAB n,h,
!         x1,y1,z1,
!         ....xn,yn,zn

SLAB 4,0.2,
 0.0,0.0,0,
 0.8,0.0,0,
 0.8,1.5,1,
 0.0,1.5,1
```

```
!SLAB_ Demonstration
!Syntax:- SLAB_ n,h,
!         x1,y1,z1,mask1,
!         ....xn,yn,zn,maskn

SLAB_ 4,0.2,
 0.0,0.0,0,15,
 0.8,0.0,0, 0,
 0.8,1.5,1, 8,
 0.0,1.5,1,15
```
With SLAB_, you can control the display of edges and edgelines, as with Prisms.

```
!SLAB_ Demonstration
!Syntax:- CSLAB_ topm,botm,sidm,
!         n, h,
!         x1,y1,z1,mask1,
!         ....xn,yn,zn,maskn

CSLAB_ "Gold","Zinc","Ice",
   4, 0.2,
 0.0,0.0,0,15,
 0.8,0.0,0,15,
 0.8,1.5,1,15,
 0.0,1.5,1,15
```

What is zzyzx?

'zzyzx' is a 'dynamic parameter' denoting HEIGHT.

We are already used to the idea that **A** and **B** are dynamic parameters, i.e. that ArchiCAD recognises them as special parameters that can make objects stretchy. 'zzyzx' (named after a small town in the Mojave desert in Nevada) can be used for height, and the height will then be displayed in the Info Box Pallette. Objects with **zzyzx** can be stretchy in the 3D view.

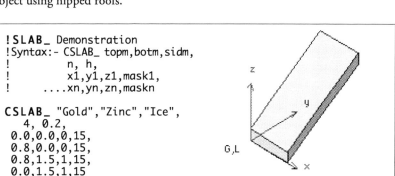

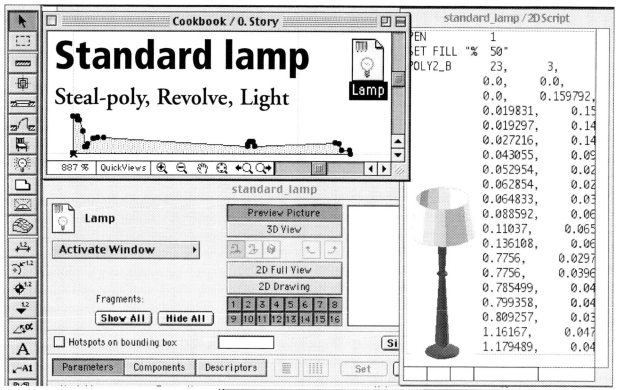

Standard lamp
Steal-poly, Revolve, Light

```
PEN        1
SET FILL "% 50"
POLY2_B      23,       3,
              0.0,       0.0,
              0.0,      0.159792,
              0.019831,      0.15
              0.019297,      0.14
              0.027216,      0.14
              0.043055,      0.09
              0.052954,      0.02
              0.062854,      0.02
              0.064833,      0.03
              0.088592,      0.06
              0.11037,      0.065
              0.136108,     0.06
              0.7756,       0.0297
              0.7756,       0.0396
              0.785499,     0.04
              0.799358,     0.04
              0.809257,     0.03
              1.16167,      0.047
              1.179489,     0.04
```

THIS teaches 4 ideas, the steal ing of a Poly from ArchiCAD, making it into a Revolve, making a Lamp, and using a flag.

Variable	Type	Name	Value
A		X Dimension	1000
B		Y Dimension	1000
C		Lamp is: On=1 Off=0	1
D		Red	1.000
E		Green	1.000
F		Blue	1.000
G		Intensity	100
stmatl		Material of Standard	16
zzyzx		Height	1550
dist		Distance for Light	3000

Procedure: First, find the origin of the Project Plan window, draw a FILL object to trace the outline of the lathing pattern for the standard lamp. make sure it is on or ABOVE the origin. Start from the centre of the base of the lamp. Now open a New Library Object – a 'Lamp', and open the 2D Script window, position it next to the Project Plan window.

Now simply D-r-a-g the Fill from the Project plan to the 2D Script window – Hey presto! Instant GDL!

3D Script: Now cut the text of the POLY2B that results, and paste it into the 3D window. Convert it into a REVOLVE, removing the first and last X-Y point and reducing the number of points in the REVOLVE by 2. Notice, the syntax for Poly2B and Revolve are almost the same! The main mask is 63, as usual for solids. Now you have got the standard pole, it's relatively easy to make the shade - but here the main mask for the object will be zero, and you have a small IF state-ment to change the material if the light is OFF or ON.

The Light: This starts with the Red/Green/Blue components, each of which is affected by the 'intensity' (G). For a general light source, shadow, radius and the three angles are zero. The distances are defined, and the brightness (intensity) governs the long distances and the fall off characteristic of the light. Place the lamp on a surface, and experiment with Photorendering to see how it performs.

2D Script: This is a series of Circles, but to indi-cate that the Lamp is on or off, you can have a loop to draw radiating lines. To save writing 2 loops, I have used C as a flag to decide whether to draw 2 or 6 lines, and the flag also calculates the angles between the lines.

```
!Standard Lamp
!2D Script
HOTSPOT2 0,0
!PROJECT2 3,270,2
CIRCLE2 0,0,0.03
CIRCLE2 0,0,0.15
CIRCLE2 0,0,0.25
CIRCLE2 0,0,0.30
 FOR k=1 TO 2+C*4
 ROT2 (360/(2+C*4))*k
 LINE2 0.03,0,0.3,0
 HOTSPOT2 0.3,0
 DEL 1
 NEXT k
```

```
!Standard Lamp 3D Script
MULz zzyzx/1.55
ROTy -90                      vertical
MATERIAL stmatl               post
RESOL 16                      routine
REVOLVE  21,360,  63,
  0.0, 0.159792,  1,
  0.019831, 0.159792,  1,
  0.019297, 0.144624,  1,
  0.027216, 0.142644,  1,
  0.043055, 0.093148,  1,
  0.052954, 0.027813,  1,
  0.062854, 0.027813,  1,
  0.064833, 0.037712,  1,
  0.088592, 0.06147,  1,
  0.11037, 0.06543,  1,
  0.136108, 0.06543,  1,
  0.7756, 0.029793,  1,
  0.7756, 0.039692,  1,
  0.785499, 0.049591,  1,
  0.799358, 0.049591,  1,
  0.809257, 0.031773,  1,
  1.16167, 0.047612,  1,
  1.179489, 0.041672,  1,
  1.189388, 0.015934,  1,
  1.227005, 0.015934,  1,
  1.228985, 0.000095,  1
IF C THEN
  MATERIAL 'Lamp'
  ELSE
  MATERIAL 'Whitewash'
  ENDIF
REVOLVE 2,360,0,
  1.20,0.3,1,             Shade
  1.55,0.25,1            routine
DEL 1

IF C THEN              Lamp making
  ADDz 1.3                routine
  RESOL 6
  SPHERE 0.03
  gb=G/100  !brightness index
  LIGHT gb*D,gb*E,gb*F,!R,G,B
  0,0,  !shad,rad
  0,0,0,!alp,bet,angfall
  0,gb*dist,(gb-1)^2!falloff
  DEL 1
  ENDIF
```

Picture Objects - Alpha channels

This model is a very important exercise in:
- Using Photoshop to make the alpha channel
- Creating the basic library object that can use any 32bit PICT or TIF file
- Rotating the object to face the camera
- Using Photorendering for the finish

The example used here is a bit of fun, and I assure you that there is no montaging done – it is rendered in ArchiCAD.

Batman visited Thailand entirely free of 3D geometrical entities!

The serious uses are as follows:

- People in buildings – populate models with photorealistic figures.
- Putting pictures of trees onto flat planes, instead of modelling them in 3D.
- Pictures and decoration on walls to gives interiors more realism.
- Attaching facades of buildings in urban models to avoid having to model them geometrically – rapidly create urban surroundings for your building.

Procedure

First catch your lion – or person, or plant, or building facade – using a digital camera or scanner.

Cutaway the background using the magic wand and eraser. It must become totally white. Use the 'Channels Pallete' to create a new channel, which you can call the Alpha Channel. You must operate in 32bit RGB colour (even if your screen only supports 16 or 8bit colour). The Red, Green and Blue channels each require 8bits (hence 24 bits for 16.7 million colours). The 8bits between 24 and 32 hold the Alpha channel, which you have created. Select and 'Cut' the WHITE area in the RGB channel (using the magic wand). Click on the alpha channel (cmd-4) and 'Paste' the same area into the Alpha channel. With the White Area still selected, fill the selected area with BLACK paint using the bucket tool.

Flatten any Layers, then Save the file as a PICT or TIFF with 32 bit colour, and avoid any form of compression, or you will lose the Alpha channel. For most Picture objects, 72 or 100dpi is enough, avoid high resolution scans. **Important:** Save it into your current Library, and Reload Libraries.

If you are intending to do this with building elevations, a picture dpi of 60 dots/m works well.

For this, you need Photoshop 2.5 or later, or any art software that can handle Alpha channels – which caxn be used by CAD software for special functions like transparency or bump-mapping.

A		X Dimension	0.700
B		Y Dimension	1.000
pictmap	Abc	name of file to map	lioness32.tif
mask	⊠	mask on=1 or off=0	On
facecam	⊠	Face Camera ON/OFF	Off
backmat		Background Material	18
helpful	⊠	Helpful ON or OFF	On

Parameters: The parameter box needs to know the name of the Pictmap that will form a picture – and it is merciless – no popup menu helps you; you just have to know the name. If the picture file is not in the library, you get very irritating error messages. Width (A) and Height (B) will stretch the pictmap to fit. In the parameter box on PCs, you <u>must</u> leave out the 3-letter suffix in the parameter box. i.e. *fat_man.tif* must be entered as *fat_man*. On Macs, you must put the suffix in!

3D Script commentary

Masking: If the photo is a building facade, you may not want the alpha channel to be made invisible, so the 'mask' has to be a choice. The Mask modifier lets the user decide if the image is 'see-through' or solid.

Size: There needs to be a rectangular frame and the photoshop image will adapt to fit the size. The frame must be the same proportions or it will look distorted. A and B make the object stretchy.

Face Camera: Many 2-D Objects such as people or trees look totally wrong if they don't face the camera. It is vital to know how to turn the object round so it looks solid. You may not want this to happen always – eg if it's a picture on the wall, or a building facade; therefore the user has to have a choice in the matter. If the object has a rotation angle in the dialog box, it will never face the camera properly; so one workaround is to use **90+dazi-W~** (W~ is the global for object's rotation angle.) If you have a rotated grid (in AC6) then this will <u>not</u> work correctly.

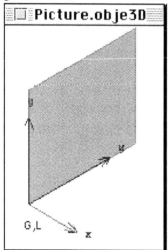

The Picture Object looks like this in 3D views. You should assign a Material like 'Whitewash' or 'Glass' to make it less obtrusive in 3D views.

The same 3D view looks like this when rendered. As the image could look distorted, you should offer a choice to 'Face the Camera'.

Rendering

The rendered object is light sensitive, so check your sun angle relative to the camera position (or you can create misleading shading on the picture.)

If the image is not to be silhouetted or transparent, you do not need to worry about alpha channels, nor about 32bit colour – for example building facades or pictures on walls. You can save files as PICT or TIFF in 8 or 12 bit colour, you can even use a modest level of compression. Make sure you reload Libraries after you save the Photoshop file into a library. By the way, if you didn't 'Flatten the Layers' in Photoshop, it may not render.

Once you get the hang of this, you can build entire models out of just the picture object! I have built whole streetscapes from this.

One problem is that you will have difficulty copying these items across to Artlantis Render – they may finish up looking like flat boards. But then there are ways of bringing in Alpha channelled images into Artlantis.

Another problem is that Alpha channelled silhouetted objects do not cast correct shadows. If SHADOW is on, you get just a rectangle(:-(so you might put a SHADOW OFF command into the script. For Graphisoft to write a Shadow algorithm that looked at the image would be difficult. But then if the Alpha channel is designated 'transparent' it should be made to work if the renderer can already use the alpha channel for other functions, such as bump-mapping.

```
!Master Script
!Location Awareness Check

dkx=K~-X~:IF dkx=0 THEN dkx=1
dly=L~-Y~
dmz=M~-Z~

dd=SQR(dkx^2+dly^2+dmz^2)!Distance
dazi=ATN(dly/dkx)      !Azimuth
```

```
!Three-D Script

 width=A: height=B
IF facecam THEN ROTz (90+dazi-W~)
  ROTx 90
  ADDx -width/2
MATERIAL backmat
SHADOW OFF
PICTURE pictmap,width,height,mask
  DEL TOP
```

A bit of trial and error was required to get the rotation angle working perfectly.

2D Script: You can simply use PROJECT2, or you could use a LINE2 or RECT2 command. You should add Hotspots if the Picture object is easy to pick and stretchy. (If you make it stretchy, you could accidentally alter the rectangular proportions, and distort the image.)

I have introduced the idea of 'Helpfulness" whereby you can project the object onto the floor for the user to stretch, using 'B'. It also names the file. To use TEXT, you should always define the text style. The idea of 'px' (an object pixel) is that it will work for very small or very large objects.

```
!ROTATING PICTURE MAP
!2DScript

!PROJECT2 3,270,1
  px=MIN(0.01,A/100)
IF facecam THEN ROT2 (90+dazi-W~)+180
  HOTSPOT2  A/2,0
  HOTSPOT2 -A/2,0

  HOTSPOT2  0,px
  CIRCLE2 0,0,px
  RECT2 -A/2,-px,
        A/2,px

  IF helpful THEN
    RECT2 -A/2,0,A/2,B
    HOTSPOT2  A/2,B
    HOTSPOT2 -A/2,B

    DEFINE STYLE "pictext" Arial,1,7,0
    STYLE "pictext"
    TEXT2 -A/2,0,pictmap
  ENDIF
DEL TOP
```

In Helpful mode, the Picture object appears to be laid flat on the ground for easy re-sizing, and its name is displayed – even though it is still standing upright.

lioness32.tif

Cutplane/Cutend

CUTPLANE is one of my favourite commands. It is much easier to make something larger than it needs to be and cut it to size, than to build it up in a positive method. The more complicated the object, the more useful CUTPLANE becomes.

The AC6 manual explains CUTPLANE much better than in AC5, and I only use and only teach one method, the Angle method.

CUTPLANE can be likened to a large spinning bacon slicer. You move the slicer into position, rotate the blade to the right angle, issue the CUTPLANE command; now you must DEL back to the origin to

```
!CUTPLANE Demonstrat'n
!Syntax: - CUTPLANE angle
!After you've made the object
!to be cut you issue a CUTEND
!
  ADDz 0.5
CUTPLANE
  DEL 1
SPHERE 1
CUTEND
```

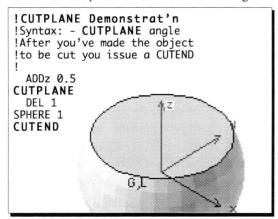

build the model that needs cutting. If your model disappears, you may have forgotten to DEL correctly.

At the end of the process, the **CUTEND** command is required to stop the blade spinning.

CUTPLANE always cuts away what is above it, and leaves behind what is below. Sometimes, you wish to do the opposite, and cut away everything below the ground plane. For this, it is handy to spin the blade through 180 degrees with a 'CUTPLANE 180' command to leave behind everything above the plane.

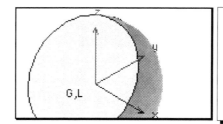

```
ADDz 0.5
CUTPLANE 45
DEL 1
SPHERE 1
CUTEND
```

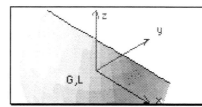

```
ADDz 0.5
CUTPLANE -45
DEL 1
SPHERE 1
CUTEND
```

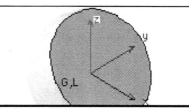

For other angles (i.e. not around X axis), you do the swivelling yourself with ROT commands and issue a CUTPLANE.

```
ADDz 0.5
ROTy 45
CUTPLANE
DEL 2
SPHERE 1
CUTEND
```

Remember to do the correct number of DELs before building the object that is to be cut.

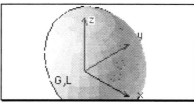

```
ADDz 0.5
ROTy 45
CUTPLANE 180
DEL 2
SPHERE 1
CUTEND
```

CUTEND is vital – otherwise the Cutting command will continue till the end of the object.

You will get a syntax error if you do not issue a CUTEND. Some models use many Cuts, and for EVERY Cutplane, you must have the right number of CUTENDs.

CUTPLANE needs to know the Material that you are using. If you do not issue a Material command before Cutplane, it will leave the cut face to the current PEN colour.

This multi-coloured model of the world can only be made by CUTPLANE, but there are so many Cuts that if you do the whole world in one go, you could need over 100megs of RAM allocated to ArchiCAD.

Multi coloured models: You could issue a Material command, issue a Cutplane, then issue another Material command, issue another Cutplane... and so on. Then build the object to be cut. In this way, you can get multi coloured models.

CUTPLANE uses a lot of memory, and if you issue a large number of them, the model rendering will slow down, or you may even be told that ArchiCAD is out of memory.

CUTPOLY and CUTSHAPE

AC 5.1 and AC 6.x bring in new Cutting commands which enhance the opportunities in 3D.

With **CUTPOLY**, you can define a convex polygonal hole shape using a syntax similar to PRISM, and then drive it through the whole model!! **CUTPOLYA** and **WALLHOLE** are variations that allows Polylines.

These appear in exercises in the **Discovery** and **Voyager** sections.

Tapering tube – with cutplane

THIS MODEL is a component in larger steel structures. It is here because it is another example of :
- The CUTPLANE command, used at angles
- POLYLINES in a PRISM

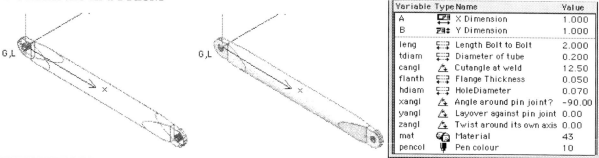

Variable	Type	Name	Value
A		X Dimension	1.000
B		Y Dimension	1.000
leng		Length Bolt to Bolt	2.000
tdiam		Diameter of tube	0.200
cangl		Cutangle at weld	12.50
flanth		Flange Thickness	0.050
hdiam		HoleDiameter	0.070
xangl		Angle around pin joint?	-90.00
yangl		Layover against pin joint	0.00
zangl		Twist around its own axis	0.00
mat		Material	43
pencol		Pen colour	10

```
!Tapered Cylindrical spar - 3D Script
PEN pencol
MATERIAL mat
 trad=tdiam/2   !tube radius
 traf=trad*0.95 !flange width slightly smaller
 clen=leng-tdiam!length of cylinder section
IF cangl<0 OR cangl>90 THEN cangl=12.5
RESOL 12

!_____ THE PROGRAM _____
ROTy yangl   !global command
ROTx xangl   !to position
ROTz zangl   !rod

GOSUB 100    !Main tube
GOSUB 200    !Bottom flange
  ADDz clen+tdiam
  MULz -1
GOSUB 200    !Top flange
  DEL 3+2    !return to origin
END:!----------------------------
```

The best way to use CUTPLANE is to move the cutting plane to a location, angle it correctly, issue the command to Cut, and then DEL back to the origin. This must be done before you make the 3D entity.

3D Script: You must issue a Material definition BEFORE issuing Cutplane, otherwise the cut face adopts the colour of the current PEN.

When you have done cutting, issue the CUTEND command, or the rest of the Library object will also be cut. You can either write simply, CUTEND:CUTEND:CUTEND:CUTEND, or you can do a short loop, FOR k=1 TO 4.

CUTPLANE is often the only way to make a geometrically complex object – where you cannot model it 'positively', it may be easier to model it by making something larger, and then carving it by subtraction (or 'negatively') to form the final object.

```
100: !main tube with cuts   200: !End Flange
 ADDz trad                    ROTz 90
GOSUB 110                     ROTx -90
 MULx -1                      ADDz -flanth/2
GOSUB 110                    PRISM_ 7,flanth,
 DEL 1 !cut bottom            -traf,-trad, 15,
                              -traf,  0, 15,
 ADDz clen                     traf,  0,1000+15,
 MULz -1                       traf,-trad, 15,
GOSUB 110                     -traf,-trad, -1,
 MULx -1
GOSUB 110                      0,0,915,
 DEL 3        !cut top         hdiam/2,360,4015
CYLIND clen,trad !draw tube      DEL 3
!cancel cuts                 RETURN
CUTEND:CUTEND:CUTEND:CUTEND
 DEL 1
RETURN
110: !Make the cut
 ADDx flanth/2
 ROTy -(90-cangl)
CUTPLANE 180
 DEL 2
RETURN
```

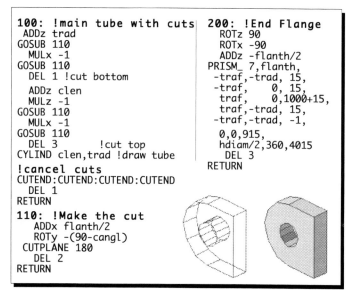

To economize on code here, the CUTPLANE is one single routine, and the script uses ADD, ROT and MULs to move the routine from place to place.

The Polyline in the flange is 1000, a tangential curve – the easiest one to use.

```
!Tapering tube 2D Script

HOTSPOT2 0,0  !Hinging point
PROJECT2 3,270,2
```

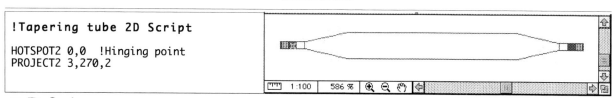

2D Script: This is a hinging component of a larger steel structure and could be any-which-way up, so you have to script it in 2D as a Project2 command. If you were building a large structure with these, you could 'encapsulate' them once they were assembled. The Hotspot is important so that it can be accurately located to the hinging point on the post.

Swivel Chair

Note: If you are doing this on a Lift Off course, you have a tutor available to help. Parts of this exercise march boldly into Voyager territory, so if you are teaching yourself, do not try it until you have tried easier tasks first!

THIS CHAIR is the ultimate 3D object of the Discovery Course. It is a very important exercise in:

- Some of the more easy and useful GDL commands – CONE, PRISM_, CYLIND
- Some of the more difficult but useful GDL commands – bPRISM, TUBE, CUTPLANE, Polylines
- Making the subroutines modular and using DEL rigorously

Parameters: In this Exercise, the seat and back are fixed sizes, and parameters A and B are ignored. You can swivel the chair in the project plan window, so it is not worth making the chair swivelable by the user. Note that this parameter box is set out in Millimetres. If you are in the USA, you might have to set it in feet and inches!!

3 D Script: This is a highly modular, structured program, in which the entire chair is analysed into essential elements – and each element is solved in an independent subroutine. **No matter how humble your object, try to apply this structured approach.**

The subroutines called in the executive script build up the chair methodically, physical element by physical element. However, if you try to run this script before the subroutines have been written, you will get a 'Subroutine not found' error. So you could write in some dummy routines, just to avoid an error. Then gradually, you fill in the details.

300: To make the foot, you need to make one toe, and repeat it around the centre. Because there are 5 toes, you rotate them by 72 degs each. Each toe is complicated because each one has its own set of Cutplane commands, so make it a subroutine 350.

350: Each toe is to be cut 3 times, once for the top surface, and two mitring cuts where the toes meet. Declare the Material before the Cuts.

With PRISM_ (underscore) you can form a curved end to the toe. First make the PRISM_ as a square ended object, ready to mitre. Then change the end to a curve by changing 13 to 1013. Now go back and insert the Cuts.

```
!Swivel Chair - 3D script

SHADOW ON
PEN 1
RESOL 12

GOSUB 300::!Foot of chair
GOSUB 400::!Vertical shaft
GOSUB 500::!Seat
GOSUB 600::!Back
END:!------------------

300:!Foot of chair
RETURN
400:!Vertical shaft
RETURN
500:!Seat                Create the Dummy
RETURN                   subroutines to avoid
600:!Back                an error – you can fill
RETURN                   them in later...
```

Variable	Type	Name	Value
sht	📏	Seat height	0.450
sth	📏	Seat thickness	0.050
smat	🎨	Seat Upholstery Material	44
mmat	🎨	Bright Metallic material	47
dmat	🎨	Dark metallic material	40

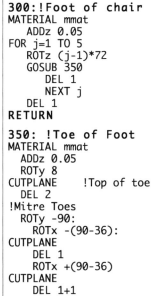

```
300:!Foot of chair
MATERIAL mmat
   ADDz 0.05
FOR j=1 TO 5
   ROTz (j-1)*72
   GOSUB 350
      DEL 1
   NEXT j
   DEL 1
RETURN

350: !Toe of Foot
MATERIAL mmat
   ADDz 0.05
   ROTy 8
CUTPLANE      !Top of toe
   DEL 2
!Mitre Toes
   ROTy -90:
      ROTx -(90-36):
CUTPLANE
   DEL 1
   ROTx +(90-36)
CUTPLANE
   DEL 1+1
```

```
!still part of 350
!Toe shape
PRISM_ 5, 0.05,
   0  , 0.04,13,
   0.2, 0.02,13,
   0.2,-0.02,1013,
   0  ,-0.04,13,
   0  , 0.04,-1

CUTEND:CUTEND:CUTEND

   ADD 0.2,0,-0.05
   !'Toenail'
   MATERIAL dmat
   CONE 0.05,0.03,0.01,
        90,90
      DEL 1
RETURN
```

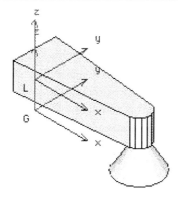

Here is the basic toe element before cutting

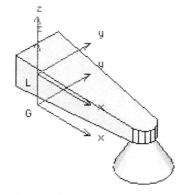

Here the top surface has been trimmed down

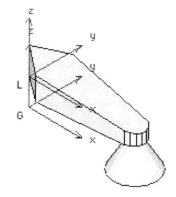

Here, the centre point has been mitred

350 continued: To give the toe more realism, the end is curved – using the 1000 polyline definition.

Hot Tip for Polylines: The 1000 must come at the node **after** the surface which you wish to have curved, but the change of 15 to 13 must come at the node **before** you wish to have a smooth curve.

Next, insert the CUTPLANE routine above the Prism forming the toe. You should attempt the routine 350 which mitres the toe correctly. You need 3 cuts altogether to make the toe into the correct shape. The mitring angle to achieve a spacing of 72° is 36° (half of 72°). Just as in picture framing, you cut wood to a mitre of 45° to achieve a joint of 90°. Every CUTPLANE has to be followed by a CUTEND.

Finally, The conical 'toenail' is added as part of each foot.

Back to 300: Finally (if you haven't already done this) having got 350 working, you return to subroutine 300: and spin the feet to produce five, using a FOR... NEXT Loop.

LEVELS of Detail: You and only you can decide what level of detail and quality to display in your models. If you did not bother to mitre the toes, it would not be noticed, and it is done here only to teach you the use of CUTPLANE. The next section, the vertical shaft, would entirely hide the centre junction.

400: When the foot is perfect, block out the foot subroutine with a ! sign, and work on the shaft.

The shaft can be done with a couple of CYLIND commands. Then manoevre the cursor to produce the adjusting knob. The heights of each part are calculated by working back from the seat heights and thickness.

500: The Seat uses the **BPRISM_** command – but to make things more interesting, it also uses **Polylines** in the definitions. Enter the seat at first as an octagonal shape so that everything ends in 15, then experiment with the 1015 definition until you get it right. The 1015 should come AFTER the line which you wish to be curved. Change the 15's to 13, and the vertical lines will be concealed. This speeds up drawing in 3D.

When you first make the BPRISM_, it comes out upside down, but the MULz -1 reverses it vertically, so it finishes up the correct way up. By the way, you can enter a minus figure as the depth of the BPRISM. This is to get tighter radii of curvature.

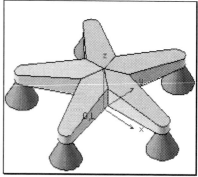

The five toes combined into a foot

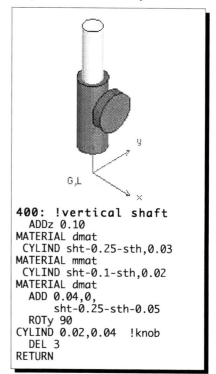

```
400: !vertical shaft
  ADDz 0.10
  MATERIAL dmat
  CYLIND sht-0.25-sth,0.03
  MATERIAL mmat
  CYLIND sht-0.1-sth,0.02
  MATERIAL dmat
  ADD 0.04,0,
       sht-0.25-sth-0.05
  ROTy 90
CYLIND 0.02,0.04  !knob
  DEL 3
RETURN
```

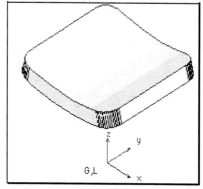

```
500: !Seat
  ADDz sht
  MULz -1
GOSUB 550 !get the seat
  DEL 2
RETURN

550: !Seat or Back
RESOL 60
BPRISM_ smat,dmat,smat,
  5+4, sth, 0.8,
  -0.15,-0.20,  13,
   0.15,-0.20,  13,
   0.20,-0.15,1013,
   0.20, 0.15,  13,
   0.15, 0.20,1013,
  -0.15, 0.20,  13,
  -0.20, 0.15,1013,
  -0.20,-0.15,  13,
  -0.15,-0.20,1013
RESOL 12
RETURN
```

The seat shape is contained in subroutine **550** because it gets called again later to do service as the back. To get the BPRISM to be curvy, you need an extremely high RESOL number like 60. Remember to change RESOL back to a safe number afterwards!

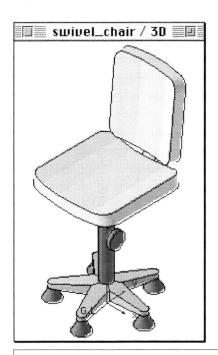

swivel_chair / 3D

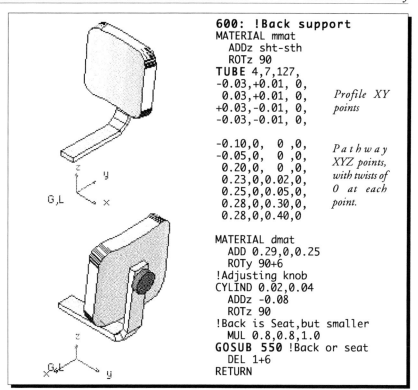

```
600: !Back support
MATERIAL mmat
  ADDz sht-sth
  ROTz 90
TUBE 4,7,127,
  -0.03,+0.01, 0,
   0.03,+0.01, 0,        Profile XY
  +0.03,-0.01, 0,        points
  -0.03,-0.01, 0,

  -0.10,0,  0 ,0,        Pathway
  -0.05,0,  0 ,0,        XYZ points,
   0.20,0,  0 ,0,        with twists of
   0.23,0,0.02,0,        0  at each
   0.25,0,0.05,0,        point.
   0.28,0,0.30,0,
   0.28,0,0.40,0

MATERIAL dmat
  ADD 0.29,0,0.25
  ROTy 90+6
!Adjusting knob
CYLIND 0.02,0.04
  ADDz -0.08
  ROTz 90
!Back is Seat,but smaller
  MUL 0.8,0.8,1.0
GOSUB 550 !Back or seat
  DEL 1+6
RETURN
```

600: The Seat back support is using the very difficult **TUBE** command. Type it in and then try changing the locations to see how it responds. Look it up in **Voyager**.

The Back Panel: The Back is the same **bPRISM** as the seat, but reduced in dimension a bit each way, using the MUL command. You can MULx, MULy or MULz, but if you just MUL, you can do all three directions in a single command.

TUBE: is a good way to get a continuous section moving through 3-D space. Once TUBE is mastered it is one of the most useful commands – and a lot easier to use.

With TUBE, you first define the cross sectional POLY shape that will travel through 3D space. You draw it on the X-Y plane, as if you were defining the outlines for a POLY2 command. Use a 'masking value' of zero for each point.

Next, you define the path that it must follow – the XYZ points along its trajectory. The trick with TUBE is that the FIRST and the LAST location points along the tube are phantom points, there to tell GDL what angle to start mitring the first and last faces on the tube. You must remember to put a zero at the end of each path X-Y-Z location to tell it you want clean junctions – it is possible to twist the section and distort the mitre by putting angle values in there.

If TUBE baffles you now, just type it in for now and enjoy looking at it. For later reference you will find more explanation and examples in the Voyager course.

2D Script: Finally, you need a 2D view. Because the chair is quite complicated, a 2D script would make it display too slowly on the Project Plan. As the chair does not change in width or depth, and as it does not swivel, there is no need for a PROJECT2 command.

Give it a PROJECT2 command temporarily, look at the 2D Full View, Select All and Copy. Open the 2D Symbol Window, and Paste to Original Location. Now you either delete the whole 2D script and the 2D symbol will take over; or you can replace the Project2 command with: **FRAGMENT2 ALL,0.** You will get bounding box Hotspots.

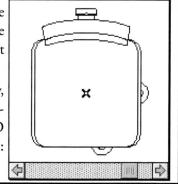

The Magic of ROTx

THIS EXERCISE is an example of 'tinkering' with existing Library Objects.

One of the slickest things you can do is to put a ROTx in front of an object and make it stand upright, or fit to a sloping site or floor.

There are many objects in the existing libraries that are not usable on sloping sites, or in unusual uses. For example the ArchiCAD and the *People and More* cars all stand horizontally, and look quite silly on a sloping carpark or driveway. A simple ROTx or ROTy can make all the difference, even to Binary objects. For these, the command ROTx 90 or ROTx -90 or ROTx rotang at the start of the script can work wonders to an existing library object.

For example, you can convert existing Graphisoft Windows into Objects by standing them upright – or take an object and make it into a window or door.

You can make shapes in Plan such as laying out a truss using the slab tool, save them as Library objects, and then ROTx them to the angle you want – this is easier than setting up the views in elevation if the angle is anything other than 90. Use ROTy if you want to lean objects in the other direction.

The Mesh Tool will not allow you to make complex shapes with undercutting. However, if you prepare Meshtool surfaces on the level, put them into GDL (by dragging into a 3D script window) and then add some ROTx and ROTy commands, you can manouvre the surfaces to the right position, and join several together to make very complex objects. This is one of the techniques used in my Motorist Car object.

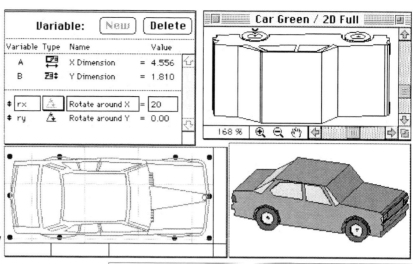

```
!3D Script            !2D Script
!ArchiCAD Car         !ArchiCAD Car
!Modified Script      !Alternative Script

ROTx rx               IF rx<>0 OR ry<>0 THEN
ROTy ry                  PROJECT2 3,270,2
                      ELSE
MULx A/4.538808          FRAGMENT2 ALL,1
MULy B/1.809472       ENDIF
Binary 1
```

2D Script: One important thing to note is that the 2D view of the object in the plan could be quite different as a result of your ROTx, so if you have made the angle a new parameter, use a script like the one above. If a rotation has been specified, then the script forces a Project2 command to take place. If not, then it will use the existing symbol – this can be invoked with the Fragment2 command, or you could use a conventionally scripted 2D symbol.

Are your HotSpots Stretchy & Squeezy?

IT has been said before, but let's repeat it! If you want objects to be Squeezy as well as Stretchy, you need to utter your HOTSPOT2 commands <BEFORE> the commands which actually draw the 2D objects. Otherwise, objects may stretch, but not reduce in size correctly.

Tips and Tricks
2D Crosshairs

IF stretchiness is a big feature of your object, the A.B points may not actually be within the object boundary. To make them visible to the user, plant a **2D crosshair** at the A,B points. e.g. for point A,0, write in the 2D script:
LINE2 A-0.02,0, A+0.02,0 : LINE2 0,A-0.02, 0,A+0.02

Don't forget that it is better to declare all your stretchy Hotspots before you issue the Project2 or the rest of the 2D script.

Tips and Tricks
General Advice and warnings

As annually issued to my First year module at the University of Nottingham School of Architecture.

Libraries

LIBRARY organisation is the biggest thing you must get right. Know where your library is, and what it is called, and how to load it. Discard libraries that are not relevant to your scheme. Use 'Load Libraries' to sort it all out.

• Avoid having duplicate libraries of the same name on the same disk, or even loaded in the project. You may have spent time improving a library object, only to see the old one come back next time, because you had the same object (the new and the old) in the same library, but in different folders.

• When you move to a different computer platform (Mac<->PC) you save as ARCHIVE (using the .PLA suffix) which will get and convert all your library objects.

• Archive does not copy across PICT and TIFF files (although it can copy textures), so these files may have to be manually copied over. If you move computer but stay on one platform, the best place for your library is a shared FileServer so it is available from every machine, and where you cannot create duplicate libraries.

Building the Model

AS you build the model, a very disciplined approach to using Layers, and storeys will save you much time and grief later. For example, you can hide the 'Roofs' layer, which will reveal the interior and let sunlight in. Or you can Hide the 'Window Tracery' or 'Trees' layer, which is slowing down your render. Or hide 'Lecture room chairs' while you render the exterior. Therefore, assign objects to layers as early as possible, as you work on the model.

• If, when starting a model, you find really wierd layer names, storey settings, dimensions, grid and materials (left there by the previous user), use the 'New and Reset' feature (by holding down 'Alt' key while you create a New file. This restores the usual default ArchiCAD settings.

• Some people try to build multi storey objects or buildings all on the one storey. ArchiCAD has the ability to work with several stories. Bet you didn't know that. (:-)

Rendering

WHILE developing the model, ALWAYS have your 3D settings as RASTER, not ANALYTIC. 3D windows also render quicker if they are smaller - there is no need for them to be 1000 pixels wide.

• Never select Vectorial Shadows or contours unless your machine is very fast.

• Frequently, Photorendering (with ambient light and no shadows) will be faster than Analytic 3D.

• To see what a camera is looking at, you must first click on the camera and then select 3D view. Dropping cameras into the plan is quicker than tweaking the perspective viewing tool in the 3D Projections window.

• Putting a 'Marquee' around the bit you are interested in will dramatically reduce rendering times, and has the effect of giving you instant sections and details. Using the 'thick' marquee will show all stories, the 'thin' one only shows the current storey.

• Don't use the 'Marquee' tool when selecting elements to make library objects because it fills the script with Cutplane commands. Select the objects using the pointer tool, then do a 3D view.

• You may spend too much time on coloured renderings, and forget that ArchiCAD produces very good scale line drawings, in 2D and 3D - and that these can be brought together in Plotmaker.

• Final colour renderings are perhaps best left to Artlantis - quicker and higher quality.

• If you feel confined by the limited set of materials offered by ArchiCAD, try making some new ones - there are oodles of spare texture images for wood, stone and brick in the ArchiCAD library that you can make into materials.

Making Library Objects

A little bit of GDL scripting - with Cones, Cylinders, Blocks etc, will produce more manageable library objects than similar objects built with curved Slabs.

• Converting groups of built elements to Library objects is a way of grouping them. (In 5.1 & 6.0, you have a group command, but making the group into a Library Object is more powerful and editable.)

• Ask for advice before embarking on complex objects, as they may already exist in the ArchiCAD or special objects library. For example, the Dome tool in ArchiCAD produces very clumsy, data heavy domes of many little roofs which fall apart if touched; whereas there is a nice little GDL Dome in the ArchiCAD Library that is more parametric and controllable.

• If you script an object from scratch, it will not have a 2D symbol unless you create a symbol. Use the PROJECT2 command to view the object in 2D. If you have the time, write a short parametric script with CIRCLE2 and RECT2 that imitates the Project 2 command; then delete the Project2 command. If the object is not intended to be parametric, use the button in the Library object window to copy a 3D view to Symbol - otherwise it will take too long to regen the Project Plan.

• Curved tracery etc, is best done with curved walls than with the slab tool. You can later control the curvature when it is saved as a Library object by inserting RESOL commands into the 3D script.

• When you make library objects, give them distinctive names, so that they are easily found with the 'Find and Select' command. If you call your object 'Column' or 'Cylinder', you will probably find that next time you open your file, you open someone else's library object which is different but has the same name. Use names like 'Column_ntc' which is unlikely to be confused with another.

CircleGrid – 2D

Object

G DL can be useful in creating 2D entities that help you to lay out models or drawings, but which do not have any 3D existence – I call them drafting aids – Dimensions, Grids and parametric furniture modules for example.

CircleGrid is a simple example. It also illustrates the usefulness of the FOR...NEXT Loop used with angles, instead of distance or number.

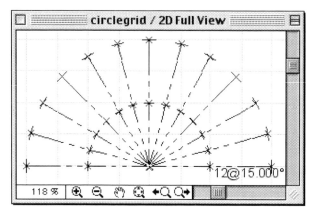

circlegrid / 2D Full View

12@15.000°

118%

Parameters: You define your own requirements. In this CircleGrid – that was written in earnest for a project and not just for the exercise, there was a main circle and a minor one. Hotspots at each point allow one to drop objects accurately into position. The grid does not trace a full circle, so a sweep angle is specified. The text block allows one to know how much rotation to give the objects, and the inner circle gives secondary hotspots which make it easier to rotate the objects to line up with the radiating lines. The object is not stretchy, so A and B are not used.

Variable	Type	Name	Value
numang	.▫▪	Number of Angles	12
fan	△	Sweep Angle of Grid 10-360	180.00
lrad	⟷	Radius of Circle (Linelength)	4.000
rhot	⟷	Main Radial Hotspot distance	4.000
rhotm	⟷	Minor Radial Hotspot distance	2.000
lindot	----	Line Type	8
shodat	⊠	Show Data=1 No=0	On
fontz	⤽	Font Size mm	3.00

If either shodat or Font height is zero then the text will not print. Text is a fixed size in mm.

```
!CircleGrid - 2D Script

IF fan<10  THEN fan=10
IF fan>360 THEN fan=360
 ang=fan/numang
HOTSPOT2 0,0
LINE_TYPE lindot

!Draw the actual grid
FOR k=0 TO fan+0.001 STEP ang
  ROT2 k
  LINE2 0,0,    lrad,0
  ARC2 0,0,rhotm,-4,4
  ARC2 0,0,rhot,-3,3
 HOTSPOT2 rhot,0
 HOTSPOT2 rhotm,0
  DEL 1
  NEXT k

!Show angular increment as Text
IF shodat AND fontz THEN
DEFINE STYLE 'angtext' 'Arial',fontz,1,0
SET STYLE 'angtext'
angstr=STR(numang,3,0)+'@'+STR('%6.3dd',ang)
TEXT2 rhotm,0,angstr
ENDIF
```

2 D Script: Firstly, title your script, even a 2D one. 'Ang' defines the angular separation of each line in the grid. Place a Hotspot at the Centre – so you can pick it up. Decide if you want it made of solid or dotted lines.

• A **FOR...NEXT loop** is used for the main routine. Rotating around the centre, each line consists of a LINE2 command, followed by ARC2 commands which place short lines to display the circle, and then Hotspots at the intersections. DEL the ROT2 command each time the loop is used. The deliberate error of 1/1000 degree is essential, or GDL makes tiny rounding down errors and miscounts the number of lines to draw.

• When you ROT2 in 2D the positive direction of rotation is anti clockwise.

• If Text quality is important, it's essential to DEFINE STYLE first. If the text element contains more than one part, you have to construct it first, using something like 'angstr' in which all parts are defined as strings joined by plus signs. In this, you can concatenate 'numang' (the number of angles) as an integer string, an @ symbol, and then, to print the degrees symbol, you can use a '%dd' method (see the manual to test this further). Try this and experiment with changing the number of digits to be displayed.

Vectorial Hatching – and Thanks

David Collins writes:

Thanks for jogging my memory about the 2d plan shadow transfer trick. Try turning on the "Special" menu (using "regedit" on PC or "resedit" on Mac, or the Control key at start up). There is a FANTAS-TIC option to turn vectorial hatching on in your sections/elevations thus eliminating the need to tediously hatch them up manually.

Lastly, just a note of appreciation for your cookbook exercises: I've been working my way through them recently, with a dawning sense of the potential of parametric GDL scripting... And I'm beginning to change sides on the great graphic vs scripted debate, having spent several unhappy weeks trying to see the point of Visual GDL.... *Many thanks*

Location-aware Capability

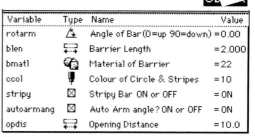

IT is possible to give a certain amount of decision making capacity to the object. Use the CAR PARK BARRIER. The barrier lifts and drops depending on the distance from the camera. Thus, if you fly or walk through the model, the barrier will appear to be active.

The same algorithm can be applied to:

- Doors, which can open as the quicktime flying camera approaches.
- 2-D trees and human figures rotate to look full bodied to the camera
- The density of branches & leaves on trees can vary.
- People and car objects can simplify hugely when camera is far.
- Lights come on in rooms, Televisions change their image.
- Curved objects change their RESOL value to higher values when the camera is near, and reduce to as little as three when it is near.
- Complex objects like Planar fittings and Louvres decide not to draw.

It works with Sun Studies, Flythoughs and with ArchiCAD6, it can also work with VR Panorama cameras.

Distance or Time?: Other aspects of animation, such as wind turbines whose blades turn, buildings stacking themselves up, cars moving, human figures waving, sea undulating, yachts heeling etc are better done by using the global variable N_ (frame number in the animation) to determine the action – which is equivalent to TIME.

The Location-aware routine makes use of the **Global Variables** used in ArchiCAD. GDL can find out from ArchiCAD what the current parameters are, in particular the Camera location and Object's own location. By comparing the distance differences in X, Y and Z (a simple subtraction that works whichever sector the model or camera is in), you can use a 3D Pythagoras calculation to reveal the real distance 'dd' from camera. *dkx* is what I call the Difference between the global variables 'K~' and 'X~' – the object and camera positions in the X direction. The same idea applies in the Y and Z direction, to generate *dly* and *dmz*.

An ArcTan (ATN) calculation reveals the Azimuth (or direction) by dividing the X distance into the Y distance.

If there is no camera, for example, in an axonometric or an elevation, you need a simple 'get-out-clause' to set a false distance from the camera. This is to avoid a 'divide by zero' error when calculating the azimuth. Thus the variable *dkx* is made equal to 1 metre. If dkx=0 you would get a 'divide by zero' error with the azimuth calculation.

3D Script commentary

150: Note that the executive script sends execution to Subroutine 150 whatever the value of 'autoarmang'. The IF... ENDIF statement decides whether to bother doing its work. All it does is to return a value of the variable 'rotarm'.

It is possible to make the barrier lift slowly, based on the number of metres distant. Here, it uses a number of IF statements to compare the actual distance with the opening distance, the script decides what angle the bar should be at.

It begins to raise the barrier when the user is twice the distance away, and at the chosen distance, the arm is fully up.

THIS location awareness routine can be used again – keep it in your Scrapbook. I have done models where EVERY GDL component was location aware to keep the rendering time under control.

Variable	Type	Name	Value
rotarm	⊿	Angle of Bar (0=up 90=down)	=0.00
blen	🔄	Barrier Length	=2.000
bmatl	🎨	Material of Barrier	=22
ccol	🖌	Colour of Circle & Stripes	=10
stripy	☒	Stripy Bar ON or OFF	= ON
autoarmang	☒	Auto Arm angle? ON or OFF	= ON
opdis	🔄	Opening Distance	=10.0

Parameters

Offer a Booleian choice, *autoarmang*, in case the user wants the Barrier to remain fixed.

The user must define the point at which the object opens or changes. Here, the barrier will lift when the camera is less than 10 metres away.

```
150: !Check distance/angle
IF autoarmang THEN
    dkx=K~ - X~:IF dkx=0 THEN dkx=1
    dly=L~ - Y~
    dmz=M~ - Z~

dr =SQR(dkx^2 + dly^2) !Plan distance
dd =SQR(dkx^2 +dly^2 +dmz^2)!Distance
azi=ATN(dly/dkx)          !Azimuth

    LET rotarm=90
    IF dd<opdis*2 THEN rotarm=45
    IF dd<opdis   THEN rotarm=0
    IF dd>opdis   THEN rotarm=90
    ENDIF
    RETURN:
```

Add this subroutine to the Car park barrier to automate the value of 'rotarm'

📄 Reserved global variables

K~, L~, M~ eye position
N~, O~, P~ target position
U~ project North direction
V~ symbol mirrored (1) or not (0)
W~ rotation angle of the symbol
X~, Y~, Z~ symbol position

The eye positions K~, L~, & M~ can also be called GLOB_EYEPOS_X, Y & Z, and the Object positions X~, Y~ & Z~ can be called SYMB_POS_X, Y & Z.

Rebuild each Frame

This routine will work for still views with different camera distances. To ensure that this works during a movie flythrough, you need a REBUILD EACH FRAME to happen during animation. In AC6, this can be enabled in the dialog box just prior to starting a Flythrough.

In AC5, this was only possible by enabling the 'Special Menu', which can be enabled with Resedit on the Mac and with Regedit on the Windows PC. Most of the Special menu is garbage – the commands are debugging commands for the programmers.

I was told by a member of Graphisoft that "Rebuild Each Frame" was added to AC6 as a result of my lobbying them to do it. If so, then **Thankyou Graphisoft!**

GDL Cookbook : Questions to ask yourself

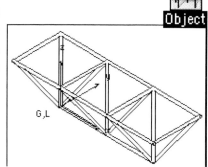

IF YOU are on a course with tutors available, you should perhaps work in pairs, or have a seminar first to plan how you would set about doing these. You should use paper to draw out your ideas. A bit of planning will save you time during scripting. For example consider:

- How can the model can be broken down into elements? – sketch it freehand.
- Which 3D commands (in GDL) would best achieve the result?
- Who is your 'User'? – will you need to check input errors?
- Where should the model's origin be?
- Can you take advantage of symmetry?
- Are there hinging elements?
- Does it want to be stretchy?
- How parametric should the model really be?
- What elements are repetitious and can be done with loops?
- What maths or circle geometry problems are involved?
- You are designers! Therefore, is your model well designed etc?

If you are by yourself, this is a test to see how you thrive without the benefit of a tutor to help you through – just the Cookbook and the Manual!

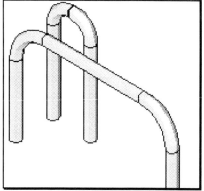

Modify Library Objects

DRAW out a Slab in the Project plan, and then make the Slab into a library object, which you can now open and view. Now copy and paste the X,Y locations to write a few mini scripts which do things like using the points for a bPRISM command, or putting a pattern of Hotspots into the 2D script, or locating a number of round columns/posts at the points on the slab.

Monopod Circular table

THIS circular table should be paramet ric in diameter and height. The leg should look stable, so you may use Cone or Revolve to form it (not Cylinder). The table should perhaps have a chamfered edge. Would you be able to make it stretchy and non circular (ie oval?) Can you do a matching 2-D script? If so, the line of the central circular support should be shown with a dotted line.

Window or Door

Using scripting (not the old slab method), make yourself a door that can be opened and shut in 2D and in 3D. Use PRISM or BLOCKs for the Door. It should be able to change material, and have a scripted 2D symbol. If you are really bold, then offer the choice to glaze the door, and have a choice of door handle or knob.

Television/Monitor

MAKE a TV or monitor with a slightly bulging, not flat screen. Trick is to use a very flat ELLIPS, then use 4 CUTPLANES to cut it to the rectangle of a TV. Then mount it into a PRISM with the rectangular hole in it.

By inserting the script for a picture object, you can form an image on the screen.

External cycle or handrail bar

DECIDE whether is it all curvy tube, or two uprights and a handrail. If it's to be a smart object, give the user the choice to make it either. If the rail length is bigger or smaller than the uprights, will that change the junction detail? It must be a 'stretchy object' – conforming to the dimension A; it could be 2D scripted, to save drawing time. Can you make it error-check to ensure that as it stretches smaller, the curve radius can be modified?

SLR camera

ALTHOUGH this is too small to ap pear in one of your architectural models, it is a good exercise in using PRISM, CYLIND, REVOLVE, and RULED. Draw it freehand first, to decide which elements you will include. You could ask the user to specify the angle of the lens – from 28mm to 200mm, this will have an effect on the length and diameter of the lens mechanism. For 2D just use Project2.

Tempietto / Bandstand

USE Cylinders for the base and ELLIPS for the dome; individual col umns should taper; think about a way of making the column bases and capitals, and use a FOR..NEXT Loop to distribute the columns. For the purpose of the test, make it parametric in height, number of steps and columns (and perhaps column fatness) and colours. Can you make it stretchy? Can you also script it in 2D, so it draws quickly?

Do not bother with complex capitals – use a short CONE or no capital at all. Remember you need to find ways of varying the resolution of curved surfaces.

Hewi style door handle set

THIS uses tubes and cylinders, and could be a subroutine of something you might add to a door design – it could be CALLed. If it is to be called, reduce the pa rameters to the minimum – size is fixed, only colour is required.

Desk Worktops

DESIGN an L-shaped desk worktop that has a curved internal corner. The sides of the L can either be 800mm or 600mm. Assume a constant thickness of 30mm. The length should be 1200mm in one direction, and 1200, 1400, 1600 or 1800 in the other. If you really want to chal lenge, you can make it stretchy to those sizes. when you drop it into the Project plan at a height of 0.00, it should automatically be at desktop height of 760mm.

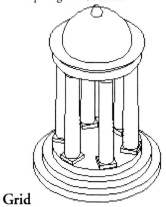

Grid

MAKE a stretchy 2D Grid tool that can vary the spacing of the verticals and horizontals.

If you are still a 'Discoverer', have a look at the task list that is at the beginning of the Voyager Course. Some of those tasks may appear to you to be something that you now feel ready to tackle.

Rules of good conduct and safe passage in GDL

Theory

- Number One! Always have paper, preferably a bound notebook (for looking back weeks later).
- Think about the investment potential of the object – or is it really a one off?
- If it's a one off, then dirty, brief coding may suffice.
- If it's an investment, you need to revisit, tidy, improve code, leave it for others to finish: so write it well. The following remarks apply to 'investment' models.

Philosophy

- You might make an object model that will be suitable for the immediate purpose – but is there any chance you can think of it as a Tool that could be used again? Are you making an object for others to use in the office, perhaps long after you have departed?

- Can the object be defined using a Value List? (Pop down menu) If so, then many of the parameters may be predetermined and do not need to be entered by the user.

Structure

Sorry for repeating these points, but they need to be drilled until they become second nature.

- Structure the program rigorously – every physical element of the model should be a subroutine.

- Use the Master Script for calculation and preparation work. This leaves the remaining scripts to focus on their jobs without clutter.

- Subroutines must always return the Cursor to the same location as where it started – so that any element of the model can be omitted without destroying the remaining model. When you exit a subroutine, you get the 3-D cursor to the same place by using the correct number of DELs.

- Remember that a few well scripted super objects (that can be changed parametrically) are far more efficient in use than a profusion of different but similar objects.

Typography and Layout

- Document the program clearly – use ! marks for 'Comment' statements; never forget to do this at the start of all subroutines.

- At the start of the script, put the object name, the date, and your name. Plus any further information that could be useful – all hidden behind comment markers (!).

- Be disciplined in your typographical layout. Always use UPPER case for COMMANDS and lower case for variables and comments.

- Indent Cursor movements by at least two spacebar taps. Indent DELs and NEXTs. Indent the XYZ dimensions in PRISMs and TUBEs. Line up commas in Prisms etc.

- Leave plenty of space (carriage returns) and rows of ----- ------------'s between sections.

- GDL ignores carriage returns in almost all cases, so that XYZ coordinates for prisms, tubes etc can be written on separate lines, providing you end each line with a comma. This looks clearer than trying to write on one line.

Maths

- Get familiarised with the X-Y-Z Cartesian universe, the Pythagoras theorem and the SOH-CAH-TOA rule of trigonometry.

- Think about the parameters that you will want to vary. Use names for your parameter variables that make sense – like 'length', 'width', 'spacing' etc. Never use a command word, like 'revolve' or 'prism' or 'del' for a variable, or any word that might be used in future versions of GDL – like 'read', 'input', 'wend' or 'while', 'do'. Use single letter variables only for Loop counters.

Development of the Script

- As the script develops, keep putting 'END' after the bit you have just done so you can keep track of the 3-D cursor location. Very early on, put an END statement in your script so you can start making subroutines.

- Block off working part of the script when you debug parts which don't work, by Commenting (!) subroutines, or by putting in temporary 'END' or 'GOTO' statements. A temporary END enables you to see where the cursor has got to.

- If you use global MUL, ROT or ADD statements, be careful not to DEL TOP during the program.

- Use temporary PRINT commands to see if the results of calculations are correct.

Good scripting practice

- Never use GOTO as part of the script unless absolutely forced. IF... THEN... ENDIF or subroutines are the best way to avoid using GOTOs.

- Avoid multi statement lines (separated by colons). like ADDz 0.1:ROTy 90. No economy is achieved by doing this, and it makes it much more difficult to debug later.

- Learn to use FOR...NEXT Loops to speed up modelling, and to introduce an extra level of parametric variation. Consider using REPEAT... UNTIL which offers more flexibility.

- When you have to use a TUBE or REVOLVE or COONS or similar, consider using a PUT routine first, to assemble the parameters in memory. It's a lot easier to dump all the XY locations (using GET(NSP)) into the TUBE if you have done all the arranging beforehand.

6.5 Mental Health Warning! Stretchy objects (which use master script) do not always stretch due to a bug in the first release of 6.5 (acknowledged by Graphisoft) The temporary work around is to move the Master Script to the beginnings of the 3D script (and 2D script if necessary).

- Make frequent use of the swivelling 3D views in AC6 to verify the shape of models.

- Don't panic if you get error messages. Errors are 98 percent YOUR fault, not the computer and a little bit of analysis or simplification of your script will reveal the error. There are some bugs in GDL and ArchiCAD.

- If using objects first created with the wall/slab tool, make sure you make them on the main model Origin in the ArchiCAD project plan view. If you use ArchiCAD's tools, use 'snap to grid' to get clean looking scripts.

User Interface

- Try to imagine how your 'user' will enter data. Write the title of a parameter with the user in mind. Can the user understand what you are asking? Radii are always best entered as Diameters and then converted in the script. Is the number you require a Dimension, a 'Real' number or an Integer?

- Can you use a Value List? This can reduce the risk or errors as it forces the user to enter data that is valid (doesn't need error checking.) Consider a Pictorial Value list, using the User Interface in ArchiCAD 6.5 onwards.

- If you offer the user more than 2 choices, you will have to use Integers instead of Boolean – for example, 'Cladding Styles 0-5'. Better still, in ArchiCAD 6.x, you can use VALUE Lists. These give the user a pop-down menu, offering choices. These are best done as Text parameters.

- Put a picture in the Preview window.

2D scripting

- Use the PROJECT2 command if the model is changing in 3D so much that it cannot be scripted. If you are able to, use 2-D scripting – have PROJECT2 turned on to make sure your script is working. When it is working correctly, turn PROJECT2 off.

- Scripting the 2-D view for articulated models will save redraw time in the main project window, and reduces model size. It's not difficult to do once you have mastered the art of 3-D scripting.

- If the model is parametrically variable, the same structure as you have in the 3D script can be followed. For example, use the same subroutine numbers. If it's exceedingly complex and parametrically variable, find out how to use FRAGMENT2, or script it fully in 2D.

- If possible, use EXTRUDE in 3D scripts instead of PRISM as the parameters can be copied and pasted to the 2D script and easily changed to POLY2_.

- Stretchy objects (using Hotspots on A,B) are useful and friendly to the user, and can reduce the number of parameters that the user must fill in. Stretchy Hotspots must occur before the 2D drawing commands or the object will stretch well but not shrink correctly.

- You can use TEXT2 to ensure that objects label themselves correctly – although you need to DEFINE STYLE of text to do this well. If you autosize the font height to fit the object, it will be free from plotting scale problems.

If you find exercises in the cookbook that do not conform to these rules, typographically or otherwise, please send me email. It may well be the case with older worksheets that have not been revised yet. None of us are perfect!

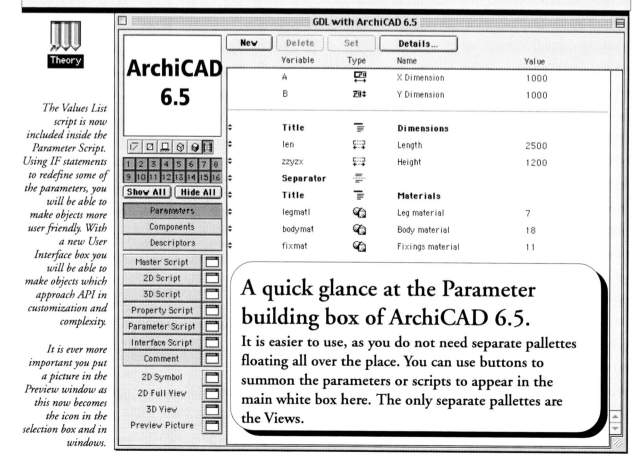

The Values List script is now included inside the Parameter Script. Using IF statements to redefine some of the parameters, you will be able to make objects more user friendly. With a new User Interface box you will be able to make objects which approach API in customization and complexity.

It is ever more important you put a picture in the Preview window as this now becomes the icon in the selection box and in windows.

A quick glance at the Parameter building box of ArchiCAD 6.5.

It is easier to use, as you do not need separate pallettes floating all over the place. You can use buttons to summon the parameters or scripts to appear in the main white box here. The only separate pallettes are the Views.

A look at GDL in ArchiCAD 6.5

THE GDL COOKBOOK will need a more thoroughgoing revision when ArchiCAD 6.5 has been around for a year, but let's list a few of the changes in GDL with 6.5.

General

• The Parameter building box (opposite) is a lot easier to work in as you do not have floating pallettes all overlaying each other (although you can have them floating if you wish it that way.)

• Organising the Parameters box to be user friendly will be easier with the opportunity to have Bold font, title lines, linefeeds, hidden parameters, lockable/unlockable parameters, and subsets of parameters that are available if certain selections are required.

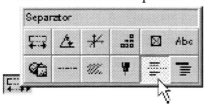

Separator and Title are new additions

• Special characteristics of an object, window, lamp and so on may now be found by clicking on a button called **Details** (including 'Hotspots on Bounding Box')

• **The GDL Debugger**, which with version 6.0 I found to be almost useless, now seems to be more capable.

• **Copy** from Mac to PC without making .PLA Archives.

3D scripting

• HOTSPOT – to remove the annoying tendency of hotspots, when seen in the 3D window to be anywhere but where you want them! So objects are easier to grab, but only hotspots on the XY plane allow stretching.

• Extension of **XWALL** to allow Log building.

• **BEAM** – has a syntax similar to **XWALL**, i.e. a lot more difficult to use than BLOCK or PRISM. But you can vary the materials of the faces. For creative programming one is likely to continue using cPRISM_. But BEAM will be the new standard for Autoscripted objects which have been constructed with the new BeamTool. The Beamtool has new and clever ways of revealing intersections with others and allowing themselves to be drilled (like Walls) or cutting slabs. In the autoscripts, these are done with CUTPOLYs. The Beamtool has many links to the ArchiCAD model through a host of new Global Variables for the purposes of listing, but it remains to be seen how the GDL writer can use this creatively. So BEAM may only be used by GDL nutcases.

• SET SECT_FILL – this will satisfy one of the biggest wishes on ArchiCAD talk, of how to control the appearance (fill pattern) of objects when cut in the Section window.

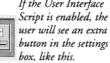

If the User Interface Script is enabled, the user will see an extra button in the settings box, like this.

2D scripting

• HOTSPOT2 – can be followed by an 'identifier ID' code. Useful if the 2D view is changing in a complex way.

• DRAWINDEX – defines the order in which 2D elements are drawn.

Properties

• DATABASE_SET – if this command is placed in the MASTER.GDL file, it will define a database set containing Descriptor, Component, Unit, Key, Criteria and List Scheme files. Along with the fact that AC_6.5 includes a special manual for the Calculate menu, this command, and what goes with it must go some way to make the whole matter of Properties easier to use.

Parameters and Values

• VALUES – the command is extended in power. If the user wants a choice that is not in the list, the CUSTOM keyword makes that possible. In addition, the RANGE keyword means that the user can enter a value falling within a range of values. VALUES commands are now written in the Parameter Script.

• PARAMETERS – I hoped this would enable one to build objects in English, French German etc. so in that respect I am disappointed. But it still has its uses, and is perhaps more useful. It will enable one to feed the object and the settings box with predetermined parameter values if the user makes a certain choice – rather as the CALL command send a list of parameter values to a Called object. For example, it can redefine and display the new values of A and B. If, in a Car model, you select 'MiniHatchback' from a Value List of cars, it can set A to 3.1 metres, B to 1.6 metres and zzyzx to 1.4. If you select Limousine, it can change them to A=6.0, B=2.1, and zzyzx=1.6. Previously, if a change of object configuration was likely to result in the outer dimensions changing, one could not use A and B. It will be a big help in Window and Door writing.

• LOCK – This enables the script to lock out parameters which are not available as a result of a decision – e.g. if the user of a smart chair object selects the model without arms, the parameters relating to chair arm height and material will be greyed out. The name must be in quotes.

• USER INTERFACE Script – the GDL writer can build a whole new series of dialog boxes with images, buttons, and boxes which the user can fill in. In particular, Pictorial Value Lists can be built which add 100% more user friendliness than before.

This is a profound improvement. the User Interface (UI) brings GDL closer to API capabilities, and of course will greatly strengthen anybody who has the will to program in API and GDL combined.

The 6.5 User Interface – part 1

FOR ArchiCAD 6.5 users, the most noticeable difference for users of Library objects is the new user interface.

First, the usual box of parameters with the scroll bar still exists, but it can now be organised into tidy groupings with hierarchical menus, bold titles and line spaces. The selection of objects is made easier as the box displays icons for each object. Secondly, it is possible to build a custom user interface that does away with the traditional parameter box altogether and makes it possible to build objects that have the sort of interface you normally expect from a well written API add-on.

Let's go to the first of these improvements and look at how to organise the parameters tidily. The object 'UI_Tester.gsm' demonstrates most of the features of the new interface. It's on your CD.

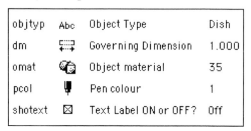

These are the dialogs we have been used to with earlier versions of ArchiCAD – now looking dull by comparison with what is available with AC-6.5

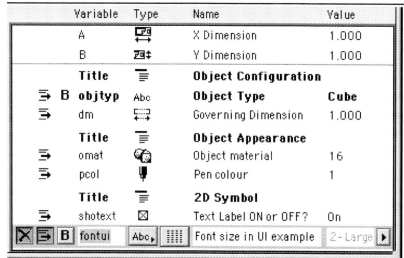

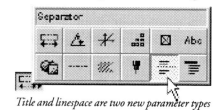

Now, let's get rocking!

Title and linespace are two new parameter types

AS you build each parameter, you have 2 new choices – you can have a Title which will be in bold type, and you can have an empty line to give a linespace in the list of parameters.

This is the user's parameter box all neat and tidy and folded up.

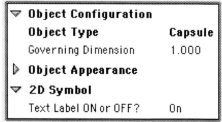

This is the user's parameter box with 2 of the groups opened up ready for inspection and use.

You also have three new buttons to touch on; the first one, with a cross (as in 'fontui') means 'hide it', in this case because it is ONLY to be used in the advanced User Interface boxes. The second button with an arrow means 'indent the parameter name', making the parameter hierarchically subservient to the nearest un-indented above it. The third button with a large 'B' means 'set parameter description to Bold'. By organising the box so that the indented parameters come under the Titles, you can make a neat and tidy job, reduce the need for the user to scroll down, and ensure that the parameters are logically grouped together – for example, 3D configuration, 2D symbol appearance.

There is no longer a Value List button – value lists automatically activate if they find a valid script in the Parameter script. In the advanced UI, you can have Pictorial Value lists.

*See the **Voyager** volume for the advanced User Interface.*

1.70

`Object`

User Interface - 2D Car symbol

WE have been used to A and B controlling width and depth, but under AC_6.5, the GDL Object can dictate a new value for these – a valuable feature as **A** and **B** control stretchiness and may be the whole basis on which the remainder of the object is dimensioned and built.

The Parameter Script is read even before the Master Script and the User Interface script. The PARAMETERS command in the Parameters script can read a VALUES list, and as a result of the user's choice, change the whole object. This example shows it clearly.

In this case the parameters have little crosses next to them because I have gone on to make a UI window and want the parameters to be hidden from the usual settings box.

```
!2-Dimensional Car Symbol
!Demonstrate PARAMETERS
!2D Executive Script

!Hood Length as fraction of 'A'
IF cartyp='MiniHatch' THEN hl=0.30
IF cartyp='Sedan'    THEN hl=0.22
IF cartyp='Jeep'     THEN hl=0.26
IF cartyp='Estate'   THEN hl=0.22

PEN carpen

LINE2 A*0.02,0,A*hl,0
LINE2 A*0.02,B*0.25,A*0.02,-B*0.25
GOSUB 1100:!hotspots
GOSUB 1000:!Body
ADD2 A*hl,0
IF cartyp='Jeep'   THEN MUL2 1.15,1.05
IF cartyp='Estate' THEN MUL2 1.22,1.00
GOSUB 1010:!Glass
GOSUB 1020:!Roof hatch
DEL TOP
END:!------------
```

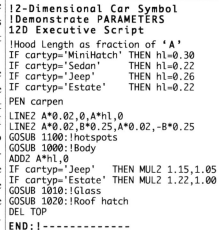

```
car_pramUI
New   Delete   Set   Details...
Variable  Type  Name              Value
    A      ⇹    X Dimension        3.400
    B      ⇳    Y Dimension        1.500

        Automobile 2D
        Symbol

Title  ☰  See the User Interface
✕ cartyp  Abc  Car Type           MiniHatch
✕ carfil  ▨    Car Body Fill pattern  24
✕ carpen  ▮    Car Pen Colour      1
✕ roofil  ▨    Roof Pattern Fill   23
✕ glasfil ▨    Glass Fill         16
```

```
!Parameter Script for 2D Car Symbol

VALUES 'cartyp' 'MiniHatch',
    'Sedan','Jeep', 'Estate'

IF cartyp='MiniHatch' THEN
    PARAMETERS A=3.4,B=1.5
ENDIF

IF cartyp='Sedan'    THEN
    PARAMETERS A=4.2,B=1.6
ENDIF

IF cartyp='Jeep'     THEN
    PARAMETERS A=4.9,B=1.8
ENDIF

IF cartyp='Estate'   THEN
    PARAMETERS A=4.2,B=1.6
ENDIF
```

Depending on the User's selection, the PARAMETERS command in this script goes off and changes the fundamental parameters of A and B – thus updating the size and also the Hotspot locations correctly.

Right: It is also possible to enjoy the pleasures of a **Pictorial Value List**; see the **Voyager course** for more details.

```
1000:!Body ALL
SET FILL carfil
PUT 0,0,
    A*0.01, B*0.45,
    A/4,    B/2,
    A*0.80, B/2,
    A*0.99, B*0.45,
    A,0,
    A*0.99,-B*0.45,
    A*0.80,-B/2,
    A/4,   -B/2,
    A*0.01,-B*0.45,
    0,0
POLY2 NSP/2,7,
    GET(NSP)
RETURN

1010:!Glass
SET FILL glasfil
PUT A*0.00, B*0.20,
    A*0.03, B*0.45,
    A*0.49, B*0.45,
    A*0.55, B*0.44,
    A*0.61, B*0.40,
    A*0.63, B*0.15,
    A*0.63,-B*0.15,
    A*0.61,-B*0.40,
    A*0.55,-B*0.44,
    A*0.49,-B*0.45,
    A*0.03,-B*0.45,
    A*0.00,-B*0.20
POLY2 NSP/2,7,
    GET(NSP)
RETURN

1020:!Roof hatch
SET FILL roofil
PUT A*0.13, B*0.10,
    A*0.14, B*0.30,
    A*0.03, B*0.45,
    A*0.07, B*0.45,
    A*0.17, B*0.35,
    A*0.48, B*0.35
IF  hl=0.3 THEN PUT
A*0.49, B*0.45
PUT A*0.55, B*0.44,
    A*0.61, B*0.40,
    A*0.52, B*0.30,
    A*0.53, B*0.10,
    A*0.53,-B*0.10,
    A*0.52,-B*0.30,
    A*0.61,-B*0.40,
```

```
    A*0.55,-B*0.44
IF hl=0.3 THEN PUT A*0.49,-B*0.45
PUT A*0.48,-B*0.35,
    A*0.17,-B*0.35,
    A*0.07,-B*0.45,
    A*0.03,-B*0.45,
    A*0.14,-B*0.30,
    A*0.13,-B*0.10
POLY2 NSP/2,7,
    GET(NSP)
RETURN

1100:!Hotspots
PUT 0,0,
    A*0.01, B*0.45,
    A/4,    B/2,
    A*0.80, B/2,
    A*0.99, B*0.45,
    A,0,
    A*0.99,-B*0.45,
    A*0.80,-B/2,
    A/4,   -B/2,
    A*0.01,-B*0.45,
    A*hl,0,A*0.02,0
REPEAT
    HOTSPOT2 GET(2)
UNTIL NSP=0
RETURN
```

Note that there is not a single Dimension here: all is controlled by parameters based on A (car length) and B (car width)

Hotspots use the same points as the Poly-points on the body outline

!Hood

Here are the resulting 2D symbols, whose fill patterns can be tweaked

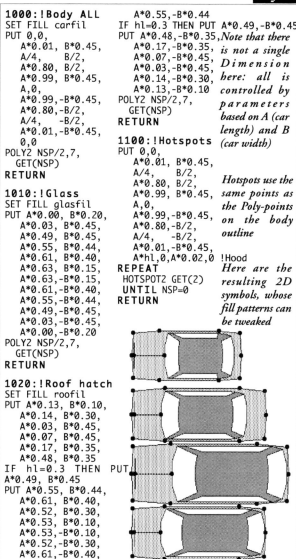

Above: Note the extensive use of PUT and GET in the subroutines. This is the first and most important thing to be covered in the Voyager Course. Without PUT and GET no serious complex task can be achieved. Note also: Hotspots are displayed to reveal their 'body hugging' quality!

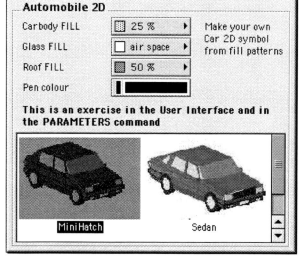

```
Automobile 2D
Car body FILL    ▨ 25 %     ▶    Make your own
Glass FILL       □ air space ▶   Car 2D symbol
Roof FILL        ▨ 50 %     ▶    from fill patterns
Pen colour       ▮▬▬▬
```

This is an exercise in the User Interface and in the PARAMETERS command

MiniHatch   Sedan

The GDL Cookbook

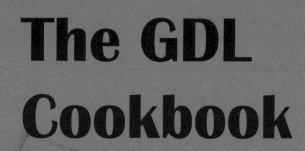

**Teach yourself GDL
by the cookbook method
& 'ArchiCAD Tips and Tricks'**

**Version 2.1
for ArchiCAD users**

Vol 2 - GDL Voyager

Marmalade

Cookbook 2.10: Voyager Course

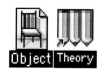

THIS is for GDL enthusiasts who have had enough experience to venture into more difficult territory. The section starts with a series of questions posed to the intrepid voyager, which (if you feel bold) you should tackle without looking at the answers. However, for those who are curious, or who have been rebuffed by the difficulty, look through the exercises and try your luck. There is a grading sequence, but less prescriptive than in the Discovery course.

Some of the exercises in the Voyager section are useful as a resource for dipping into when you need to remind yourself of certain routines. I wouldn't go on any consultancy mission without having the GDL Cookbook with me as a reference.

Voyager Task List

IF you attempt some of the following tasks, assume a high level of parametricity in all objects, but try to keep to the point of the exercise, to keep each one within 1.5 - 2.0 hours. If you are on a Lift Off course, then you are not on your own during these exercises – the idea is to be thoroughly briefed by a tutor at the start, and to work on it with a tutor close at hand, but not writing it for you. Many of the tasks in the course are covered by model scripts and worksheets in the rest of the Cookbook.

If you are teaching yourself with the Cookbook, try to do these with a fellow enthusiast. Talk over the best approach to each problem.

You do not have time to make each one a totally finished product with total error checking, and perfect user friendliness - but do the best you can in the time. Keep focussed on the learning requirement of each exercise, and avoid distracting side issues.

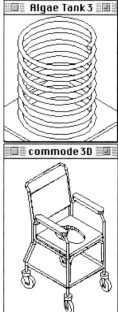

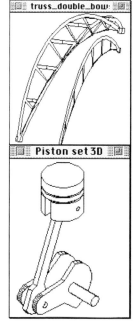

Some useful guidelines

WHENEVER possible you should apply rules of quality control to all objects. Some of these quality control aspects are:

- Even for the smallest model, try to structure the script into subroutines that represent physical components of the model. When you start a model, it is OK to tap in preliminary code, but the moment you are getting it to work, enclose it into subroutines.

- Ensure that the subroutines are totally self contained in terms of cursor location. DEL the exact number of cursor moves in each subroutine.

- Distinguish between parameters that the 'user' will be allowed to change and ones that your script needs to know. Make sure that the user parameters are clearly explained in the dialog box.

- Can the parameters be grouped into hierarchical menus? Can you form a series of User Interface pages?

- Pay attention to RESOL on all circular elements - part of 'quality' is the factor of efficiency in speed of rendering.

- Always work with copious quantities of paper and pen handy, and be prepared to sketch out every small problem on paper - this is more efficient that tapping things into the script and being annoyed by error messages.

- Make frequent use of the ! to document your subroutines and moves.

- Put all key words into UPPER CASE (e.g. BLOCK, MUL, DEL etc) and keep all variables in Lower case (e.g. len, wid, higt, x1, z0 etc). Do this even for quick and dirty library objects. It makes it easier to debug later.

- Although it is tempting to use PROJECT2 3,270,2 for all 2D scripts, try to replace these with 2-D scripts if you want efficiency in display in the Project Plan.

- Do not be afraid to try new commands and polylines and masks in GDL - some of these may be better than ones you have got set in your ways of using. Use Trial and Error if at first you do not get them working.

- No matter how experienced you are, make frequent use of the HELP windows and manual.

Table Lamp

LIGHT, Revolve, Articulating form, Lamp, Cylind, Sphere, Ellips.

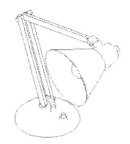

MAKE a small anglepoise lamp. Avoid excessive detail in the body of the lamp, as the purpose of this is to use the Light command. Include a toggle switch. The Lamp head should swivel. Set two of the lights on a table, and photorender to see how the pools of light work together.

Extruded Section

DXF Conversion, CutPlane, Revolve, BPrism

OPEN a 2D DXF or DWG file from Autocad or similar, convert it to a slab, then convert to a library object and either:

• write a 4 directional Mitring routine for the 3-D section, or:

• write a Curving routine for the 3-D section, with parametric curvature.

In either case the section should be able to be tilted around X and Y.

If you dont have a DXF sectional drawing like this to hand, draw one quickly in ArchiCAD (using floor slab) view the object in plan, and save it as a DWG or a DXF 2D drawing. Reload it, convert it to a SLAB using space bar snap, and view in plan. This time, save it as a library object.

Staircase

PUT & GET, BPRISM, REVOLVE, TUBE

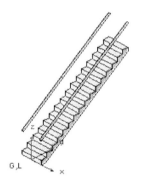

CREATE a routine for generating a staircase with parametric rules for number of steps, risers, tread, material etc. Plan ahead to see how you would organise this, if you wanted:

a] Straight stair with handrail

b] Theatre seating in the round,

c] Spiral Staircase

Although these stairs would be used in different parts of a building the routines are similar and if you have time, write both main routines in the same object.

Handrails

TUBE, PUT & GET, Circle Geometry, RESOL

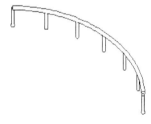

DESIGN a long handrail for exterior use, such as for a racecourse. One of the problems here is that you cannot use ELBOW and RADIUS, because if you get the RESOL right for the curve, you have an unacceptable number of polygons for the surface. Also, you need to distribute uprights evenly along the circular rail. The user needs an easy way to define the parametric properties of the rail in the dialog box.

Ensure (by masking values) that the tube looks clean and is not cluttered with lines. Try to make it go up a slope – by defining an upper and lower height (e.g. round a stair).

Geodesic Exercise

Can you build using trigonometry?

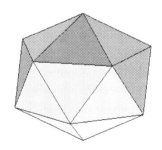

THIS exercise is surprisingly easy if you combine the power of loops and trigonometry, because the icosahedron (20 sided) is so very regular. It has a pentagonal pyramid shape at the top and at the bottom, and ten equal triangles forming the sides. If you use arrays, you can remember the locations, and line all the panels with tubular edges, in fact, hide all the panels altogether, and perhaps put ball joints at all the junctions.

Constant Rectangle

2D Scripting, Global Variables

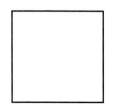

Draw a Rectangular outline to your project that can be a frame for printing on paper - that stays the same size regardless of the scale of the drawing. i.e. if it is equivalent to A2 in outline when in 1:100 scale, it is still A2 when your drawing is 1:500, and your building is reduced to a speck. The Size of the rectangle is set with A and B, but need not be stretchy. (Hint, you need globals, and it's 1-line)

Catamaran

COONS, MUL, GOSUB, CYLIND

THIS exercise if a must if you are interested in making meshes, and in structured programming.

a) Make the hull of the CAT. First the floats must be made by making half of one float as a COONs and then doubling it to make one float, and then doubling that. The width of the float and the length and width of the Cat should be parametric.

b) If you have time and the interest, take the Cat a bit further. Make a central Mast and forestay. The mast should be oval in profile. Make a parametric sail and jib that can be to Port or Starboard tack.

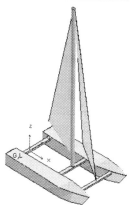

User Interface

Mastering the UI command set

TAKE an object you already know well, and develop a page or a set of pages using the User Interface command set in ArchiCAD 6.5 onwards. If it has Value lists in it, see if these can be converted to a Pictorial Value list.

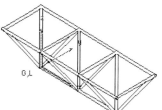

Spaceframe / Lattice

Cylind, Nested FOR..NEXT Loops

A spaceframe Lattice beam was part of the Discovery Course. This pays some reinspection, this time in the form of a spaceframe roof. This should be parametric in number of bays, depth and spacing, diameters etc. It involves some FOR... NEXT loops. For the real challenge, you could make its dimensions based on A and B, and the script work out the number of bays. But this is not essential.

Ideally, the upper sections should be square, and the diagonals and lower lattice should be round.

Derrick Crane

Circle geometry, Cylind, Tube, Elbow

ALTHOUGH this is a very simplified model of a Derrick crane, it is a good exercise in knowing the XYZ coordinates of objects in circular space and using TUBE to construct it.

Making a hook for the crane, and making this lowerable.

The crane should be able to swivel round.

As the arm of the crane is lowered, the cable should always reach to the pulley at the end of the arm. Try to keep the hook at a constant height.

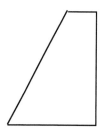

Hollow Elbow

Sweep, Cutplane, Prism_, Loops

This can be made in two ways - by Defining a hollow tube profile, and drawing it with a Sweep command through a curve, or by Revolve. Make the main radius, the tube radius, the tube resolution, the surface resolution, the sweep angle, and the wall thickness parametric.

Stretchy Battered Wall tool

ARCHICAD does not provide a tool for this purpose (how many times do architects use battered walls?), but this tool could serve for ramps and earthberms. Like a Wall, it should have user definable colour on the sides and top Faces, Internal Face, and external Face. You can also do it without GDL, to include windows. Do you know how?

It is an even greater challenge to make it mitre or turn corners (anglar or rounded), or to include windows, so do not attempt this unless you manage the main task with ease.

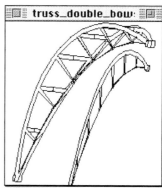

Bowstring Truss - 2D

TUBE, ELBOW, Circle Geometry, PUT, GET, For... Next

IF you are short of time, do not attempt a 3-D Bowstring truss - which has 7 different circle centres and radii! This 2D truss is a development of the Handrail task in the Voyager course - using the TUBE command.

A 2-D truss only has two circles. It should be parametric in span, height and depth, and in the quantity of lattice members. But you will need circle geometry to work backwards from Span and Height to calculate Center and Radius. The components of the truss can be made with the ELBOW command, or the TUBE command, but for realism and model quality, both the compression member and the tension member are best done with Tube.

Picture objects and textures

Picture, Alpha channels, making materials, global variables

YOUR models can acheive added realism if you can put scans of photos of people or plants onto a surface. They are even more effective if you can have the surroundings of the sihouette made transparent by using alpha channels. The same can be done with textures and materials for entire objects. Scan or photograph something and do the Photoshop editing on it to achieve a silhouetted outline.

At this point it is useful to learn the routine for making objects 'Location Aware' so that flat 2-D objects look more solid.

Smooth rounded Bodies!

COONS, MUL, Prism, Polylines

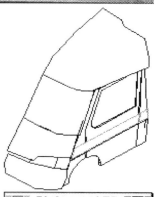

FORM part of the front end cabin of a Ford Transit Van. This is done by using COONS meshes. As the van is symmetrical, you only need to make half of it, and MUL to generate the other half. It is not as difficult as it looks. You do not need to make it parametric as the van shape is fixed. Every dimensional location of the front end should relate to the same origin. Also, each COON surface is adjacent to the next, so you have fewer XYZ points to calculate. It is worth maintaining a consistent grid in the Y direction to reduce the workload.

Animation in time

Cameras, Global Variables, Articulating Model, TEXT

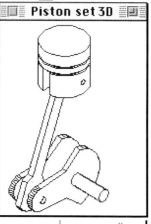

IT is possible to make animated objects change with time. This may not be so useful in practical architecture, but is a demonstration of the powers of ArchiCAD. Try one of these ideas, or one of your own.

• 3-D clock whose hands turn.

• LCD type clock whose numbers change with each frame.

• Neon lettering for a club/bar, whose letters light up or rotate in sequence.

• Reciprocating single cylinder piston and crankshaft.

With each frame of a 'Path' it is possible for the library object to read the frame number (N_)and react accordingly. If you position 2 cameras in identical locations with many in between frames, the object will animate. You must have "Rebuild each Frame" set up in the special menu.

Carved Polyhedra

SPHERE, CUTPLANE, CUTEND, FOR... NEXT

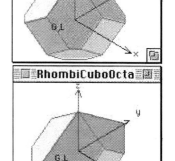

MAKE Cubes (hexahedron) and Spheres your starting objects. Using Cutplane, form these into truncated polyhedra. Make a cube from a sphere. Then try the rhombicuboctahadron from a cube. Carving, as a way of making these, is considerably easier than building these up. There may be a problem with the way that cut surfaces are displayed, and you have to get Pen colours and materials right.

Another thing you may try is a sphere that has every facet in random colours (as shown in the Primer in the Cutplane section).

Fun with Helical forms

BPRISM, TUBE, Polylines, Trigonometry

FIRST make a helical shape with the BPRISM command - experiment with this. Then make a smooth tubular helix using the TUBE command, making the frequency, total and tubular diameters parametric. Finally, try making something like the penguin pool type ramp that is shown in the GDL manual.

Perforated Wall Panel

Parametric Holes in a PRISM_, PUT, GET, FOR...Next

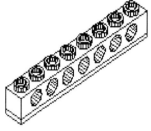

TRY making a wall panel, perforated with a number of holes. You can make the choice of Round and Square holes parametrically selectable. Given a number of rows and columns of holes, your program should work out appropriate sizes and spacing. Use PUT to organise the array of holes, and use PRISM and GET to produce it in 3-D.

Can you use the same technique with EXTRUDE, or make a curving object with REVOLVE?

Flexible Tube

File Input, TUBE, PUT, GET

TUBE command allows one to make tubes which are mitred at all junctions. A sequence of tubing could be made by reading a list of points within the script. These can be in the TUBE command, or can be put into the buffer first using PUT and GET). This is how the spirals are done.

You can also try writing a script that can read in a text file, the SAME script could generate a great variety of tubular structures by reading in text files of XYZ points. Thus, complex structures for piping, geodesics etc could be constructed more easily than with conventional GDL.

Kitchen Chair

Cone, Structured subroutines, Polylines, BPRISM

THIS elegant traditional chair model can be made almost totally from the CONE command, except for the Seat, Arm and Back made with PRISM and BPRISM commands. You should only need to build half of it, and MUL to make the whole chair.

Stretchy Objects

Using A and B

THE user finds it easiest to place objects into the Project plan if they can be stretched. Conventionally made objects will stretch, but all the elements of the models will then be wrongly sized. Make a stretchy object that preserves or recalculates the size of elements. Try one of these:

- Soldier, coping or Dental course
- Wall radiator (with pipes and valve)
- Table (so leg sizes are retained)
- Trussed Rafter
- Railing with spaced verticals

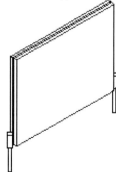

Report Writing

Properties Scripting or File I/O

GET the stretchy radiator (or something similar), to be able to read the global variables, and output a report to file, with a unique filename, defining data such as its location in XYZ, storey, orientation, surface area. Assuming you made it clickable to be double or single panel, make extra clickable choices for the 2D symbol to report on the surface area of the radiator. Instead of the radiator, you could try something structural. For example, a stretchy Universal Beam/Column - has a sectional area, moment of inertia, modulus of elasticity, radius of gyration. The formulae are available in the Metric Handbook. Or just get it to write a report to the Components window, using a Properties Script.

Irregular Surfaces

TERRAIN is one of the more difficult tasks in ArchiCAD - the Slab tool is too flat, the roof tool is another solution, but requires careful tweaking. COONS is only controllable at the edges. MESH combined with RND is a useful way of randomizing terrain - especially when you combine two together, of different colours. MASS is good, but difficult to exploit randomisation. Try it.

Window 3D (Modelled)

MAKE a window using slabs within the working environment, then projected in the 3D window and saved as a Window or Door. It can then be edited by opening the library element as a Window or Door.
- Now try adding a cill to the window.
- Now try making the window head arched.
- Now ensure that the window fits into walls of varying thickness and materials.
- Allow user to show glass or hide glass.

Smart Structural objects

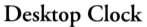

MAKE a stretchy object containing a number of spaced out three D elements or spaced out holes - such as a cellular or castellated beam (with parametrically calculated hole positions). Make this beam react to its length by changing in width and height – with the holes and hole spacing being re-calculated intelligently.

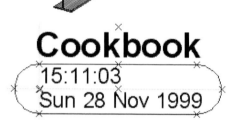

Desktop Clock

THIS can be a totally 2-D object, designed to float about on the drawing - either capable of being to scale with the building (whatever the drawing scale) or to be a constant height (whatever the drawing scale). This can display the time to the user, and record accurately the time and date of printing a document. You need to look at REQUEST, Style definition and drawing scale.

More things you might like to try:
- Define Text Styles in 2-D symbol, getting 2D symbol to report info.
- Making Text autosize, whatever the plotting scale.
- Define Materials or Lights in the script.
- Revolve, Sweep, Extrude, Pyramid, Tube
- Slab, CSlab, Croof, CWall, Bwall etc.
- Make a Macro and CALL it.
- Time and Date
- File Input and Output
- Make a scene entirely using Picture Objects
- A task requiring Circle Geometry

- Try a 3D truss - using tube or trig.
- Try a tree trunk, with random generation of the next set of branches (Difficult)
- Try making a simple assembly of shapes, (as used for example in the demo of materials in ArchiCAD) and then create materials (in either script or in working environment) which exploit alpha channels, for transparency, bump mapping etc.
- Some clever railings that can be level or follow up a stair, and be stretchy
- Something that changes position or state as each animation frame progresses.
- Something (such as curved glazing) that uses arrays, either in the script, or even as part of the user input in a parameter box.

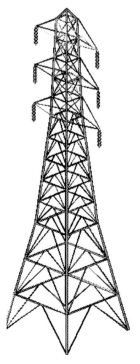

Door - 2D Scripted

Arc2, Line2, Globals

MAKE a simple opening door in 3D. Use 2D scripting to generate the 2D door image, and use global variables to make sure it is always the right width to fit the thickness of the wall it is put into. Make it show different levels of detail between 1/50 scale, or 1/100 scale.

MAKE a copy of the same door, but do the 2D using 2D symbol and make sure that it responds to scale in the same way, using the Fragment2 command.

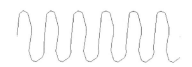

Ridge and Hip tiles

Stretchy objects, Tube or extrude

MAKE a roof similar to the one here, and make a universal stretchy hip and ridge tile that can follow all the hips and ridges. Make it so that it stretches horizontally in plan, according to the dimension A. Make it so that the pitch is defined as an angle.

MAKE a copy of the hip-ridge tile, and redefine it so that you use the dimension B to define the upper height of the tile (so that it is no longer based on angle).

User Defined Lines

'Squiffle'

DRAW 2D lines in the Project Plan. Select the lines drawn and copy them to clipboard. From the Options menu, select 'Line Types' and make a new Symbol line. Try making a 'squiffle' line, and then use that to turn a 3D axonometric into something that looks hand-drawn. Use the same technique to make insulation, or concrete texture, or lines including text or images.

Library Object conversion

PUT and GET, Sweep or RULED

DRAW out a slab in the Project Plan, and save it as a Library object. Look at the script: you will see a cPRISM. Modify it so that you have a PUT statement of the X,Y locations of the points. Now write an EX-TRUDE statement that uses GET, to feed the locations into the extrusion. Use NSP to determine how many points to put in the extrude.

NOW, try it again this time to make a more complex shape. Spacebar snap a polygon to the slab, and then shrink the polygon (so that it has the same number of vertices as the first slab) Move the polygon aside slightly. Spacebar snap another slab to the new polygon. Now save the two slabs as library objects. Now use PUT and GET in the same way (stealing the X,Y locations so conveniently given to you) and make a RULED command. By the way, note that this could also be done with a SWEEP command, using only the first set of points used for the Extrude exercise above.

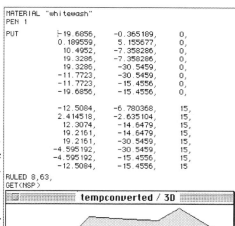

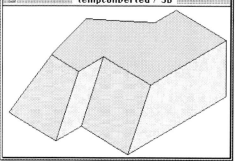

Using another monitor

PCI cards are very cheap now; if you have a redundant monitor lying around the office, why not get a second video card, and have a second monitor attached to the computer? It is very helpful to have a second screen where the 3D view gets generated, or where you can store your pallettes.

Writing for older versions

IF you are using ArchiCAD 6.x, the people you send work to could be dismayed to find that nothing you write works in version 5.0 or 5.1. Do not despair. If you have written in 5.0 compatible code (avoiding Fprism, Cutpoly, arrays and a few other things) you can email them the 3D script, the 2D script and a list of parameters as text files, and these can be dropped into place. Re-writing the parameters is the longest task.

Tips and Tricks
Squiffle

COMPUTER line drawings look too perfect and determinate and often mislead the client into thinking that your sketch design drawings are looking like a finished scheme. School of Architecture tutors are especially prone to be hostile at crits when faced with hard exact line drawings when the other students are still in the soft pencil stage.

Try using **'squiffle'**. Create a Line Type by drawing some feathery or wiggly lines in 2D, Copy them to clipboard. Go to Options:Linetypes, make a new one and call it Squiffle (or somethig similar). Paste in the wiggly line. Modify the scale options if it's too big or small.

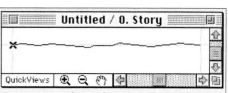

Now view your model in 3D. Save the model as a 3D Pict, with VECTORED lines and polygons. Then bring back the 3D view into the Project plan with a 'Merge' command. Now select all of the 3D view you have brought in. Double click on the line tool in the toolbox. Now select 'squiffle' for the line type.

Lo, your 3D drawing is converted into something that looks informal, even hand drawn to the casual viewer. this can be printed direct, or popped into Plotmaker.

Draw your own line in the Project Plan window, using the 2D line tool.

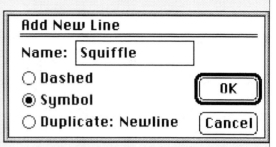

Above: Ask for a 'New' line, and click on 'Symbol'. That will allow you to paste in some lines.

Below: The line can be solid or dashed: move the little flag markers. The normal Paste command doesn't work, you have to hit the Paste Line Components button.

Right: You will have to play with 'Scale' to give the line the 'squiffliness' that you wish for.

Left: Your 3D drawing now looks more informal.

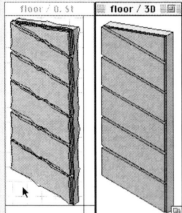

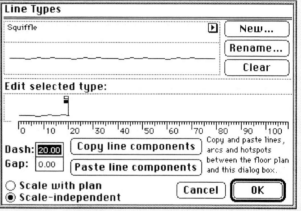

Picture Objects

PEOPLE often have trouble getting PICTURE to work - see the exercise in Discovery, called Lioness.

To remind you...

The image to be rendered has to be saved from Photoshop into **a currently loaded library**. It must be TIFF or PICT for Macs and TIFF for PCs. Some PC users recommend ticking the 'Mac tiff file format' button in Photoshop.

In the parameter box, with Macs, you must **call the file by its real name**, e.g. *tree01.tiff*, whereas with PC, you have to **omit the suffix** (and let Windows add it on for you), and write just *tree01*. This is a real pain, as archives which are ported from Mac to PC or back usually transfer parameters directly, and could result in images not rendering on the alternative platform.

Even if you use channels (for alpha channel transparency) make sure you

This street scene is easier to model by photographing the buildings and making them into picture objects. Only the building on the right is 3D modelled.

'flatten the layers'. After a modest amount of copying and pasting, a photoshop file may have generated half a dozen or more layers - which prevent the file being saved as *tiff* or *pict*.

Picture objects lie flat on the floor, so if you want it to stand up like a tree, you need to **ROTx 90** before you issue the command : such as

    ROTx 90
    PICTURE "tree01" 8.0,12.0,1
    DEL 1

When you write an archive for transfer PC to Mac or back, the Pictures used in the Picture objects do not get included - you must **copy them over separately.**

Picture objects should be 2D scripted to **make them stretchy** - it's more user friendly.

If you use tiffs on Macs (for portability to PCs) note that tiff alpha channels DO NOT WORK on AC 5.0, but they do work on 5.1 & 6.0.

For facades, it is vital to record the number of pixels horizontally and vertically, and to ensure that the proportions of the PICTURE rectangle are perfectly matching. 60 dots per metre of building is an ideal density.

Tips and Tricks

Use the GDL Manual!

MANY ArchiCAD GDL commands are covered in various sections in the GDL Cookbook. But please note that it is not the function of the Cookbook to replace the manual. You need to use both. You will find the GDL Manual a lot easier to read now you have tried the Cookbook.

Congratulations to Graphisoft on making the AC6 GDL manual better than its predecessors.

The main ArchiCAD reference manual chapter on Libraries is an essential read for anybody starting GDL, as it contains fundamental information of library object writing (which I believe ought to be in the GDL manual.)

PICT or TIFF or JPEG?

WHEN rendering textures you may be wanting to use Alpha channels – to get transparency. These have to be made in Photoshop (or similar). Save as PICT or TIFF on Mac, and TIFF on PC's. If you want to make your files truly cross platform (through saving as archive files) use only TIFFs.

These files should be saved in uncompressed form. If you apply compression such as JPEG, one of the first things to be squeezed out during compression is the alpha channel. If you are not using alpha channels, you can use a small amount of compression and can lower the colour level.

Rendering – Speed

IF the project is large, photorendering often appears faster than 3D drawing, analytic or raster. Before embarking on a VR walkabout or a flythrough animation or series of pictures, ArchiCAD tries to draw a 3D of the most recent camera used – which can take ages. It does this for good reasons – it has the effect of an integrity check on the whole model to make sure that there are no objects, pictures or textures missing.

Therefore, set up one 3D camera facing <u>away</u> from the model in Raster mode (so that it draws nothing), and immediately after, proceed with the VR or Flythrough. It will start with the rendering almost immediately.

Preview images

IT improves the presentation of your Library objects if you can give them a Preview window. If you look in the preview image in the File/Open dialog box, it always says 'No Preview'.

The answer is to render an image of your object in 200x130 resolution, select it and copy to clipboard, open project preview window and paste image; save. Now try and see if you have a preview.

This is especially good if you are making objects for other users. It will make an icon for your object.

The Digital Architect
by John Stebbins, Digital Vision, Irvine CA

SOME people think that ArchiCAD needs to do everything well. I have never believed this. It does MOST things well and as far as project THROUGHPUT is concerned, it can't be beat for most things. I believe there is no other product out there as efficient as Archicad for most of what architects do, but occasionally, we have to create spaces, objects and wierd things with lots of curves.

But, I have always maintained that the DIGITAL ARCHITECT needs a "tabouret of tools" – a chest of tools – to get the job done. Can you build a building with just a hammer?

The supplemental tools the ArchiCAD Digital Architect needs to master and to invest in, in my humble opinion are, in order of importance:

- **Photoshop** – for image manipulation and photomontage
- **FormZ** – for modelling wierd things
- **PowerPoint** – for slide show, speaker support presentations
- **Macromedia Director** – for multimedia, interactive presentations

Of course there are other tools, but as an instructor of digital architecture (UC Ivine Extension), I see these as the most important.

Everyone needs to ask themselves: how digital do I want to be? The more digital you want to be, the more of the above tools you will need to master (or have a master as part of your team).

I also believe that the more digital you are, the more 'of service' you can be to your clients, the more additional services you have to sell, the more efficient you can be, and if digital tools are properly deployed, the better architecture you can create.

How digital do you want to be?
John Stebbins

FormZ *(John Stebbins continues...)*
I have been a dealer for FormZ since 1991(and an ArchiCAD dealer since 1989) and find it is a perfect complement to ArchiCAD for modelling organic, spline-based shapes, like certain furniture, light fixtures, hyperbolic paraboloids, etc.

The way you bring these things into ArchiCAD is to use the 'Open Library Part' command, choose 'New Object' and bring the FormZ model in as an ArchiCAD object via DXF or 3D Metafile, saving it in your loaded library.

[**Editors note**: Graphisoft have launched a multimedia product combining the virtues of Powerpoint and Director. It's too soon to judge how successful this will be. There is also an interesting presentation product from Tribeworks called 'iShel'. Adobe Acrobat can also be used for building cross platform presentation.]

Roof Cutting

IN AC5 you have a choice of cutting roof edges vertical, or perpendicular to the surface. With AC6, you can do more. Just Alt-click on a roof, and then hold the mouse button down on a roof edge until the menu pops up. You now get an option that looks like an XACTO knife blade – with which you can customise the cutting angle of the edge.

Tips and Tricks

Use your BODY!

YOU may have noticed that all autoscripted library objects in ArchiCAD put the BODY -1 command after all PRISMs, MESH and other 3D commands. BODY -1 ensures the integrity of the preceding group of 3D commands. It is not essential for user scripted routines, but 3D GDL is more reliable if you use BODY -1; especially the troublesome TUBE command.

Recording contract drawings, long term

Duane Valencia writes:

I have been RECORDING the sets that go out by writing PLOT files instead of duplicate layouts. I find this a bit safer and more efficient. Safer in that 3 years from now, I don't have to worry about backwards compatibility with plotmaker. I don't even need plotmaker to do the plotting.

Theo de Klerk writes:

SECOND that! We keep a copy of the PLT file in a folder with the date with the project folder as an electronic record of what drawings were issued. If someone asks for extra copies of a particular drawing just duplicate the PLT files and drop them all in the spool folder – very quick!

Editor's Note: Another question is, which media is safest for long term storage. At the time of writing, it seems CD is guaranteed the longest life into the future. Ferromagnetic media (zip/tape/disk) have a limited life, as do the mechanisms. DVD is still undergoing development of standards.

True Line weights in 2D

YOU can set up the Pen pallette to give you different colours, and you can set up the line weight too, in millimetres or points. But they persistently remain as hairlines, no matter how much you zoom in. The answer to this perplexing problem is to look at the Options; Display Options.. menu where, if you set 'True line weights', they suddenly work. You need to be pretty settled on the scale that you will be printing at; now that you have set *absolute* thicknesses, the *relative* line weights will change if you change the drawing scale.

Stationery File – keep your settings

YOU want to preserve all your hard won material, layer and line settings for the next project? On the Mac, you can save a 'Stationery file'. Take a COPY of a file that has all the ideal settings, linetypes, layers and materials. Clear all stories, clear all objects – so that the file is empty. Save it as 'AC_template', or some such name. Back in the Finder, Get_Info on the file, and tick the 'Stationery' checkbox, and Lock it. When this file is next opened, it will offer you a new untitled window, retain all your preferred settings, but not altering your original template.

If your project has already started, you can use the 'Merge' command to bring in another template file that already has the Pen settings etc that you want.

Desktop Printing

Glenn Lym <grlym@well.com> writes:

I have found that disabling desktop printing for my HP455CA on macs has eliminated an occasional, random freeze that we would get on our two workstations. This is a known bug. You don't need desktop printing to use the HP plotter when using the postscript RIP (and not necessary when going directly from AC, Plotmaker or PlotFlow). To disable desktop printing (assume you don't have other printers that need it), turn off 'desktop print spooler' and 'desktop PrintMonitor' extensions from inside the Extensions Manager.

Pens changing when opening dwg files

From: Matthew J. Pastula <mpastula@saed.kent.edu>

I recently opened a dwg file from AutoCAD 14 on the PC side and it changed all the standard pens and colors all around. I really liked the default settings before I opened this file. Is there any way to get the pens and colors back without reloading ArchiCAD?

Duane Valencia writes:

THERE are a couple of ways to achieve this...

1. If you have an old file that has the pens you want... Just open it. Then start a new drawing. This new drawing will maintain the pens from the previous drawing and then become part of the new file.

2. If you like the factory presets... hold the option(alt) key down and choose NEW & RESET from the file menu. This will bring all defaults back to factory.

If you are asking how you get this AUTOCAD file to use your old pen setup... then just copy all the elements from the .dwg file and paste into one of the scenarios above. The pens will remain as they were defined for the blank file.

CAUTION: this means the pen weights will also be "preset" and may make your dwg elements different from that intended.

Transferring favourite settings

from Daniel Lindahl to Brian:

I and a lot of others got used to the pallette in AC5 and dislike the seemingly random default pallette that came with AC6.

Colours don't automatically affect line thicknesses, but from within the colour pallette you can change the default line thicknesses for any given pen number.

When I first discovered this after already having begun a new plan file in AC6, I managed to transfer my preferred colour and line thickness set up to this file in the following way:

1) open an old file that has your preferences.

2) from there open a new (blank) document. This will then have your pallette preferences.

3) merge the file with the "wrong" colour pallette into this open blank file. It will now have your preferences.

4) save this as [filename] of "wrong colour" file to overwrite it.

Tips and Tricks
Making scripted objects stretchy or squeezy

THIS topic is addressed in several of the Cookbook exercises, but in a nutshell, here are some guidelines.

• Make the width and depth of the object dependent on 'A' and 'B' in the 3D script.

• Your 2D script, which will either be scripted or based on a PROJECT2 must include HOTSPOT2's based on A and B.

For example, in one rectangular object:	For another example, in a concentric rectangular object:
HOTSPOT2 0,0	HOTSPOT2 -A/2,-B/2
HOTSPOT2 A,0	HOTSPOT2 A/2,-B/2
HOTSPOT2 A,B	HOTSPOT2 A/2, B/2
HOTSPOT2 0,B	HOTSPOT2 -A/2, B/2
RECT2 0,0, A,B	RECT2 -A/2,-B/2,A/2,B/2

As long as there are Hotspots whose distance apart is equal to A and B, this routine will work. For items which are linear, you can use HOTSPOT2 0,0 and HOTSPOT2 A,0.

Because these Hotspots are dangerous (move them and your object will be distorted) you will always have to use Cmd-D to move them. It is better to plant additional hotspots at places where it is safe to pick the object up.

If stretchiness is a big feature, plant a **2D crosshair** at the A,B points (LINE2 A-0.02,0,A+0.02,0:LINE2 0,A-0.02,0,A+0.02)

Compression Advice

WHEN you save an Flythrough or VR file using Quicktime, you will be offered the chance to set options for compression. Quicktime is not only about digital video, it also contains 'CODECs' which are algorithms for COmpression and DECompression.

The listed types in AC6.0 are: Animation, BMP, Cinepak, Component Video, DV-NTSC, DV-PAL, Graphics, H.263, Intel Indeo Video 4.4, Motion JPeg A, Motion JPeg B, Photo-JPeg, Planar RGB, Sorenson Video, and Video.

The most commonly used are Animation, Cinepak and JPEGs. 'Cinepak' achieves astonishing compression, but has a serious loss of quality, and can take too long for the movie to decompress as it is read in from disk. I use 'Animation' most often. You also have a slider bar from Worst quality to Maximum quality. If you haven't got a problem with disk space (for example you are saving to Jaz cartridge or to CD), my advice is to set the slider to Maximum quality, or to No compression at all.

There is a balance to be achieved – with no compression, the disk (or CD) can be too slow to deliver the frames – if there is some compression, the disk can deliver faster, but then you need a fast processor to decompress each frame. A smaller frame size (320x240) and a slower frame rate (16fps instead of 24fps) will also help the speed.

Servers with Teamwork – try iMac!

THERE has been discussion about getting Teamwork functions to work swiftly with a file server during Send and Receive. The key isn't just the speed of transmission, but how fast ArchiCAD takes to process the changes. There is as little as 10% difference between 10base-T (normal ethernet) and 100-base-T even though 100-base-T sends files 10 times faster. Ultra fast SCSI or IDE give the biggest speed increases over computers with normal disks, even if equipped with fast processors.

One cost saving solution that surprised many: *John Zdralek writes:*

"Are you running ACTW on a Mac network and are *NOT* currently using a G3 for a server? Here's a tip. Buy an iMac. The best $1,199 you will ever spend.

I was using a PM7200/120 as a server on a 100bT Ethernet Network. Opening an 8.2mb ACTW file with a 200mb library on a G3/300 client took 5 minutes, 48 seconds. Two weeks ago I bought and setup the iMac as the office server, (running plain old appletalk, NOT appleshare). Are you ready? Same file and library, opening on the same G3/300 client: 1 min 47 seconds! OK, so you think, "but we need a REAL workhorse for our server. The imac is only 233mz and has an IDE drive." Check out this test – I ALSO setup a G3/300 minitower WITH Ultra Wide SCSI drive as the server, and opened the SAME file on the G3/300 client desktop. The elapsed time to open: 1 min 40 seconds!!! I am VERY glad I saved $1,100.00, (PLUS the cost of a monitor) by buying the iMac."

Wirelines in Rendering
Aaron Sills<lucid@ihug.co.nz>

SOMEONE mentioned wanting to produce wireframe within a rendered view.

Save a hiddenline view as 2D elements (2DL) and then render the exact same view and save that as a tiff or pict. Lay the lines directly over the top of the rendering in Plotmaker. This gives a rendering that is a bit more graphic (for want of a better word) because of the outlines. The 2DL can be edited before putting it into Plotmaker to remove any lines that aren't needed in the final image (all those extra lines on 3D people for example).

Tracing Scans

MUCH could be written on this. I believe that you are better tracing into ArchiCAD yourself, so you selectively draw what is significant information. For mechanised tracing, CorelDraw (with CorelTrace) is highly recommended, if set to 'centreline trace'. Bitmap scans cause an unpleasant slow down in AC, and should be deleted as soon as possible after tracing, or moved to an invisible layer, or storey.

If the map you are scanning from has a grid (e.g. UK Ordnance Survey maps have a 100metre grid), set the ArchiCAD grid to the same grid. Rotate the scan until it is level with the grid. Then you can stretch the scan. To keep the scan in

proportion, tweak the top right corner away, then return it to the previous location, hit Alt-A (which locks the diagonal angle of the scan, and then you can stretch or shrink it, knowing that the scan retains the correct proportions. You might have to do this several times.

If you can get a site plan that is already vectorised – e.g. a UK Ordnance Survey map in .dwg format, you can use the 'Find and Select by pen colour number' to reduce the multitude of layers to just a few, such as building outlines, building names, kerbs, levels etc. When all colours are copied over, delete all the original layers.

Tips and Tricks
Bounding Boxes in 2D

THERE are occasions when even DNC uses the conventional method of making Library objects using walls and slabs. I often make composite objects using GDL objects previously made. (By this method, you get the correct syntax with the CALL command.)

ArchiCAD puts Hotspots at the 'bounding box' of the object – which can be a nuisance if the object is very complex or curvy, as it may not relate to the real object's position. It also fills the Project plan with undesired Hotspots which show up when you marquee another object. You also get one at the centre point of the bounding box.

If the 2D view of the object is just a 2D Symbol, you should put one hotspot at the origin of the symbol window, then put hotspots on the real points that you want hotspotted. Turn off 'bounding box' hotspots in the Library object box, and save. The bounding box will go. In AC5, you have to put a hotspot at the Origin of the 2D symbol window (even for a scripted object) before it will obey the command to hide the bounding box.

In AC6, 2D symbols have fallen into disuse. Autoscripted objects generate many scripted Hotspots, so you can more readily turn off the bounding box.

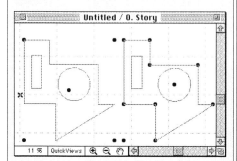

Object on left is what ArchiCAD gives you. But you can change it to the one on the right.

Batch Rendering Stills

YOU can make several camera layers in the camera settings box. Make one layer called 'overnight images'. Set up in this layer a no. of camera positions in views that you need. Make sure that 'Photorendering settings' are all correct. Before you go home or to bed, start up a Flythrough, set to *render Keyframes only*. Turn off the screen and forget it.

Next morning, you have a disk full of images that you would never have had the patience to wait for in the daytime.

Animation / Flythroughs

Flythroughs (or drivebys or what ever) can be good but can also become boring. It take hours or days of computer processing to produce just a minute or two of the 'witches broomstick' flying effect. But just think... the TV and film industry has accustomed us to pans and zooms, cuts to another scene, or from face to face. You could do better to stitch together a series of shorter clips.

Some collected Tips and Tricks on effective animation:

• Use Storyboards and plan your final animation before touching the camera tool. Most viewers get bored quickly, so think of some variety.

• Use recognisable items (for example a fountain) in views so that the viewer does not get disorientated.

• Look at varying the speed at which you 'fly' (vary the distance between cameras.)

• Compile the animation first with only 3 or 5 'tweens' per keyframe to make sure you like the route.

• Dropping the camera and zooming into a building is much more effective than the orbiting or landing by helicopter effect.

• Zooming could mean having a series of cameras getting closer to the object (with the target fixed on the object). But if you place two cameras in identical location and target, you can have one set on a zoom angle of 90 degrees, and the other on 30 degrees. With 20 frames in between, you have an effective zoom. Because the perspective doesn't change, it seems smoother.

• Avoid making the target switch about crazily – as you zoom towards something or orbit around it, make all the cameras share the same target location.

• At least one level if not more of Anti-Aliasing is essential, otherwise thin objects flash on and off erratically.

• Overall don't try and create the animation in one go. Use some video editing software and include stills and photographs to get your point across.

• Adobe Premiere is good but there is shareware quicktime editing software on the web if you look. MoviePlayer 2.51 for the Mac allows no-cost movie editing.

• Blending or 'morphing' one still image to another still image using Premiere or Director will give you several seconds of animation with negligible toil.

• You could use something like Director for final assembly.

• VR walkabouts can be more interesting than a flythrough because they are interactive – take less space on disk – are easier to download from web pages – can be combined with real photographic environments.

• It is becoming more commonplace to view animations on CD on a computer than on VHS. So don't worry so much about getting it onto tape.

• Save animations multi-platform & write CD's in hybrid format so that Macs and PCs can share the fun.

• If you use animation resolution bigger that 320X200, then it is going to take longer to render and it will display more slowly off the CD.

• Save the animation sequence in 'PICS' files on the Mac, and 'Sequence targa' files on the PC; this way, they are "in the bank" even if the machine crashes later. 'PlayBack' is good at joining PICS files together.

• Avoid over compression – gives you fast delivery, but poor image quality.

• Avoid zero compression – best image quality, but if your flythrough is coming from a CD, it will be leaving out many frames in its effort to keep up.

• If you use Sound, try it several times, including from CD. Set Sound to be the device which determines speed of display. Broken or missing images are not as bad as broken or missing sound.

• Make your objects Location Aware so that they are 'simple' when distant from the camera – and Rebuild Each Frame. The time of rebuilding is saved by the vast reduction in polygons and light fittings..

Tips and Tricks
Vertical Stretchy Objects – zzyzx

O NE innovation of ArchiCAD 6.x is to permit GDL users to provide a quick way to enter heights of objects without having to open the settings box. With AC5 and with window/door making, you can use B for the height, so you can make the object vertically stretchy. 'zzyzx' is the new way of entering heights, if you use them as the height parameter, ArchiCAD will give special treatment to it.

Amusingly, the GS team spelt ZZYZX in the final english language manual, but I gather it did't cause much amusement in Budapest after thousands had been printed.

I quote some recent correspondence on the Internet which brought me a special email from Budapest - read on.

Lazlo Vertesi of Graphisoft-HU wrote in ArchiCAD-Talk,
Page 210 of the 6.0 GDL reference is wrong. Stretching in 3D in AC 6.o requires that the LAST additional parameter is named 'ZZYZX'.

David N-C replied,
Ha Ha!! Do I guess that some of your programming team used to play the famous game 'Collossal Cave'?? Wasn't that was the password to get from the Sapphire room back to the House in the Forest??? (and back down again)

Lazlo Sparing of Graphisoft-HU replied,
Dear David, I was the fool who suggested this stupid name for this standard parameter. I looked for a unique name which doesn't make any old library part obsolete. Names like Z, ZZ, ZVALUE, ZPARAM etc. can be used anywhere in the ArchiCAD world, but I hope, this name is strange enough, difficult to remember, and that's why ideal for the above goal.

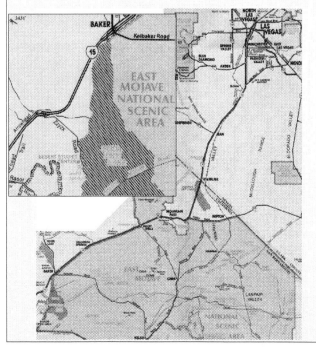

W hat is ZZYZX? – The enclosed picture shows you the solution: a guide-post in California, close to the Mojave desert. If you drive from Los Angeles to Las Vegas, you can find it. I've never been in this village(?), but its name was so strange, I made a short video about it. The picture was digitized from this film. So, no computer game, only a short visit to the city of Casinos after a conference.
>Best Regards, Laszlo Sparing, CTO, Graphisoft R&D

To which I replied, firstly to the effect that I was gathering that almost everybody who works for Graphisoft seems to be christened Lazlo, but secondly, I have actually driven a car through the Mojave desert from LA to LV, and although I didnt see that sign, I noted that there is a lot of wierdness out there - and it doesn't surprise me if there's someone trying to make their town the last in the alphabet.

Postscript
ZZYZX is good and bad....

Good in that it's quick to enter new heights; objects viewed in the 3D window get high level hotspots and are vertically stretchy.

Bad, in that they are not stretchy in the section view, and the height displayed in the info box is an absolute not a relative height, so if you enter a new altitude for the object which is higher than the zzyzx factor, the object finishes up inverted!

Protecting your Scripts

I F you wish to protect your scripts, you may try saving your Library objects as Binary..... bad idea!! they lose all parametric qualities.

There is no easy fix for this within the legal syntax of GDL. However, if you talk nicely to the Graphisoft distributor in the country of your residence, and make out a case that you are writing objects and wish to protect your code, they do have a little application that is only about 25k, that they can send you. Run it, and select the object you wish to protect, and it will do it. The object is fully parametric, but if someone tries to read your scripts, they are politely told that the scripts are unavailable.

However, there is no unprotect or undo command, and you must be sure to do it to a copy!!

My recent information is that this has not been extended to AC 6.x so will only hide the 3D and 2D scripts.

Tips and Tricks

Rendering – textures

MOST of the material definitions in ArchiCAD are in surfaces of a non specific nature with attributes like colour, transparency and reflectivity applied, but no texture - for Example 'Whitewash' and 'Stainless Steel'. A number of them also include textures - for example 'Grass' and 'Pine Shiny'. In renders, these untextured surfaces are prone to look posterised with areas of slightly wierd shading - disturbingly visible in VR panoramas.

My tip here is to apply textures to most of the surfaces you use, even when the texture you apply is largely a little square of nothing (just white). With Photoshop, you can introduce the tiniest bit of 'Noise' to make sure that there is something in the little white square. The bit map can be a tiny tile as there is zero grain in the tile.

You can still set attribute like shininess, transparency. But the main point is that you seem to get better play of light over the surface.

Alpha Channels – Another tip is to have a hard look at these. If you have a wall panel perforated with holes, that would be a very complicated GDL task to model the holes, and would add to the rendering load (all those polygons!!) By using a texture that is just a Bitmap with an alpha channelled hole in it, and making that into a material, you can apply the material to solids and they look completely perforated. It's great for trees, hedges and shrubberies! Use it for wire netting, wired glazing, venetian blinds.

Building Slabs to use for GDL

THE easiest way to make a list of XY locations for a GDL Prism, Ruled, Revolve, or even the pathway of a TUBE may be to draw a piece of floorslab in the project plan, make it into an object, and then copy and paste the XY's.

Have 'snap to small-grid' turned on if you want to avoid millionths of a metre dimensions. ALWAYS set a part of the slab on the origin of the main Project, so that you can delete all the autoscripted clutter, including any ADD offsets.

DWG Export advice

jawar3@earthlink.net writes:

WHEN opening an ArchiCAD generated building cross section in AutoCad R14, the windows came in as blocks which could not be exploded for editing.

Duane Valencia <VFrontiers@aol.com> writes:

IN light of our conversation of PURGING LAYERS, I recommend the following sequence BEFORE sending out DWG's....

1. Create Layer Set for dwg export.
2. Change to HAIRLINES and no wall fills (unless they are needed).
3. Export to .dwg.
4. Import back into ArchiCAD w/ EXPLODE BLOCKS INTO ELEMENTS selected.
5. PURGE unused layers by the method previously discussed.
6. RE-export to dwg over the previous file.
7. ZIP the file for emailing.

Memory Management

THESE days RAM is so cheap, there is no point trying to struggle along with 16 or 24 megs. 'Slam in the Ram', I say!

However, if you are still struggling – for example doing a long VR render and anxious to avoid having to run out of RAM on the last panorama - two small tips can be used. Options/Preferences/Data Safety gives you the chance to reduce the number of Undo steps, which normally force AC to allocate quite a lot of RAM for the purpose. Turn off virus checkers and your desktop picture if RAM is critically short. Forget lights and shadows - you have no hope without enough RAM. Ensure that your model does not have excessive polygons, textures or picture objects.

Macs can use Virtual RAM, and with MacOS 8.x, this can be used efficiently. The ideal arrangement is 50% more than your real RAM. For a 64 meg machine, increase it to 96meg with VMemory.

Ignore the ArchiCAD warning against using VM, it is officially obsolete with OS8+.

In Windows, memory allocation is managed differently.

DWG Import - Layers

IF you do this you find that you inherit all the AutoCAD layers which need to be changed or at least you have to create all new layers for your drawing - not to mention all the default settings for everything has to be reset. This is very time consuming. Any ideas?

Open that AutoCAD I/O config file (using a text editor) and go to the Layer Convert section. Follow the directions to 'automatically convert layers'.

Also, if your imported file has a bunch of layers with nothing on them do the following...

- Open dwg file into ArchiCAD
- Select all (make sure no layers are locked first)
- Copy
- CLEAR all layers (in layer dialog box)
- PASTE back all the elements; only the needed layers remain.

If you want the whole DWG file in a simpler layer arrangement of your own making, make a layer for the 2D-dwg, a Layer for the Text-dwg. Now click in the 2D lines button in the tools pallette and

Select-All. All lines will respond and you can move them to the 2D-dwg. Do the same for round/wavy 2D lines. Now click in the text button, select-all and move to the text layer.

Now hide those two layers. If anything remains visible, move it to a layer of your choice.

When this is done, go to Layer settings and Clear all the imported AutoCAD layers except your two new ones.

3D DXF/DWG Conversion

IF you open one of these files directly into ArchiCAD's Project plan window, you invariably end up with a set of 2D lines.

If you want to use the 3D information in the file you need to bring it in as a library part. Go to "File", then "Open library part". Click on the pop up menu of file types and choose either DXF or DWG as the file type you wish to open. This will bring in the file as a single 3D entity. By the way, you may be surprised by how big it is, and you will find the result virtually uneditable, as it could contain thousands of lines. The DXF will have been converted into the more obscure GDL commands like VERT, EDGE and PGON.

DXF's are big Text Files and DWG are Binary, but Macs can read them from PC disks without any pain.

Tips and Tricks
Triangulating Polygons

Michael Hohmann wrote (7 Oct 98)

ON the bottom of the Tools menu in AC6 is a command "Triangulate Selected Polygons" for which I find no explanation in the Reference Guide. What is it good for?

Matiu Carr replied (8 Oct 98)

It will split any selected polygons (ie. the faces that make up walls and slabs, etc) so that they are made up of a bunch of three sided polygons (ie. triangles). This is useful for a number of things.

1. Faces with holes are problematic for many renderers, or file formats.

2. Sometimes you get problems with hidden line algorithms when you have long polygons intersected and wrapping about other objects. The rendering procedure can incorrectly "layer" polygons in the resulting 2D image. Splitting these large polygons to more simple smaller ones can help alleviate this problem.

3. A three sided polygon is guaranteed to be a legitimate planar surface. Some surface generating algorithms will happily create 4 or more sided figures where the vertices are non-coplanar. This can cause trouble in some renderers, and with some exchange formats.

What is (or was) Visual GDL? ... and coloured script

PEOPLE often ask me if they should use Visual GDL instead of learning GDL. VGDL is (was) an elemental 3D modelling environment – where you build objects with stretchy primitives (cubic, cylindrical, conical shapes etc). As you add shapes you can lift them to position, and rotate or resize to fit. The 3D script is updated as you do each manoevre. It writes totally unstructured code – for each primitive in the library part, the script goes from the origin to a location, draws a primitive, and then Dels back to the origin.

With AC6.0, Graphisoft dropped Visual GDL (and I think nobody bought VGDL) because you can now edit and build in 3D, and could more easily build furniture and building components in AC6.0. If Graphisoft in the future sell a separate GDL writing engine, I and many others who get by with only one dongle will be quite delighted.

In particular, I do wish that Graphisoft would bring back a good feature of VGDL, which was **coloured script**. Commands one colour, comments another, variables and numerals another – it is common to other languages like C++, and helps the programmer in both writing and debugging.

Tips and Tricks – Memory Settings

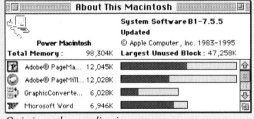

Quitting other applications releases more memory!

GDL *per se* requires very little memory, but Rendering, especially with shadows or with VR panoramas requires a lot of memory.

IF you start making beautiful tubular structures now that you have learnt GDL, you will notice that rendering and shadow representations are slowed, even when you have tried hard to reduce excessive detail and smooth curvature. At some point, ArchiCAD may even pack up with insufficient memory to complete the rendering.

On Macs, it is easy.

MAKE sure first that you have enough memory. Then 'Get Info...' on the ArchiCAD application Icon, and enter a Minimum and a Preferred size for ArchiCAD. Always leave more than 10megs free for System.

Activities like Printing, File sharing and Quick draw 3D rendering take place in the System memory, OUTSIDE of the memory used by ArchiCAD. Leave enough!

On PCs, it is more complex – beware!

1. **QUIT** all applications, use the Run... command from the Windows Start Menu, type in 'Regedit', and click 'OK'.

2. Double-Click 'HKEY_CURRENT_USER'. Double-click 'Software'. Double-click 'Graphisoft'. Double-click 'ArchiCAD'.

3. Double-click 'Fixed Partition' and change value from 0 to 1. Quit Regedit.

4. Run ArchiCAD briefly, then close it again.

5. Repeat operation 1. and 2. again.

6. Now you see something called 'Partition Size'. Double-click. Change it to Decimal with the button, then enter an amount of RAM to allocate to ArchiCAD. Try not to exceed 112megs.

7. Quit Regedit, and run ArchiCAD. If it doesn't run, you may have given it too much memory; repeat the whole operation with a smaller number. Windows needs at least 16megs.

8. If it's gone very wrong, you may have to re-instal ArchiCAD!

GDL Syntax – PUT, GET and NSP

Theory

IN the GDL manuals PUT&GET are explained in a way that requires considerable perseverance to understand. Even when you 'sort-of' understand it, it is very difficult to work out what you could use them for.

The Voyager course starts off with these, by the use of examples. If you are to do anything ambitious with GDL it is essential to learn the use of PUT and GET, and you will then use it frequently – because it reduces the risk of errors. You need to learn Put&Get to use TUBE. It is also useful in solving difficult COONS and MESH problems.

ArchiCAD allows you to use an area of memory as a temporary store (or buffer) to hold numbers. The amount

seems to be related to the total amount of RAM allocated to AC.

PUTting into the memory buffer is a bit like pushing tennis balls through a one way tube.

Every time you use a **'PUT item'** command, that item gets put in the tube. Everytime you issue a **GET(1)** command, the number that has been stored longest is popped out of the far end of the tube. GET(3) would get 3 items. GET(NSP) empties the entire buffer. **NSP** is a variable (number of stored points) that tells you how many numbers are stored in the buffer.

Sadly, you cannot store strings (text) in the buffer.

Print x=NSP is a way of finding how many numbers are stored. If the points for a Plane are stored in the buffer then there are 3 numbers for each point – the number of points in the Plane will be NSP/3.

The numbers in the buffer are stored with commas between each one. So when you get them out, they are in the perfect condition to drop straight into a PRISM or EXTRUDE statement and produce a 3D result. For example, if the buffer contains alternating X and Y points for a prism, the statement,
```
PRISM NSP/2,0.5,
        GET(NSP)
```
will produce a prism.

Put and Get Practical: 1

Object

This is the •first• exercise in the Voyager course, because it is vital to master this technique for most of the later exercises. First, we modify an existing library object. Then we look at how the PUT buffer works.

```
! Name    : temp
! Date    : Wednesday,May 5,1999
! Version : 6.00
! Written by ArchiCAD
!
MULX   A/  8.599127
MULY   B/  5.354173
MULZ   ZZYZX/   0.2
ADD       0.012093,5.922268,0.2
RESOL  36
GLOB_SCRIPT_TYPE =    3
GLOB_CONTEXT =       3
GLOB_SCALE      100
GLOB_NO                    90.0
GLOB_F
GLOB_
GLOB_
GLOB_
GLOB_                      .259
GLOB_                     .035
GLOB_TA              89.381
GLOB_TARG            184.934
GLOB_TARG              1.7
GLOB_HSTORY_HEIGHT =     2.9
!!Slab-001
PEN       1
ADDZ     -0.2
GLOB_LAYER = "Floors"
GLOB_ID = "Slab-001"
GLOB_INTID =    3
BODY     -1
cPRISM_ "Pine","Pine","Pine",
          7,     0.2,
  -0.012093,   -0.568094,   15,
  -0.012093,   -5.922268,   15,
   5.991071,   -5.922268,   15,
   5.991071,   -3.618351,   15,
   8.587034,   -3.618351,   15,
   8.587034,   -3.196507,   15,
  -0.012093,   -0.568094,   -1
BODY     -1
DEL      1
```

This is what your Auto-scripted 3D Script looks like

Modifying Library Objects: this script was first looked at in the Discovery Course.

```
! Name :temp - Edited small

ADD   0.012093,5.922268,zzyzx
PEN   1
ADDZ    -zzyzx
MATERIAL "Pine"
PRISM 7, zzyzx,
  -0.012,  -0.568,
  -0.012,  -5.922,
   5.991,  -5.922,
   5.991,  -3.618,
   8.587,  -3.618,
   8.587,  -3.197,
  -0.012,  -0.568
DEL TOP
```

This is what it looks like after pruning. The maskings (15) have been removed and the PRISM_ reduced to a PRISM.

Editing the Script

As you did with 'Modify Library Object', make a simple form with a piece of floorslab and turn it into a Library Object. Now, instead of modifying it as in the middle panel, use copy and paste to modify it as in the right hand panel. You can put the word PUT at the start of the list of XY locations; ensure that you do not change the comma positions.

Why do this?? Well you can prove it to yourself by inserting some extra XY locations somewhere in the middle of the list. Ensure that you maintain the flow of commas. What you find is that the Prism continues to work. This is because the number of points in the Prism is recalculated each time. As the number of stored points (NSP) is the X and Y of each prism-point, then the number of prism-points must be NSP/2.

```
! Name :temp - Edited PUT+GET

ADD   0.012093,5.922268,0
PUT -0.012, -0.568,
    -0.012, -5.922,
     5.991, -5.922,
     5.991, -3.618,
     8.587, -3.618,
     8.587, -3.197,
    -0.012, -0.568
MATERIAL "Pine"
PRISM NSP/2, zzyzx,
     GET(NSP)
DEL TOP
```

Now edited using PUT and GET

The number of points in the PRISM (7) has been replaced with NSP/2

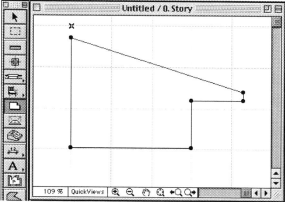

Put and Get Practical: 2

PUT and GET analysed

This exercise shows how the PUT and GET commands work. The Print command displays what is in the buffer. PUT and GET will become a favourite technique with you, once learnt.

PUT&GET is a form of single dimensional array, but seriously volatile! When you use it, it evaporates.

PRINT This routine will issue print dialogue boxes which show you how the data is stored in the buffer. It's a bit annoying, but keep pressing 'Continue', and you can see the buffer contents reducing as each block is generated. You are unlikely to put this into a Project plan, but if you do, put in a Project2 command for the 2D.

NSP (Number of Stored Points) shows the total number of items remaining in the buffer, and as you GET groups of numbers out of the buffer, the NSP reduces. You do not need to know how many items are in the buffer. NSP knows how many there are.

When you PUT a string of data in, you must separate each item with a comma. When the PUT buffer is used for a Prism, GDL puts commas in all the correct places when it GETs the numbers.

One thing you cannot do is to say **FOR k=1 TO NSP**, because the value of **NSP** is dynamically reducing in value every time you issue a GET command. But you can say **REPEAT... .... UNTIL NSP<=0** if you wish to.

USE() command enables you to use the contents of the buffer without destroying it, so it can be used again. It's only useful when you USE the whole contents of the buffer.

Applications: The Staircase, later in the book, is a good demonstration of the situation where you MUST KNOW HOW TO USE the Buffer. It is made with a **PRISM**; if it is to be a parametric stair, you can use a **FOR...NEXT** loop to store the points. Then, with a **GET(NSP)** command (as above) you get the stair drawn for you.

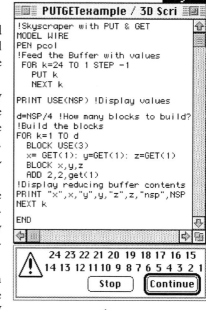

```
PUTGETexample / 3D Scri
!Skyscraper with PUT & GET
MODEL WIRE
PEN pcol
!Feed the Buffer with values
 FOR k=24 TO 1 STEP -1
   PUT k
   NEXT k

PRINT USE(NSP) !Display values

d=NSP/4 !How many blocks to build?
!Build the blocks
FOR k=1 TO d
  BLOCK USE(3)
  x= GET(1): y=GET(1): z=GET(1)
  BLOCK x,y,z
  ADD 2,2,get(1)
!Display reducing buffer contents
PRINT "x",x,"y",y,"z",z,"nsp",NSP
NEXT k

END
```

```
24 23 22 21 20 19 18 17 16 15
14 13 12 11 10 9 8 7 6 5 4 3 2 1
          [ Stop ]   [ Continue ]
```

Put and Get Practical: 3

Modify Library Object again

In this exercise, you should make •two• slabs: and then with PUT and GET, you can make a RULED command which connects them. Each polygonal piece of slab must have the same number of points.

Clean the script up as in exercise 1, and you should have two prisms. Remove the end XYM (X-location, Y-location, Mask) point of each prism (because it is a repeat of the first point). Copy and paste the two lists of XYM values to become part of a PUT command, as in the script window here. Make sure that you organise your commas correctly. PUT must be followed by a continuous flow of numbers that are separated by commas, but must end with NO comma.

Now replace all the 15's for the first prism with zero's - this is a status value, but could also be thought of as the height. Now replace the 15's in the second prism with a height. In this case, I have changed them to 12 – in RULED, this last number is not a masking value, but means a height – in this case 12 metres.

You get interesting effects if you deliberately move the X,Y locations on one step, and then tweak the masking value from 63 to something else - see illustration, right. Try it.

```
slabshape / 3D Script
! Name    : slabshape
! Date    : September, 1998
! Version : 5.10
! Written by ArchiCAD

MULX A/ 39.0141
MULY B/ 35.7016
MULZ V_SCALE/ 0.1
ADDZ 0.18
ADD 0.0, 0.0, 0.0
RESOL 36
!A_ = 100
!N_ = -1
!K~ = 15.7401
!L~ = 0.763003
!M~ = 4.0
!N~ = 9.82733
!O~ = 0.755212
!P~ = 4.0
!T~ = 3
!U~ = 90.0
!Q_ = 3.1
!!Slab-020
PEN 78
ADDZ -0.18
BODY -1
cPRISM_ "Zinc", "Zinc", "Zinc",
   9, 0.1,
   -19.6856,   -0.365189, 15,
   0.189559, 5.155677, 15,
   10.4952,  -7.358286, 15,
   19.3286,  -7.358286, 15,
   19.3286,  -30.5459, 15,
   -11.7723, -30.5459, 15,
   -11.7723, -15.4556, 15,
   -19.6856, -15.4556, 15,
   -19.6856, -0.365189, -1
BODY -1
DEL 1
!!Slab-021
ADDZ -0.18
BODY -1
cPRISM_ "Zinc", "Zinc", "Zinc",
   9, 0.1,
   -12.5084,   -6.780368, 15,
   2.414518,  -2.635104, 15,
   12.3074,  -14.6479, 15,
   19.2161,  -14.6479, 15,
   19.2161,  -30.5459, 15,
   -4.595192, -30.5459, 15,
   -4.595192, -15.4556, 15,
   -12.5084, -15.4556, 15,
   -12.5084, -6.780368, -1
```

```
MATERIAL "Zinc"
PEN 1

PUT -19.6856,   -0.365189,0,
   0.189559, 5.155677, 0,
   10.4952, -7.358286, 0,
   19.3286, -7.358286, 0,
   19.3286, -30.5459, 0,
   -11.7723, -30.5459, 0,
   -11.7723, -15.4556, 0,
   -19.6856, -15.4556, 0,

   -12.5084,  -6.780368, 12,
   2.414518,  -2.635104, 12,
   12.3074, -14.6479, 12,
   19.2161, -14.6479, 12,
   19.2161, -30.5459, 12,
   -4.595192, -30.5459, 12,
   -4.595192, -15.4556, 12,
   -12.5084, -15.4556, 12

RULED 8,63,
GET(NSP)
```

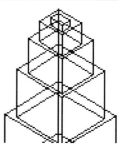

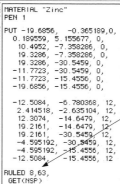

Replace Masking Values with heights, in this case zero and 12 metres

If this figure (8) is replaced with NSP/6, you would then be able to add more points or change points without difficulty.

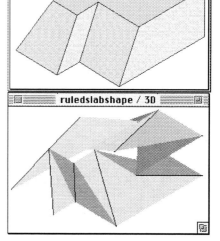

```
ruledslabshape / 3D
```

Advanced 3D Commands

TUBE

TUBE is a profoundly useful command. You can draw a section through a series of X-Y-Z points in 3D space, thus creating complex frameworks without having to use Trigonometry. TUBE does its best to work out a mitring solution at each change in the pathway.

TUBE Profile –With TUBE, you define the 2D outline, just as you do in **Extrude** or **Poly2**.

TUBE Pathways – You define a number of path points that the section must pass through – as in **Sweep**. At each joint, GDL mitres the junction.

```
!TUBE Demonstration
!Syntax:-  TUBE n,m,mask,
! section-> u1,v1,s1,...un,vn,sn,
! pathway-> x1,y1,z1,angle1,...
!        ->...xn,yn,zn,anglen
LET p=0.05  !one pixel

BODY -1
TUBE 4,5+2,63,            Note, again, the
  0,0,0,                 use of 'p' to save
  0,p,0,                 having to type in
  p,p,0,                 many zeroes.
  p,0,0,

  0 ,0  ,-p ,0, !phantom start
  0 ,0  ,0  ,0, !real start
 -p ,0  ,p*3,0,
 p*2,0 ,p*4,0,
  0 ,0  ,p*5,0,
  0 ,0  ,p*6,0, !real end
  0 ,0  ,p*7,0  !phantom end
BODY -1
```

TUBE works out its own mitres, and wierd things happen if you start trying to twist the section. For safety, always use a mitre/twist value of zero. In this example, I have used the mysterious command called BODY -1 which does an integrity check on the 3D form. It's a lifesaver with TUBE which can often display irrational errors.

```
!Display Phantom points
MATERIAL 0
  ADD 0,0,p*7
SPHERE 0.01
  DEL 1
  ADD 0,0,-p
SPHERE 0.01
  DEL 1
```

Phantom Start and End
In this script, a little ball has been placed at the Phantom Start & Phantom End points to illustrate the principle.

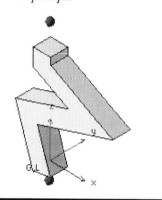

Design Problems: Because the Mitring and Rotational angle can be set with each joint, TUBE requires a Starting and Ending Direction, so it knows how to treat the start and end surfaces.

So you must position a 'Phantom Start' and 'Phantom End' point. This will correctly mitre the start and end of the tube object. You need to type in some examples to appreciate quite how it works. The example here puts a black ball at each phantom point.

The Pathway is defined in XYZ locations – a bit like in Sweep. In Sweep, the section changes by the same scale and angle change, and moves from XYZ point to XYZ point. In Tube, the section remains constant, but you can have a different twist angle, at each mitring opportunity.

TUBE works best if the section is kept simple, and is axially centred on the origin – like a cylindrical or rectangular profile.

One trick you can do is to lay out a floorslab in plan, save it as a temporary library object, and then steal the XY locations, copying and pasting them to a TUBE command. These can be the path or profile points for a Tube. this is how the Add-On 'Profiler' works.

Masking: 1=Base surface, 2=End surface, 16=Base edges, 32=End edges, 64=Cross section edges visible

TUBEA

ARCHICAD 6.x has a **TUBEA** command. It's different from TUBE, in that there is no Twist Angle involved at each junction; it is not better than TUBE, just different. The section defined is drawn onto the YZ plane using the same syntax as REVOLVE (which has to be drawn onto the XY plane), and is 'extruded' along the X axis. The section defined is the section at the mitres, so there seems to be a danger of the actual linear section changing erratically along its length if the pathway is moving a lot. What it seems best at is that if you leave the section description unclosed, it will force the section to 'grow' downwards to meet the XY plane, like a wall of changing height. The GDL manual does not explain it clearly, and it took me an hour to work out what was happening. The very interesting illustrated example is unscripted, and the scripted example carries insufficient explanation. That's the usual case for new commands – MASS, VALUES and TUBEA. But future editions of the manual and of the Cookbook will cover these powerful commands in greater detail.

TUBE+TUBEA Mental Health Warning!

TUBE causes more grief that most – because if you don't get it right, you get error messages. Once you understand it, though, you may find yourself typing in TUBE scripts with confidence. My solution is to use a series of PUT statements first to ensure that one major source of syntax errors is removed.

However, the way that the sectional outline is drawn in TUBE is verging on the irrational. It is supposed to follow the 'looking from above' rules of the other 3D elements. But then it jumps about the origin once the location points are entered. It works more reliably if the direction of the tube is mainly horizontal. A lot of trial and error may be involved to get it right. A BODY -1 command before and after the TUBE is advisable.

MESH

MESH – is limited by being applicable to rectangular entities only.

However, it is easy to use, as you only need to enter the Z – the height – of each point. Write the mesh out with all points zero at first. Set them out with the same grid as the 'n' and 'm' factors. Then try tweaking some points upwards.

```
!MESH Demonstration
!Syntax:- MESH a_width,b_length,
!          m,n,mask,
!          z11,z12,z13,z14,..z1m,
!          z21,z22,z23,z24,..z2m,
!          ...zn1,zn2,zn3,zn4,..znm
MESH 15,12,6,5,63,
     0, 0, 0, 0, 0, 0,
     0, 0, 0, 0, 0, 0,
     0, 0, 0, 0, 0, 0,
     0, 0, 0, 0, 0, 0,
     0, 0, 0, 0, 0, 0
```

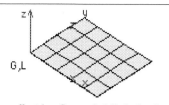

Start off with a flat mesh (all the heights at zero), then tweak the points up and down.

MESH – Try putting in some heights to tweak the terrain up and down.

Unfortunately, as you view it in the script and then in the window, the positions of the meshes appear inverted. The bottom left on the mesh is the top left in the script. The top right of the mesh is the bottom right in the script. It is as if you were viewing it from upside down.

```
!MESH Demonstration
MESH 15,12,6,5,63,
     1,0, 0, 0,0,0,
     0,0,-1, 0,0,0,
     0,0,-1,-1,0,0,
     1,0, 1, 2,2,2,
     1,2, 4, 7,6,4
```

Masking: 1=Base surface, 4=Side surface, 16=Base & side edges, 32=Top edges, 64=Top edges & surface rough.

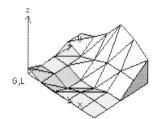

Above – it appears inverted
Below – it now appears corrected with the MULy -1 command

Hot MESH Tip!

If you precede the MESH command with a MULy -1 then the script and the object will be the same way up, and it is easy to enter heights (even though the top left corner is now at the origin).

```
!MESH Demonstration

MULy -1
MESH 15,12,6,5,63,
     1,0, 0, 0,0,0,
     0,0,-1, 0,0,0,
     0,0,-1,-1,0,0,
     1,0, 1, 2,2,2,
     1,2, 4, 7,6,4
DEL 1
```

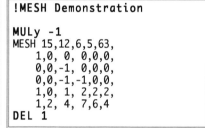

Notice that the grid is rectangular, but if a surface within a rectangle of the mesh is not planar, it is divided into two triangles, and thus can be rendered as two planar surfaces. With triangular subdivisions, ANY surface, however complex can be rendered. It could be quite useful for doing a site, but you cannot drill holes in it, or increase local detail, or vary its outline. The new MASS command of AC6.x is more useful for sites, and permits holes to be drilled.

COONS

Freeform surface making

BY defining the **XYZs** of the **corners** and **edgepoints** of a **rectangular object**, GDL will work out all the in between locations; the whole surface will be rendered as a myriad of small triangles. It can therefore adopt any shape.

The overall object need not be an exact Rectangle – it just requires 4 corners (so that it is 'quasi-rectangular'), and almost anything can happen in between. GDL interpolates and smooths all the points within the surface.

More complex surfaces can be made up with tiles of COONS elements. Sometimes the edge points are determined by mathematical procedure, not by guesswork, so for this you MUST use the PUT statement.

Masking: 4=1st boundary edge, 8=2nd boundary edge, 16=3rd boundary edge, 32=4th boundary edge, 64=Top edges & surface rough.

Now we come to one of the most intriguing 3D Commands of all – COONS. I used to theorise that this meant something like **Co-ordinated Network Surface**, but when I asked Graphisoft, it turned out to be named after a mathematician called **Robert Coons** who is admired by the programming team!

I have evolved a fairly unburstable routine for doing COONS successfully, and very rarely get an error using this method. Try this one out.

```
!COONS Demonstration
!Syntax:- COONS n,m,mask,
!    all XYZs from Point 1 to 2
!    all XYZs from Point 4 to 3
!    all XYZs from Point 1 to 4
!    all XYZs from Point 2 to 3

COONS 2,2,63+64,
     0.0, 0.0, 1.0, ! 1 to 2
     0.0, 2.0, 1.5,

     2.0, 0.0, 0.7, ! 4 to 3
     2.2, 2.4, 1.9,

     0.0, 0.0, 1.0, ! 1 to 4
     2.0, 0.0, 0.7,

     0.0, 2.0, 1.5, ! 2 to 3
     2.2, 2.4, 1.9
```

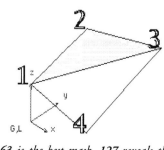

63 is the best mask, 127 reveals the triangles, and can be written as 63+64

Start with the corners only:

If you follow the rigorous discipline of Points 1 to 2, Points 4 to 3, Points 1 to 4, Points 2 to 3, then you will be able to use COONS successfully.

Once it works, then insert the interpolated points along the edge. Don't forget to increase the stated number of points on the first line of the statement.

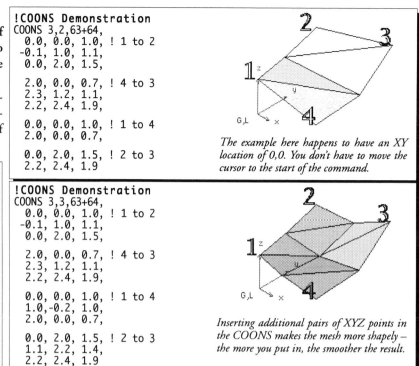

```
!COONS Demonstration
COONS 3,2,63+64,
  0.0, 0.0, 1.0, ! 1 to 2
 -0.1, 1.0, 1.1,
  0.0, 2.0, 1.5,

  2.0, 0.0, 0.7, ! 4 to 3
  2.3, 1.2, 1.1,
  2.2, 2.4, 1.9,

  0.0, 0.0, 1.0, ! 1 to 4
  2.0, 0.0, 0.7,

  0.0, 2.0, 1.5, ! 2 to 3
  2.2, 2.4, 1.9
```

The example here happens to have an XY location of 0,0. You don't have to move the cursor to the start of the command.

```
!COONS Demonstration
COONS 3,3,63+64,
  0.0, 0.0, 1.0, ! 1 to 2
 -0.1, 1.0, 1.1,
  0.0, 2.0, 1.5,

  2.0, 0.0, 0.7, ! 4 to 3
  2.3, 1.2, 1.1,
  2.2, 2.4, 1.9,

  0.0, 0.0, 1.0, ! 1 to 4
  1.0,-0.2, 1.0,
  2.0, 0.0, 0.7,

  0.0, 2.0, 1.5, ! 2 to 3
  1.1, 2.2, 1.4,
  2.2, 2.4, 1.9
```

Inserting additional pairs of XYZ points in the COONS makes the mesh more shapely – the more you put in, the smoother the result.

Hot Tip!

PUT and GET

COONS statements can get very long, and increasingly complex. The same applies to **MASS**. Once this happens the chance of errors increases.

By using a series of **PUT** statements to 'build' the coons or mass, and by using an **NSP** statement to define the number of points on the surface, you will have greater freedom to interpolate edge points.

I also use PUT and GET for most Prisms and Tubes – it reduces syntax errors.

O K! so **COONS** looks terrifying. But if you take the gradual, systematic approach demonstrated here, you can get COONS to be useful for you. It is the only way to do smooth interpolated surfaces in ArchiCAD or in GDL.

MASS

M ASS is good. MASS is very good. It is the GDL equivalent of the **Mesh tool in AC6.x**, and forms a surface from a number of X-Y-Z node locations by resolving the resulting surface into triangles. It is a great help for surface and site making.

A neat trick is to use the mesh tool direct in AC to get the basic shape worked out, then you can edit the details of the resulting MASS script in GDL. With some thought, you could generate new shapes with MASS such as trigonometrical or random surfaces, an interesting adventure to try some time.

After the opening lines of materials and masking, you first define the XYZ nodes in the boundary. Then, if you have any points within the surface, you define them as a series of small 'ridges'. As the ridges are added, the whole surface responds with yet more triangles to ensure that the whole surface will shade. By playing with the object mask, you can also show or omit the side wall (skirt) or the base, and invoke object smoothing.

The XYZ's of **Holes** are considered to be 'external points', but they need a minus 1 after the external shape, as in PRISM_holes.

```
MASS topmat, botmat, sidemat,
numbextpoints,numbintpoints,mask,skirtheight,
xe1,ye1,ze1,se1,...xen,yen,zen,sen, list of external points,
xi1,yi1,zi1,si1,...xin,yin,zin,sin, list of internal points
```

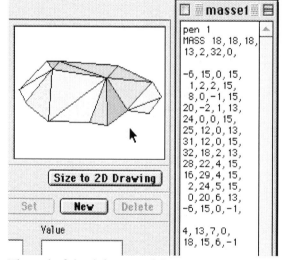

The end of the definition of the perimeter is marked by a masking code of -1, and the later XYZ definitions are ridges or points – also each ending in a -1. The overall object masking code (here, 32) can decide if the sides or bottom are to be displayed, or if the object is to appear smooth in renderings.

Masking: 1=Show base, 4=Show skirt, 16=Show edge lines for base and skirt, 32=Edge lines for top are visible, 64=Top edges visible, top surface is not smooth.

The difference between COONS and MASS in a Nutshell

C OONS makes a skin, and requires you only to describe the edges of a surface and it tries to interpolate all the other points – sometimes producing excellent results. If the surface is too complex in shape to tolerate smooth interpolation because it has more complex detail, MASS will allows you to be more prescriptive about the exact height of points, in addition to making skins or solid objects. Both are difficult to write. **MASS** has the advantage that you can build it in ArchiCAD's normal project window with the **MESH** tool, then copy it to GDL and edit to its final form. **COONS** can only be built the hard way. MASS permits holes to be drilled, or plateaux to be formed.

RULED

RULED gives you a 'tweaked' solid – whereby you lay out the plan first, and specify an equal number of points higher than the base (by their X-Y-Z location) and it will try to form the solid.

RULED is most useful, even though it lacks Polylines. You always have to start from flat on the local X-Y plane, and define the lower lines in the same way as you do for Extrude. Use Status values of zero (0).

The XYZ locations of the upper points can, theoretically be anywhere. But they should still be planar if possible. If the top is not planar, it may not draw properly.

However, you can take risks with the sides and it will subdivide the surfaces into triangles in order to make them

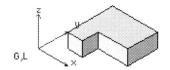

```
!RULED Demonstration
!Syntax:- RULED n,mask,
!          u1,v1,s1,...un,vn,sn,
!          x1,y1,z1,...xn,yn,zn

LET p=0.05  !one pixel
RULED 6,63,
  p  ,p  ,0,     !No polylines possible
  p  ,p*4,0,
  p*4,p*4,0,
  p*4,p*2,0,
  p*2,p*2,0,
  p*2,p  ,0,     Masking: 1=Base surface,
                   2=Top surface (if planar),
  p  ,p  ,p,       4=Side surface, 16=Edges
  p  ,p*4,p,       on planar (base) curve,
  p*4,p*4,p,       32=Edges on space curve,
  p*4,p*2,p,       64=Side edges  edges vis-
  p*2,p*2,p,       ible, object rough.
  p*2,p  ,p,
```

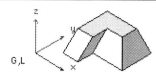

```
!RULED Demonstration
LET p=0.05  !one pixel
RULED 6,63,
  p  ,p  ,0,
  p  ,p*4,0,
  p*4,p*4,0,
  p*4,p*2,0,
  p*2,p*2,0,
  p*2,p  ,0,
                   In this case I used the
  p  ,p*2,p,       word 'LET'. This is
  p  ,p*4,p,       voluntary. If you wish
  p*3,p*4,p,       your scripts to be
  p*3,p*3,p,       rigorously correct. then
  p*2,p*3,p,       use 'LET'.
  p*2,p*2,p
```

capable of rendering.

The mask is 63 (as usual) if you want a top and bottom drawn.

This is one solid where you should NOT close the polygon. When you get to the penultimate point at the lower level, start defining the upper level.

Use a 3D 'Pixel' size

Notice a neat trick that I have used here. If you can define your smallest dimension, in this case 0.05 metres, as an 'object pixel', you can use the variable 'p' instead of typing out dozens of decimal figures.

SWEEP

SWEEP – pulls a 2D outline (defined on the X-Y plane) upwards through a series of pathway points.

SWEEP is also capable of twisting the 2D outline, and rescaling it as it passes. It also attempts to mitre the joints on the way. If the sides are not planar, it tries to divide them into triangles to get the best shading effects.

```
!SWEEP Demonstration
!Syntax:- SWEEP n,m,alpha,
!          scale,mask,
!          u1,w1,s1,...un,wn,sn,
!          x1,y1,z1,...xn,yn,zn

LET p=0.05  !one pixel

SWEEP 6,3,15,0.7,63,
  p  ,p  ,0, !Outline of section
  p  ,p*4,0,
  p*4,p*4,0,
  p*4,p*2,0,
  p*2,p*2,0,
  p*2,p  ,0,

  0  ,0, 0,   !Pathway begins
  p  ,p,p*3,
  p*2,0,p*6
```

Sweep can be erratic to control - but there are times when it is the only solution to a problem.

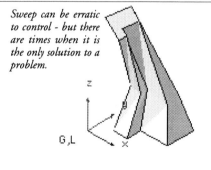

Masking: 1=Base surface, 2=Top surface, 4=Side surface, 16=Edges on base, 32=Edges on top, 64=Side edges edges visible, object rough.

PYRAMID

PYRAMID – it takes the outline (using the same syntax and status values and masking as described as in EXTRUDE) and pulls all to one point at 0,0, on the Z-line.

It is useful for building a church spire (the example in the AC 6.x manual)

```
!PYRAMID Demonstration
!Syntax:- PYRAMID n,height,mask,
!          x1,y1,s1,....xn,yn,sn
PYRAMID 9,0.3,63,
  0.00,0.00,0,
 -0.10,0.30,0,
  0.10,0.30,0,
  0.10,0.40,0,
  0.20,0.40,0,
  0.20,0.10,1000,
  0.15,0.10,0,
  0.15,0.00,0,
  0.00,0.00,-1
```

Pyramid supports Polylines

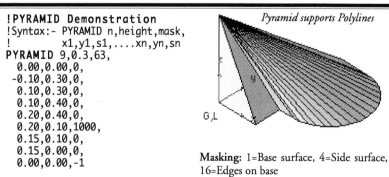

Masking: 1=Base surface, 4=Side surface, 16=Edges on base

MOST 3D commands require you to enter the **'number'** of **X-Y** coordinates in the object, e.g. RULED 6,63 means that there are 6 points on the shape, with a mask of 63. Similar rules apply to REVOLVE, SWEEP and most complex 3D forms.
Masking Values: All complex 3D commands use a Masking value for the whole object – usually 63. Each command has a different way of using these. As I have decided that the Cookbook is not intended to be a total replacement for the manual, I haven't printed the keys to these values for each and every object. This is a case for delving into the manual, where they are quite well explained.

EXTRUDE

EXTRUDE – allows you to define an outline, and then lift it to a different XYZ location. Simple as that. Along with the other similar commands, the subtle variations offered by Polylines, Status values and Masking values can help. With 63 as mask, the whole form is drawn. Extrude can give you skins or solid forms.

Masking: 1=Base surface, 2=Top surface, 4=Side (closing) surface, 16=Edges on base, 32=Edges on top

```
!EXTRUDE Demonstration
!Syntax:- EXTRUDE n,dx,dy,dz,mask,
!          x1,y1,s1,....xn,yn,sn
EXTRUDE 9+2,0,0,0.1,16+32,
   0.00,0.00,0,
  -0.10,0.30,0,
   0.10,0.30,0,
   0.10,0.40,0,
   0.20,0.40,0,
   0.20,0.10,1000,
   0.15,0.10,0,
   0.15,0.00,0,
   0.00,0.00,-1,

   0.05,0.1,900, !hole
   0.05,360,4000 !hole
RETURN
```

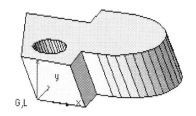

EXTRUDE – Masking value here is 63 above, all surfaces visible.

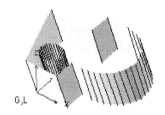

EXTRUDE – Masking value here is 0 above, only the edge surfaces visible. (Vertical lines are controlled by Status values)

Extrude vs. Prism

If you are making an object that is likely to be 2D scripted, make Prism shapes using the EXTRUDE command, not PRISM. The XY locations have the same syntax as POLY2_. Copy the 3Dscript to 2D, then convert.

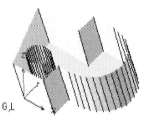

EXTRUDE – Masking value here is 1 (one) which means draw the bottom, but no top, no top or bottom edge lines. (Vertical lines are controlled by Status values)

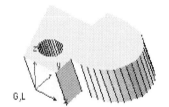

EXTRUDE – Masking value here is 2, which means draw the top surface, but omit the upper edge lines.

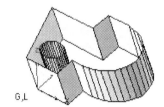

EXTRUDE – Masking value here is 32+16, which means draw neither top nor bottom, but draw the upper and lower edge lines for top and bottom.

If you have typed in the previous EXTRUDE commands, play with different ways of writing masking values. Notice that for all these examples, the same set of X-Y values are used – so you can copy and paste, then modify.

You can write masking values as single numbers, or you can use them analytically, as I have done here on the right. It will not slow the machine down to do this. It just helps you remember what you put in or left out.

You can also multiply the numbers by Booleian flags of 1 or zero, which switch the values on or off.
For example:
$32*0 + 16*1 + 8*1 + 4*0 + 2*1 + 1*0 = 27$

```
!EXTRUDE Demonstration
EXTRUDE 9+2,0,0,0.1,16+32,
   0.00,0.00,0,
  -0.10,0.30,0,
```

Analytic way of writing a masking value

SKIN (or 'LOFTER')

No, sorry, SKIN does not exist. But it ought to. If you had a SKIN command which was a combination of RULED, TUBE and SWEEP, how happy we would be. The syntax would be to state the number of points in the section, the number of pathway points, and then a sequence of Skin polygon definitions, and angle. The function would then skin the results to form a shape. My friend Oleg Shmidt has written a GDL Macro called LOFTER that does just this, although it is complex to use. Let's hope Graphisoft adopt LOFTER in a future edition.

Polylines, Status and Masking values

THESE are the very stuff of getting effective power out of the 3D commands on these pages. The basic idea of **Polylines, Status and Masking codes** is covered in **Discovery**, and if you are now a Voyager, you should by now be happy with reading more about it in the manual. The masking values for the sides of a Prism are the easiest way to start understanding Masking. Objects can have masking values too. The masking values relevant to a 3D object are different for each object; for example, in a REVOLVE, you can have the ends open or closed, whereas this would not apply to a TUBE or COONS. Many of the **Voyager** exercises illustrate ways of using Polylines, Masking and Status values.

Advanced 2D

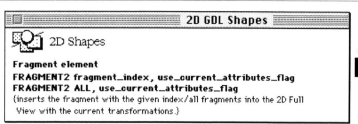

FRAGMENT2

FRAGMENT2 is a system of layering in the 2D environment of GDL.

All 2D lines, text, circles etc that you would normally draw in a 2D symbol are put into the top drawing layer, called Fragment 1. Now try this – open the 2D symbol window, click in the toolbox on the line tool and select all, it will select all the lines in the symbol. Now Cmd-T for the settings and you are offered the chance to move it all to a different layer (just like, in 3D, you can move a roof object to the Site and landscaping layer, if it is a sloping lawn). Select Fragment 2.

If you are using a complicated symbol, you might have to repeat this process for all Text, Circle and Fill objects.

Once the whole symbol is in Fragment 2, you could draw another symbol into Fragment 1, and then move it by the same process to Fragment 3. In this way, you could build up a whole series of quite different drawings or im-

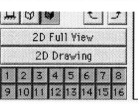

Under AC_6.0, it is a lot easier to hide and show the Fragments

ages in each fragment. You can draw directly in a fragment, but have to 'choose' that as the drawing fragment first.

In the Library part main dialog box, you will find that all fragments are normally displayed, as a series of dark or light numbered buttons. But click on the buttons (popup menus in AC5), and you find that you can select all, or one only, or any group of fragments to be displayed.

Normally when a 2D symbol is drawn, it is immediately disabled when there is an active 2D script. However, the two work together if the FRAGMENT2 command is invoked.

FRAGMENT2 in action

For a very simple example, suppose you had a Chair object that had 5 different Styles. A style might be chosen with a number, or with a value list.

For examples of the styles,
1=a stool; 2=chair with a back; 3=chair with arms and back; 4=chair with arms and back and headrest; 5=chair with arms and back and headrest and footrest.

Now if you used a PROJECT2 command, there could be an unacceptably long wait while the whole object had to be converted to a 3D plan view before it would come up in the Project Plan window.

Procedure

For AC5: Set a chair to each style, then view it in Plan, and send '3D View to Symbol'. It will go into Fragment 1.

For AC6: Place the object in the Project Plan. Configure to the required shape, select it, then Explode it. 'Cut' the resulting lines, and paste them into the 2D Symbol window of the GDL object. The pasted result will be put into Fragment 1.

Start with style 5; now select all lines in the symbol, Cmd-T (Ctrl-T for PCs) the lines and move them all to Fragment 5. Now do the same for style 4 and so on, down to 1.

In the 2D script, include a routine like this:

```
IF cstyl=1 THEN FRAGMENT2 1,1
IF cstyl=2 THEN FRAGMENT2 2,1
IF cstyl=3 THEN FRAGMENT2 3,1
IF cstyl=4 THEN FRAGMENT2 4,1
IF cstyl=5 THEN FRAGMENT2 5,1
!the 1 after the command is an
!attributes flag. Leave it as 1.
```

A practical use for FRAGMENT2...

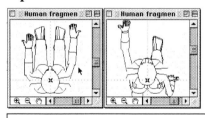

...is in my Human Figure model. It has a number of preset positions, such as running, jumping, sitting and standing. As Project2 is too slow to wait for, each pose is stored as a 2D symbol in plan view and saved into different fragments.

POLY2_A and POLY2_B

– are extensions of the POLY2 and POLY2_ statements. Simply, they give you ultimate control over the PEN colours, not just of the lines, but of the Fill and the Background colour to the Fill.

It may be my version of AC, but I have never got the BackGround Pen colour to work correctly in POLY2_B, but you can make good use of POLY2_A.

2D Scripts using CIRCLE2, RECT2 etc will be 'transparent'. If you wish your 2D objects to be opaque, e.g. furniture to show clearly over a textured floor, then you have to get a hold of POLY2_A, and Polyline syntax.

```
740:!POLY2_A & B demonstration
!Copy and paste to the 2D Script
POLY2_B 9,7,4,10,
  0.00,0.00,1,
  -0.10,0.30,1,
  0.10,0.30,1,
  0.10,0.40,1,
  0.20,0.40,1,
  0.20,0.10,1,
  0.15,0.10,1,
  0.15,0.00,1,
  0.00,0.00,1
```

SPLINE2 and SPLINE2_A

are usually the result of autoscripted 2D library objects, and it may take you longer than it is worth to make parametric splines based on typing in coordinates.

If it had some equivalent command in 3D, it would be more useful.

Fragment Tester

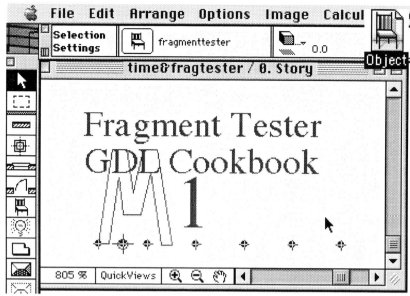

THIS EXERCISE takes the cover off the mystery of how to use the FRAGMENT2 command. It also demonstrates the use of the stretchy properties of 'A' as a joystick to change an object.

Fragments are used a bit like you could use Layers in 3D ArchiCAD. In 3D Project window, you can click on an object, and put it into the landscaping layer, or the roofs layer, or special constructions. In 2D, you have layer (or fragment) number 1, 2, 3, 4, etc. Anything you draw initially gets stored in fragment 1, but can be moved to another fragment by you.

2D symbols in the project plan are generated in one of three ways:
• A 2D Symbol that has been drawn by yourself, or copied and pasted from the main project window into the symbol window.
• A 2D script that you have written, and that uses the parameters in the library box.
• A 2D symbol that is stored in fragments, that could be one of several 2D images that you may previously have drawn, and which is revealed as a result of your script.

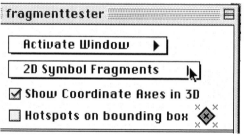

This is one exercise where you need to load the example from the diskette and analyse what it does, because it is not all scripted. For your own example, you could draw different things, and then select them, and move them to the fragment number in which you want them to live. Have another look at Fragment2 in the 'Advanced 2D' to remind yourself how it is done. The exercise also give you another example of making object stretchy. As you vary the value of 'A', the object changes to different fragments.

Illustrations of Fragment

1: Typical view in ArchiCAD of the object with a small value of A.

2: Use the popdown menu in the library box to show and hide different fragments.

3: Parameters for this exercise – as there is no 3D involved, only A is used, and it's used by stretching a Hotspot.

4: Draw what you want to draw in each fragment, using the 2D drawing tools.

5: Select all 2D objects and move them to the final fragment.

6: In this example, there are 6 different fragments, and the cross hairs are put in to show how the fragment changes as the stretching hotspot moves sideways.

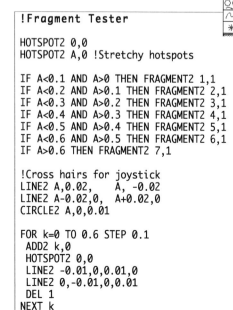

```
!Fragment Tester

HOTSPOT2 0,0
HOTSPOT2 A,0 !Stretchy hotspots

IF A<0.1 AND A>0 THEN FRAGMENT2 1,1
IF A<0.2 AND A>0.1 THEN FRAGMENT2 2,1
IF A<0.3 AND A>0.2 THEN FRAGMENT2 3,1
IF A<0.4 AND A>0.3 THEN FRAGMENT2 4,1
IF A<0.5 AND A>0.4 THEN FRAGMENT2 5,1
IF A<0.6 AND A>0.5 THEN FRAGMENT2 6,1
IF A>0.6 THEN FRAGMENT2 7,1

!Cross hairs for joystick
LINE2 A,0.02,   A, -0.02
LINE2 A-0.02,0, A+0.02,0
CIRCLE2 A,0,0.01

FOR k=0 TO 0.6 STEP 0.1
  ADD2 k,0
  HOTSPOT2 0,0
  LINE2 -0.01,0,0.01,0
  LINE2 0,-0.01,0,0.01
  DEL 1
NEXT k
```

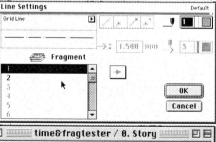

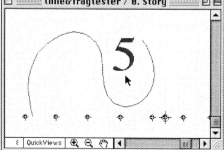

The 7 line fragment2 routine here could be rewritten as simply:-

$$x = \text{MIN}(7, \text{INT}(A \times 10) + 1)$$
FRAGMENT2 x,1

Master Scripts

Programming Concepts

A MAJOR BENEFIT for GDL users in AC6 is the **Master Script.**

Previous to ArchiCAD 6.0, any internal parameters that needed to be calculated (such as the circumference and sweep angle of an arch) had to be done separately in the 2D and 3D scripts – and perhaps in the Properties script too. You might have needed several IF statements to check for bad user parameters. If you subsequently changed or added to these, you had to go to each script, copying and pasting. Now, with Value Lists, there is even more parsing of internal parameters to be done.

You can put all this error checking and parameter calculation into the **Master Script.** GDL executes the Master Script early (it reads the Values Lists earlier!) and retains all the internal parameters, passing these on to the 2D and 3D scripts as needed. This way, you only have one place to check when you want to modify your error checking routines. You can make the 2D and 3D scripts concentrate solely on their main job.

(A small bug in early releases of AC_6.5 stops objects being stretchy if they havea complex Master Script – if this occurs, move the script to the 3D Script area.)

How do GDL scripts get information with which to build 3D and 2D objects?

Input

Hard coded parameters: First, many parameters can be 'hard coded' in the script. These are not user modifiable. You might want your script to include the tensile and compressive properties of steel or timber, so that sizes in a truss can be checked by a calculation. As these quantities never change there is no point in forcing the user to enter them in the settings.

User modifiable parameters: When you create an object, you build a list of user modifiable parameters in the main library control window – you have in effect built your own dialog box which controls the object. Parameters can be dimensions and angles, numbers and integers, materials and pens, text or fill patterns, or ON/OFF choices.

Calculated Parameters: As the object is stretched, or as a result of some user entered parameters, certain calculations may be made which will change the object. For example, if the slenderness ratio of a steel strut is exceeded, the diameter can be increased.

Arrays: The most interesting of the user modifiable settings is that you can offer the user a spreadsheet-like display which they can fill with an array of numbers, which then get used by the script.

Text File input: The GDL Script can read information from a text file placed in the ArchiCAD Data folder. Of course, the script needs to know how the data will be offered. It is equivalent to the READ or the INPUT# commands in BASIC.

Hotspots: Every object has hotspots, to enable it to be picked up or selected. But Hotspots in the right places can be used to make the object stretchy, or in some cases, the user's movement of hotspots can change some other characteristic of the object - analogous to a joystick control.

Global Variables: The GDL script can request information from the current project such as the current drawing scale, the current pen and material settings, the storey. the most useful application of this idea is in Window/Door design where the window can find out the thickness, materials, radius of curvature and other properties of the Wall which holds the window.

Output

3D-Output: The first result of GDL is the object in 3-D. This is the main purpose of using GDL.

2D-Output: [1] Many objects are solely in the form of 2-D, such as grids, or sanitary/hospital fittings/machines etc for layouts where 3D is not required. However, you can also get the 2D to be scripted as carefully as the 3D, so that the 2D symbol can be used to label the object, or even display a warning when something is wrong and needs modifying - such as warning that a beam is unsafe, or a tube is too slender. 2D can also do useful things like displaying the span of a beam that has been stretched to fit between supports, or to print chevrons to indicate the upwards direction in an object that has been tilted.

2D output: [2] The object can also be viewed in section or elevation. this can be saved as a plotmaker file, or as other re-usable forms, such as JPEG. Or if you select the section, Copy it, and paste into the Plan, you have a 2d drawing which can now be grouped, merged, edited, or saved as a DXF. Perhaps you need it in DXF to drive a cutting machine, or simply for sending to your engineer or fabrication shop.

Text Output: The GDL script, while executing, can be made to open a text file, write data to it and close. This could be a table or listing of useful data, such as a cutting schedule for a trussed rafter.

Properties/Components/Descriptors: This is another way of printing out listings and is more powerful than the text file, as it can include plans, section/elevations or 3D views of the object for the purpose of creating schedules or databases.

Tips and Tricks
Lost your Toolbar?
Windows users! There is nothing in the preferences or display settings or in the manual that can help you. Do you despair? No, because you can 'right-button' click the grey bar at the bottom of the A'cad screen and get it back.

Arrays

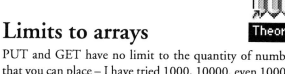

Arrays - a table of numbers

ANYBODY who has programmed in BASIC will welcome the power of Arrays. An 'array' is just a row or a table of numbers.

Imagine a single row of 16 numbers in a spreadsheet called 'pt'. This is a one dimensional array (e.g. DIM pt[16]). Now just imagine a spreadsheet table of 4 columns and 16 rows (DIM pt[4][16]). This is a 2 dimensional array. These numbers are stored in memory. A statement like LET eavht= pt[4]*1.723 will modify the fourth item in an array.

The essential difference between an Array and the Put & Get system in GDL is that an Array of numbers can be played with – manipulated, sorted, used again and again.

With Put and Get, you Put numbers into a temporary memory buffer, somewhat like a one dimensional array; but you can only get them out in the order they went in, and the moment you Get them out, you have cleared the buffer – it is emptied! Lost!

The array can be filled from a series of numbers generated in the script – for example, by a routine that worked out the outline of a curved window. With AC-6.x, the script writer can set up a single or 2D array that is visible to the user in the Library settings dialog box, and the user can edit it.

When I first read about PUT and GET, I couldn't think of a use for them. After a few models, one realised that they were an essential aid for everyday use (with prisms, extrude, tube etc.) and one could not manage complicated 3D modelling without them. I felt the same way about Arrays. Now I use arrays with many of my objects.

Limits to arrays

PUT and GET have no limit to the quantity of numbers that you can place – I have tried 1000, 10000, even 100000 without trouble; Arrays have to be declared first with a numerical DIM statement, declaring their size e.g. DIM vx[32]. It is not possible to declare an array with a variable, e.g.: pn=32: DIM vx[pn], in which the quantity in the array results from user input or an earlier calculation. However, it is possible to write it so that the user can edit small arrays from within the Library object settings box. It is very powerful.

Declaring an Array

You first declare the size of the array with a DIM command. If the array is to be 16 numbers called 'eavht', and you have another array for X, Y, and masks for a floor slab, you would write (early on in the Master or 3D script),

DIM eavht[20],xym[8][3]

The idea of writing a few more than 16 is that it doesn't do you harm to reserve more memory in case you decide to use more numbers in the future. 2D arrays go in the order [rows][columns] so **xym[8][3]** is 8 rows of numbers, 3 columns deep.

Using an Array

Once the array is filled, you can use the numbers in the array as variables, such as:- **ADDz eavht[8]**, which would lift the cursor to the height of the eighth eaves height in your list, say for placing a gutter. To go to the third point on the floor slab, you could write:-

ADD xym[3][1],xym[3][2],0

In certain cases, such as with PRINT or PUT, you can dump the entire contents of the array in one go. e.g. **PRINT xym**, or **PUT xym**, but I have tried and it will not work directly with PRISM because it doesn't insert commas. What will work though is:-

PUT xym !fill buffer with array contents
PRISM NSP/3,0.2,
        GET(NSP) !do it!

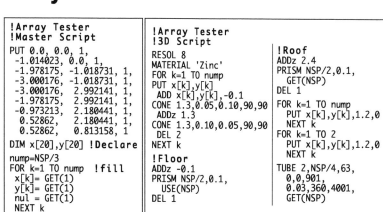

Arrays can be 1-dimensional (like this), or can be 2dimensional, like a table of numbers. Arrays can contain strings(alphabetical characters.)

Arrays in action

```
!Array Tester
!Master Script
PUT 0.0, 0.0, 1,
   -1.014023, 0.0, 1,
   -1.978175, -1.018731, 1,
   -3.000176, -1.018731, 1,
   -3.000176, 2.992141, 1,
   -1.978175, 2.992141, 1,
   -0.973213, 2.180441, 1,
   0.52862, 2.180441, 1,
   0.52862, 0.813158, 1
DIM x[20],y[20] !Declare
nump=NSP/3
FOR k=1 TO nump   !fill
   x[k]= GET(1)
   y[k]= GET(1)
   nul = GET(1)
NEXT k
```

```
!Array Tester
!3D Script
RESOL 8
MATERIAL 'Zinc'
FOR k=1 TO nump
   PUT x[k],y[k]
   ADD x[k],y[k],-0.1
CONE 1.3,0.05,0.10,90,90
   ADDz 1.3
CONE 1.3,0.10,0.05,90,90
   DEL 2
NEXT k
!Floor
ADDz -0.1
PRISM NSP/2,0.1,
   USE(NSP)
DEL 1
```

```
!Roof
ADDz 2.4
PRISM NSP/2,0.1,
   GET(NSP)
DEL 1
FOR k=1 TO nump
   PUT x[k],y[k],1.2,0
NEXT k
FOR k=1 TO 2
   PUT x[k],y[k],1.2,0
NEXT k
TUBE 2,NSP/4,63,
   0,0,901,
   0.03,360,4001,
   GET(NSP)
```

I dont know what this structure is, but it perfectly exemplifies the use of arrays – when you have a number of X-Y positions which are needed repeatedly for different purposes.

```
!Array Tester
!2D Script
HOTSPOT2 0,0
FOR k=1 TO nump
   PUT x[k],y[k]
   HOTSPOT2 x[k],y[k]
NEXT k
POLY2 NSP/2,7,
   GET(NSP)
```

GDL Control

B INARY: is what all Binary converted Library objects begin with, and either have a value of 3, 2, 1 or 0. There is no use for the command in your creative GDL. Binary objects are not editable (except for the odd MUL or ROT in front of them, and there cannot be parameters for them, except for the MUL or ROTs.

C ALL: is used to bring an existing library object in, to work as part of your existing object, and you have to opportunity to use the default or new parameters. Whenever you make an Autoscripted library object that involves nesting already made objects, the CALL command is always used.

It is not a good idea to use CALL in creative GDL objects. It slows the system down (having to read in from disk) but more importantly runs the risk that if you change the name of the called script, or even one of the parameter names of the imported object and then forget to update the new object, the new object will then have a chunk missing.

```
┌──────────────────────────────────────────────────────┐
│  ☐                    Control Statements    ▤▤▤▤▤▤▤▤▤  │
├──────────────────────────────────────────────────────┤
│  ▦  Control statements                                 │
│                                                        │
│ BINARY mode {includes inline binary objects;           │
│          mode=0 to override original colors, mode=1 to use original colors} │
│                                                        │
│ [CALL] "macro_name_string" parameter_list or           │
│ CALL macro_name_string PARAMETERS [name1 = value, ..., name_n = value_n] │
└──────────────────────────────────────────────────────┘
```

One of the whole points of creative GDL programming is that you can have smart, integrated objects that do not rely on making CALLs. It is better in my mind, to copy and paste the script of the other object into your new object, as a subroutine, and make sure that parameters you wish to use match up with the ones you have already set up. Or write a list of parameters at the beginning of the subroutine.

It is most useful when you make a range of objects, and some small component is repeated many many times, such as a door handle, or a sink tap; so that a door or a sink unit can call in a handle or a tap script. The CALLed file might not even be a full object in its own right – it may be saved as a **GDL Macro**, a chunk of pure 3D script which can be read in.

Encapsulating: If you wish to use the CALL command, the best way is to view the old object in the Project Plan, select it, Save-Special as a library object and you then get the CALL command perfectly autoscripted for you by ArchiCAD, with all the parameters correctly spelt. Copy and paste that to your new object, and use it as a subroutine. I call this process 'encapsulating' the object.

```
BODY    -1
CALL    "swivel_chair" PARAMETERS A=0.450466, B=0.544259,
     sht=0.45, sth=0.05, smat=IND(MATERIAL,"DEFAULT"),
     mmat=IND(MATERIAL,"Zinc"), dmat=IND(MATERIAL,"Asphalt")
BODY    -1
```

GDL Macros

M ANY OF GRAPHISOFT's Library objects – windows, kitchenware etc – make use of macros. A macro is a script or object that is used to often that it is stored as a special component.

An example is a window sash, that could be called from the Library to join a whole variety of window designs. It saves having to write it all out again. The same applies to a kitchen tap – which can be called to a variety of sink unit configurations. AngleRod (in the Voyager Course) could be used as a macro in a cable or spaceframe structure.

Macros can be used with the CALL command or they can be used directly as if they were a command. They may bring their own parameters (that they were first saved with) or may be told to adopt new values in the current script.

An even simpler use of the concept of Macro is to use a subroutine inside a script that can be used again and again, with different parameters being passed to it. The exercise 'Kitchen Chair' is an example of this, whereby the conical wood turned elements of the chair are all based on one macro.

Here is a tiny example. Supposing you want a Square sectioned solid that always behaved like a Cylinder - that rises axially about the Z axis. I call it a **Squilinder.**

```
LET squilinder=100
!.....
!.....
w=0.3: hit=0.85
GOSUB squilinder
  ADDx 1.0
GOSUB squilinder
  DEL 1
```

```
100:!Squilinder
PRISM 4,hit,
    w/2,w/2,
   -w/2,w/2,
   -w/2,-w/2,
    w/2,-w/2
RETURN
```

Keeping the macro within your existing 3D script
In this case it is a subroutine, and you just pass parameters to it. To make things smoother, you even apply the name to the subroutine.

CALLing the Macro from another script
Save the left hand routine as an object in its own right (without the return) and with only 'hit' and 'w' as parameters. Now your current script can get it from the library with a

```
!Squilinder macro
PRISM 4,hit,
    w/2,w/2,
   -w/2,w/2,
   -w/2,-w/2,
    w/2,-w/2
```

```
MATERIAL "whitewash"
CALL squilinder PARAMETERS
            w=12",hit=2"-10"
  ADDx 40"
squilinder w=12",hit=2"-10"
  DEL 1
```

CALL command, or, if you want to cut corners, you do not even have to use the CALL command. Just name the macro, as above. However, to make it easier to debug your own script months after you have written it, I advise you to use the CALL command on every occasion.

Maths Primer

Theory

GDL requires a 3-D spatial awareness, and an essential minimal knowl edge of Triangle and Circle Geometry. Architects usually have no problems with the former, but may need help with the latter.

Let us assume that you are familiar with basic Arithmetic and Algebra. As a Voyager, you have a working knowledge of BASIC. However, there are 3D problems which require considerable analysis before you begin, and I find these pages useful for myself when tackling new problems. Sketch onto paper the essential geometry of the problem. Then plan the solution.

Nostalgia trip
Suddenly all those distant memories of Maths you did back at school can be dusted off and made useful.
Isn't it marvellous!!

Rotation Directions

The Geophysical world works with the vertical north (0°) at the top and east (90°) is in a positive direction clockwise. West is either –90° or +270°, depending on how you travel there. The hands of a clock work that way.

In Mathematics, the horizontal is Zero°, and an angle grows in the anti clockwise direction, so that 90° is facing up the page. This is how the diagram for the camera works in 3D Projection Settings, in ArchiCAD.

When you talk about the azimuth of the Sun relative to the site and entering site survey information, this causes endless confusion. But at least, for GDL use, I hope this is clear.

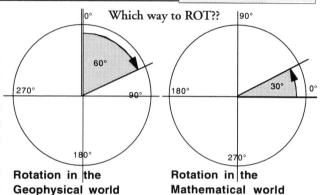

Rotation in the Geophysical world

Rotation in the Mathematical world

Right Angle Triangles

Next you need a basic knowledge of the right angle triangle – in fact all you need to know is the motto SOH CAH TOA so that you can always calculate the characteristics of a triangle from minimal information. If you don't know this already, learn it by saying it to yourself as a mantra whilst in traffic queues.

Coordinate Geometry is based on Pythagoras.

The distance between any two points is simply $SQR((x1-x2)^2 + (y1-y2)^2)$. This works even when points have negative values. The gradient 'm' of a line is $=(y1-y2)/(x1-x2)$ – the same as the TAN of its angle.

The formula for a straight line is $y=mx+c$, or $ax+by+c=0$. If two lines intersect (straight or curved), you can derive a simultaneous equation – both 'y' values equal each other. The gradient 'm1' of a line equals $(-1)/(m2)$, m2 being the gradient of its perpendicular line – or you can say that $m1*m2=(-1)$.

Remember: "SOH CAH TOA"

SIN(angl)=Opposite/Hypoteneuse
COS(angl)=Adjacent/Hypoteneuse
TAN(angl)=Opposite/Adjacent

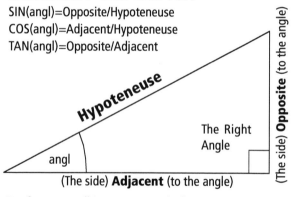

Pythagoras (him smart cookie) says: Hypoteneuse squared equals sum of the squares of the other two sides. In other words, Hypoteneuse=SQR(Adjacent^2 + Opposite^2)

Irregular Triangles

Irregular triangles can be analysed by breaking into small right angled ones and using SOH CAH TOA. The SIN and COS rules will enable you to derive all the facts from any three pieces of information.

Powers can be written with two asterisks e.g. num**2, or as num^2 and square root is SQR(num) or num^0.5. Cube and other roots would be written as num^(1/3).

Any three points in space, no matter how irregularly disposed can be joined up to form a planar (flat) triangle; a planar circle can be drawn through the points. ArchiCAD's circle tool provides a means of finding this centre. The calculation is more difficult.

An Isosceles triangle has two equal sides and two equal angles. The angles of any triangle add up to 180°.

From this diagram you can work out any triangle from any three known facts

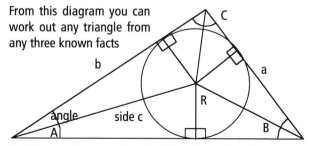

A circle can always be inscribed in an irregular triangle. From this, several right angle triangles can be derived.
SIN Rule: a/SIN(A)=b/SIN(B)=c/SIN(C)=2*R
COS Rule: a^2= b^2 + c^2 – 2*b*c*COS(A)
Hence, if you know the sides,
Angle A=ACS((b^2+c^2-a^2)/(2*b*c))
Area=(length of any side)*(height relative to that side)/2

3D Pythagoras

ONE FACT that I worked out for myself, but must be in a book somewhere, and which I have used for some time, is the Pythagoras' Theorem in 3-D. The diagonal of a cuboid shape is the Square Root of the sum of the squares of the Length, Width and Height. diaglen=SQR(x^{**2} + y^{**2} + z^{**2}) [can also be written as SQR(x^2+y^2+z^2)]

The script here demonstrates it fully. Thus if you have a linear object arcing around in 3D space (like the arm of a crane) you know its length and its declination angle from the simple formulae demonstrated here. (Declination is the elevational angle from vertical).

From this theorem, you can work out the reverse of the 3D Pythagoras, using Trig. If you know the crane arm's length, its Rotational angle, and its Elevational angle (from horizontal), you can know its X,Y,Z location in space.

In the diagram, 'rotang' is the rotational angle of the arm from the Y axis, and elvang' is the elevational angle from flat on the floor. 'clen' is the length of the Cylinder. Hence,

- X=SIN(rotang)*COS(elvang)*diaglen
- Y=COS(rotang)*COS(elvang)*diaglen
- Z=SIN(elvang)*diaglen

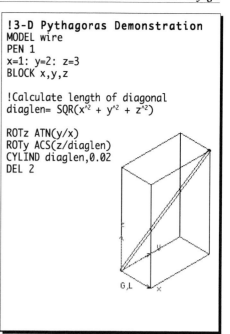

```
!3-D Pythagoras Demonstration
MODEL wire
PEN 1
x=1: y=2: z=3
BLOCK x,y,z

!Calculate length of diagonal
diaglen= SQR(x^2 + y^2 + z^2)

ROTz ATN(y/x)
ROTy ACS(z/diaglen)
CYLIND diaglen,0.02
DEL 2
```

Circles

THERE will be many situations where the object you are making is circular (curved truss), or parts of it trace a circular path through space (a swinging arm). In coordinate geometry, the Formula for a Circle is $R^2 = x^2 + y^2$.

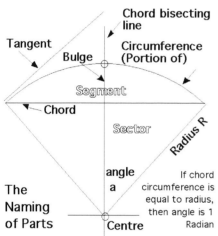

The diagram displays the terminology of parts of circles that I mention in many of the worksheets in the CookBook.

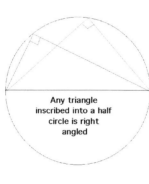

All triangles can be drawn into a circle. It is useful to know that in a right angle triangle, the hypoteneuse is also the diameter of an enclosing circle, and its half way point is the Circle centre.

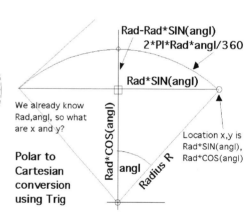

If you are distributing things in a circle (e.g. mullions in a bay window), you usually know the centre, the radius and the angle in which you are pointing.

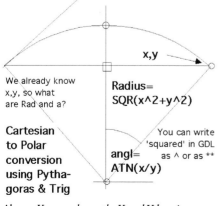

Above: *You may know the X and Y location, but need to know the Radius and Angle – perhaps you have a diagonal cylindrical tube which must connect the two points. Only works if 0,0 is the centre.*

Right: *On many occasions, you need to derive the factors of Circles and their inscribed triangles when you only know the CHORD length and the BULGE (segment height). For instance, you need this when dealing with handrails of long distance, bowstring trusses, curved mullions or transom sections and arches. This helps you work out where the centre must be.*

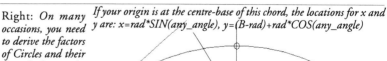

If your origin is at the centre-base of this chord, the locations for x and y are: x=rad*SIN(any_angle), y=(B-rad)+rad*COS(any_angle)

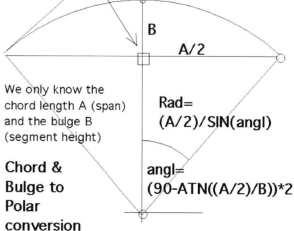

Chord & Bulge to Polar conversion

Arch Forms

I have developed formulae which can be used for raised arches or hanging cables. (See the 'Arches and Waves' exercise in Voyager). The parabola is the perfect form to display the effect of gravity on a linear pathway.

An arch or cable with self weight describes a Parabola distorted into a Catenary, which is based on hyperbolic trig (COSH & SINH) and cannot be covered in this edition.

The formulae below compute values for 'z' derived from distance 'x' from the origin, based on nothing more than span and height.

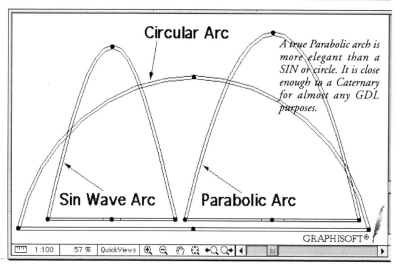

A true Parabolic arch is more elegant than a SIN or circle. It is close enough to a Caternary for almost any GDL purposes.

GRAPHISOFT®

Flattish Round Arch

(less than 180 degrees of sweep):
radius=(span/2)/SIN(2*(90-ATN((span/2)/height)))
Z=radius*COS(ASN(x/radius))-(radius-height)
(Circles and ellipses are much better done by a radial method. For an ellipse, you can use the above, but add, LET Z =Z*height/(span/2)).
The cartesian formula for a Circle is $R^2=x^2+y^2$ so you can use y=SQR(R*2 -x*2) for short circular forms.

SIN Wave Arch

Z=height*SIN(X*180/span)

Parabolic Arch

Z=height–(4*height/(span^2))*X^2
or, Z=height*(1 – (2*X/span)^2)
dydx=(8*height/(span^2))*X
'dydx' is TAN of the slope at point X – important if you want to attach panels.

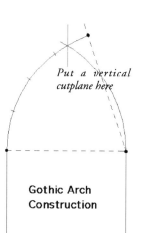

Put a vertical cutplane here

Gothic Arch

This may not be as the medieval master builders planned; but if you do a circular form centred from the top of the opposite jamb, it looks very passable. You can run a profile of the doorway with REVOLVE or TUBE.

Elliptical Arch

... is best done by applying MULz to a Circular arch, but this may distort the section of the tubing. Use the Radial method or ELBOW to draw the arch.

Gothic Arch Construction

Ways of avoiding Trig

Using the TUBE or the SWEEP command, it is possible to link two XYZ locations with a cylinder without needing to know the angle and length.

If you are distributing objects in a circle – like mullions in a curved window – you may not need to do a polar to cartesian conversion. Just keep swivelling the cursor, and push out an object, delete back, then swivel to the next location. e.g.
`ROTz ang: ADDy R: GOSUB 250: DEL 2.0`
This will make sense when you try an exercise (eg the CircleGrid or the Tempietto).

Points to remember:

- PI exists as an accurate constant in GDL. Useful...
- There are 360 degrees in a circle. But you can safely issue commands like SIN(angl) when angl is a number like 535° (greater than 360) and GDL will not turn a hair (it will return a result of SIN(175)).
- A circle's circumference is 2*PI*R.
- You can make Ellipses by using the MUL command to shrink or stretch Circular forms into ellipses.

Besides the matter of geometry, you need to know some of the arithmetic functions offered by GDL, such as ABS( ) and INT( ), MAX() and MIN(), MOD and FRA().

If you are handy at deriving things from first principles and thinking logically, all you need really is Pythagoras and SOH CAH TOA !

Tips and Tricks – Maths bits

You frequently need to 'toggle' or convert numbers, especially when Booleian choices are involved.

- To find out if a number is odd or even :-
  IF INT(item/2)=item/2 THEN even=1 ELSE even=0
  or IF item MOD 2=0 (it is even)
- To find out if number is Negative or Positive (& set a flag):
  IF item<>0 THEN flag=item/ABS(item) ELSE flag=0
  (makes 1 or -1, or 0 if item is zero)
- To force a number to be positive: item=ABS(item)

• To turn 1 & 2 into 0 & 1	(item-1)
• To turn 1 & 2 into -1 & +1	(item-1)*2-1
• To turn 0 & 1 into -1 & +1	item*2-1
• To toggle values of -1 & +1	item*(-1)
• To generate 1 or 0 randomly	INT(RND(2))
• To toggle values of 0 &1	(1 – item)
• To make 0=0, and 1,2,3 etc=1	INT(x/(x-0.1))
• To make 1 & -1 into 0 & 1	-(item-1)/2
• To make -1 & 1 into 0 & 1	(item+1)/2

The Binary System – for Voyagers

Theory

Only read this if you want to...

IF you are a GDL beginner, or if your eyes glaze over at maths, do not bother with this page right yet. Come back to it, when you are trying to understand 'status codes' and 'masking values'.

Binary is the key to understanding how to use the Status and Masking values. It's the way that all computers work actually, but low level programming code converts decimal numbers to binary without our knowing or needing to know how it does it.

Binary is a numbering system based on 2, rather than ten, which is what we use in normal life – because we were born with ten fingers. With decimal, we have to develop a notation for all the numbers between 0 and ten, hence 1,2,3,4 etc. With Binary, you have a simple choice – 0 or 1.

Binary is quite efficient at dealing with CHOICES – which could be simplified down to YES or NO situations. Do you draw a LINE? If yes, it's *zero* if no, then it's *one*. That is how status codes work in 2D entities in GDL.

If the base is 2, then to write a number in Binary, you use a series of 1 and 0's . For example, the number 3, being the sum of 2+1 is written as 11. The number 9 is made up of 8+ 0+ 0+ 1, so it is written as 1001. 147 is 128+ 0+ 0+ 16+ 0+ 0+ 2+ 1, so it is 10010011.

Using Binary to choose Status Values - 1 to 1

IN 2D GDL, you only need to decide whether a line is to be drawn or not. Therefore there is a simple choice, *Yes* or *No*. In the example here, Status codes have been used to define whether lines are to be drawn or not. Zero (0) means draw the line, and one (1) means do not draw it. Even when mixed with Polyline commands such as 900 and 1000, you ADD one or zero to achieve the same effect.

Using Binary for Masking Values in Prisms – 0 to 15

IN 3D Prisms, you need not only to know if lines are to be drawn, but if surfaces are to be visible. This has 16 possibilities – from 0 to 15. Here is a table of all the numbers up to 16 so you can see how they are made; these cover all the masking values for the sides of PRISMs. In this case, [1] means do the action, and [zero] means do not. So 8 means draw the face, 4 means draw the top line, 2 means draw the side line, and 1 means draw the bottom line. Any combination of these can be expressed with a number from 0 to 15.

It is puzzling that with Status Codes for profiles in Extrude and Tube, zero means draw the line, but with Masks, the opposite applies. Graphisoft! – why??

```
420:!POLY_ Demo with hole
!Syntax:- POLY_ number,
!         x1,y1,mask,
!         x2,y2,mask, etc
POLY_ 9+2,
  0.00,0.00,1,
 -0.10,0.30,1,
  0.10,0.30,0,
  0.10,0.40,1,
  0.20,0.40,1,
  0.20,0.10,1001,
  0.15,0.10,0,
  0.15,0.00,1,
  0.00,0.00,-1,

  0.05,0.1,900,
  0.05,360,4000
```

Analysis	Binary	Decimal
1	1	1
2+0	10	2
2+1	11	3
4+0+0	100	4
4+0+1	101	5
4+2+0	110	6
4+2+1	111	7
8+0+0+0	1000	8
8+0+0+1	1001	9
8+0+2+0	1010	10
8+0+2+1	1011	11
8+4+0+0	1100	12
8+4+0+1	1101	13
8+4+2+0	1110	14
8+4+2+1	1111	15

In this example (reading from the table) we want to draw the face, and the top line and the bottom line, but neither of the side lines. So we need 8 + 4 + 1 which gives us 13.

Masking codes 0-7

POLY2_ in 2D scripting uses a binary group of *three* choices, draw the Line (1), draw the Fill (2), and Close the polygon (4). Therefore the range of decimal numbers is from 0 to 7. WALLHOLE also uses 7.

Masking codes up to 127

USING the same principle, you can now analyse how the masking values work, up to 127. These are used by EXTRUDE, PYRAMID, REVOLVE, RULED, SWEEP, TUBE, MESH, MASS and COONS. If you use 127 or 63, you cover almost all eventualities, but you may find this table helpful to understand how to achieve results. By the way, each of the 3D forms mentioned here use masking values slightly differently, so you still need to check the manual in each case.

Analysis	Binary	Decimal	
16+0+0+0+0	10000	16	
16+8+0+2+1	11011	27	
32+ 0 +8+0+0+1	101001	39	
32+ 0 +8+0+2+1	101011	43	
32+16+0+0+0+1	110001	49	
32+16+8+4+0+0	111100	60	
32+16+8+4+2+1	111111	63	all on
64 or 127-63	1000000	64	
64+ 0 +16+0+4+0+1	1010101	85	
64+32+16+8+4+2+1	1111111	127	all on

Analytical combinations can be done by subtraction as well as addition. For example, '127-2' is a convenient way to say "draw everything except the top surface".

Some people use numbers up to 255, but as things stand, it is clear from the manual that 127 is the highest number necessary.

Ridge & Hiptool

Variable	Type	Name	Value
A	⬌	X Dimension	2.000
B	⬍	Y Dimension	1.000
rad		Radius of Ridge tile	0.100
shape	Abc	Base it on Angle or Height?	Base it on Angle
pitch	△	Pitch of roof	30.00
hit		Height of ridge/hip end	1.000
higl	⊠	Highlight Ridge/Hip ON/OFF?	On

THIS is a useful item to put on your buildings, to give them added authenticity. You have to use the Section view to nudge them into final position.

PEN L_ and MATERIAL M_ is a useful way to enable someone to use the library dialog box (as above) to define Pen and Material – thus reducing the amount of clutter in the parameter settings. Once in the Project plan, it adopts the material setting given to it.

While developing your model, it may have the unfortunate appearance of being green, so you could put a temporary MATERIAL "whitewash" command in.

The idea of highlighting, is to make sure that you have remembered all the ridges and hips, and to make it easier to pick them up in plan (gives you more hotspots). As it can cause visual clutter in the plan, they should be a boolean choice to be turned off.

```
!Ridge and Hip tile
!3D Script

MATERIAL M_
PEN L_

IF shape='Base it on Angle' THEN
  len=A/COS(pitch)
 ENDIF
IF shape='Base it on Height' THEN
  pitch = ATN(hit/A)
  len   = A/COS(pitch)
ENDIF

 ROTz 90
 ROTx 90-pitch

RESOL 10
BODY -1
EXTRUDE 4,0,0,len,55,
   rad,    0,      1,
   0,      0,    901,
   rad,  180,   4001,
   0,      0,      1
BODY -1
DEL 2
```

```
!Values List Script
VALUES 'shape' 'Base it on Angle',
  'Base it on Height'
```

*Use a **Value list** to decide between using the Ridge by naming a Pitch or a final Height. It's more user friendly than a Booleian choice.*

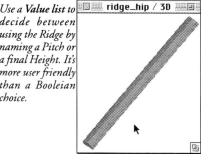

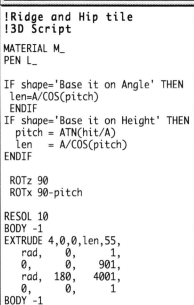

```
!Ridge and Hip tile
!2D Script

PEN L_

  HOTSPOT2 0,0
  HOTSPOT2 A/2,0
  HOTSPOT2 A,0
  PROJECT2 3,270,2

  IF higl THEN
  HOTSPOT2 A/2, 0.5
  HOTSPOT2 A/2,-0.5

  LINE2 0,0, A/2, 0.5
  LINE2 0,0, A/2,-0.5
  LINE2 A/2, 0.5, A,0
  LINE2 A/2,-0.5, A,0
  ENDIF
```

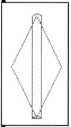

The 2D symbol can be highlighted so that you can pick it up

Obscure Commands

THE GDL Cookbook does not cover **ARMC** and **ARME** at the moment, as their use is very rare. In most tubular assemblies, one can allow Cylinders to flow into each other. I guess that ARMC

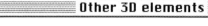

Other 3D elements

ARMC r1 , r2 , l, h, d, alpha {a piece of tube starting from another tube

ARME l, r1 , r2 , h, d {a piece of tube starting from an ellipsoid in the x-y plane

and ARME must be the last remains of the RaDar piping design software that was the birth of ArchiCAD.

AngleRod – Useful stretchy tool object with TUBE

A NGLEROD is an example of a STRETCHY Object. Angle Rod is most useful for building up anything tubular – by placing the object in the project window, stretching it to its endpoint, and then defining height.

Parameters: Stretchy objects are made by using A and B as the defining dimensions of the object – most useful for railings, cornices, kerbs, special walls, beams. Once you have used this, you will always try to make your objects stretchy.

3 D Script: The 3D Script uses the TUBE command – this requires that you specify a 'phantom' location above and below the real tube start and end points. By using the A and B dimensions to define these, you get cleanly cut butt ends to the cylinders.

The routine 0,0,901, followed by cdiam/2,360,4001 is the standard routine for defining a circular section in an extrude, revolve, tube or in several other commands. You might as well get used to it.

2 D Script: The key to stretchy objects is to place the Hotspots in the 2D script. Hotspot2 0,0, and A,B.

As a complex group of tubes could have end and bounding box hotspots which would interfere with each other, you should plant Hotspots along the line of the tube, so you can be sure which one you have grasped.

You can get rid of the bounding box by placing a 2D hotspot at the origin in the 2D Symbol window – then turning off bounding boxes in the main library box.

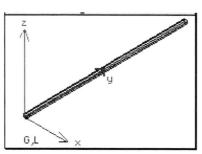

Variable	Type	Name	Value
A		X Dimension	1.000
B		Y Dimension	1.000
z1		Z (height) of final point	1.000
cdiam		Diameter of Cable/Rod	0.050
cmat		Material of Cable/Rod	11
rsl		Resolution of curvature	16
endshape	Abc	Design of ends of the Rod	Rounded Ends

It is important to allow user control over the Resolution. The anglerod could be used for fine cables (use resol 3) or the giant sections for a bridge or pier.

```
!AngleRod
!3D Script

MATERIAL cmat
PEN 1

RESOL rsl

TUBE 2,4,63,
    0,0,901,
    cdiam/2,360,4001,

    -A,-B,-z1,0,
    0,0,0,0,
    A,B,z1,0,
    2*A,2*B,2*z1,0
```

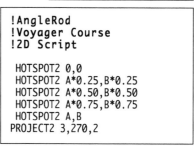

```
!AngleRod
!Voyager Course
!2D Script

HOTSPOT2 0,0
HOTSPOT2 A*0.25,B*0.25
HOTSPOT2 A*0.50,B*0.50
HOTSPOT2 A*0.75,B*0.75
HOTSPOT2 A,B
PROJECT2 3,270,2
```

Notice that with the Tube command, you get linear lines along the cylinder. By changing the 900 and 4000 commands to 901 and 4001, the lines are cleared.

*2D Script: Plant Hotspots along the line of the tube. Specify Hotspots **before** you issue the Project2 command. 2D View below:*

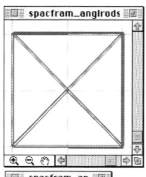

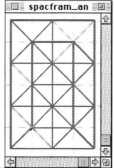

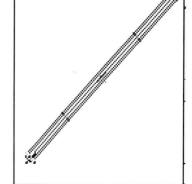

Use it as a Component or as a Macro!

By combining AngleRod into tetrahedral groups, and by grouping the groups in encapsulated library objects, you can assemble complex tubular and cable/strut structures without any need to use GDL or trigonometry!

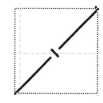

Using AngleRod: When you enter the anglerod into the plan, it's best to have the stretchy box selected in the control box. If you dont, you have to place it first, and then stretch it later.

This is what it looks like as it is being stretched. One rod on its own doesn't look very exciting, but the rods can be combined to create complex frameworks.

Value List: *By adding an extra parameter to choose Butt ends or Rounded ends, you can add a Sphere at each end of the Tube, giving a rounded end. Put this in the Value List.*

```
!Extension to 3D Script
IF endshape='Rounded Ends' THEN
SPHERE cdiam/2
    ADD A,B,z1
SPHERE cdiam/2
    DEL 1
    ENDIF
```

```
VALUES 'endshape' 'Rounded Ends'
                  'Butt Ends'
```

Round ends will add hundreds or thousands of polygons to your model – Beware!

Stair – Parametric

Object

This exercise demonstrates of the use of:
• The PUT statement in a FOR NEXT loop.
• PRISM using GET
• CYLIND, TUBE & Polylines for the Handrail
• Using Pythagoras and ArcTan to work out the details

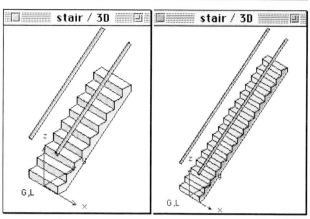

The Result
The Stair can be any number of risers, any riser height or going! You can opt to have handrails or none, on the left or the right side, or on both!!

O NE of the problems with any object •stepping• like a staircase is how to make the number of steps as a parametric quantity.

First, you could make each step a separate object, and use a loop to draw them. But this would be ugly with many surplus lines. It is better programming to do the stair as one object, and thus ensure a smooth soffit to the underside with faster rendering.

You can make most Staircases with Stairmaker, but how much more fun it is to make your own, and with a greater degree of control. The technique used in this example is used later in the Theatre seating and other stepping objects.

Parameters: First put in the parameters that affect the stair itself. Leave all the handrail questions till later. The stair will be stretchy in width, so use A. The stair risers will be slightly raked - the user can decide on the size of 'rak'.

Variable	Type	Name	Value
A	↔	X Dimension	0.900
B	↕	Y Dimension	1.000
numrisr		Number of Stair Risers	6
riser		Stair Riser Height	0.200
going		Stair Going Size	0.250
matl		Stair Material	5
rak		Rake of Nosing	0.050
pcol		Pen colour	1

3 D Script: As is common with the Cookbook ethic, a very structured approach is used, whereby the executive script is as SHORT as possible, with most of the workload delegated to the subroutines.

The majority of shapes used in GDL can be done with **PRISM** commands. These always rise up the Z-axis. You have to lay out the PRISM on the X-Y plane, and up it goes. On some paper, draw an X-Y diagram like this. To make it the right way up, it will have to rotate it 90 degrees around Y.

• **First**, doing it NON parametrically, you get the 'Bad Stair' 100: – in which the treads and risers have been individually dimensioned, and no parametric possibility is offered.

• **Second**, you try the 'Good Stair' 200: – in which you store all the points in the prism in a PUT buffer first - allowing you freedom in the number of risers that the staircase will have.

PUT & GET: Please observe how economical the PUT and GET routine is – it replaces the long list of dimensions above with a perfectly parametric solution.

The **GET** command: If you want a number of items from the buffer, you write GET(4) if you want 4, GET(12) if you want 12 etc. You can GET the entire buffer by defining NSP as the quantity; you get what the PRISM command requires – a set of numbers, separated by commas. As the numbers are extracted, the commas are inserted by the GET procedure. The PRISM requires 2 numbers on every line, so the number of points in the prism is NSP/2

```
!Stair parametric - 3D Script

MATERIAL matl: PEN pcol

LET width=A        !make it stretchy
!GOSUB 100: !Stair non parametric
 GOSUB 200: !Stair parametric

!Left  handrail
 IF hrstyl=1 or hrstyl=3 THEN GOSUB 300
!Right handrail
 IF hrstyl=2 or hrstyl=3 THEN GOSUB 400

END !_____
```

The Handrails will be done on the next page

```
!*WARNING* - do not bother typing
!subroutine 100 - it's here as
!an example of inefficient
!programming - Use subroutine 200

100: !Bad Stair, Nine Risers
ADDx width/2
ROTy -90

PRISM 22,width,
0.0,0.00,
0.0,0.25,
1.6,2.25,        1.8,2.25,
1.8,2.00,        1.6,2.00,
1.6,1.75,        1.4,1.75,
1.4,1.50,        1.2,1.50,
1.2,1.25,        1.0,1.25,
1.0,1.00,        0.8,1.00,
0.8,0.75,        0.6,0.75,
0.6,0.50,        0.4,0.50,
0.4,0.25,        0.2,0.25,
0.2,0.0,         0.0,0.00,

DEL 2
RETURN !----------------
```

First, the BAD stair
You can knock up a quick and dirty stair like this by doing it in ArchiCAD's Project plan using Slab tool, then bring it into GDL to tidy it up. But it would be non parametric!

The Good Stair: In this routine, the loop follows its way round the prism shape on the previous page.

Handrails

The user needs to enter their choice of hand-rail configuration. To show you two different methods of doing it, the left has been done with a **TUBE**, and the right has been done with a **CYLIND** and some **Trig**. In reality, use one method or the other, and use the MULx -1 command to draw it other side.

```
!Parameter Script
VALUES 'hrconf' 'No handrail',
  'Left handrail only',
  'Right handrail only',
  'Both handrails'
```

First make a **Value List** offering the user some choice in the configuration. Then use the Master Script to read the Value List and turn it into numbers (flags).

Variable Type Name			Value
pcol	✏	Pen colour	1
shodata	☒	Show Information? ON/OFF?	Off
hrconf	Abc	Handrail Configuration	Left handrail
hrht	⊟	Handrail Height	0.850
hrdiam	⊟	Handrail Diameter	0.080
hrmatl	◉	Handrail Material	11

Handrail with TUBE Command

SUBROUTINE 300 uses the TUBE command. People find TUBE hard to learn, but it is very rewarding.

Tube Section: The cross section is determined by two Polyline commands, one to set the centre of the circle, and the other to describe a circle around it. Radius is half the diameter, 360 is the sweep angle, and 4000 tells it to draw the circle. The extra one [1] on the end makes the rail smooth - to avoid the longitudinal lines you may get along the handrail.

Tube Path: TUBE goes from XYZ location to XYZ location, so there is no need for Trigonometric calculations. The Tube must overshoot at each end by one node. So a two point TUBE needs 4 defined XYZ locations. The start and end locations serve to define the mitring of each end, so a small overshoot of one centimetre is used. Make sure that they go in the right direction to get the mitring to work correctly.

Handrail with CYLIND command

SUBROUTINE 400 uses CYLIND. This is easier to do, but requires Pythagoras to work out the length, and ArcTan to work out the angle of the rail.

Getting it right: depends on the real requirements of the Handrail design - do you need balusters, do you need the tubing to turn at each end, or what? This may determine your choice of TUBE or CYLIND.

```
!2D script for Stair

HOTSPOT2 0,0
HOTSPOT2 0,leng
HOTSPOT2 -A/2,0
HOTSPOT2  A/2,0
  PEN pcol
PROJECT2 3,270,2
  leng = numrisr*going
  pitc = ATN(riser/going)

LINE2 0,0,0,leng
LINE2 0,leng,-A/2,leng-A/2
LINE2 0,leng, A/2,leng-A/2

IF shodata THEN
  fontz=going*1000/A_
  DEFINE STYLE 'show' Arial,
              fontz,4,0
  SET STYLE 'show'
  ROT2 90
  TEXT2 0,0,STR(pitc,4,2)
ENDIF
```

2 D Script: IT IS possible to write a fully parametric 2-D script for this object, but if the redraw time is not unacceptable, it can be left as a PROJECT2. However, even with Project2, you should use the script to place HOTSPOTs at the key positions – makes it easier to pick up. You can also add an arrow to the 2D symbol, to indicate direction.

The 2-D script that DEFINEs a style is there so that you can offer an option for the 2-D symbol to display its pitch to the user, and when the pitch is correct, the user can turn that feature off. The Font is autosized to be the height of one going of the stair.

```
200:!Parametric Stair
!   using PUT&GET
!Using square or raked risers
ADDx width/2
ROTy -90

PUT 0,0
PUT 0,going
PUT (numrisr-1)*riser,
    numrisr*going

FOR N=numrisr to 1 step -1
  PUT N*riser,  N*going
  PUT N*riser, (N-1)*going-rak
NEXT N
PUT 0,0

!Now draw the Stair
PRISM nsp/2,width,
  GET(nsp)

DEL 2
RETURN !----------------
```

```
!Stair Master Script
  LET width=A      !make it stretchy
IF hrconf='No handrail' THEN hrstyl=0
IF hrconf='Left handrail only' THEN hrstyl=1
IF hrconf='Right handrail only' THEN hrstyl=2
IF hrconf='Both handrails' THEN hrstyl=3
```

```
300: !Left Handrail - TUBE
startht=hrht+riser
endht  =(numrisr+1)*riser+hrht
 d=0.01 !one cm overshoot

ADDx width/2-hrdiam/2

MATERIAL hrmatl
RESOL 12
TUBE 2,4,63,
  0,0,901, !Sets Circle centre
  hrdiam/2,360,4000+1,

  0,-d,startht-d,0,
  0,  0,startht,0,
  0,numrisr*going,  endht,  0,
  0,numrisr*going+d,endht+d,0
DEL 1
RETURN !----------------
```

```
400: !Right H'rail - CYLIND
!This requires Trigonometry
startht =hrht+riser
hgoing  =numrisr*going
hriser  =numrisr*riser
hrailen =SQR(hgoing^2+hriser^2)
hrailang =ATN(hriser/hgoing)

ADDx -width/2+hrdiam/2
ADDz  startht
ROTx -90+hrailang

MATERIAL hrmatl
RESOL 12
CYLIND hrailen,hrdiam/2
DEL 3
RETURN !---------------
```

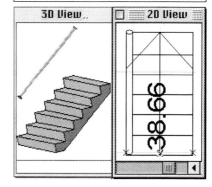

Theatre in the Round Seating

Object

198x182

The result - The Nudist convention meets in Epidaurus!

This exercise is an interesting demonstration of:
- REVOLVE with a parametric profile
- PUT and GET statement
- Using a parametric offset in the REVOLVE command
- Planning the location of the object and the origin

This is a continuation of the Staircase example earlier in the GDL Cookbook.

As with the staircase, the problem is how to make the number of steps as a parametric quantity. You can make each step a separate object (as a prism in plan), and use a loop to draw them. Theatre seating could be done that way.

However, it is better programming to do the bank of seats as one object, and ensure a smooth soffit to the underside. Instead of laying down prisms in plan, draw the **section** of the seating as a prism outline, and then **REVOLVE** that outline.

Parameters: The Bank of seating can be any number of seats, any height or going, any radius of curvature and any sweep angle! You can opt to have staircases or none, on the left or the right side, or on both!! This is important if you are planning to join them together to make larger assemblies. The seating banks do not contain actual seats - like plastic flip up seats - but that may the the subject of a future variation on the model.

It is important to have a 'curviness factor', because the usual default curve resolution of 36 on such a small sweep angle will make the model look too polygonal. Be warned that making it more curvy will add more polygons. You have to balance smoothness with rendering speed!

When you offer your user two choices, you can use the Boolian command, but for more complex requirements, an integer number has to be given, as in stair style.

The steps at the side sit correctly relative to the seats. On the underside, there is a perfectly smooth soffit - because the location of the points for the underside are defined by the same subroutine.

Variable	Type	Name	Value
A		X Dimension	=1.000
B		Y Dimension	=1.000
numrisr		Number of Seat Risers	=8
alphangl		Sweep alpha angle of seating	=60.00
srisrht		Seat Riser Height	=0.500
stgoing		Seat Going Size	=0.900
cent		Distance of front from Centre	=8.000
rs		Resolution (curviness)	=80
sstyl		Stair Style 0=N,1=L,2=R,3=Both	=3
stangl		Stair sweep angle	=10.00
matl		Material	=5
pcol		Pen colour	=68

Structured Approach.... & use PUT and GET

3D Script: A structured approach is employed, whereby the program is as SHORT as possible, with most of the workload delegated to the subroutines.

If you build it with REVOLVE commands using real dimensional data, it will work, but will be non-parametric. If you use a PUT GET routine first, like the one in the Staircase example, you can modify this as freely as the staircase.

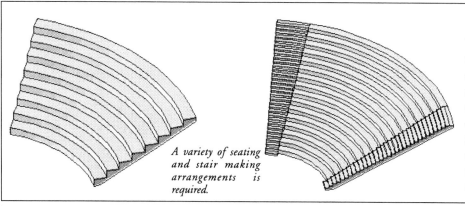

A variety of seating and stair making arrangements is required.

This doesn't have to be used in a greek theatre - this object can be used in an ultra modern stadium, and this curved structure could be set into a steel frame (as one of my students has done) and then tweaked with the parameters to fit.

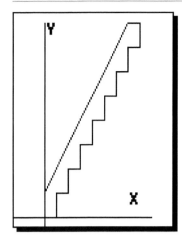

Draw it out first!

As with the Staircase, draw out the shape as if you were to make it with a PRISM command - these always rise up the Z-axis. Draw it first.

The REVOLVE command spins the object around the X-Axis, so one has to be careful how one lays out the prismatic outline. It is done on an X-Y diagram like this. The example shown appears not just to spin around the X-axis, but to touch it. It is a lot easier to work this way, and to apply a parametric OFF-SET, here called 'cent'. So design it according to this diagram.

The Seats and the Stair use virtually the same subroutine - before calling the subroutine, you prime the program with the values of the variables that will produce either a seat or a stair - 'num', 'ris' and 'gon'.

In addition, we add the 'f' flag, to tell the subroutine which structure it is building.

All these 'alphangl' rotations are very important to ensure that the Origin stays at the front row of seats - and that the axis of symmetry of the seats remains down the centre. If you had the origin of the model at the centre of Rotation of the seats and stairs, you would have an easier time programming it; but the user would have a nightmare – everytime they changed the parameters, the whole assembly would jump backwards or forwards, because the origin would be 10s or 100s of metres away.

Looking at the Staircase (previous exercise), one had to feed in the location of the starting points of the stair, followed by the repetition of the x,y coordinates for the stairs themselves. We do the same here. The seats are just like a stair, a similar profile, but bigger. Instead of a PRISM, it's a REVOLVE.

PUT & GET: and 'flags'

PUT&GET were explained in the Staircase example. A difference here is that the same subroutine 400: is used for the seating as for the staircase even though there are a different number of stairs and seats. Another complication is that you must bring the stair forward the length of a step so that the junction of the stairs and the seats is correct. Thus one cannot follow exactly the same algorithm and simply change the riser and going. Here I use the idea of 'flags' which the subroutine checks to see what the current setting is. The flag is called 'f' which can be '0' when drawing the seats and '1' when drawing the stair. A flag can also be used as a factor. If you multiply something by '0', you get zero. Thus, by subtracting an amount equal to the distance of the Risers from the centre which is multiplied by 'f', you finish up with the correct location. Type it in, try it with and without and you will see how it works.

```
!2D script - Theatre Seating

PROJECT2 3,270,3
HOTSPOT2 0,0
HOTSPOT2 0,numrisr*stgoing
   ADD2 0,-cent
   ROT2 90+alphangl/2
GOSUB 100
   ROT2 stangl
GOSUB 100
   DEL 2
   ROT2 90-alphangl/2
GOSUB 100
   ROT2 -stangl
GOSUB 100
   DEL 2
END !_____

100: !draw hotspots
HOTSPOT2 cent,0
HOTSPOT2 cent+numrisr*stgoing,0
RETURN
```

```
!Curved Theatre Seating
!3D Script

IF rs<36 THEN rs=36
RESOL rs: MATERIAL matl: PEN pcol

   GOSUB 100   !seats parametric

IF sstyl=1 or sstyl=3 THEN !Left Stair
   GOSUB 200   !stairs one side
   ENDIF

IF sstyl=2 or sstyl=3 THEN !Right Stair
   MULx -1
   GOSUB 200   !stairs other side
   DEL 1
   ENDIF

END !_____
```

```
100: !Parametric Seats
         !using PUT & GET
ADDy -cent
ROTz -alphangl/2
ROTy -90

num=numrisr: rak=ABS(rak)
ris=srisrht:gon=stgoing: f=0
GOSUB 400   !PUT all the values

!Now draw the seats
REVOLVE nsp/3,alphangl,63,
   GET(nsp)

   DEL 3
RETURN !-----------------------
```

```
200: !Draw the stairs
ADDy -cent
ROTz +alphangl/2+stangl/2
ADDy +cent
   GOSUB 300
   DEL 3
RETURN

300: !Parametric Stairs
         !using PUT & GET
num=numrisr*2:
ris=srisrht/2:
gon=stgoing/2
f=1            !'f'=stepsflag
GOSUB 400      !PUT all values

!Now draw the stair
ADDy -cent
ROTz -stangl/2
ROTy -90

REVOLVE nsp/3,stangl,63,
   GET(nsp)      !Do it!!

   DEL 3
RETURN !-----------------------
```

```
400:!----- PUT routine ---
PUT 0,0 + cent -f*gon,0
PUT 0,stgoing/2+cent,0
PUT  numrisr*srisrht-srisrht/2,
     numrisr*stgoing+cent,0
PUT num*ris,(num)*gon+cent,0

FOR N=num to 1 step -1
  PUT N*ris,(N - f)*gon+cent,0
  PUT N*ris,(N-1-f)*gon+cent-rak,0
  IF bulrak THEN
    PUT N*ris-rak,(N-1-f)*gon+cent-rak,0
    PUT N*ris-rak,(N-1-f)*gon+cent,0
    ENDIF
  NEXT N
  PUT 0,0+cent-f*gon,0
RETURN !---------------------+
```

theatre_seating / 2D Full

40 %

2D Script: You need a Project2, but you also need a bit of tricky thinking to work out the location of Hotspots – needed to help you pick the object up. You could borrow the script from the Staircase which prints out the pitch (angle) and have it displayed on the 2D symbol so that you can tweak the seating to fit a steel frame.

Spiral Staircase

Object

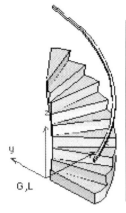

Variable	Type	Name	Value
A		X Dimension	2.000
B		Y Dimension	2.000
numrisr		Number of Stair Risers	9
width		Width of Stair	0.900
riser		Stair Riser Height	0.200
going		Stair Going Size	0.250
matl		Stair Material	5
pcol		Pen colour	1
rakd		Rake dimension	0.020
hrhit		Handrail Height (0=none)	0.800
stret		Make it Stretchy ON/OFF?	On

bPRISM **is special:** The Spiral Staircase follows on logically from the two previous examples. It is an important example though, because it shows a reason why Graphisoft made bPRISM exceptional in being able to tolerate a negative figure for depth. If 'width' had to be positive, the stairwell radius could never be smaller than the stairwidth.

As with all the staircases, the only way to make it parametric is to master the use of the PUT command in a FOR... NEXT loop to allow a variable number of risers.

If you wish the origin to be in the centre of the staircase, you need an offset at the start of the 3D script. You also need a ROTx move at the start to make the staircase stand upright.

It is very timesaving if you can use the same technique, with minor variations, to define the handrail. The drawback of this is that it has to be a rectangular section. If you wanted a round tubular section, you would have to use a helical TUBE routine.

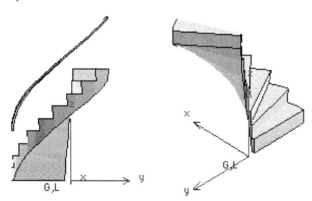

ArchiCAD Training

No matter how long one has been driving, or parenting, or architecting (for that matter) there is always something useful one can learn from others – no matter whether they are equals, experts, or newcomers with open eyes.

In the United States, you can attend ArchiCAMP sessions – Weekends or Daycamps in many locations. You can also attend some great one-day specials with Digital Vision in Anaheim, California.

In Europe, you can have an invigorating weekend in the company of ArchiCAD University, held in every September in Nottingham, England.

```
!Stair spiral - 3D Script
!
 MATERIAL matl: PEN pcol

GOSUB 50:!Error checking

!Globals
ADDy -A/2
ROTx 90

GOSUB 100:!Put the locations for Stair

!Now draw the Stair
bPRISM_ matl,matl,matl,
  nsp/3,-width,A/2,
  GET(nsp)

IF hrhit>riser THEN GOSUB 200:!Handrail

DEL top

END:!-----------------------

50:!Error checking
IF width>A/2 THEN width=A/2.01
IF rakd>going/3 THEN rakd=going/3
RETURN

100:!Put the locations for Stair
PUT 0,0,15
PUT going,0,15
PUT numrisr*going,(numrisr-1)*riser,15

FOR N=numrisr to 1 step -1
  PUT  N*going+rakd,N*riser, 15
  PUT  (N-1)*going,N*riser, 15
  NEXT N
  PUT 0,0,15
RETURN

200:!PUT locations for Handrail
PUT 0,0,15,
    0,0.04,15
PUT numrisr*going,numrisr*riser+0.04,15,
    numrisr*going,numrisr*riser,15

!Now draw the Handrail
ADDy hrhit
bPRISM_ matl,matl,matl,
  nsp/3,-0.04,A/2,
  GET(nsp)
DEL 1
RETURN
```

```
!Spiral Staircase - 2D script

HOTSPOT2 0,0
HOTSPOT2 0,-A/2
HOTSPOT2 0,-A/2+width
HOTSPOT2 A/2,0

IF stret THEN HOTSPOT2 -A/2,0

PROJECT2 3,270,2 !Do it last
```

2D **Script:** It would be very tiresome to script this fully in 2-D, and unless you have dozens of spiral stairs in the building, you would not get a speed benefit from doing so: therefore you can be contented with a PROJECT2 command. what you must do is to ensure that you have HOTSPOTs in the right places to help you pick up the stair. There is a little IF statement that allows you to make the stair stretchy. If you stretch it, the diameter of the well is changed.

3D GDL –Building Elements

C WALL and bWALL: are commands that GDL users do not penetrate, as they are typical of the most difficult parts of the GDL manual; strangely, they spend pages detailing the use of GDL commands that are only likely to be used in autoscripting. You get to the point where the difficulty of writing something in GDL is only justifiable if you are going to get parametric objects. Otherwise, you are better creating it with the normal ArchiCAD tools, and saving the result as an object. I have tried making objects with them, but these are all easier to make with SLAB, PRISM and so forth.

There is also **XWALL**, for walls with holes, cuts and everything.

cROOF The same can be said for CROOF, although CROOF is less difficult for someone really determined to get custom window shapes for rooflighting. I guess these commands are not really intended for people using creative GDL scripting. If you are a Voyager, you will be able to cope with the example given in the manual.

```
======= Wall & Primitive Elements =======   Theory
[====]  Wall elements

CWALL_ leftmat, rightmat, sidemat, height, x1, x2, x3, x4, t, mask1, mask2,
mask3, mask4, n, xbeg1, lower1, xend1, upper1, framevis1, ... xbegn, lowern,
xendn, uppern, framevisn, m, a1, b1, c1, d1, ... am, bm, cm, dm {a straight wall}
BWALL_ leftmat, rightmat, sidemat, height, x1, x2, x3, x4, t, radius, mask1, mask2,
mask3, mask4, n, xbeg1, lower1, xend1, upper1, framevis1, ... xbegn, lowern,
xendn, uppern, framevisn, m, a1, b1, c1, d1, ... am, bm, cm, dm {a smooth curved wall}

  Primitive elements
VERT x, y, z {the definition of a node}
VECT x, y, z {the normal vector of a polygon}
EDGE vert1, vert2, pgon1, pgon2, status {the definition of an edge}
PGON n, ivect, status, edge1, edge2, ... edgen {the definition of a polygon}
BODY status {the condition of a body defined by the primitive elements}
PIPG filename, a, b, mask, n, ivect, status, edge1, edge2, ... edgen
            {picture polygon definition}

COOR wrap, vert1, vert2, vert3, vert4 {Local coordinate system of a BODY for the
       fill mapping. wrap 1: planar, 2: box, 3: cylindrical, 4: spherical}
```

VERT, EDGE, PGON, BODY, PIPG, BASE, VERT, TEVE and COOR.

These commands are vital to imported Autoscripted objects. If you import DXF files, you get them condensed into pages of scripted garbage using these commands. So while it's useful to have a way of interpreting DXF imports, I doubt if you will use them for making new objects.

VERT and COOR can be used to exert greater control over mapped textures in photo rendering, but the example in the manual works, but does not carry an explanation of how it works, and it seems to work erratically. Future Cookbooks will investigate.

BODY can be used to do a check on the integrity of 3D commands, and I recommend you to use it in the form BODY -1. All autoscripted object commands have BODY -1 before and after them, and Graphisoft write these in to improve the reliability of objects in the script. So it cannot do any harm to write this in after long Prisms, Revolves and other bodies. I have found in practice that occasions when objects made with TUBE (remember the 'mental health warning') render more reliably with the BODY -1 command nearby.

Conclusion: Use BODY -1

SPECIAL PRISMs

F PRISM allow you to chamfer the top edge of a prism, and to have different materials for each surface. Put an angle in and you get a hipped roof effect. Put in zero for angle, and you get round edges.

RESOL works differently. Usually, in a 90degree curve, you would get 1/4 of the resolution i.e. resol 40 would give 10 edges. Here, you get your exact resol figure; resol 10 gives 10 edges.

Most realistic furnishing and other objects have rounded edges; this FPRISM function is a real help.

Bug Report:

FPRISM does not have masking to hide the many horizontal lines on rounded surfaces on the 'hill'.

FPRISM was bad in early AC releases – could not work with MULZ -1, and the Hill material determined the side and bottom materials. Upgrade to AC 6.5 if this troubles you.

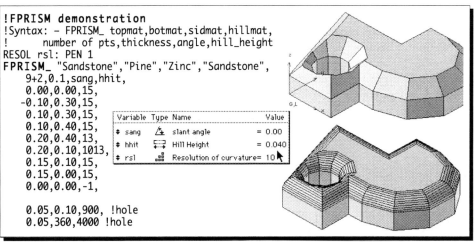

```
!FPRISM demonstration
!Syntax: - FPRISM_ topmat,botmat,sidmat,hillmat,
!       number of pts,thickness,angle,hill_height
RESOL rsl: PEN 1
FPRISM_ "Sandstone","Pine","Zinc","Sandstone",
    9+2,0.1,sang,hhit,
    0.00,0.00,15,
    -0.10,0.30,15,
    0.10,0.30,15,
    0.10,0.40,15,
    0.20,0.40,13,
    0.20,0.10,1013,
    0.15,0.10,15,
    0.15,0.00,15,
    0.00,0.00,-1,

    0.05,0.10,900,  !hole
    0.05,360,4000  !hole
```

Variable	Type	Name	Value
sang	slant angle		= 0.00
hhit	Hill Height		= 0.040
rsl	Resolution of curvature		= 10

More 3D GDL

Theory

SPRISM is a routine for cutting a roofplane through the top of a Prism. It is not as useful as FPRISM, in that you can use a normal prism with a Cutplane to achieve the same result, where as FPRISM is unique. It has always been difficult to use any of the FDL commands which use **Vectors** (ROT, and one version of CUTPLANE) because of the effort to imagine the result, so some trial and error is required. In this case the vector draws a line on the X,Y plane, and the roof is cut at right angles to that line, at the height and angle specified.

If the roofplane is cutting too harshly (i.e. it cuts through the floor of the Prism) it will not get drawn.

```
!SPRISM demonstration
!Syntax: - SPRISM_ topmat,botmat,sidmat,hillmat,
!   number of points,X_begin,Y_begin,X_end,Y_end,height,angle,
!   x1,y1,mask, x2,y2,mask..... xn,yn,mask

RESOL 10: PEN 1
SPRISM_ "Sandstone","Pine","Zinc",          0.20,0.10,1013,
    9+2,0,0,0.1,0.1,0.2,-30,                 0.15,0.10,15,
    0.00,0.00,15,                            0.15,0.00,15,
    -0.10,0.30,15,                           0.00,0.00,-1,
    0.10,0.30,15,
    0.10,0.40,15,                            0.05,0.10,900, !hole
    0.20,0.40,13,                            0.05,360,4000 !hole
```

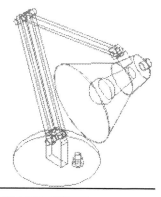

Frankly, it's easier to use CUTPLANE, once you have got the hang of it.

LIGHT I offer an example of the LIGHT command in the Discovery Cookbook (Standard Lamp), and there is one example in the Voyager, in the Anglepoise lamp.

It is a topic I have been looking at hard recently (in the Smart Car), in which the car headlights are the only lightsources in a model several miles wide!

Remember that an object (eg bulb in the light fitting) that emits light can be assigned Material indices. For example, when the light is ON, it can be 'Lamp' and when OFF, it can be 'Whitewash'.

Only when the light is directional can it cast shadows – a general brightener does not cast shadows. Directional LIGHT travels along the X-axis. Lamps are only effective if you turn 'Lamps' on as a light source in the PhotoRendering settings box.

CUTPOLY has huge advantages over CUTPLANE in that it operates like a cookie cutter through the model.

You define the profile of CUTPOLY with similar syntax to a common PRISM. It grows up from the X-Y plane. The direction of the cut can be modified by maneouvring it into position (like I advise for CUTPLANE, and just like you would do if you were trying to manoevre a PRISM to the same location) or it can defined with a final x,y,z statement at the end of the CUTPOLY statement which defines a vector (from 0,0,0).

A limitation is that the profiles MUST be CONVEX. Concave or more complex shapes would have to be built from a succession of convex CUTPOLY statements.

CUTPOLYA If you want holes with Polylines enabled, you can use a variation called **CUTPOLYA** which is analogous to PRISM_ in that every XY location has to be followed by a masking value, usually 15. You are supposed to be able to point CUTPOLYA in a certain direction and fire it off a defined distance, but this feature does not work in AC_6 or 6.5 and it is best to assume that the cut profile is infinite in length.

There is also **CUTSHAPE** but I have not had occasion to use it yet.

```
!CUTPOLY demonstration
!Syntax: - CUTPOLY no_of_cutting points,
!         x1,y1,x2,y2,...xn,yn
!         (define a poly cut plane)
!         [,x,y,z] (optional)
!         defines the vector direction
!         of cutting.
!Remember to issue a CUTEND after
!you have made your object

PEN 1
MATERIAL "Gold"
RESOL 16
    ADDz 0.02
    ROTx 90
CUTPOLY 4,
    -0.02, 0,
    0.02, 0,
    0.02, 0.02
    -0.02, 0.02
DEL 2

!Now for the object!
CONE 0.04,0.04,0.06,90,90
CUTEND    !Close with a Cutend
```

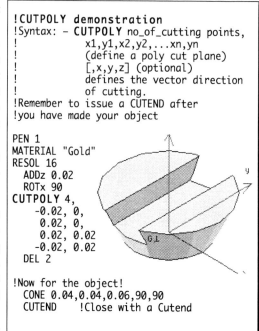

WALLHOLE has almost identical syntax to CUTPOLYA, but only operates when part of a window object. It supports polylines. It drills a holes through a wall, but must not have any complicated peninsulas, or it will not happen, and the window will default to a rectangle based on A and B. See the Curvy Windows in both the Discovery and Voyager courses for examples. Like CUTPOLY, you maneouvre it to its destination as if you were moving a PRISM, and the job is done.

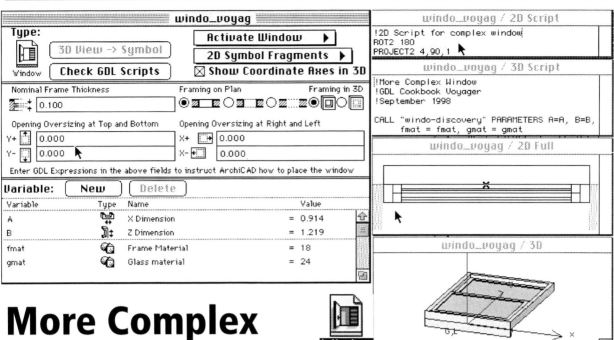

More Complex Window

IN THE DISCOVERY volume, you will find the exercise called 'Simple Window'. This laid down rules for building windows with a script. Quite often, you need a window with special jamb details, a curved lintel, a projecting sill, or some other complication. This exercise shows how to provide some of these complications.

To save typing the original window again, try using the CALL command. You can either type in the CALL manually, or you can make a small wall, put the window into it, save that as a temporary library object, then open that and copy the little bit of text above. As we want to be able to redefine materials etc, and use the same A and B as before, you can use A=A, and so on, using identical parameter names.

Window and Doors always cut a rectangular shape in a wall, so it is important that your A and B parameters apply to the window itself; but you may need to cut a hole much bigger to accommodate arched lintels or the like.

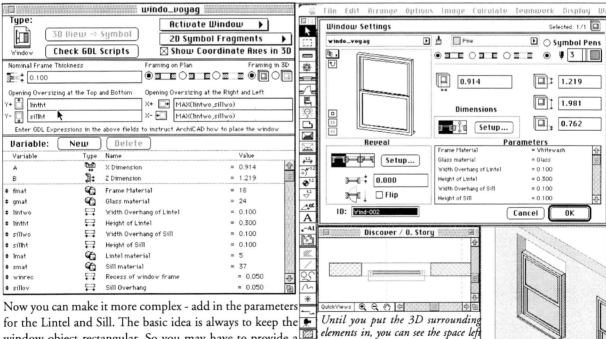

Until you put the 3D surrounding elements in, you can see the space left around the window

Now you can make it more complex - add in the parameters for the Lintel and Sill. The basic idea is always to keep the window object rectangular. So you may have to provide a jamb around the window.

If the lintel and sill both project from the face of the wall, you can keep things simple. Just add them to the 3D model, and they will exist in the 3D model. This exercise shows you the 'pukka' method whereby you might also have to build jambs around the window. This also ensure that you have

the correct materials on the reveals. A plain window in an ArchiCAD wall will have brick on the inside reveals, or plaster on the outside reveals – not good! By building a jamb element, you ensure that the reveals render correctly.

In the Library box where you enter new parameters, you can enter 'Oversize' parameters for width and height. You can enter real dimensions, or can put in variables, or expressions. Here, we want it to cut a hole to conform to the widest element - either the lintel or the sill. Use the MAX factor.

```
!More Complex Window
!Voyager

ADDz winrec
CALL "windo-discovery" PARAMETERS
    A=A,B=B,fmat=fmat,gmat=gmat
DEL 1

wmax=MAX(lintwo,sillwo) !largest width
recp=winrec+0.05 !centre point of frame

!Jambs & wall above & below
!External face
MATERIAL "Red Brick"!H_
PRISM_ 5+5,winrec+0.05,
  -A/2-wmax,-sillht,    8,
  -A/2-wmax,B+lintht,   8,
   A/2+wmax,B+lintht,   8,
   A/2+wmax,-sillht,    8,
  -A/2-wmax,-sillht,   -1,

  -A/2,0-0.01,15,
  -A/2,B+0.01,15,
   A/2,B+0.01,15,
   A/2,0-0.01,15,
  -A/2,0-0.01,-1

!Internal face
 ADDz winrec+0.05
MATERIAL "whitewash"!G_
PRISM_ 5+5,C_-winrec-0.05,
  -A/2-wmax,-sillht,    8,
  -A/2-wmax,B+lintht,   8,
   A/2+wmax,B+lintht,   8,
   A/2+wmax,-sillht,    8,
  -A/2-wmax,-sillht,   -1,

  -A/2,0,15,
  -A/2,B,15,
   A/2,B,15,
   A/2,0,15,
  -A/2,0,-1
DEL 1

!Lintel face
 ADDz -0.01
MATERIAL lmat
PRISM 4,winrec+0.05,
  -A/2-lintwo,B,
  -A/2-lintwo,B+lintht,
   A/2+lintwo,B+lintht,
   A/2+lintwo,B

!Sill Piece
 ADD  -A/2-sillwo,0,winrec
ROTy 90
MATERIAL smat
PRISM 5,A+sillwo*2,
   0,0,
   winrec,0,
   winrec+0.05,-sillht/2,
   winrec+0.05,-sillht,
   0,-sillht
 DEL 2
END:!-------------------
```

```
!2D - complex window
!This could be better
!if fully scripted
ROT2 180
PROJECT2 4,90,1
DEL 1
```

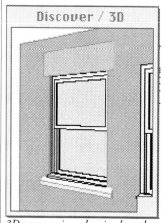

3D view in the 'bottom plan view position' showing the whole assembly of jamb, linto and sill.

3D camera view, showing how there are no lines around the jamb element - buy using 8 as the masking value.

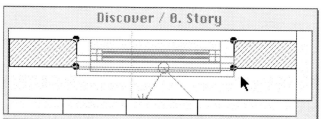

Just to remind you, you only need to do the jamb element if you have receding or hollow elements in the window (such as a fanlight). It isnt really necessary in this particular model.

3D Script commentary

The window is CALLED from the previous exercise. the Call command refers to the same parameter names, A,B, fmat and gmat. Lift the window frame if you wish to control the amount it is recessed into the opening (if you use ArchiCAD's control, it may recess the whole assembly - not good!)

wmax and *recp* just save you typing later by establishing them as 'internal parameters' (calculated from main parameters) to define window width and recess distance to the centre of the frame. As it was a 100mm frame, the distance is *winrec+0.05*.

The Jamb is just a prism built around the window frame. It is important to make full use of masking, to get it looking right. The outside of the prism has a masking value of 8 (show face only, no lines) to avoid a line showing around the opening. The inside face of the prism, showing the reveals, is done with 15, because you want the lines to show.

Two prisms are drawn, one for the external wall surface, and one for the internal wall surface. the materials and thicknesses are based on Global variables G_, H_, I_ and C_.

The lintel face is just another prism.

The Sill is more complicated. Because it is profiled, it has to be built upwards as a prism and then a ROTy 90 lays it down into position.

2D script: The one here is simple, but it is not ideal. The Project2 command (first shown to you in the Simple Window exercise) has to be in wireline, but then it shows too much of the construction lines. If the window is to be used a lot, it is better to be fully scripted, in which you could also add fill pattern, more hotspots, change the constructional detail at different scales and so on. The A and B dimensions in the Library settings box will continue to apply to the window frame only.

Glazing Assembly

Object

Variable	Type	Name	Value
A	⇄	X Dimension	2.400
B	⇅	Y Dimension	0.120
zzyzx	⇶	Vertical Height	2.400
numbay	▫	Number of Bays in WindowWall	4
mmatl	⊚	Material of Mullions	11
transm	⇶	Transom heights (see table)	[5]
shoglas	☒	Show Glass? Y=1 No=1	On
gmatl	⊚	Material of Glass	29
tiltang	∠	Tilt angle of Glazing	0.00

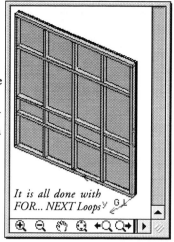
It is all done with FOR... NEXT Loops

Remember, this is an Object, not a Window. You can make it into a 'window' by applying a ROTx -90 to the whole 3D thing, saving it as a window, and writing the 2D script that I recommend for Windows.

THIS GLAZING infil panel could be useful, and the exercise illustrates:

- Using Subroutines to ensure modularity
- Using FOR...NEXT loops for repetition
- PUT and GET
- 2-D scripting, where PROJECT2 would not work well
- Using an Array in the Parameter box

Parameters: You should use A to define window width, zzyzx the height.

The user is offered a TILT to the glazing, because when I first did this, the client had tilted glazing.

Although this is a Glazing system, it is NOT SAVED AS A 'WINDOW' (in the ArchiCAD definition). This is because it is designed to sit in a frame construction building as an OBJECT - not to be punched into a wall. If it's in a wall, you have to put an empty hole in the wall first.

'Transm' is an Array and you can click on the array button – make 5 heights, which can be all zero or any combination of heights.

```
!WindowWall
!MasterScript
wid=A
height=zzyzx
mulwid = 0.05
muldep=0.12
mulspac=(wid-mulwid)/numbay

PUT 0.000, 0.0,
  0.000, 0.05,
  0.077, 0.05,
  0.077, 0.031,
  0.106, 0.031,
  0.106, 0.05,
  0.121, 0.05,
  0.121, 0.0,
  0.106, 0.0,
  0.106, 0.019,
  0.077, 0.019,
  0.077, 0.0,
  0.000, 0.0,
```

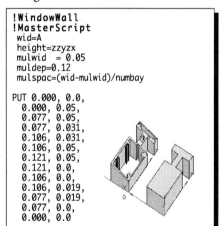

2 D Script: It is not practical to use PROJECT2 unless the window is tilted. If you do it hidden line, you cannot see the mullions; if you do it wireline, you get a excessive mass of detail in the lines.

The 2D script is similar to the 3-D script; it draws the mullions as a subroutine in a FOR... NEXT loop, using the same Subroutine number in each script (here, 150:). The 2-D script reads parameters from the main Parameter box, but also from the Master Script.

3 D Script: The executive script is resolved into subroutines, so that each part of the model can be separately drawn.

Use the Master Script to up variables that are NOT in the parameter box, but will be used in the script, such as *mulspac*. These are 'internal parameters' – they are there to help you, but are not modifiable by the user.

As this exercise is for general 3-D modelling, it doesn't go in for special features like mitring the ends of the transoms - they just cross through the mullions, and butt against the jamb sections.

Here, a simplified mullion is provided, but you could CALL one that exists as a separate object, if you were using proprietary components - which may have been supplied to you as manufacturers DXF profiles.

```
!WindowWall - 2D script

HOTSPOT2 0,0
HOTSPOT2 A,0

IF tiltang THEN
  PROJECT2 3,270,2
  HOTSPOT2 0,-height*SIN(tiltang)
  HOTSPOT2 A,-height*SIN(tiltang)
ENDIF

RECT2 0,0, A,-0.121 !Outline
FOR k=1 TO numbay+1 !Mullions
  ADD2 mulspac*(k-1),0
  GOSUB 150: !mullion
  DEL 1
NEXT k

!Glass
RECT2 0.032,-0.1,A-0.032,-0.08

END:!-----------------

150: !Mullion
  ROT2 -90
  POLY2 NSP/2,1,
  USE(NSP)
  DEL 1
RETURN
```

```
!WindowWall 3D Script

ROTx tiltang    !global tilt
MATERIAL mmatl
GOSUB 100: !Sole & Head
GOSUB 200: !Mullions
GOSUB 300: !Transoms
IF shoglas THEN GOSUB 600: !Glass

END !-----------------------

150: !Mullion section
!simplified Astrawall
PRISM NSP/2,len,
  USE(NSP)
RETURN

200: !MULLIONS
len=height-mulwid*2
ADDz mulwid
FOR k=1 TO numbay+1
  ADDx mulspac*(k-1)
  ROTz -90
  GOSUB 150 !Draw it!
  DEL 2
NEXT k
DEL 1
RETURN

300: !TRANSOMS
len=A-mulwid*2
FOR k=1 TO 5
  IF transm[k] THEN
    ADD mulwid,0, transm[k]+mulwid
    ROTy 90: ROTz -90: GOSUB 150
    DEL 3
  ENDIF
NEXT k
RETURN

600: !SHOW GLASS
MATERIAL gmatl
  ADD mulwid,-0.1,mulwid:
  BLOCK A-mulwid*2,0.015,
      height-mulwid*2
  DEL 1
RETURN
```

If you use GET here (instead of USE), you will empty the buffer and no more mullions could be drawn

Values of transm [5]	
	1
1	1.900
2	1.800
3	0.000
4	0.000
5	0.000

The user enters heights for up to 5 transoms in the array

PUT & GET: This demonstrates a economical use of PUT and GET. The Mullion outline is PUT once only, in the Master Script. The 2D and 3D script use the USE(NSP) command, which uses the outline without emptying the buffer.

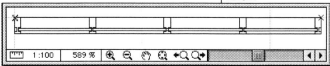

Curvy Window

PREVIOUSLY, making windows any shape other than a rectangle was a bit of a nightmare; you had to construct chunks of wall around the window, investing it with the exact qualities of the wall around it, and paying deep attention to the line drawing of the PRISM that makes the wall, and mimicking in reverse the profile of the window.

ArchiCAD 6 brings you the command **WALLHOLE** which is a boon to all GDL users. You can define any shape, no matter how complex, providing it does not have any concavities, and the shape will be made for you. If you have concavities in the window outline, then you can use additional Wallholes until the job is done. Thus you can concentrate on building the window only, letting the Wall reshape itself as if made of liquid, around the window.

This window is a portion of a much larger 'Super Window' project that I am working on, which contains 10 different window shapes in one script. This exercise shows two of them.
There is a simpler version of this window in the Discovery section

This exercise is useful in several things:
• **Using Value Lists to set up the parameters**
• **Using Arrays to store numbers**
• **Using TUBE command to make the frame**
• **PUT and GET to build elements**
• **Using circle trigonometry to calculate curvature variables**
• **Using the WALLHOLE command**
• **Making an object stretchy**

Values List (in Parameter script)
The window shape is a parameter called 'winshape', and you have a choice of putting in a 'transom'. I tend to use Value lists even for simple Booleian choices, as it is more user friendly, and leaves the option of adding more choices later with easier coding. Thus, Value lists allow you a more structured approach.

```
VALUES "winshape" "Arched","Pointed"
VALUES "transom"  "None",
                  "Horizontal at Jamb ht"
```

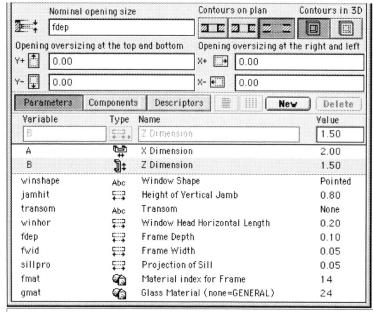

Variable	Type	Name	Value
B		Z Dimension	1.50
A		X Dimension	2.00
B		Z Dimension	1.50
winshape	Abc	Window Shape	Pointed
jamhit		Height of Vertical Jamb	0.80
transom	Abc	Transom	None
winhor		Window Head Horizontal Length	0.20
fdep		Frame Depth	0.10
fwid		Frame Width	0.05
sillpro		Projection of Sill	0.05
fmat		Material index for Frame	14
gmat		Glass Material (none=GENERAL)	24

Parameters: A and B are always the most important parameters in window design as these are what make the window stretchy in its outline dimensions. You need to specify a Jamb height – the difference between the jamb height and the total height will determine the curvature. In case the window is to have a flat top, specify a length for the horizontal element, 'winhor'. The frame is defined ('fdep' and 'fwid') and the projection of the sill element. Finally, you need to specify the materials in case the user has modified the material index for Glass.

Master Script: Here, it reads and converts the Value list into numbers, converts A and B into english, checks for user's errors (such as negative quantities) on the entry of parameters 'winhor', 'sillpro' and 'jamhit'.

```
!Curved top window
!for GDL Cookbook
!Part of Super-window - Master Script

!Window Shape
IF winshape="Arched"  THEN wsh=4
IF winshape="Pointed" THEN wsh=8

!Transom Option
IF transom="None" THEN trnsm=0
IF transom="Horizontal at Jamb ht" THEN trnsm=1

tothit=B        !Total Height
winwid=A        !Window width
```
Always parse the Value Lists first

```
!Limit length of window head
 winhor=ABS(winhor)
IF winhor<fwid THEN winhor=fwid
IF winhor>winwid*2/3 THEN winhor=winwid*2/3

 fd=fdep/2      !Half Frame Depth
IF jamhit<=fwid THEN jamhit=fwid

!Sill Check
sillpro=ABS(sillpro) !make sure it's positive
```

```
!Curved top window - 3D Script
!Part of Super-window
!See MASTER SCRIPT for Parameter organisation

!Array for window X and Y's
DIM winxy[3][60]

!3D Script begins..........................
ADDz fdep/2

!Arched Window ))))))
IF wsh=4 THEN GOSUB 140

!Pointed Central>>>>>
IF wsh=8 THEN GOSUB 180

nfp=NSP/3 !Number of points in frame
GOSUB 210:!Store numbers in an array
GOSUB 250:!Wallhole command
GOSUB 260:!Draw Glass
GOSUB 270:!Draw Frame
GOSUB 300:!Transom
GOSUB 310:!Projecting Sill
DEL 1
END:!------------------------
```

Where did subroutines 100, 110, 120, 130 etc go to?? They are part of my 'Super window', offering a variety of shapes.

Remember the Golden rule of Window making is that you build it with the external face flat on the ground, with the origin at the mid-width if possible.

Subroutines 140 and 180 go off and calculate the X,Y coordinates of the outline shape of the window. Then the remaining subroutines perform tasks (as annotated in the script).

3 **D Script: Curvature:** The two calculations here establish the Radius and sweep angle of the two curves. They appear the same but are not. The arched window goes from round to flat, but the pointed window goes from round to pointed. So 'curvwid' and 'curvhit' change places.

Control: If the user stretches or shrinks the window beyond reasonable limits, you will get an error. To avoid this, get it to devise a new value for 'jamhit' (jamb height), so a new 'curvhit' gets calculated which always produces a correct result (avoiding a 'divide by zero error').

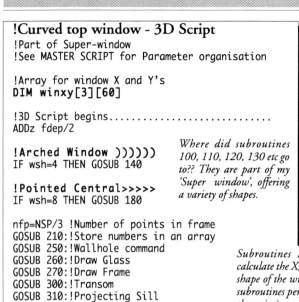

3D view of the two window shapes, set into a wall. If you put the frame thickness 'fdep' into the frame thickness box in the parameters box, the window can be pushed deeper into the wall.

```
140:!Arched Window ))))))
!Calculate Curve dimensions
 curvwid=(A-winhor)/2 !width of curved section
 curvhit=tothit-jamhit!Height of Curve

!Allows window to modify jamb height
IF curvhit<=fwid THEN !Control Minimum
  jamhit=tothit-fwid
  curvhit=fwid
  ENDIF
IF curvhit>curvwid THEN !Control Maximum
  jamhit=tothit-curvwid
  curvhit=curvwid
  ENDIF

angl=(90-ATN(curvwid/curvhit))*2
crad=curvwid/SIN(angl)
stng=ABS(angl/10)    !Stepping angle

!Locate points on the surface-----------
PUT -A/2,0,15,
    -A/2,jamhit,15

FOR k=-angl+stng TO -stng STEP stng
 PUT  crad*SIN(k)-winhor/2
 PUT -crad+curvhit+jamhit+crad*COS(k),13
 NEXT k

PUT -winhor/2,tothit,15, !Centre section
    winhor/2,tothit,15

FOR k=stng TO angl-stng STEP stng
PUT  crad*SIN(k)+winhor/2
PUT -crad+curvhit+jamhit+crad*COS(k),13
 NEXT k

PUT A/2,jamhit,15,
    A/2,0,15
RETURN
```

'curvwid' and 'curvhit' change places

```
180:!Pointed Arch (Gothic style)>>>>>>
!Calculate Curve dimensions
 curvwid=A/2 !width of curved section
 curvhit=tothit-jamhit   !Height of Curve

!Control jamb height
IF curvhit<=curvwid THEN !Minimum
  jamhit=tothit-curvwid
  curvhit=curvwid
  ENDIF  !No need to control maximum

angl=(90-ATN(curvhit/curvwid))*2
crad=curvhit/SIN(angl)
stng=ABS(angl/10)    !Stepping angle

!Locate points on the surface------
PUT -A/2,0,15,
    -A/2,jamhit,15

FOR k=stng TO angl-stng STEP  stng
 PUT -crad*COS(k)+crad-A/2,jamhit+crad*SIN(k),13
 NEXT k

PUT 0,tothit,13  !Centre point

FOR k=angl-stng TO stng STEP -stng
 PUT crad*COS(k)-crad+A/2,jamhit+crad*SIN(k),13
 NEXT k

PUT A/2,jamhit,15,
    A/2,0,15
RETURN
```

Note that the Masking value for the points on the Curve are 13, not 15, to make it look smoother. The start and end points are 15, to draw the corners correctly.

Note: All that these two routines are doing is calculating the outlines of the window opening and PUTTING them into memory. Nothing else.

```
210:!Store numbers in an array
FOR k=1 TO nfp  !Put number into array
 winxy[1][k]=GET(1) !X coordinate
 winxy[2][k]=GET(1) !Y coordinate
 winxy[3][k]=GET(1) !Masking for hole
NEXT k

FOR k=1 TO 4 !Extend array to enable TUBE
 winxy[1][nfp+k]=winxy[1][k]
 winxy[2][nfp+k]=winxy[2][k]
 winxy[3][nfp+k]=winxy[3][k]
NEXT k
RETURN

220:!Frame Outline Locations
PUT  0.00,-fd,0,
     0.00, fd,0,
     -fwid, fd,0,
     -fwid,-fd,0,
     0.00,-fd,0
np=5 !Number of points
RETURN

250:!Wallhole command for all types
FOR k=1 TO nfp  !Read in array
  PUT winxy[1][k], winxy[2][k],15
  NEXT k
WALLHOLE NSP/3,1,
  GET(NSP)
RETURN

260:!Draw Glass for all types
IF gmat>0 THEN
FOR k=1 TO nfp+1  !Read in array
  PUT winxy[1][k], winxy[2][k],1
  NEXT k
MATERIAL gmat
POLY_ NSP/3,
  GET(NSP)
  ENDIF
RETURN
```

210: This routine is putting the contents of the memory buffer into an array for future use. The same numbers are used for the Wallhole, the Glass and the Frame. The array has to be extended by a further four points to accommodate the TUBE routine.

220: This routine is defining the frame outline, to save having to type it in again for each window type.

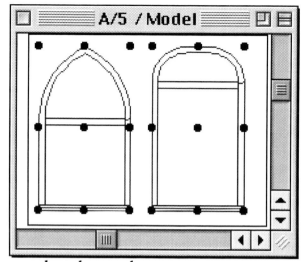

Remember these rules:

• The polygon of points in a Wallhole must not close up.

• The ones in the Glass MUST close up.

• The ones for the frame must go round an extra two lengths because of the 'phantom points'.

This highlights the benefit of using an array – without it, you would have to do a complete recalculation every time.

Finally, if the user wants a transom, they can have it, as a simple block of the same dimension as the frame. I have not built in more complex routines such as small glazing bars, but you could have a go at this yourself.

```
270:!Draw Frame for all types
GOSUB 220:!Get Frame Profile
!Frame
FOR k=1 TO nfp+3  !Read in array
  PUT winxy[1][k],winxy[2][k],0,0
  NEXT k
MATERIAL fmat
TUBE np,nfp+3,63,
  GET(NSP)
RETURN

300:!Transom
IF trnsm THEN
   ADD -A/2+fwid,jamhit-fwid,-fd
   MATERIAL fmat
   BLOCK A-fwid*2,fwid,fdep
   DEL 1
   ENDIF
RETURN

310:!Projecting Sill
IF sillpro THEN
   ROTy -90
   ADDz -winwid/2
MATERIAL fmat
PRISM 5,winwid,
  -fd,0,
  -fd,fwid,
  fd,fwid,
  fd+sillpro,fwid/2,
  fd+sillpro,0
  DEL 2
  ENDIF
RETURN
```

2D Script: It is always worth starting with a PROJECT2 4,90,1 – which draws a wireline from the position and angle that you would see it if building the window from slabs. Gradually you build in a scripted solution that exactly matches with the project2 command.

The Frames, the Outline, the Sill and finally the Glass.

Bugs in Value Lists

I was warned by Graphisoft not to put comments in Value Lists, as these can introduce misbehaviour. But I have included complex IF statements without a problem.

Also, I have seen value lists disappearing, due apparently to a conflict with REQUEST statements in the Master script, or Master Scripts exceeding 10k. wierd....

```
!Curved top window
!2D Script
!for GDL Cookbook Feb 1999
!David Nicholsoncole
!Part of Super-window

ROT2 180
!Just to check that 2D works
!PROJECT2 4,90,1
DEL 1

!Main Frame
ADD2 -winwid/2,-fd
RECT2 0,-fd,fwid,fd
DEL 1
ADD2  winwid/2,-fd
RECT2 0,-fd,-fwid,fd
DEL 1
!Outline
RECT2 -winwid/2,0, winwid/2,-fdep
!Sill
RECT2 -winwid/2,0,winwid/2,sillpro

!Glass
IF gmat THEN
  LINE2 -winwid/2+fwid,-fd,
        winwid/2-fwid,-fd
  ENDIF
```

Anglepoise Lamp

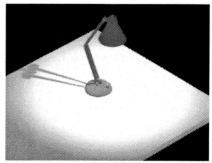

This is an exercise in the use of :
- LIGHT
- REVOLVE
- PRISM_ with Poly lines.
- Mirroring objects using the MUL command

FOR the model to have any credibility in an interior view, it has to be able to hinge like a real lamp, and to be able to switch on its light. This one does both of these things. I use it in interiors.

First of all, my technique is to hammer in some rough script, to get the model started (as on the left). Once I get to the point where it needs to be structured (certain elements need to go into Subroutines) I convert the text, as shown below, by wrapping Line numbers and 'Returns' around the blocks of text, putting an END statement in near the top, and then inserting GOSUB to each of the newly created subroutines. For example, here, I got one main arm working well, and then I want to mirror the main arm on the other side of the pivot.

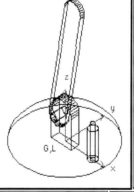

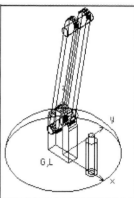

```
!Anglepoise Lamp
!3D Script

PEN 1

!Lamp Base
ELLIPS 0.05,0.1

!basepivot
 ADD -0.025,0.01,0
 ROTx 90
 PRISM_ 5,0.02,
   0,0,15,
   0.05,0.00,15,
   0.05,0.06,15-2,
   0.00,0.06,1015,
   0,0,-1
 DEL 2

!button
 ADD  0.07,0,0.025
 CONE 0.02,0.013,
      0.011,90,90
 CYLIND 0.03,0.007
 DEL 1
```

Left: is a first working script
Right: is the same script, 'massaged' into shape by converting it into two subroutines numberd 100 and 200, not forgetting the button at 110:.

Now that the script has been structured into subroutines, the arm routine (in 210) can be MULled around the Y-axis, which means that you get a mirror image – this is done in subroutine 200.

As the Main arm prism will be used again for the Second arm, the PRISM command is, itself, a small subroutine (220)

```
!Anglepoise Lamp
!3D Script

MATERIAL 0
PEN lcol
RADIUS 0.02,0.03

 GOSUB 100 !Lamp base
 GOSUB 110 !switch
 GOSUB 200 !Lamp arm
END!_____

100: !Lamp Base
ELLIPS 0.05,0.1 !base

 ADD -0.025,0.01,0
 ROTx 90
 PRISM_ 5,0.02,!basepivot
   0,0,15,
   0.05,0.00,15,
   0.05,0.06,15-2,
   0.00,0.06,1015,
   0,0,-1
 DEL 2
RETURN
```

```
110: !Switch
 ADD  0.07,0,0.025
 CONE 0.02,0.013,0.011,
      90,90!base
 GOSUB 230 !Steel button
 DEL 1
RETURN

200: !Lamp Arm
GOSUB 210 !arm part
 MULy -1
GOSUB 210
 DEL 1
RETURN

210: !Arm part
 ADDz 0.065
 ROTx 90
  GOSUB 230 !axle
 ADDz 0.01
 ROTz -armang1
GOSUB 220    !arm prism
 ADD  0,armlen,-0.01
  GOSUB 230 !axle
 DEL 5
RETURN

220: !arm prism
PRISM_ 5,0.01,    !arm
 -0.01,0.00,15,
 -0.01,armlen,15,
  0.01,armlen,1015,
  0.01,0.00,15,
 -0.01,0.00,1000
RETURN

230: !axle / switch
MATERIAL "stainless Steel"
  CYLIND 0.03,0.007 !axle
MATERIAL 0
RETURN
```

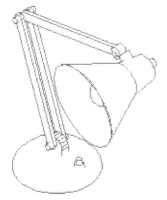

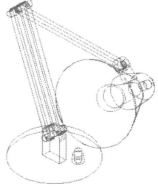

This is the final shape we are aiming at – it helps to draw it freehand in your book, or at least to think out the junction details simplify then appropriately. Avoid over complex levels of detail. For example, there is no point in making the steel springs for the anglepoise unless the lamp is the central point of the model. If it is furniture in an interior design, the level of detail shown here is adequate.

The bright stainless button for the switch is also used as an axle for the arms, so it is a subroutine, called by the other subroutines.

Make a Lamp: The time comes when you need to convert it from an OBJECT to a LAMP. Save the GDL object, and close it. 'Open Library Part' again, and you can say what you want it opened as. This time, make it

come back as a LAMP, and you can now save it as a LAMP. It will add more parameters, all concerned with Lighting, and all starting with single letters, which cannot be edited – but which can be used.

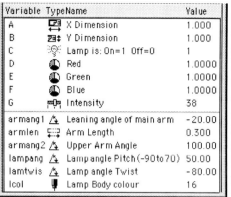

Variable	Type	Name	Value
A		X Dimension	1.000
B		Y Dimension	1.000
C		Lamp is: On=1 Off=0	1
D		Red	1.0000
E		Green	1.0000
F		Blue	1.0000
G		Intensity	38
armang1		Leaning angle of main arm	-20.00
armlen		Arm Length	0.300
armang2		Upper Arm Angle	100.00
lampang		Lamp angle Pitch (-90to70)	50.00
lamtwis		Lamp angle Twist	-80.00
lcol		Lamp Body colour	16

Below is the final script - in the form of a LAMP, not an OBJECT. All this means is that a few parameters are used in the subroutine containing the light bulb. When you have saved the lamp, you may be a bit perturbed that you can no longer find it, but this is because it has been saved as a LAMP and can only be brought back with the lamp icon in the tools pallette.

```
!Angle Poise
!Master Script
IF lampang> 70 THEN lampang= 70
IF lampang<-90 THEN lampang=-90
IF armang1> 80 THEN armang1= 80
IF armang1<-80 THEN armang1=-80
IF armang2>120 THEN armang2=120
IF armang2< 0  THEN armang2=  0
```

Master Script: You can use this to prevent the user defying gravity and materiality by bending the lamp until it goes into its own arms.

```
300: !upperarm
  ADDz 0.065    !lift
  ADDy 0.005    !centralise
  ROTy armang1
  ADDz armlen
  ROTy armang2
  ROTx 90
GOSUB 220      !arm prism
  ADDy armlen
  ADDz -0.01
   GOSUB 230 !axle
  ADDz 0.005
  CYLIND 0.02,0.015!shade swivel
DEL 9
RETURN

400: !Lamp itself
  ADDz 0.065    !lift
  ROTy armang1
  ADDz armlen
  ROTy armang2
  ADDz armlen
  ROTy lampang
  ROTz lamtwis
GOSUB 410 !Lampshade
DEL 7
RETURN
```

```
410: !Lampshade Body
  ADDz 0.01   !lift
  CYLIND 0.02,0.015 !swivel
  ADDz 0.05 !total is 0.06
GOSUB 420   !outercolorshell
  ADDx 0.001
  MULy 0.98
  MATERIAL "whitewash"
  IF C THEN MATERIAL "lamp"
   GOSUB 420 !innerwhiteshell
   GOSUB 430 !bulb
DEL 4
RETURN

420: !lampshade lathe
REVOLVE 5,360,1,
  -0.05,0.01,0,
  -0.03,0.01,0,
  -0.03,0.03,0,
   0.03,0.04,0,
   0.15,0.10,0
RETURN

430: !Lightbulb
  ROTy 90
  CONE 0.08,0.015,0.025,90,90
  ADDz 0.09
  SPHERE 0.03
DEL 2
  !Light points along X
  IF C=1 THEN
    LIGHT G/100*D,!set intensity
          G/100*E,
          G/100*F,!RGB
    1,         !shadow on
    0.2,       !start radius
    30,50,     !Alpha beta
    0.1,       !anglefalloff
    0,2,       !distances
    0.1        !distfalloff
  ENDIF
RETURN
```

Script Commentary: As an articulated model gets longer, you get an increasingly long chain of cursor commands that has to be followed each time you do the next element of the object - you can see what I mean in the script for the Upper Arm.

The Lamp element itself can also twist/rotate, as well as vary its light level and colour. Notice that the cone of the lampshade is drawn twice, the outer shell is coloured, and the inner shell is Lamp coloured.

As one wants the lamp to have bright colours, the Lamp body MATERIAL is set to *zero* and you use PEN to decide on its colour.

You may have to use Trial and Error to get the Distance Falloff and other factors just as you want them – by doing some photorenders, with Lamps active.

Don't forget to update the Executive script regularly as you add in subroutines for the lamp and arms. The RADIUS command is the final touch, to make sure you are not adding too many polygons.

```
!Anglepoise Lamp
!light object
!Final Executive 3DScript

MATERIAL 0
PEN lcol
RADIUS 0.02,0.03

GOSUB 100 !Lamp base
GOSUB 110 !Switch
GOSUB 200 !Lamp arm
GOSUB 300 !upperarm
GOSUB 400 !Lamp itself

END!_____
```

```
!2D Script
HOTSPOT2 0,0
PROJECT2 3,270,2
```

2D Script – Because the lamp can hinge and move, it has to be scripted as a PROJECT2, but it's is a good idea to have a Hotspot at the Origin, so that you can pick it up easily.

Recursive Tree

The Tree as a series of Cones

TREES are one of the biggest problems in 3D modelling because it is difficult to make them look natural random, and they take a very long time to render due to the high number of polygons.

This example of a winter deciduous is a remarkable piece of programming written by a GDL friend, Phil Cannon, who has been using GDL longer than anyone in the UK. It has a very natural look, and if used in a partially 2D form, it has few polygons.

I have adapted it (with permission from Phil) for the Cookbook, because the recursive CALL statement is so wickedly daring that I cannot imagine how he dared to even try it out in the first place. He says it was one of those '2 in the morning' decisions!

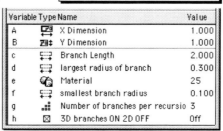

The tree as a series of Planes

The Tree itself: I have adapted it so that the trunk is always solid and rather knarled looking (by using SWEEP) and the rest of the tree can be done as a set of branch structures, using either a series of 2D Planes, or solid Cones.

Needless to say (even with a resol of 5) the Cones take vastly longer to render than the Planes, having 7 polygons each, compared with 2. They also look far too heavy; and it's in the nature of the algorithm that if you made the cones small enough to reduce to the size of real twigs, the iterations would produce so many that it would take all your computer's time to draw just one or a few trees. In silhouette, the Plane-based tree looks more realistic than the Cone-based one. The buildings in your model can be glimpsed more easily through a winter tree than a fully foliated one.

The parameters are kept very simple in naming, to one letter, so that the first 6 letters, c, d, e, f, g, h are all the same meaning in the Tree as in the Branch. In that way, the CALL command is reduced to the most simple form, CALL "recursive_Branch" a,b,c,d,e,f,g,h. (not needing the word PARAMETERs, or a long line of c=c, d=d, e=e, f=f etc etc.)

Variable	Type	Name	Value
A		X Dimension	11.500
B		Y Dimension	11.500
c		Branch Length	2.000
d		largest radius of branch	0.200
e		Material	25
f		smallest branch radius	0.100
g		Number of branches per recursio	3
h		3D branches=ON 2D =OFF	Off
thit		Trunk Height	3.000
twid		Trunk width at base	0.800
pcol		Pen colour	1

Parameter box for the TREE

```
!Recursive Branch
!3D Script
!Phil Cannon
!Adapted by DNC

RESOL 15/g
MATERIAL e
ROTx (10+rnd(25))

IF h THEN !3D
  CONE c,d,d*0.8,90,90
ELSE
  ROTx 90
  POLY 4,!2D
  -d,0,
  d,0,
  d*0.8,c,
  -d*0.8,c
DEL 1
ENDIF

BODY 1
ADDz c
IF d<0.14 AND d>f THEN
  GOSUB 1100
ENDIF
c=c*0.8
d=d*0.8
IF d<f THEN 1099

FOR t= 1 TO g STEP 1
ROTz 360/g
CALL "recursive_Branch"
a, b, c, d, e, f, g, h
NEXT t

1099: DEL TOP
END:!----------

1100:
LET g=5
ROTx 5
RETURN
```

The 3D option – a CONE

The 2D option – a PLANE

Variable	Type	Name	Value
A		X Dimension	1.000
B		Y Dimension	1.000
c		Branch Length	2.000
d		largest radius of branch	0.300
e		Material	25
f		smallest branch radius	0.100
g		Number of branches per recursion	3
h		3D branches ON 2D OFF	Off

```
!Recursive Tree
!3Dscript
!!1996 Phil Cannon
!Modified, with
!PC's permission
!by David NC, Dec 1999

!Trunk
MATERIAL e
GOSUB 100:!trunk

!Branching System
MUL A/9,B/9,1

ADDz thit-thit/3
ROTx 9+rnd(2)
CALL "recursive_Branch" a, b,
c, d, e, f, g, h
DEL 2

ADDz thit
!Centre branch
ROTx -10-RND(25)
CALL "recursive_Branch" a, b,
c, d, e, f, g, h
DEL 2

ADDz thit
ROTz 180
ROTx 9+rnd(2)
CALL "recursive_Branch"
a,b,c,d,e,f,g,h
DEL 1

ROTz 90
ROTx 9+rnd(2)
CALL "recursive_Branch"
a,b,c,d,e,f,g,h
DEL 1

ROTz 180
ROTx 9+rnd(2)
CALL "recursive_Branch" a, b,
c, d, e, f, g, h
DEL TOP

END:!-------------
100:!more realistic trunk
MUL twid/0.6,twid/0.6,1
ROTz RND(180)
SWEEP 10,2,RND(60),0.6,63,
0.1,0.2,0,
0.1,0.1,0,
0.3,0,0,
0.1,-0.25,0,
0,-0.2,0,
-0.05,-0.25,0,
-0.3,-0.05,0,
-0.25,0,0,
-0.2,0.15,0,
0.1,0.2,0,

0,0,0,
0,0,thit
DEL 2
RETURN
```

Phil's original trunk was a Cone, but the SWEEP gives a more irregular section, and the twist makes it look knarled

Normally, if a library object calls itself, the effect is similar to a Subroutine GOSUB-bing itself – but worse. GOSUB can be cancelled with Ctrl-Stop, but the CALL causes the computer to freeze until rebooted. In this case, the diameter and length of the cones or planes are being reduced by 0.8 each time, so when they reach a minimum diameter, they stop proliferating.

2 D Script: The 2D would be too slow if you have a PROJECT2; so you first save the object with Project2. Then explode a copy of the object into 2D, copy and paste it into the 2D Symbol window of the tree. Centre it carefully. make sure it is the right way round. If you add your own 2D hotspots to the symbol, the object will not be stretchy, so you write the stretchiness into the 2D Script – using FRAGMENT2 to call up and display the 2D Symbol. PEN L_ means that the user selected pen will be used, even if the hotspots are black.

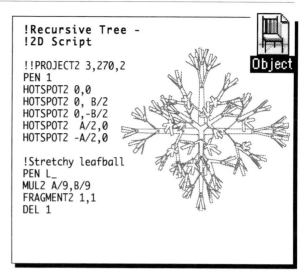

```
!Recursive Tree -
!2D Script

!!PROJECT2 3,270,2
PEN 1
HOTSPOT2 0,0
HOTSPOT2 0, B/2
HOTSPOT2 0,-B/2
HOTSPOT2 A/2,0
HOTSPOT2 -A/2,0

!Stretchy leafball
PEN L_
MUL2 A/9,B/9
FRAGMENT2 1,1
DEL 1
```

A NOTHER way (type 3 below) to make a tree more realistic is to use a scanned or generated image of a tree, create an Alpha Channel for the sky to show through; and impose that on a Picture library object with the ability to turn towards the camera. You can satisfy a wider variety of trees. PhotoTrees cause a high memory overhead despite fewer polygons, because ArchiCAD tries to remember every tree it has already done.

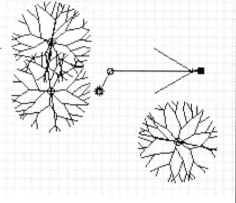

Houses by Letts Wheeler, model by DNC, 2D Tree image by Mick Kingsbury

All the Trees are aware of the camera position, and look most solid from the camera's view. A version of this is in the Cookbook Library.

Tree questions

How do others generate large quantities of trees in their site model renders?

There are several ways of doing trees. Trees on their own are a potential disaster, due to the potential for thousands of polygons in each tree. If the trees are distant, there is no point in a model that faithfully and geometrically tries to build every leaf. But if you are doing a close up, and a tree is important for authenticity, then a geometrically modelled tree is what you want.

So,

First you can have a 3D geometrically modelled tree - if it's any good, it will have randomised branches, and variable height and leafdensity and colour, and leafball shape. I've got one, but the best I know of is one done by Mick Kingsbury in Nottingham, but it's not for sale.

Second, you can have a 3D 'lollipop' style tree, basically a ball on a stick which sounds dreadful, but you can have subtle variations such as using a texture with alpha channels to make it look leafy, shape variations to make it tall+thin, or squat shape, and can reduce the resolution of curvature to make it more polygonal than ball shaped. The result, grouped together with a randomiser to vary the height of each, the trunk height and diameter, the leafball shape and height, can look very effective and have only a fraction of the polygons.

Third, you can have 2D trees, which turn to face the camera. These can be Picture objects (in which case you have to have some alpha chanelled photos of tree types - these can be purchased from library suppliers (look on the Graphisoft web site, someone advertises them). There is a simple one in the GDL Cookbook Library.

Fourth, you can have 2D tree using 3D elements displayed in a 2D arrangement, which turn to face the camera.

The GDL Cookbook could do with a longer feature on trees of all four types, that's an idea for a future edition.

I have been doing a University Campus model, doing the general building shapes (a 3D figure ground plan really) and found that the Lollipop trees are the best solution, with randomised heights and diameters, and a texture that has alpha channels (to make them look filigree)

Kitchen Chair

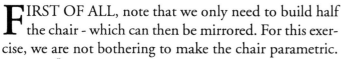

This chair exercise is an example of:
- BPRISM - Bent Prism
- Polylines in Prisms
- Using CONE
- Passing parameters to a macro
- Using symmetry

FIRST OF ALL, note that we only need to build half the chair - which can then be mirrored. For this exercise, we are not bothering to make the chair parametric.

First hammer in the outline of the seat of the chair. Do it as a chamfered shape first, and you will be able to curve the chamfers later. We use PRISM_, not PRISM, because we want to add in curves at the corners using Polylines.

By the way, there is only one Parameter in the parameter box, 'cmat' for the Material.

As I do in almost every exercise, now convert that seat prism to a Subroutine. In addition, convert the chamfers to curves, by adding 1000 to the original masking value of 15. Then subtract 2 from 15 to remove the vertical lines in the curve. Add the ADD command to lift the seat to the correct height.

Variable	Type	Name	Value
A	⟷	X Dimension	1.000
B	↕	Y Dimension	1.000
cmat		Chair Material	16
arms	Abc	Include or Hide Arms?	Include arms

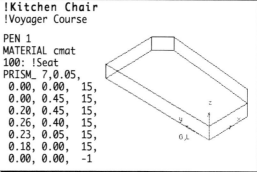

```
!Kitchen Chair
!Voyager Course

PEN 1
MATERIAL cmat
100: !Seat
PRISM_ 7,0.05,
  0.00, 0.00,  15,
  0.00, 0.45,  15,
  0.20, 0.45,  15,
  0.26, 0.40,  15,
  0.23, 0.05,  15,
  0.18, 0.00,  15,
  0.00, 0.00,  -1
```

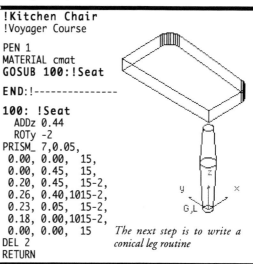

```
!Kitchen Chair
!Voyager Course

PEN 1
MATERIAL cmat
GOSUB 100:!Seat

END:!---------------

100: !Seat
  ADDz 0.44
  ROTy -2
PRISM_ 7,0.05,
  0.00, 0.00,  15,
  0.00, 0.45,  15,
  0.20, 0.45,  15-2,
  0.26, 0.40,1015-2,
  0.23, 0.05,  15-2,
  0.18, 0.00,1015-2,
  0.00, 0.00,  15
DEL 2
RETURN
```

The next step is to write a conical leg routine

```
!Kitchen Chair
!Voyager Course

PEN 1
MATERIAL cmat
GOSUB 100:!Seat

  d1=0.20: d2=0.25
  r1=0.02: r2=0.03
CONE d1,r1,r2,90,90
  ADDz d1
CONE d2,r2,r1,90,90
  DEL 1
```
This next little routine will be the basis of all future leg and braces for the chair. Copy the routine above and make it into two routines, number 200: and 210:. Thus you get one leg working.

```
PEN 1
MATERIAL cmat
GOSUB 100:!Seat
GOSUB 200:!Legs

END:!---------------

100:!Seat
(see text box above)
RETURN

200:!Chair Legs etc
  d1=0.20: d2=0.25
  r1=0.02: r2=0.03
GOSUB 210: !Rearleg
RETURN

210:!ConeLeg
CONE d1,r1,r2,90,90
  ADDz d1
CONE d2,r2,r1,90,90
  DEL 1
RETURN
```

Now extend it to include the other leg Initially, the legs are vertical.

By a bit of pushing and pulling and twisting with ROT commands, you can get the legs to splay correctly.

```
200:!Chair Legs etc
  d1=0.20: d2=0.25
  r1=0.02: r2=0.03
ADD 0.20,0.40,0.45
GOSUB 210 !Frontleg
  DEL 1
ADD 0.17,0.05,0.45
GOSUB 210: !Rearleg
  DEL 1
RETURN

210:!ConeLeg
CONE d1,r1,r2,90,90
  ADDz d1
CONE d2,r2,r1,90,90
  DEL 1
RETURN
```

```
200:!Chair Legs etc
  d1=0.20: d2=0.25
  r1=0.02: r2=0.03
ADD 0.20,0.40,0.45
  ROTx 180
  ROTx 5
  ROTy 5
GOSUB 210 !Frontleg
  DEL 4
ADD 0.17,0.05,0.45
  ROTx 180
  ROTx -5
  ROTy 5
GOSUB 210: !Rearleg
  DEL 4
RETURN
```

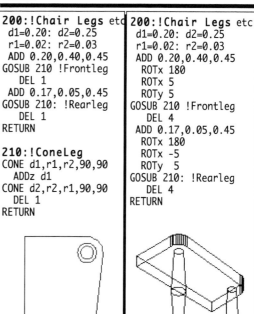

Next, you need to develop a conical form to use for the legs, leg braces and many other parts of the chair. This is an example of 'passing parameters', because the conical legs are of different lengths and diameters. Having got it working, store it as a subroutine, and make sure it works by first using it for the legs of the chair. then you have to use it for the arms.

```
300:!Arms
  ADD 0.22,0.38,0.50
  ROTy 9
  ROTx -6
  d1=0.10: d2=0.10
  r1=0.01: r2=0.02
  GOSUB 210 !ArmSupport
  DEL 3
  RETURN
```

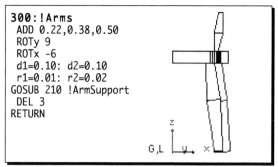

G,L

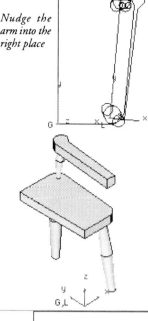

Nudge the arm into the right place

```
300:!Arms
IF arms='Include arms' THEN
  ADD 0.22,0.38,0.50
  ROTy 9
  ROTx -6
  d1=0.10: d2=0.10
  r1=0.01: r2=0.02
  GOSUB 210 !ArmSupport
  DEL 3
  ADD 0.18,0.02,0.69
  ROTz -3
PRISM_ 8,0.04,    !Arm
  0.00,0.00,   15,
  0.02,0.10,   15,
  0.02,0.39,   15-2,
  0.10,0.39,1015-2,
  0.08,0.36,   15,
  0.07,0.12,   15,
  0.05,0.00,   15,
  0.00,0.00,   -1
  DEL 2
ENDIF
RETURN
```

```
VALUES 'arms' 'Include arms',
       'Hide arms'
```

Next, place a coneleg in the location for the Arm upright support - slightly angled forward.

Then add in the Prism for the Arm itself. This has a curvy end - could be done by a simpler prism and a Cylinder at the end. But here it is done with a masking value that gives you a Polyline rounded profile.

VALUES: You can use a Values List to decide if arms are to be included or not.

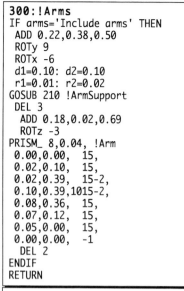

Making the whole chair

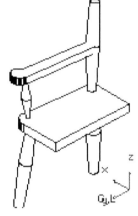

Your main 'executive' script should now look like this on the left, and once you start to add in the back, will look like this drawing on the left. Half the chair, is drawn.

Modify the script using a **MULx -1** so that the whole thing is repeated with it mirroring in the X direction.

Your Executive script grows as subroutines are added.

```
!Kitchen Chair
!Voyager Course

PEN 1
MATERIAL cmat
GOSUB 100:!Seat
GOSUB 200:!Legs
GOSUB 300:!Arms

  MULx -1
GOSUB 100:!Seat
GOSUB 200:!Legs
GOSUB 300:!Arms
  DEL 1

END:!---------------
```

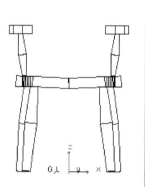

G,L

The Back

Put in the double cone for the back pillars - leaning over, of course. Now, it's time to build the Curved Back shape - using bPRISM !

```
400: !Back
  ADD 0.18,0.05,0.50
  ROTx 8
  ROTy 6
  d1=0.23: d2=0.33
  r1=0.02: r2=0.03
  GOSUB 210 !BackSupport
  DEL 3
  RETURN
```

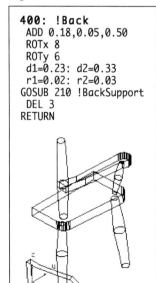

G,L

```
400: !Back
  ADD 0.18,0.05,0.50
  ROTx 8
  ROTy 6
  d1=0.23: d2=0.33
  r1=0.02: r2=0.03
  GOSUB 210 !BackSupport
  DEL 3
  GOSUB 410:!CurveBack
  GOSUB 420:!Slats
  RETURN

410:!CurvedBack
  ADD 0,-0.04,1.05
  ROTx 96
BPRISM_ cmat,cmat,cmat,
        7,0.045,0.8,
  0.00,0.00,   15,
  0.00,0.15,   15,
  0.27,0.15,   15-2,
  0.31,0.10,1015-2,
  0.30,0.04,   15-2,
  0.25,0.00,1015-2,
  0.00,0.00,   -1
DEL 2
RETURN
```

This uses the same macro routine (210:) that was used for the legs; just pass it larger parameters.

Making the Back: The trick with Polylines is to create the Prism object first with simple chamfered corners. Once you get the Prism working correctly, add in the 1000 polylines to make the corners curve. Then lift it into position and rotate as required to make it fit.

When you start making a component, do not worry about first making it on the floor, and leaving out the curved bits.

Leg braces

The legbraces are important enough to deserve their own subroutine. You can use the coneleg (210) for the fore-and-aft brace, but the cross brace simply needs a Cone. Nudge them into position with the ADD commands, using a planview in wireline. Use the number 250: to keep it near the other leg routines.

```
250:!Leg Braces
  ADD 0.19,0.03,0.25
  ROTz -4
  ROTx -90
  d1=0.19: d2=0.19
  r1=0.01: r2=0.02
  GOSUB 210:!Legbrace
  DEL 3
  ADD 0.21,0.22,0.25
  ROTy -90
  CONE 0.21,r1,r2,90,90
  DEL 2
  RETURN
```

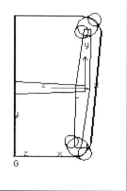

G

Back slats

Finally, you add in the back slats. These need individual nudging into position, and rotating to the correct angle - using the wireline view in plan and side elevation.

This subroutine for the Slats is called from within subroutine number 400 – it's part of the back assembly. It could also be called from the executive script as it is a tidily self contained object. That's structured programming in action – objects!

```
420:!Slats
  ADD 0.02,0.01,0.50
  ROTx 7
BLOCK 0.05,0.01,0.56
  DEL 1
  ROTz 5
  ADDx 0.08
  ROTz 5
  ROTx 7
BLOCK 0.05,0.01,0.56
  DEL 5
RETURN
```

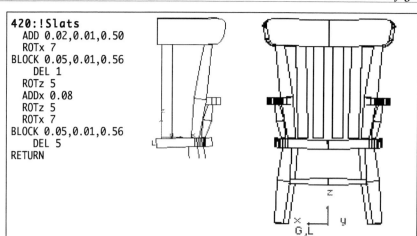

```
!Kitchen Chair
!Voyager Course

PEN 1
MATERIAL cmat
GOSUB 100:!Seat
GOSUB 200:!Legs
GOSUB 250:!Leg Braces
GOSUB 300:!Arms
GOSUB 400:!Back

  MULx -1
GOSUB 100:!Seat
GOSUB 200:!Legs
GOSUB 250:!Leg Braces
GOSUB 300:!Arms
GOSUB 400:!Back
  DEL 1

END:!--------------
```

Your final 'executive' script should look like this – neatly tabulated and documented.

Your final chair should look like this. The curved edges have had their vertical lines tidied away by using 1013 instead of 1015 in the PRISMs.

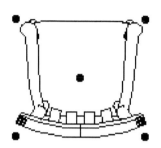

2D Script or Symbol?

As this chair is not parametric, you would find it best for use in the project plan to use a Symbol. First use Project2, then save. Place it in your Project Plan. Select the chair and apply the Explode! command to it. This makes it to a 2D symbol. Copy and paste that into the 2D 2D Symbol window of the chair object. Then remove the Project2 command from the 2D Script. Add some hotspots to make it easier to pickup.

Tips and Tricks: Special Menu

THERE is a hidden menu called **SPECIAL** which is used by programmers at Graphisoft for debugging, and can be enabled by users with a bit of daring. Some of the commands are hostile, so try them out on an unimportant file.

• When you boot up ArchiCAD hold down the Alt-Cmd (or Alt-Ctrl keys on PC) to enable this menu. Alternatively, you can make SPECIAL menu permanently available with RESEDIT on the Mac or REGEDIT on the PC. On the Mac, find the 'menu' resource, find 'special' and enable it. On the PC, find the flag for the 'special menu' and change it from 0 to 1.

• Since ArchiCAD 6.0 permits <Transparency in 3D views> and <Rebuild Each Frame>, I have not needed to use this Special menu, so do not fret if you cannot get it working.

Top Maths Trivia - Find the Circle Centre

I have always wanted to know how to find the centre of a circle which runs through the node points of an irregular triangle (right angled triangles are no problem, the mid point of the hypoteneuse is the centre.) Now I know. It's difficult. The proof is in the Cookbook CD. Here is the answer:

```
XCentre=-((y1+y2)/2+(x1-x2)/(y1-y2)*(x1+x2)/2 - ((y2+y3)/
2+(x2-x3)/(y2-y3)*(x2+x3)/2)) / (((x2-x1)/(y1-y2))+(x2-x3)/(y2-
y3))

YCentre= Xcentre*(x2-x1)/(y1-y2) + (y1+y2)/2 + (x1-x2)/(y1-
y2)*(x1+x2)/2
```

This is as compact as it gets without resorting to squares and roots.

Some more GDL Syntax

Theory

STR( ) is very useful in 2D and Properties Scripting – when you often need to combine many numbers together to make a long string of letters.

You can use it most in 2D Scripting, when you wish to annotate a symbol. For example, if you have a stretchy staircase, you can get it to display a string like: "Pitch= 38.462 degrees". This would indicate that you need to stretch it a bit more to reduce the pitch, or squeeze it if the stair is in a house.

The most common use of STR is in the first form above, whereby you say

how many digits will be needed to represent an entire number, and how many of those digits will occur after the decimal point.

For example: item=123.456
STR(item,6,3) gives you '123.456'
STR(item,6,1) gives you '123.4'
STR(item,4,3) might give you a syntax error,
STR(item,7,2) gives you '123.45'
You might then say:
lstr="Length=" + STR(item,6,2)
and get a string variable called 'lstr'.

REQUEST and REQ – If you get as far as needing these, then you probably have got beyond the Cookbook, and can understand the manual. **For examples of the STW, STR and REQUEST commands, the Filestamp/ Desktop Clock gives a good example.**

IND( ) is used by the autoscripting routines (when you get ArchiCAD to make a library object for you) in determining, and putting into a CALL statement the index number of a Material, Style, Line_type or Fill.

It is most useful where you think that users have tweaked their materials library and changed some of the default numbers. For example, IND(MATERIAL, "Whitewash") will guarantee getting 'Whitewash', whereas MATERIAL 18 might get a quite different result. You can use it to do the same if users have tweaked their Linetype and fill numbers.

When you make your own material in GDL using the DEFINE command the new material gets allocated a number by ArchiCAD – but you don't know it. To be sure, type in:
MATERIAL IND(MATERIAL, "dnc_brick")

SPLIT( ) This is an interesting command that convert strings back into numbers – complicated to use, but worth exploring for the Voyager. See the 'Bendibar' for an example. It half-does what VAL( ) could do in BASIC. To me, its most useful purpose has been rapid parsing of Value List answers – reducing the need for many IF statements.

Variable	Type	Name	Value
A	⟷	X Dimension	= 3.000
B	↕	Y Dimension	= 6.000
C	✏	Pen pattern	= 1
D	▨	fill pattern	= 53
E	▦	Font height mm	= 5
ft	Abc	Font	= geneva

northpoint / 2D Full

N

Northpoint

2D Script: This script was emailed to me by Brian Frank because it didn't quite work. I tidied it up and sent it back, and it's a useful demonstration of 2D.

By using A and B as the determinants of size it is completely stretchy. It also has the bounding box removed.

The northpoint used a filled POLY2, and LINE2 to form the cross shape. Hotspots are also positioned at key positions. The Fill pattern and Pen colour are settable by the user.

The script shows how to set a text style in a 2D script, and how to control font and fontsize.

northpoint / 2D Script

```
!North Arrow Development
!by Brian M. Frank
!Melville Thomas Mobley Architects
!Modified by David Nicholsoncole

PEN C
!Ideal size A=3 B=6
LINE2 0,-B/2, 0,B/2
LINE2 -A/2,0, A/2,0
LINE2 A/4,0, 0,-B/2.5

SET FILL D

POLY2_ 4,3,

   0,0,1,
   0,B/2.5,1,
   -A/4,0,1,
   0,0,1

PEN c
DEFINE STYLE "north" ft, E,5,0
!E is Font size,FT is Font type
SET STYLE "north"
string = "N"
TEXT2 0,B/1.75,string

!Hotspots
HOTSPOT2 0,0
HOTSPOT2 A/2,0
HOTSPOT2 -A/2,0
HOTSPOT2 0,B/2
HOTSPOT2 0,-B/2
!turn off bounding boxes
```

Long Handrail

THIS handrail is an example of how to do long curvy objects without having to use ELBOW - and making them stretchy. This is a situation where you must use **TUBE** to make the object (no matter how long you have tried to avoid using TUBE!). It is also a way to organise the angular distribution of elements, in this case, the uprights of the handrail.

ELBOW is a problem, especially in large curves, as it requires a very high **RESOL** to look good, but when you do that, you have a massive number of surfaces to render, because RESOL also applies that number to the tube surface. You cannot use **RADIUS** either, because its highest value is 36; in such a long sweeping curve, 36 would still seem too polygonal.

There are several ways of defining a curve. The obvious one is based on **1. the Location of the Centre, 2. the Radius, and 3. the Sweep angle**. In a very large curve like this, the user does not know any of these factors. They are only likely to know the distance between the ends of the chord created by the curve, and consequently, the bulge of the curve. From this, you can work out the centre-location, radius and sweep – in this case, I have devoted Subroutine 100 to working those out. These start as A and B, which makes it stretchy, but I prefer to change their names to 'lenc' and 'bulg'.

Variable	Type	Name	Value
A	X Dimension	X Dimension	= 6.000
B	Y Dimension	Y Dimension	= 1.000
diam1		Main Tubing Diameter	= 0.200
diam2		Upright Tubing Diameter	= 0.150
matt		Material of Main Tube	= 11
matu		Material of Uprights	= 23
tcol		Pen Colour	= 1
nupr		Number of Uprights	= 7
thit		Height of Handrail	= 1.000
rs		Resol: Rail curvature(40-360)	= 360
rst		Resol: Tube curvature (8-16)	= 12

```
!Curved Handrail,external
!For Racecourse scheme
!3D Script

GOSUB 100 : !Work out parameters
GOSUB 200 : !Main Tube using TUBE
GOSUB 300 : !Round ends

IF nupr>1 THEN GOSUB 400:!Uprights

END:!_____
```

```
100 : !Work out Parameters
        !(could be in master Script)

lenc=A: bulg=B
!car = Angl of centreline & radius
!bulg= the 'bulge' for the rail
  car     = (90-ATN((lenc/2)/bulg))*2
  trad1   = diam1/2 !Rad of Main tube
  trad2   = diam2/2 !Rad of Uprights
  radtube = (lenc/2)/sin(car)
!radtube is Rad of whole rail
  radtdif = radtube-bulg  !Chordline to centre

IF bulg>radtube*2 THEN bulg=lenc/2
RETURN
```

3D Script: The executive script is simply 4 lines, because there are only 4 operations to carry out. I have put round ends onto the tube, but these could have been a Booleian choice.

In case the user wants zero uprights, there is an IF statement, to avoid 'divide by zero' errors which would occur if you tried to calculate the positions of zero uprights.

The user is able to set a resolution for the main curve, which could be as high as 360 (1 degree increments). The calculation works out the angular increment (anginc).

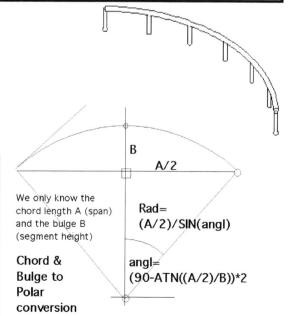

We only know the chord length A (span) and the bulge B (segment height)

B
A/2

Rad= (A/2)/SIN(angl)

Chord & Bulge to Polar conversion

angl= (90-ATN((A/2)/B))*2

These algorithms for calculating the Radius and sweep angle are in the Maths Primer.

Building the TUBE in 3D

Next, the PUT statement is used to store all the X,Y locations. (The Z locations are zero). This is the ONLY practical way to set up a large TUBE statement. It is done in a FOR... NEXT Loop. Notice that (to create the phantom start and end points) you need to make the loop start one stepping angle earlier and one later than is needed for the real sweep angle.

You then move to the centre of the circle, and deliver the Tube statement. The 901 and 4001 numbers are required to draw the tube as a clean cylinder. (Try using 900 and 4000 to see the difference it makes.)

It is useful to know that when you want to know X and Y, but already know Radius and Angle (we are talking Cartesian to Polar conversion), it is usually X=R*SIN(a) and Y=R*COS(a).

```
200:  !Main Truss Tubing for 3D
!Tube algorithm to avoid
!having to use a high resol
RESOL rst    !Set surface resolution
MATERIAL matt: PEN tcol:
  angd=360/rs              !angular diff
  nrs=INT((car*2)/angd)+1!Make angd fit curv
  anginc=car*2/nrs        !angular increment

FOR k=-car-anginc TO car+anginc+0.1 STEP anginc
  PUT radtube*SIN(k),radtube*COS(k),0,0
  NEXT k
```
Notice that the sweep angle is deliberately exceeded by 1/10 of a degree to avoid a decimal> binary> machine code conversion error
```
ADD 0,-radtdif,thit

TUBE 2,NSP/4,63,
  0,0,901,            !Formula for
  trad1,360,4001, ! round section
  GET(nsp)

DEL 1
RETURN
```

```
300:  !rounded ends
  ADD lenc/2,0,this
SPHERE diam1/2
  ADDx -lenc
SPHERE diam1/2
  DEL 2
RETURN
```

It is an easy job to put a sphere at the end of the tube. The RESOL is the same as for the tube – I recommend 12 or less.

```
400 :  !Uprights
RESOL rst
angup= (car*2)/(nupr-1)
!angle diff between uprights

FOR k=1 TO nupr
  ADDy -radtdif
  ROTz  car-(k-1)*angup
  ADDy radtube
CYLIND thit,trad2
  DEL 3
  NEXT k
RETURN
```

Finally, you calculate the angular difference between the uprights. Then retreat to the centre of the circle, and 'spray' out the uprights, retreating back to the centre before doing the next one.

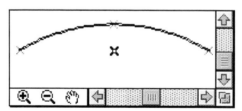

```
!2-D script for
!long handrail

HOTSPOT2 0,B
HOTSPOT2  A/2,0
HOTSPOT2  -A/2,0

PROJECT2 3,270,2
```

2D Script: is simply a PROJECT2 command, with a routine to draw Hotspots to make sure you can stretch the handrail to the right size.

Tips and Tricks

Remove that annoying Error message

WHEN you start up, you often get the 'Missing or Duplicate library Objects' message. Check 'Load Libraries'. Only load libraries that you need for that project.

There are four reasons for this:

1. You probably DO have Missing objects. Find them and make sure that they are in the currently used libraries. Re-load libraries.

2. If not, then you MAY have Duplicates, and this is bad as you take pot luck which ones of the same name load first - maybe the one you spent a lot of time writing or editing will not load – last year's library object of the same name will load instead and you will not notice until you have spent hours rendering.

3. If not, then you MAY have greyed out libraries in the 'Load Libraries' window. If you ignore this you will get the error mes-

sage every time. 'Remove' libraries that you are not using or don't need.

4. If not, and you have followed the advice above, then you MAY have material definitions (such as Grass, Walnut, RedBrick etc) which depend on textures to render but they cannot find the library that includes textures.

When you buy an object from Objects on Line, Object Factory or myself, you will always get that error message. In order to keep the file size to a minimum, the object developer will have saved an archive which includes absolutely nothing except the object you want – thus omitting textures etc. When you have created the temporary library folder that came with the archive, copy the new object to your regularly used Library, then re-load libraries and all will be good again.

CONE-shapes
or... Fun with Cutplane

Object

```
VALUES "shape" "Ellipse", "Parabola",
               "Hyperbola"
VALUES "hlp2d" "True View","Show stretchy 2D"
VALUES "twk" 10,20,30,40,50,60,70,80,90
```

Values List – you set up the contents of the Pop-down menus. Values which are Text have to be in quotes.

A	X Dimension		2000.0
B	Y Dimension		2000.0
shape	Abc	Resulting Shape of cut	Ellipse
hlp2d	Abc	Helpfulness of 2D symbol	Show stretchy 2D
twk		Tweak Index (10-90%)	50

THERE are various ways of defining the three important mathematical shapes of **Ellipse, Parabola and Hyperbola**. This can be done with a formula using X and Y and Radius, with string and nails stuck in a wooden board, hanging chains, or with bullets fired into the air. The easiest way is to cut a cone at different angles and observe the result.

This exercise is to explore the use of VALUE LISTs, and to get the hang of manoevring CUTPLANE around the model. It also shows stretchiness and the benefit of a 'helpful' 2D symbol.

Parameters: In this case, all the user options in the setting box are defined by Pop-down menu. A Value List parameter can be an 'ABC' text type or a number, and you have to click the little button next to the word 'descriptors' to activate the pop-down effect.

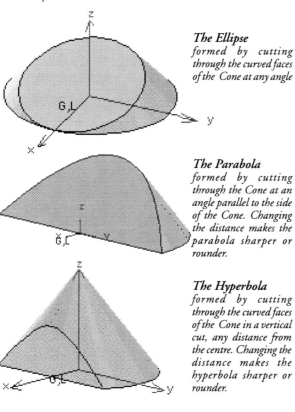

The Ellipse
formed by cutting through the curved faces of the Cone at any angle

The Parabola
formed by cutting through the Cone at an angle parallel to the side of the Cone. Changing the distance makes the parabola sharper or rounder.

The Hyperbola
formed by cutting through the curved faces of the Cone in a vertical cut, any distance from the centre. Changing the distance makes the hyperbola sharper or rounder.

```
!Shapemaking with Cone and Cutplane
!GDL Cookbook - 3D Script

MATERIAL 'whitewash'
PEN 1

!Make an ellipse
IF shape="Ellipse" THEN
ADDx A/2
ROTy ATN(B/(A/2))*twk/100
CUTPLANE
DEL 2
ENDIF

!Make a Parabola
IF shape="Parabola" THEN
ADDx -A/2+A*twk/100
ROTy ATN(B/(A/2))
CUTPLANE
DEL 2
ENDIF

!Make a Hyperbola
IF shape="Hyperbola" THEN
ADDx A/2-(A/2)*twk/100
ROTy 90
CUTPLANE
DEL 2
ENDIF

!Draw it
CONE B,A/2,0,90,90

CUTEND
END
```

You must declare Materials and Pen BEFORE you start cutting planes.

The 'TWEAK' here changes the form of the shape: for the Ellipse by changing the angle of the Cutplane, for the Parabola and Hyperbola by changing its distance from the centre.

Cutplane cuts away everything ABOVE it, so you only have to rotate it to the right angle, so that what you want is UNDER the CUTPLANE.

The Value list of shapes decide which of the IF... ENDIF routines will be carried out. Whichever you choose will result in ONE Cutplane, so you only need one CUTEND after you have drawn the cone.

If the Values list result in changing both 2D and 3D shapes, you may have to write some short script to parse the list in the Master Script.

```
!Shapemaking
!with Cone&Cutplane
!2D Script

PROJECT2 3,270,2
  HOTSPOT2 0,0.001
  HOTSPOT2 -A/2,0
  HOTSPOT2 A/2,0
  HOTSPOT2 0, A/2
  HOTSPOT2 0,-A/2

IF hlp2d="Show stretchy 2D" THEN
  HOTSPOT2 0,B
  POLY2 3,1,
  -A/2,0,
  0,B,
  A/2,0
ENDIF
```

Show All **Hide**

☑ Hotspots on bounding box

Helpful 2D Scripting

This little routine draws an elevation of the Cone on the 2D symbol, with a stretchy Hotspot button at 0,B.

If you put enough of your own Hotspots in, you are best to remove the Bounding Box, which will just confuse the 2D symbol.

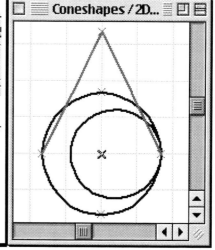

Coneshapes / 2D...

RhombiCubOctahedron
or... More fun with 'Cutplane'

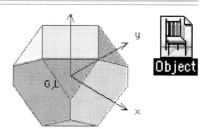

CUTPLANE enables you to produce objects (by subtraction) that cannot be sculpted positively.

For example, one can make a CUBE by cutting a SPHERE with 6 different faces. In this case, one can take a cube, and cut the corners off to create a Truncated Hexahedron, and ultimately a RhombiCubOctahedron. By varying the dimensions of the cube, and the distance of the cutting plane, one gets interesting shapes.

Variable	Type	Name	Value
A		X Dimension	= 1.000
B		Y Dimension	= 1.000
clen		Cutting Distance	= 0.700

```
!RhombiCuboOctaHedron
!Stretchy Using Cutplane

MATERIAL "Whitewash"

ADDz -(A+B)/4
PRISM 4,(A+B)/2,
    A/2, B/2,
    -A/2, B/2,
    -A/2,-B/2,
    A/2,-B/2
DEL 1
```
Stage 1: Make Prism

First - make a CUBE.

There is, sadly, no command in GDL that generates a cube or cuboid from a central location. So one uses a PRISM to make it with. The parameters of width and length are made using A and B - this will make the cuboid 'stretchy'. The height of the cuboid is an average of A + B.

Having got the CUBE working, convert it to a subroutine by putting in the END statement, and boxing the routine with a number and a RETURN statement: as shown here.

```
!RhombiCuboOctaHedron
!Stretchy Using Cutplane

MATERIAL "Whitewash"

GOSUB 100 !Cube

END:!--------------------

100: !Make the Cube!
ADDz -(A+B)/4
PRISM 4,(A+B)/2,
    A/2, B/2,
    -A/2, B/2,
    -A/2,-B/2,
    A/2,-B/2
DEL 1
RETURN
```
Stage 2: Make Prism command into a subroutine

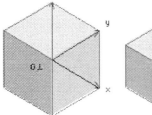 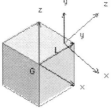 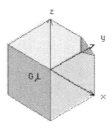 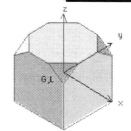 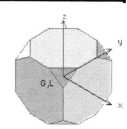

CUTPLANE

Next thing to do it to move a cutting plane to the places where the cut is to be made. Think of the cutting plane as a large revolving bacon-slicing blade that has to be manoeuvred to the right place, and then set in motion. You then DEL back to the origin and build your model - or perhaps set up other blades in motion.

The CUTPLANE command leaves behind everything BELOW the blade. You can swivel the blade by a stated angle - so if you wanted the blade to leave everything ABOVE it, you would issue a CUTPLANE 180 command.

Avoid using the other methods of Cutplane. The manual does not explain them well and they cause headaches getting them to work.

```
MATERIAL "Whitewash"

ROTz 45
ROTy 45
ADDz clen
CUTPLANE
DEL 3

GOSUB 100 !Cube
CUTEND
END:!-----------------
```
Stage 3: Get one CUT working correctly

Take our CUBE - you move the cutting plane to the correct place by a rotation around Z, point towards the corner by rotating around Y and then move out a stated amount (ADDz). Apply the CUT, then DEL 3 to get back to the origin. You have to plan all this ahead, because you havent actually built the cube yet! In the examples here, I have shown how the cursor goes to the place, and the result when it goes back.

Next you need to devise a way to cut all four upper corners in one go! The FOR... NEXT routine.

```
!RhombiCuboOctaHedron
!Stretchy Using Cutplane

MATERIAL "Whitewash"

ROTz 45
FOR k=1 TO 4
    ROTz 90*k
    ROTy 45
    ADDz clen
    CUTPLANE
    DEL 3
NEXT k
DEL 1

GOSUB 100 !Cube

    CUTEND: CUTEND:
    CUTEND: CUTEND:

END:!-----------------
```
Stage 4: Apply the CUT to all four corners of the top of the cube

Notice in the this routine that we had to do a CUTEND after building the cube. If you don't do this, the blades continue spinning, and the rest of the model gets cut. Each cut needs a CUTEND.

In the FOR... NEXT Loop here, you have to start by an initial turn of 45, thereafter, turn at right angles to do each cut. At the end, you do 4 CUTENDS.

Controlling CUTEND

In this development of the script, the idea is to set up a counter called "kut" which is incremented every time you issue a CUTPLANE command. This way, you can have FOR...NEXT loops issuing any number of Cutplane commands, and the correct number of Cutends will always be issued – in a matching FOR...NEXT Loop.

Making it into Subroutines

Once you have that working, you now encapsulate that whole cutting routine into a subroutine called 200: You need to do this, because you are going to repeat the whole thing for the underside of the cube; whenever you have to repeat an operation, use a FOR.. NEXT or a GOSUB to save typing.

```
!RhombiCuboOctaHedron
!Stretchy Using Cutplane

MATERIAL "Whitewash"

 ROTz 45
 FOR k=1 TO 4
  ROTz 90*k
  ROTy 45
  ADDz clen
   CUTPLANE: kut=kut+1
 DEL 3
 NEXT k
 DEL 1

GOSUB 100 !Cube

 FOR n=1 TO kut
 CUTEND
 NEXT n

END:!-------------------
```

Stage 5: Neater way to keep track of the number of CUTs and to perform CUTEND

```
MATERIAL "Whitewash"

GOSUB 200 !upper 4-CUT
GOSUB 100 !Cube

FOR n=1 TO kut
  CUTEND
  NEXT n

END:!----------------

100: !Make the Cube!
.........
Prism etc, etc, etc
.........
RETURN

200: !Make the 4-CUT
  ROTz 45
FOR k=1 TO 4
  ROTz 90*k
  ROTy 45
  ADDz clen
   CUTPLANE: kut=kut+1
  DEL 3
  NEXT k
  DEL 1
RETURN
```

Stage 6: Make the whole CUT routine into a subroutine

```
!RhombiCuboOctaHedron
!Stretchy Using Cutplane

MATERIAL "Whitewash"

GOSUB 200 !upper 4-CUT
  MULz -1
GOSUB 200 !lower 4-CUT
  DEL 1

GOSUB 100 !Cube

FOR n=1 TO kut
  CUTEND
  NEXT n

END:!--------------------

100: !Make the Cube!
.........
Prism etc, etc, etc
.........
RETURN

200: !Make the 4-CUT
  etc, etc, etc, etc .....
```

Stage 7: The Cutting routine can now be Mirrored in Z to cut all the underside of the Cube.

Once you have got the routine at 200: working, you can Invert it to make it cut the bottom of the cube. Multiply the Z values by *minus 1* to make it invert. The MUL command is a 'cursor movement' so it needs a DEL command after.

After you have issued Cutplane commands, you always have to retreat back to the origin to do the next Cutplane sequence, or to build the object which is to be cut.

This is a Stretchy Object - its dimensions are defined by A and B. Or you can type in new values for A and B.

As you can also define the distance of the CUT from the origin, you can create interesting effects by interplaying the two.

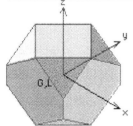

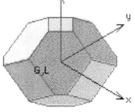

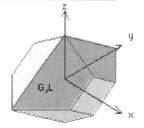

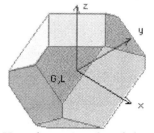

The cube in the script so far has used a size of 1 meter for the cube, and a cutting distance of 0.7m diagonally from the centre. In this one the cut distance is only 0.6m.

This one has a cutting distance of 0.45m. The cut faces now form a more predominant part of the appearance than the original cube. Now it has truly become a Rhombicuboctahedron.

Here, the cut is also 0.45, but the long dimension of the cube is 2 metres.

Here, the cut is 0.6, and the long dimension of the cube is 2 metres.

```
!Rhombi
!2D script
HOTSPOT2 -A/2,0
HOTSPOT2 A/2,0
HOTSPOT2 0, B/2
HOTSPOT2 0,-B/2
PROJECT2 3,270,2
```

2D Script: As the object is ever changing, give it the minimal commands required to make it stretchy.

Tips and Tricks: '3D View to Symbol'

This command has been lost in ArchiCAD 6. Autoscripted objects are now fully scripted. If you want a simple 2D Symbol, give the object a 2D script of PROJECT2 3,270,2. Drop the object into the Project Plan. EXPLODE it. Select the Lines in the exploded 2D symbol, Copy them. Open the 2D symbol window, and Paste it. It will be in the right place and scale, and if not adjust it so that it is in the right place relative to the object's origin. Add some 2D Hotspots. Replace the PROJECT2 command with FRAGMENT2 ALL,1.

Making a Cube from a Sphere: The same technique can be borrowed to have fun with making one common shape from another. The routine in this exercise has been adapted to make a cuboid from a sphere. The top picture has a cutting distance (from the origin) of 0.5 metres - it remains a sphere. The middle one is 0.4 metres - interesting. At 0.33, you get back to the Truncated Hexahedron that we were making before - with rounded corners. Finally, at 0.3 metres, the sphere becomes a cube. Note that you MUL X, Y, and Z with a single command.

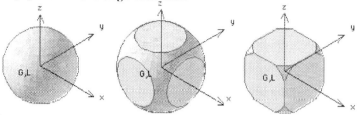

In this case, the CUTPLANEs are symmetrical, and there is no difficulty in issuing all the CUTENDs at one go. However, in some more complex models, some CUTPLANEs remain in operation, other need to be ended. The order of CUTEND is similar to DEL, in that the most RECENT cut command will be ended. So if the model has many cuts, you need to plan the order of cuts carefully.

ArchiCAD 6.X includes CUTPOLY, CUTPOLYA and CUTSHAPE commands which extend the power of 'subtractive' model making even further.

```
!Cube From a Sphere
!Stretchy Using Cutplane

MATERIAL "Whitewash"
  GOSUB 200 !3-CUTs
  MUL -1,-1,-1
  GOSUB 200 !other 3-CUTs
  DEL 1

SPHERE A/2 !Sphere

FOR n=1 TO kut
  CUTEND
  NEXT n

END:!--------------------

200: !the 3-CUT
  ADDz clen
  CUTPLANE: kut=kut+1
  DEL 1
  ROTx -90
  ADDz clen
  CUTPLANE: kut=kut+1
  DEL 2
  ROTy -90
  ADDz clen
  CUTPLANE: kut=kut+1
  DEL 2
RETURN
```

DesktopClock / Filestamp

Variable	Type	Name	Value
A		X Dimension	1.000
B		Y Dimension	1.000
htxt		Height Index of text in mm	5.00
clockscale	Abc	Clock Scale Plot/Plan?	Scale to PLAN
clockshape	Abc	Show Projectname or Clock?	Clock and Project
projpen		Pen colour	3
fontnam	Abc	Font Name	Arial

Adventures in 2D GDL Scripting
This covers: REQUEST, Defining Style, Value List,
              Making fonts to autosize to drawing scale.

ALTHOUGH all of us enjoy the luxury of a clock displayed on the menu bar of our computer or on our wrists, this clock is useful because it can be scaled to fit the building you are working on, or the scale of the document for plotting. So it will accurately datestamp the time and date of a Plot. It gets updated everytime there is a Reload of the file. This has been adapted to show Project Name.

Parameters: are simple - If you are plotting, you can fix the size to the Plot, and then the height in millimetres will be the height of the text. If you tick the box to fit the Plan, it will always relate to the size of the building, whatever the scale of the drawing. Plotting height is defined strictly in millimetres, you must set the Type as a number, not dimension. Use a Value List for the Plot/Plan choice. A and B are not used.

REQUEST: The REQUEST command must be amongst the most difficult of all the GDL commands, since the manual does not clearly explain – but then the same applies to Polylines, File Input/Output, TUBE, DEFINE and much else. Added to which DateTime does not appear in the manual anyway. Read the DateTime Readme file in your Graphisoft folder for deeper information. The 'x=' before REQUEST creates a value for x of 1 or 0 if the command succeeds.

STW(): is a way of determining in metres, the length of a string when printed on the page in the defined style. It is difficult to set the clock size to follow the Plot or the Plan, and the script here is the result of much trial and error research - but it works! Many people use this!

Comment: GDL doesn't have a VAL() function to convert text strings into numbers like BASIC. The Time and Date info, even when apparently returned in numbers, is actually a string. GDL's SPLIT command is the equivalent of VAL(). With SPLIT to read numbers, you can make an analog clock with revolving hands. *(Ana-Clock by Trevor Grant 1999)*

Cookbook   *Use this to mark up your drawings*

15:11:03
Sun 28 Nov 1999

Object

```
!Desktop clock/ Filestamp
IF clockshape='Project Title' THEN clkshp=1
IF clockshape='Clock and Project' THEN clkshp=2
IF clockscale='Scale to PLOT' THEN clspln=1
IF clspln THEN htx=htxt ELSE htx=htxt*10/A_

PEN projpen
  DEFINE STYLE 'clock' fontnam,htx,0,(1-clkshp/2)
  SET STYLE 'clock'
  REQUEST('Height_of_Style','clock',height)
  len =STW('day 00 mon year')*A_/1000
  hit= height*A_/1000

!Hotspots
HOTSPOT2 0,  0
HOTSPOT2 0,  hit
HOTSPOT2 len,hit

IF clkshp<>1 THEN
  x=REQUEST('DateTime','%a %d %b %Y',dstr)
  x=REQUEST('DateTime','%X',tstr)

!Display date and time
  TEXT2 0, ,dstr
  TEXT2 0,hit,tstr

!Body of Clock
  ARC2 0.0,0,hit,90,270
  ARC2 len,0,hit,270,90
  LINE2 0, hit,len, hit
  LINE2 0,-hit,len,-hit
HOTSPOT2 0,      -hit
HOTSPOT2 len,    -hit
HOTSPOT2 -hit,    0
HOTSPOT2 len+hit, 0
HOTSPOT2 len/2,   0
ENDIF

!Show Project Name
IF clkshp THEN
IF clkshp=1 THEN ADD2 0,-hit
DEFINE STYLE 'title' fontnam,htx*1.6,2,1
SET STYLE 'title'
x=REQUEST('Name_of_plan','',filename)
  TEXT2 len/2,hit*2.5,filename

HOTSPOT2 len/2, hit*2.5
HOTSPOT2 len/2, hit*1
ENDIF
```

In Europe, AC plots in millimetres, but my readers in USA can adapt this to points.

'dstr' is the Date String
'tstr' is the Time String

Put this below in the Value List script

```
VALUES 'clockshape' 'Clock Only',
       'Project Title','Clock and Project'
VALUES 'clockscale' 'Scale to PLOT',
       'Scale to PLAN'
```

Simple Crane

THIS may not look like a wonderful crane, but as a Cookbook Model, it looks at:

- **Trigonometry**
- **PUT and GET**
- **Animation of model**
- **TUBE, RULED, PRISM_**
- **Object oriented approach**

Parameters: The main things to be parametric here are the ones which demonstrate the trigonometric game being played. The main script is organised in a totally modular way, using GOSUBs.

By using the frame number of a sequence between cameras, the crane will move.

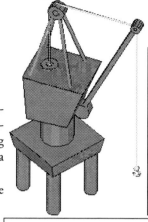

Variable	Type	Name	Value
A		X Dimension	1.000
B		Y Dimension	1.000
cabdir		Direction of Cabin	30.00
blen		Beam length	8.000
bmang		Beam Angle	65.000
hhit		Hook height above Ground	3.000
abim		Animate Beam ON/OFF?	On
cabmat		Crane and Cab Material	40
cablmat		Material of Cable and Hook	3

```
!Simple Crane
!Demo of Trigonometry
!& ObjectOriented approach

!3D Script

MATERIAL cabmat: PEN 1

GOSUB  50 !animation info
GOSUB 100 !Base
GOSUB 200 !Upper structure
GOSUB 300 !Beam
GOSUB 400 !Cable+Hook

END:!--------------------
```

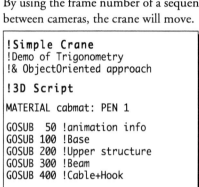

3D Script: Although the executive script looks neatly structured, this will report an error unless you create dummy subroutines first e.g.
```
200: !Upper structure
RETURN
300: !Beam
RETURN
```
Then you start to fill these in.

100: The script includes a loop to build the 4 cylinder columns, and the same type of loop is used in the upper structure too. At almost all times, the cursor remains in the centre of the crane, darts outwards, draws something, and then DELs back to the centre.

RULED is used to build the crane platform and platform.

200: 4 hoist legs are made with a loop. The exithole and roller are made with PRISMs using Polylines to make them hollow.

300: The range of movements of the beam angle ('bmang') are defined. The main beam is rectangular.

The ROTz cabdir is restated for each subroutine to ensure that the beam and other parts rotate when the cabin rotates.

```
100: !Base
RESOL 12
FOR k=1 TO 4          Loop to build
  ROTz 45+90*k          the legs
  ADDx 2.0
  CYLIND 3.0,0.4 !Leg
  DEL 2
    NEXT k

  ADDz 3.0
RULED 4,63,         !Platform
  1.8, 1.8, 0,
  -1.8, 1.8, 0,
  -1.8,-1.8, 0,
  1.8,-1.8, 0,
  2.0, 2.0, 1,
  -2.0, 2.0, 1,
  -2.0,-2.0, 1,
  2.0,-2.0, 1

  ROTz cabdir  !Cab direction
  ADDz 1.0
CYLIND 2.0,1.0 !Cabin base
  ADDz 2.0
RULED 4,63,         !Cabin
  1.1, 1.4,0,
  -1.4, 1.4,0,
  -1.4,-1.4,0,
  1.1,-1.4,0,
  2.2, 1.6,3,
  -1.6, 1.6,3.2,
  -1.6,-1.6,3.2,
  2.2,-1.6,3
DEL 3+1
RETURN
```

RULED always has to have the bottom surface at level zero. You do not 'close' the polygon as you often do with a prism.

400: It requires a bit of addition and trigonometry to work out the X-distance and height of the roller at the top of the crane beam. You have to put in some precautionary IFs to ensure that the hook position isn't too low or too high. Making the TUBE: You could write the tube locations directly into the tube statement, but you will find it is ALWAYS better to organise them first into a set of PUT statements, so that you can simply define NSP/4 as the number of points for the cable. This way you can add or subtract extra points without getting an error message.

```
200:!Hoisting Structure
RESOL 12
  ROTz cabdir
  ADDz 9  !height of roof
PRISM_ 3,0.3, !Exithole for cable
  -0.5,0,915,
  0.5,360,4013,
  0.2,360,4013

FOR k=1 TO 4          Loop to build
  ROTz 45+90*k          the legs
  ADDx 1.8
  ROTy -20          PRISM_ is used to
  CYLIND 4.5,0.1 make Cylinders that
  DEL 3             have holes through
  NEXT k            them.  The  900
    ADDz 4.5        command defines the
    ROTx 90         Centre, and the 4000
    ADDz -0.3       command tells it to
PRISM_ 3,0.6,       draw the line in a
  0.0,0,915,        circular form
  0.5,360,4013,
  0.2,360,4013 !Topmost Roller
    DEL 4+1
RETURN
```

```
300: !Hoisting beam
IF bmang>85 OR bmang<-10 THEN
    bmang=45
    ENDIF
    ROTz cabdir
    ADD 1.6,0,6.5
    ROTx 90
    ADDz -0.3
CYLIND 0.6,0.5 !Hinge mechanism
    DEL 2

    ROTy 90-bmang
PRISM 4,blen,!Actual beam
  0.15, 0.20,
  -0.15, 0.20,
  -0.15,-0.20,
  0.15,-0.20
  ADDz blen

    ROTx 90
    ADDz -0.3
PRISM_ 3,0.6,!Roller end of Beam
  0,0,915,
  0.3,360,4013,
  0.1,360,4013
    DEL 6
RETURN
```

420: Then you move to the hook position and call up the hook. This should be written as an object, so it draws the right size and way up. It is a slightly elaborate job using Elbows.

```
420: !Hook
    ADDx 0.2
    MULz -1
    ADDx -0.2
    SPHERE 0.15
    ELBOW 0.2,60,0.05
    DEL 1
    ROTy 60
    ADDx -0.2
    ROTz 180
    ELBOW 0.2,225,0.05
    DEL 5
    RETURN
```

```
400: !Upper cables
MATERIAL cablmat
LET cabx=1.6+blen*COS(bmang)
LET cabz=6.5+blen*SIN(bmang)
IF hhit<1    THEN hhit=1
IF hhit>cabz THEN hhit=cabz-1
 PUT 0,0,0
 PUT -0.5,0,9,0
 PUT -0.5,0,13.5,0
!Go round the big pulley
 PUT -0.5*COS(22),0,13.5+0.5*SIN(22),0
 PUT -0.5*COS(45),0,13.5+0.5*SIN(45),0
 PUT -0.5*COS(68),0,13.5+0.5*SIN(68),0
```

It requires some Trig to do a realistic display of the cable passing over the top pulley. Cos & Sin enable you to determine the X,Y locations of any point where you know radius & angle.

```
 PUT  0,0,14,0
 PUT  0,0,14,0
 PUT cabx,0,cabz,0
 PUT cabx,0,hhit,0
 PUT cabx,0,0,0
```

```
    ROTz cabdir
 TUBE 2,nsp/4,63,
    0,0,901,
    0.03,360,4001,
    GET(NSP)
```

```
ADD cabx,0,hhit
GOSUB 420  !Hook
DEL 2
RETURN
```

Animating the Model

50: If you want to animate the crane, you can link the position of the beam and hook to the frame number. 'N_' is the number of a frame in the animation. The new values of cabdir and bmang override the numbers in the parameters box.

If you model is to animate, you must have 'Rebuild Each Frame' enabled just before you save the animation.

Reserved global variables

L_ pen number of the symbol
M_ material index of the symbol
N_ frame number in animation
O_ first frame index in fly-through
P_ last frame index in fly-through
Q_ height of home story
R_ radius of the bended wall
S_...Z_ free for users

| abim | ☒ | Animate Beam ON/OFF? | On |

```
50: !Animation Info
IF abim THEN
    LET cabdir= N_*2 -30
    LET bmang = 5+ N_*2
ENDIF
RETURN
```

We could also animate the hook up and down, but there isn't enough space in the book for that level of detail – have a try at it yourself.

2D script: It is best done with Project2. The task here is to put in Hotspots - using the same trig calculation you used in the 3D script.

The 'cabx' could have been put into the Master Script, saving you a line or 2 of typing.

```
!Animated Crane
!2D Script
HOTSPOT2 0,0
PROJECT2 3,270,2

 ROT2 cabdir
cabx=1.6+blen*COS(bmang)
HOTSPOT2 cabx,0
 DEL 1
```

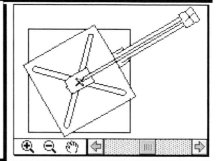

Tips and Tricks
Building Lattices

WE CAN easily make non parametric lattices with the slab tool, laying out the shape, and then inserting holes, and finishing up with rectangular sectioned members. But if you stretch them, the sizes of all the members are distorted. Making a 3D truss this way is almost out of the question.

Home built Parametric Lattice trusses are one way to impress people who think that everything should be done with AutoCAD. Challenge them to match that with AutoLisp! Here are four methods to think about.

The Prism method: A lattice can be made as a PRISM_ with holes drilled. You can use arithmetic to work out how many holes to draw, PUT to store the outlines of the holes, and GET to draw the prism. You could also make the web of a castellated beam this way. This is somewhat limited to 2D trusses.

The Trigonometry and Loop method: Using the technique of the Lattice truss in the Discovery course, you can use arithmetic to work out how many lattice modules required (or to calculate the module size) then use a For Next Loop. The cursor runs along the length of the truss, building each module. Along the way, you will have to use trigonometry to work out the angles of the truss members, and either Cylinder, or a Squilinder (prism) to draw the members. (I call this 'knitting'). This needs some serious maths if the truss is curved or irregular in shape.

CUTPOLY method: First build your lattice as a solid block; then apply a series of CUTPOLYs to drill holes, leaving behind the structural members. This is a laborious method for a 2D lattice, but for a 3D lattice, it could be the easiest! Use Loops and PUT and GET to place them.

The 'AngleRod' method: is useful if the truss departs from regular spacings or layout, and has members in which there are so many angles and geometries that the trigonometry gives you a headache. (I like trig, but you may not). In this case, you just use a macro like AngleRod in the Voyager course, and just specify the start and end points, the sectional diameter, and whether the rod is square or round. You do not actually need to call Anglerod, because the routine using TUBE is so short, it can be copied and pasted as a subroutine into your main script.

Spiral Handrail

Object

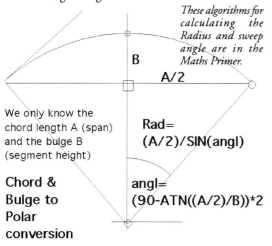

THIS handrail is similar to the 'Long Handrail' earlier in the Cookbook, but this one goes further in that it follows a spiral staircase and has more sophisticated treatment of the ends and the infil panel.

Again, you must use TUBE to make the object because ELBOW is too feeble. Even with the RADIUS command active, the Elbow can look too chunky. You need the mathematical method of the FOR...NEXT loop to organise the angular distribution of elements, in this case, the points on the handrail, the downrights of the handrail and the points on the Infil Panel. Yes, for GDL nutcases, there is the chance to try a COONS object, the infil panel. By the way, this is a mega useful object, and worth buying the Cookbook for on its own!

The infil panel can be glass, or you can apply an alpha channeled wiremesh texture

Parameters & Master Script: First establish the basic geometry of the circle. This is to be stretchy, based on a CHORD of a circle, the width being A and the bulge being B.

These algorithms for calculating the Radius and sweep angle are in the Maths Primer.

B

A/2

We only know the chord length A (span) and the bulge B (segment height)

$$Rad = (A/2)/SIN(angl)$$

Chord & Bulge to Polar conversion

$$angl = (90-ATN((A/2)/B))*2$$

Variable	Type	Name	Value
A		X Dimension	2.000
B		Y Dimension	1.000
diam		Tubing diameter in millimetres	50.00
zzyzx		Height difference between ends	1.000
matl		Material of Tubing	11
chunk		No. of chunks in Rail 3-80	16

```
!Handrail Sloping
!Round with infil
!3D Script
PEN pcol
!Tube locations
 h=-hitd !height counter
FOR k=-angl-angd TO angl+angd+0.2 STEP angd
  PUT crad*SIN(k),crad*COS(k),h,0
  h=h+hitd
NEXT k
```

This is all it takes to make a lovely stretchy 3D handrail for a spiral staircase (although it depends on the master script for the angles and the 2D script for the hotspots

```
!Draw the handrail
RADIUS trad*0.7,trad*1.4
ADDy -(crad-B)
MATERIAL matl
BODY -1
TUBE 2,NSP/4,63,
  0,0,901,
  trad,360,4001,
  GET(NSP)
BODY -1
DEL 1
```

Radius is used here instead of Resol because later we are dealing with elbows and ellips to treat the handrail ends

```
VALUES 'endstyl' 'Butt cut ends',
  'Downward Elbows','Rounded ends'

VALUES 'infil' 'Infil Panel',
  'NO Infil Panel'
```

*As always, use **Value Lists** to ensure that your objects are user friendly*

```
!Handrail
!Master Script

!Parameters for handrail
IF chunk<3 THEN chunk=3
 angl=(90-ATN((A/2)/B))*2 !Sweep angle
 crad=(A/2)/SIN(angl)    !Curve Radius
 trad=diam/2000     !HRail Tube Radius
 angd=angl*2/chunk !angle difference
 hitd=zzyzx/chunk  !height difference/chunk

!Parameters for downrights & ends & infil
 dnrad=ddiam/2000 !Downright Radius
 dnnum=ABS(dnnum)    !make it positive
 IF dimen<trad THEN dimen=trad
 IF endstyl='Butt cut ends'   THEN es=0
 IF endstyl='Downward Elbows' THEN es=1
 IF endstyl='Rounded ends'    THEN es=2
 IF dropin<0 THEN dropin=0
 IF lenin<=dropin THEN lenin=dropin+0.001
IF dnnum>1 THEN
 angdw=angl*2/(dnnum-1) !angle diff
 hitdif=zzyzx/(dnnum-1)  !height diff
 ENDIF     !avoids divide by zero error

!Parameters for ends
!sloping angle at end
anglen=ATN(hitd/(2*PI*crad*angd/360))
```

This first bit is all you need at first to get the handrail working. Do the downrights later.

```
!Downrights
!3D script
IF dnnum THEN
 ADDy -(crad-B)
 FOR k=1 TO dnnum
  ROTz angl-angdw*(k-1)
  ADD  0,crad,hitdif*(k-1)
  ROTx 180
  CYLIND dnlen,dnrad
  DEL 3
 NEXT k
 DEL 1
ENDIF
```

Handrail 3D: A FOR...NEXT Loop runs through, calculating all the points along the handrail. Do not forget that for a TUBE, you have a phantom Start and End point. Using PUT & GET, it is almost impossible to get an error. But I still advise the use of the BODY -1 command, to be sure.

Downrights 3D: The first FOR...NEXT loop was based on angle, this one is based on number.

Handrail Ends 3D: This is an example of using Value Lists and using flags (in this case 's') to toggle values and angles. I suggest three methods, as a simple end of the handrail results in a very ugly detail where it meets the downrights.

```
!Handrail Ends 3D
ADDy -(crad-B)
  s=(-1)      !'s' is the flag
  GOSUB 100:!Handrail end
ADDz zzyzx
  s=(+1)
  GOSUB 100:!Handrail end
DEL 2

END:!-----------------------

100:!One Handrail end
ROTz -s*angl
ADDy crad
ROTy s*(90-s*anglen)
ROTz -180*(s-1)/2
GOSUB 110+es
DEL 4
RETURN

!End Treatments
110:CYLIND dimen,trad!Butt-end
    RETURN

111:CYLIND trad,trad !Elbows
    ADDz trad
    ELBOW dimen,90+anglen*s,trad
    DEL 1
    RETURN

112:CYLIND dimen,trad!Rounded
    ADDz dimen
    ELLIPS trad,trad
    DEL 1
    RETURN
```

```
!Handrail
!2D Script

PEN pcol

HOTSPOT2 0,0
HOTSPOT2 -A/2,0
HOTSPOT2 A/2,0
HOTSPOT2 0,B

!display stretchspot location
CIRCLE2 0,B,diam/6000

PROJECT2 3,270,2!DRAW IT!!

!Downrights
IF dnnum THEN !downrights
  ADD2 0,-(crad-B)
  FOR k=1 TO dnnum
  ROT2 angl-angdw*(k-1)
  ADD2 0,crad
  HOTSPOT2 0,0
  CIRCLE2 0,0,dnrad
  DEL 2
  NEXT k
  DEL 1
    ELSE        !stretchspots
    CIRCLE2 A/2,0,diam/6000
    CIRCLE2 -A/2,0,diam/6000
    ENDIF
```

Handrail Ends 3D: I must advise that you cannot write code like this straight off. You get each handrail end working as two routines. I am always anxious to make my Cookbook exercises fit one or 2 pages, 3 at the most. So you discover that the difference between the routines is some pluses and minuses here and there. By using the flag ('s') you can toggle the angles and rotations and do the both with the same routine. These toggling routines are contained in the **Tips & Tricks** in the Voyager Maths Primer.

To do one of the three choices for an End-solution, the flag 'es' is used to decide which subroutine to run.

2D Script: As the object is stretchy, place the hotspots FIRST in the script. Use PROJECT2 (although a 2D script with ARC2 could be written if you have time). The downrights need hotspots, and if there are no downrights, you need little circles to help the user find the stretching points.

dnlen		Downright length	0.800
ddiam		Downright diameter millimetres	35.00
dnnum		Number of Downrights	5
endstyl	Abc	Handrail end style	Rounded ends
dimen		Overhand at Handrail ends	0.000
infil	Abc	Infil Panel below??	Infil Panel
lenin		Downward Height of Infil	0.600
dropin		Gap between Infil & handrail	0.100
matin		Material of Downstanding Infil	29
pcol		Pen colour 2D and 3D	1

Additional Parameters for Downrights and Infil Panel

```
!Glass locations for COONS infil
IF infil='Infil Panel' THEN

!Points 1 to 2
  h=-dropin       !height counter
PUT crad*SIN(-angl),crad*COS(-angl),-dropin
FOR k=-angl+angd TO angl-angd+0.002 STEP angd
  h=h+hitd
  PUT crad*SIN(k),crad*COS(k),h
  NEXT k
PUT crad*SIN(angl),crad*COS(angl),zzyzx-dropin

!Points 4 to 3
  h=-lenin        !height counter
PUT crad*SIN(-angl),crad*COS(-angl),-lenin
FOR k=-angl+angd TO angl-angd+0.002 STEP angd
  h=h+hitd
  PUT crad*SIN(k),crad*COS(k),h
  NEXT k
PUT crad*SIN(angl),crad*COS(angl),zzyzx-lenin

!Points 1 to 4
PUT crad*SIN(-angl),crad*COS(-angl),-dropin
PUT crad*SIN(-angl),crad*COS(-angl),-lenin

!Points 2 to 3
PUT crad*SIN(angl),crad*COS(angl),zzyzx-dropin
PUT crad*SIN(angl),crad*COS(angl),zzyzx-lenin

ADDy -(crad-B)
MATERIAL matin
BODY -1
COONS 17,2,63,
  GET(NSP)
BODY -1
ENDIF
```

Infil Panel 3D: COONS can make it! It has the Power! Another method (slightly easier) would be bPRiSM_, but you need care in calculating and locating it.

Follow the routine I advocate in the tutorial on COONS. Use a similar FOR...NEXT routine to the one used for the TUBE.

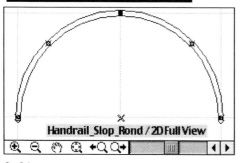

Handrail_Slop_Rond / 2D Full View

Tips and Tricks
Getting Strings to Work Correctly

YOU may have problems with SPLIT and STR commands if GDL does not know if a variable is a string or a numeral. Parameter variables and ones already in use in the script are already known. Variables imported from an external file or table e.g. from a command like:

nr=INPUT (ch, 1,1,varnam).

If GDL receives varnam as "44-22-22", is it to accept it as the value 0, or is it a string for a telephone number? You can define in advance the form of a variable by initialising it. e.g.

varnam1=" "   etc. Then ArchiCAD will know that these
varnam2=" "   variables must be handled as strings and
stitem=" ": lent=0 not as integers or whatever...

THERE is a new statement in AC_6.5, **VARTYPE(exprn)**, which returns a 1 if the expression is a number and 0 if it is a string. The main use for this is in IF statements when reading text file from disk.

Hotel Canopy

THIS CANOPY is based on something bigger and much more complicated, designed in Aug 1997 for the entrance to the Bradford Royal Infirmary Accident and Emergency Unit. This is an exercise in:

- TUBE command
- PUT and GET for many uses
- Polylines in PRISMs
- Nudging elements to fit
- Using subroutines for elements
- Using symmetry

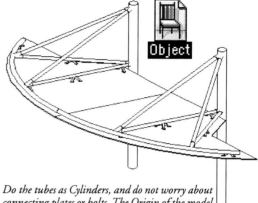

Do the tubes as Cylinders, and do not worry about connecting plates or bolts. The Origin of the model is the midpoint between the main masts.

```
!Hotel Canopy
!Voyager Course

PRISM_ 7,0.02,
   0 ,   0,15,
   1.8,   0,15,
   2.4,-0.9,15,
   3.9,-0.9,15,
   0.0, 0.9,900,
   0.0,  -3.4,3015,
   0 ,   0,15
```

```
!Hotel Canopy
!Voyager Course
PEN 1:
GOSUB 120:!half sheet

END!-----------------

120: !Canopy Glass
MATERIAL "Glass":
   ADDy -0.15
PRISM_ 7,0.02,
   0 ,   0,15,
   1.8,   0,15,
   2.4,-0.9,15,
   3.9,-0.9,15,
   0.0, 0.9,900,
   0.0,  -3.4,3015,
   0 ,   0,15
DEL 1
RETURN
```

In the way that we have done with many worksheets, convert this to a subroutine in the usual way, with line numbering, an END statement and a RETURN statement.

```
!Hotel Canopy
!Voyager Course

PEN 1:
GOSUB 100:!Glass sheet

END!-----------------

100: !Canopy Glass
   ADDz 3.0
   ROTx -10
GOSUB 120 !halfsheet
   MULx -1
GOSUB 120 !halfsheet
   DEL 3
RETURN

120: !Half of Glass
MATERIAL "Glass":
   ADDy -0.15
PRISM_ 7,0.02,
....... etc etc etc
.........
   0 ,   0,15
DEL 1
RETURN
```

First, hammer in HALF the glass shape - you can do this because the whole assembly is symmetrical. The polyline to use here is 3000. With 3000, you reach a point, you define a centre-circle, followed by a second point, and it moves around that circle from the previous point.

3000 does not go exactly to the second point, but it goes as close to it as it

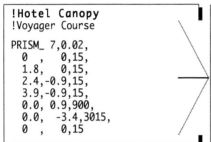

can, and regards the circle as its primary definition. It is therefore down to you to work out where the ideal centre should be, so it hits the end point correctly. If you tried to use the 4000 polyline, you would need to know the sweep angle of the curve.

Now convert this to a subroutine. Move the edges of the glass forward of

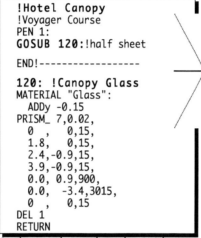

the centre line of the masts with ADDy -0.15.

We would like to have this Half sheet duplicated symmetrically, so it is better to change the actual PRISM subroutine into a number like 120 (that comes after 100:) so that 100 becomes the mirroring routine.

In your 100, first, you lift the cursor

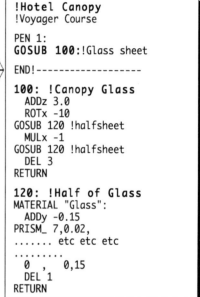

to the correct height, tilt the glass, issue the first 120 command, mirror around X and issue 120 again. Finally, DEL the cursor moves to complete subroutine 100.

```
GOSUB 200: !Both Masts
END:!--------------

200: !Both Masts
GOSUB 220 !Mast
   MULx -1
GOSUB 220 !Mast
   DEL 1
RETURN

220: !Masts and diags
MATERIAL "Paint, gloss"
   ADDx 1.5
CYLIND 5,0.1
   DEL 1
RETURN
```

MULy -1 is a simple mirror-around-Y-axis command

Mast and tubing system

You should only build half of it, as it can be mirrored. Start a subroutine number 200: to hold the tubes. The easiest bit is the two Main Masts. Put them in first.

The curved tube is much more difficult. This can be part of the Glass subroutine, as it must be tilted with the glass. The lower diagonal tubes must also tilt with the glass.

```
120: !Half of Glass
MATERIAL "Glass":
  ADDy -0.15
PRISM_ 7,0.02,
  0  ,  0,15,
  1.8,  0,15,
  2.4,-0.9,15,
  3.9,-0.9,15,
  0.0, 0.9,900,
  0.0,  -3.4,3015,
  0  ,  0,15,
  DEL 1

! Curved Tube ----
MATERIAL "Paint, gloss"
  ADDy 0.9-0.15
FOR k=-5 TO 65 STEP 5
 PUT 4.2*SIN(k),
  -4.2*COS(k),0.15,0
    NEXT k

TUBE 2,NSP/4,63,
  0,0,901,
  0.05,360,4001,
  GET(NSP)
    DEL 1
RETURN
```

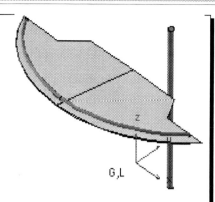

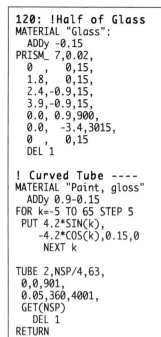

G,L

This could also be done with Elbow, but the technique used here is more interesting

In FOR... NEXT Loops we usually use a Stepping value of ONE, but in loops involving angles, one often uses the angle as the step - in this case, 5 degrees.

```
!Lower diagonal
  ADD 1.5, 0 ,0.15
  ROTx 90
CYLIND 3.15,0.04
  ROTy 34
CYLIND 2.65,0.04
  DEL 3
RETURN
```

Add this little routine to the bottom of subroutine 120

Curved Tube

This tilts, so it is parallel to the glass. Whenever doing a curved TUBE command, it is easiest to use a FOR... NEXT loop that feeds values into the PUT statement.

In this case, (starting from the same centre of radius as the glass curve itself) you define X and Y values using SIN and COS. Generally, SIN gives the X-value, and COS gives the Y-value. Z is 0.15 above the glass, and the mitring angle is assumed to be Zero. With Tube, you always start ONE place earlier, and finish one place later to form the tube.

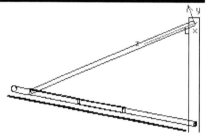

The diagonals could be done with TUBE, but there is a danger that in the mitring at the junction with the curved tube, you might get a spiky point coming through.
(See the Long Handrail problem in the GDL Cookbook)

Diagonal Tubes

Using Cylind, and burying the butt ends inside the masts and curved tubes, you will get a neat result. By the way, this exercise does not include making special plates on the masts, or doing fancy nut and bolt ends to the tubes.

It would be possible to make the tilting angle and dimensions of the glass parametric, in which case, you would have to use trigonometry to determine the ends of the diagonal Cylinders.

As this is not parametric, you can use the lazy man's solution of setting up the Cylinder start point, and then juggling the length and angles to get the ends into the right position. I call it 'docking', like nudging a ship into its berth.

```
200: !Both Masts
GOSUB 220 !Mast
  MULx -1
GOSUB 220 !Mast
  DEL 1
RETURN

220: !Masts and diags
MATERIAL "Paint, gloss"
  ADDx 1.5
CYLIND 5,0.1
  DEL 1

!Upper diagonals
  ADD 1.5,0,4.9
  ROTx 111.5
CYLIND 3.28,0.04
  DEL 1
  ROTz 35
  ROTx 118
CYLIND 2.95,0.04
  DEL 3
RETURN
```

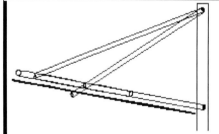

Docking the angled tubes is more difficult, but by using a combination of the elevation and plan windows, you can get the cylinder ends to meet. (You have thus lost the parametric opportunity of changing angles and tilt - but never mind.)

Notice that 200 has now changed to use the same routine for mirroring the structure as we used for the glass in 100:. So the actual masts and diagonals move to 220:.

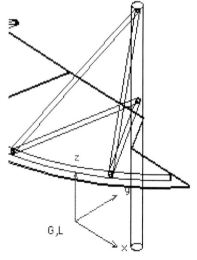

G,L

Notice that (because of the tilting of the tubes) the upper tube is angled at 35 degrees, and the lower one at 34.

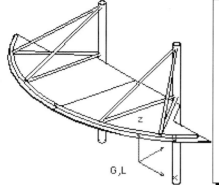

```
!Hotel Canopy
!2D Script

PROJECT2 3,270,2
HOTSPOT2 0,-3.4
HOTSPOT2 1.5,0
HOTSPOT2 -1.5,0
HOTSPOT2 1.5,-3.15
HOTSPOT2 -1.5,-3.15
```

2D Script

The final touch is to write the simple 2-D script so that the model appears in the plan.

You should make the whole thing easy to pick up by putting HOTSPOTs at sensitive locations. In fact, if the structure is not at all parametric in dimension, you might be best to view the 3D structure in plan, then save the 3D view as a symbol.

You have now finished the main structure and glass. However, if you wish to continue, you can add the Mastic joints in the glass, the Planar fittings, and put conical ends on the tubes.

Adding in the details

Mastic Joints

Because the Mastic joints follow the glass, they should be a subroutine inserted into the glass object. Here it is 130: inserted immediately after the PRISM command.

'p', the 'pixel' idea

Again, one uses the TUBE command. First, one describes a small square section, but to avoid many zeroes and decimal points, one defines a 'pixel' called 'p', in this case 1 centimetre. So the joint is a square section 20mm x 20mm in size. The tube must have a phantom start and end point, and arbitrarily, I have selected points 1000 metres in each direction (the equivalent of selecting 'Infinity' on your camera focus setting.)

Get one working, to test out the TUBE command. If this works, then put in all the remaining mastic joints – for only the right half of the glass, of course. When they are working, tweak, or nudge the points to get the starts and ends just where you want them.

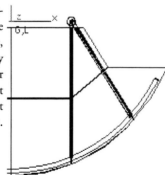

```
120: !Half of Glass
MATERIAL "Glass":
  ADDy -0.15
PRISM_ 7,0.02,
  0  ,  0,15,
  1.8,  0,15,
  2.4,-0.9,15,
  3.9,-0.9,15,
  0.0, 0.9,900,
  0.0, -3.4,3015,
  0   0,15
GOSUB 130!Mastic Joints
  DEL 1

RETURN

130: !Mastic Joints
PUT 1.50, 0.00,0,0,
    1.50,-3.10,0,0

p=0.01 !One GlassPixel!
FOR k=1 TO NSP/8 STEP 1
  TUBE 4,4,63,
    p, p,0,
   -p, p,0,
   -p,-p,0,
    p,-p,0,
  0,1000,0,0,
  GET(8),
  0,-1000,0,0

NEXT k
RETURN
```

Assume that Z and mitres are all zero. The mastic joints will be part of the glass and will get tilted with it. The nearest Material to clear glazing Mastic (in appearance) is ICE.

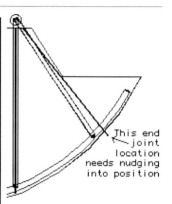

This end joint location needs nudging into position

```
130:!Mastic Joints
PUT 1.50, 0.00,0,0,
    1.50,-3.10,0,0,
    2.40,-0.90,0,0,
    1.50,-1.60,0,0,
    0.00,-1.60,0,0,
    1.50,-1.60,0,0

p=0.01 !One GlassPixel!
FOR k=1 TO NSP/8 STEP 1
  TUBE 4,4,63,
    p, p,0,
   -p, p,0,
   -p,-p,0,
    p,-p,0,
  0,1000,0,0,
  GET(8),
  0,-1000,0,0

NEXT k
RETURN
```

Planar Fittings

Next is to tackle the Pilkington Planar fittings (or something that looks like them!) These are going to be either in pairs or in fours, so one needs to make both types.

Again, because the structure is symmetrical, you only need do half the planars, then mirror them across X, just as with subroutines 100 and 200.

```
600: !Planars
IF shoplan THEN
  MATERIAL "Stainless Steel"
  GOSUB 620 !half planars
    MULx -1
  GOSUB 620 !other half
    DEL 1
    ENDIF
RETURN
```

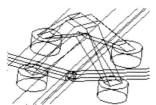

Planar fittings, continued

It is a good idea to put documention into the subroutine, if it contains syntax that you may want to remember later.

This routine is a bit complicated. (If you are actively on the Voyager course, you have a tutor to help). The width of the PRISM in the quad planar needs to be wider than for the double. Because it is rotated at 45 degs, it is widened by (Root-2)/2 which is 1.4. To enable the same prism command to be used for both, a factor called 'qp' is set to 1 or 1.4.

When the routine in 620 discovers either a 2 or a 4 (in the GET statement), that number is added to 650, so it knows whether to run either 652 or 654. Subroutine 652 defines the actual form of the planar, and 654 repeats 652 twice with a 90-degree twist, to make a quad shape.

```
620: !Draw half Planars
!PUT all the figures
!N.B. Syntax of PUT is
!Xloc, Yloc,Angl,Type
!Type=2 double or 4 quad
!Tilt with the glass
PUT 1.5,-0.20,    0, 2,
    1.5,-1.53,   15, 4,
    1.5,-2.85,    0, 2,
    3.5,-1.35,   58, 2,
    2.28,-0.95,-56, 2

  ADDz 3.10 !height
  ROTx -10  !tilt of glass
  ADDy -0.15
np=NSP/4:
FOR planar=1 TO np
  ADD GET(1),GET(1),0
  ROTz GET(1)
  qp=1 !Set to double
GOSUB 650+GET(1)
  DEL 2
  NEXT planar
  DEL 3
RETURN
```

```
652: !Double Planar
ph=0.07!Planar height
pt=0.04!Planar thickness
RESOL 12
  ROTx 90
  ADDz -pt/2
PRISM 8,pt,    !Arms
  0,0,      0.10*qp, -ph,
  0.12*qp,-ph,      pt,pt,
  -pt,pt,    -0.12*qp,-ph,
  -0.10*qp,-ph,     0,0
  DEL 2
ADD -0.11*qp,0,-ph-pt
CYLIND pt,pt  !Pad
  ADDx 0.22*qp
CYLIND pt,pt  !Pad
  DEL 2
RETURN

654: !Quad Planar
qp=1.4  !It's a quad!
  ROTz 45
GOSUB 652
  ROTz 90
GOSUB 652
  DEL 2
RETURN
```

Passing Parameters (Macros)
Improving the fine detail

As a final turn, you might like to give a more sophisticated ending to each Cylinder for the diagonal tubing. As each tube is a different length, this could become tedious. Set up a single subroutine 250 to describe one cylinder with conical ends, using common parameters (here called 'clen' and 'crad'.)

Thus, before you draw each cylinder, 'pass the parameters' to the subroutine, as you see in the script example, and the improved cylinder will be drawn. The old one is left in the script, with a comment mark, so you can remember the required length. Go back and replace some of the old Cylinders with subroutine 250.

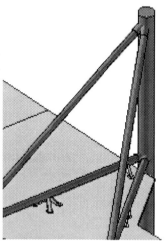

```
!Upper diagonals
  ADD 1.5,0,4.9
  ROTx 111.5
!CYLIND 3.28,0.04
clen=3.28:crad=0.04
GOSUB 250 !ConedCylin
  DEL 1
  ROTz 35
  ROTx 118
!CYLIND 2.95,0.04
clen=2.95:crad=0.04
GOSUB 250
  DEL 3
RETURN

  250:!Cylind with ends
CYLIND clen,crad
CONE 0.2,crad*1.2,
    crad*1.1,90,90
  ADDz clen
  ROTx 180
CONE 0.2,crad*1.2,
    crad*1.1,90,90
  DEL 2
RETURN
```

Storey Sensitivity

Global variables, 2D Scripting

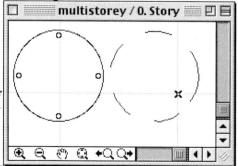

O FTEN an object needs to appear on other storeys, such as main Beam lines, ventilation ducts, drainage lines, lighting fittings etc. Here is an example of Storey Sensitivity, using a simple stretchy round table. On its own storey, the Global variable S~ is zero, on others it's a number e.g. 1 for the storey above. So it can be displayed on the home storey in all its glorious detail, and on other storeys it will show more simply using a linetype of the user's choosing.

S~ can also be known (to aliens) as GLOB_CH_STORY_DIST.

```
!Simple Table
!3D Script

RESOL 12
MATERIAL 'Whitewash'
PEN 1
FOR k=1 TO 4
  ROTz k*90
  ADDx A/2-thk
  CYLIND hit-thk,thk/2
  DEL 2
  NEXT k

RESOL 24
  ADDz hit-thk
  CYLIND thk,A/2
  DEL 1
```

[Object]

```
!Simple Object to demo
!Storey sensitivity
!2D Script - where it all happens

HOTSPOT2 0,0
HOTSPOT2 -A/2,0
HOTSPOT2 A/2,0
HOTSPOT2 0,-A/2
HOTSPOT2 0, A/2

IF S~=0 THEN   !Legs
FOR k=1 TO 4
  ROTz k*90
  CIRCLE2 A/2-thk,0,thk/2
  DEL 1
  NEXT k
ENDIF

IF S~<>0 THEN LINE_TYPE lint
CIRCLE2 0,0,A/2   !Tabletop
```

This could also be done with an IF... THEN... ELSE... ENDIF routine

Variable	Type	Name	Value
A		X Dimension	1.000
thk		Sectional thickness	0.050
hit		Height of Table	0.800
lint		LineType on other Storeys	8

multistorey / 0. Story

Stretchy Edging Tool

THIS OBJECT is almost like a macro – in the sense that the routine is standardised, and can be used over an over again. All you have to do is put a different profile into the PRISM statement, and whatever you define will become a stretchy cornice/ skirting/ eaves piece/ metal flashing/ cladding panel, or whatever it is intended to be. The mitring routine allows it to follows a wall or roof edge, however angular (except curved).

In terms of GDL, it is interesting in that it uses:
- Polylines in the Prism shape - essential for most cornice shapes.
- CUTPLANE and CUTEND.
- PUT and GET as a way of making a PRISM.

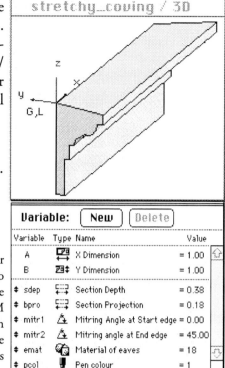

3 D Script: The mitring could be for an internal or an external corner. To make sure that there is always substance to the Prism, you must make the PRISM its full length, plus at least twice its depth at each end. Use CUTPLANE to make it the correct length – even when there is no mitre. This will allow pretty extreme angles to be chosen by the user.

Variable:	**New**	Delete	
Variable	Type	Name	Value
A	⟷	X Dimension	= 1.00
B	↕	Y Dimension	= 1.00
↕ sdep		Section Depth	= 0.38
↕ bpro		Section Projection	= 0.18
↕ mitr1	△	Mitring Angle at Start edge	= 0.00
↕ mitr2	△	Mitring angle at End edge	= 45.00
↕ emat		Material of eaves	= 18
↕ pcol		Pen colour	= 1

It may be difficult for the user to know which is the start and the end, and whether mitres should be positive or negative angles – but they soon find out by trial and error.

The Section Depth and Projection give you an opportunity to build into the PRISM definition as much parametric control as you want.

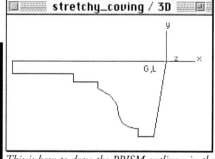

This is how to draw the PRISM outline - in the NEGATIVE quadrant of the X-Y plane.

2 D Script: In most things, 2D scripting is useful, but for stretchy objects, good 2D scripting is vital. Some trig is required to make the hotspots land on the corners, however extreme the mitring angle. Unless there are many of these items, it is acceptable to use PROJECT2 in the 2D script, which saves one some hard work with trigonometry. However, if you need trig to work out the hotspots, you could just as well script the entire 2D object.

```
!External coving
!3D Script        Material
                  command must
MATERIAL emat     always   come
PEN pcol          B E F O R E
RESOL 16          Cutplane!

50:!Organise cutplanes
ROTy -90
ROTx -mitr1
CUTPLANE
DEL 2             People who find
                  this doesn't work
ADDx A            have    usually
ROTy 90           forgotten to DEL
ROTx -mitr2       after issuing the
CUTPLANE          C u t p l a n e
DEL 3             commands.


100:!Make the Prism
ROTy -90
ADDz -A-bpro*2

!Put values for
!main Cornice panel
PUT 0,0,15,
 -0.030,-bpro, 15,
 -0.070,-bpro, 15,
 -0.070,-0.160,15,
 -0.075,-0.160,13,
 -0.120,-0.110,1013,
 -0.125,-0.100,13,
 -0.165,-0.066,1015,
 -0.170,-0.065,15,
 -0.170,-0.050,15,
 -0.230,-0.050,15,
 -0.230,-0.030,15,
 -sdep, -0.030,15,
 -sdep, -0.000,15,
  0,    0,    -1

!Now Do it!
PRISM_ NSP/3,A+bpro*4,
 GET(NSP)

DEL 2

!Finish
CUTEND
CUTEND

END:!----------------
```

```
!External coving
!2D Script

IF mitr1<>0 OR mitr2<>0 THEN
PROJECT2 3,270,2
 ELSE
RECT2 0,0,A,-bpro
 ENDIF

LINE2 -bpro*TAN(mitr1),-bpro,
      A+bpro*TAN(mitr2),-bpro

HOTSPOT2 0,0
HOTSPOT2 A,0
HOTSPOT2 0,-bpro
HOTSPOT2 A,-bpro
HOTSPOT2 A/2,0
HOTSPOT2 A/2,-bpro

HOTSPOT2  -bpro*TAN(mitr1),-bpro
HOTSPOT2 A+bpro*TAN(mitr2),-bpro
```

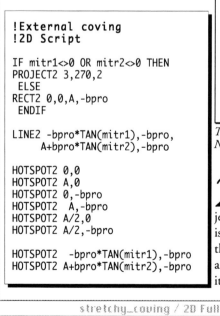

Boundary Survey Tool

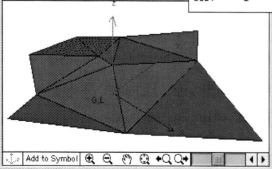 Object

THIS is a 'survey assistant' – you can set up a theodolite on a tripod on a site in one place, measure distances to all corners and some points on the site, note their angle (azimuth) from the instrument. Write these with a text editor and you can produce a topographically accurate site model.

It is an interesting example of:

- File input - reading in from a data text file
- Using Arrays
- Define Style and Autosizing forms
- Using the PUT and GET functions
- Loops where only REPEAT... UNTIL will do

Variable	Type	Name	Value
A		X Dimension	1.000
B		Y Dimension	1.000
fnam	Abc	Filename for site	siteboun.dat
ft	Abc	Font name	geneva
fh		Font Height in millimetres	2.00
shol	☒	Show Levels? ON/OFF	On
slin	☒	Site Lines? ON/ OFF	On

Arrays have to be 'declared' first – here the array is declared with the DIM command, and must not exceed 20 numbers. You could increase this number.

Survey Textfile: the user types in the name of the project, followed by a list of the points (in order) of the boundary using Angle, Distance, Altitude and a flag of 0 for boundary. This is followed by internal points, which are written the same, with a flag of 1. The file is saved into 'ArchiCAD Data folder'.

Master Script: does the whole reading operation and puts the coordinates and levels into an array. The flags f[ ] tell it if it's part of the boundary or internal. This example is limited to 20 points.

OPEN and INPUT are some of the most difficult of commands to understand – by writing a statement that somehow determines the value of a useless number ('n'), you discover the value of variables and strings. Read the appendix to the manual on this function, and try this ('n' is the number of items found). 'n' is -1 when the file end is reached.

To make practical use of ARRAYS you must be prepared to use the PUT and GET statements to build and use the arrays.

Derivation of the x[] and y[] values is a piece of Circle geometry – the X and Y of every point defined by radius and azimuth is found with a SIN and COS statement.

With AC 6.0 & 6.5, we can use this routine to make a MASS command. This forms the site with correct levels.

```
!Boundary Survey Tool
!Master Script

DIM angl[20], dist[20], alti[20],
    x[20], y[20], z[20], f[20]

!titlestr will be title
ch1=OPEN("TEXT",fnam,"SEPARATOR=',',MODE=RO")
n=INPUT(ch1,1,1,titlestr)  !title

!REPEAT Loop - necessary because
!FOR NEXT loop cannot be used with INPUT
REPEAT          !Fill the array
  p=p+1
  n=INPUT(ch1,1+p,1,ang,dis,alt,flg)
  angl[p]=ang: dist[p]=dis:
alti[p]=alt:f[p]=flg
  UNTIL n<=0
CLOSE ch1
pall=p-1 !Number of all Points

FOR k=1 TO pall
  x[k]=SIN(angl[k])*dist[k]
  y[k]=COS(angl[k])*dist[k]
NEXT k

p=0 !Find how many external & intenal
REPEAT
p=p+1
UNTIL f[p]<>0 OR p>=20

pext=p-1        !No of External points
pint=pall-pext !No of Internal points
```

When you open a file, you have to define the channel ('ch1'), and the characteristics (mode, separator etc) that GDL will expect to find.

3D Script: The MASS command is a delight to use, but you need to learn it. The first points are the boundary points, with a masking code of 15, ending in a -1 (like Prisms). The internal points are all separately listed, ending in -1.

```
!Survey Tool - 2D Script

PEN L_
DEFINE STYLE "boundy" ft, fh,1,1
SET STYLE "boundy"

!Draw the Site
  PROJECT2 3,270,1

FOR k=1 TO pall
HOTSPOT2 x[k],y[k]
CIRCLE2 x[k],y[k],A_*fh/2000
  IF shol THEN
    altstr=STR(alti[k],4,2)
    TEXT2 x[k],y[k],altstr
  ENDIF
NEXT k
```
The circles are autosized to be the same height as Font, taking note of the drawing scale A_.

```
!Survey Tool - 3D Script

PEN     L_    !uses variables
MATERIAL M_    !in settings box

!Draw the Site
FOR k=1 TO pext-1 !External
  PUT x[k],y[k],alti[k],15
  NEXT k
  PUT x[1],y[1],alti[1],-1

FOR k=pext+1 TO pall !Internal
  PUT x[k],y[k],alti[k],-1
  NEXT k

BODY   -1
MASS  M_,M_,M_,
  pext,pint,16+64*slin,0,
  GET(NSP)
BODY   -1
```

Survey Textfile: You type in the survey details in any text editor, save it as an ascii (text) file and put it into the 'ArchiCAD Data Folder'. Put a title on the first line. Write in the order: Azimuth, Distance, Altitude, Flag. Use commas to separate numbers. Boundary points come first with a '0' flag, then interior points follow using the '1' flag

```
Site survey
  10, 12.65, 2.7,0,
  30, 10.55, 2.0,0,
  80, 21.55, 2.3,0,
  128, 10.55, 2.2,0,
  196, 14.55, 1.9,0,
  210, 9.50, 1.7,0,
  245, 10.55, 2.5,0,
  285, 8.55, 2.0,0,
  325, 6.55, 2.6,0,
  360, 6.75, 2.1,0,
  0, 0, 3.6,    1,
  270, 2.35, 3.6,1,
```

Winged Truss

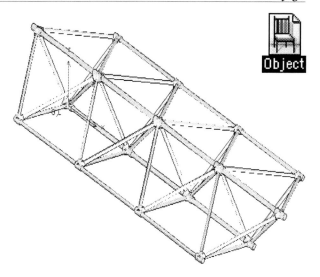

Object

THIS is an interesting truss form, which I call a 'winged truss'. The truss in detail, has cast metal sleeved joints to the tubes. However, for general perspective drawing, or animation, one would like to shorten the drawing time - hence the truss can also be drawn with all the joints concealed. It also prints an engineer/fabricator's report.

This is a valuable learning exercise: It includes:

- Offering the user alternative forms of 3D: simple & complex
- Outputting data to file to inform the user of details and risks
- Reading the system clock
- Extensive 2D scripting, to save redraw time
- Passing parameters to a subroutine
- Defining and Autosizing text in 2D symbols

Variable Type Name			Value
A		X Dimension	4.500
B		Y Dimension	3.600
iden	Abc	Truss Identification	MainHall
thit		Height of Truss	1.200
tlen		Length of one Truss module	2.100
t1diam		Diameter Top+Bottom main tube	0.100
t2diam		Diameter Longitudinal tubing	0.070
t3diam		Diameter Upper wing tubing	0.070
t4diam		Diameter Lower wing tubing	0.070
truvu	☒	Truview=ON Scripted View=OFF	Off
tmat		Material of Tubing	11
simcom	☒	Simple=OFF Complex=OFF	On
outdat	☒	OutPut DataFile ON / OFF?	On
shownam	☒	Show Name in 2D symbol ON/OFF	On

Parameters: The truss has four different radii of tubing. Every linear element is parametrically definable. A and B are used to make the truss stretchy. The Master Script converts the A and B into 'tnum' and 'twid', from which the rest of the truss can be drawn.

Leave the parameters at the bottom of the list until later.

```
!Winged 3D truss
!Master Script

tnum=INT(A/tlen)   !Number of Trusses
twid=B             !Width of Truss

!Longitudinal Diagonal Tubing
dtang=ATN(thit/(tlen/2))
dlen =SQR(thit**2+(tlen/2)**2)

!Upper Wing tubing
ang1=ATN(tlen/twid)
ang2=ATN((thit/2)/((tlen/2)/SIN(ang1)))
utlen=(thit/2)/SIN(ang2)

!Lower Wing Tubing
ltang=ATN(thit/twid)
ltlen=SQR(thit*thit+twid*twid)/2
```

3D Script: Subroutine 100 is called to deal with calculating essential data like the angle and length of diagonal tubes. Therefore, at this early stage, do not forget the END statement. An early subroutine like this is a good place to store all internal parameters, and to put in ones that you think of during the development.

```
!Winged 3D truss
!3D Script

PEN 1:MATERIAL tmat

!Lower member
RESOL 8
  ROTy 90
CYLIND tlen*(tnum-1),t1diam/2
DEL 1

!Upper tube
  ADD -tlen/2,0,thit
GOSUB 400
  DEL 1
  END:!----------------------
```

The Lower and Upper and outer tube members (300: and 400:) are easy enough to do. Use Cylinders which point along the line of the truss.

Once you have got 300: and 400: in place, you can finish the main script of the truss (next page).

The main tubes include Sleeve joints. For the Upper and the Outer tube, they are included in Subroutine 300: and 400: whereas the ones for the lower tube are better done in the subroutine for the diagonals.

```
300: !Outer Tube
ROTy 90
CYLIND tlen*(tnum-1),t2diam/2
IF simcom THEN !Sleeve
FOR k=1 TO tnum
ADDz -t2diam*1.5
ADDz tlen*(k-1)
CYLIND t2diam*3, t2diam/1.2
DEL 2
NEXT k
ENDIF
DEL 1
RETURN

400: !Upper Tube
  ROTy 90
CYLIND tlen*tnum,t1diam/2

IF simcom THEN !Sleeve
FOR k=1 TO tnum+1
    ADDz -t1diam*1.5
    ADDz tlen*(k-1)
CYLIND t1diam*3, t1diam/1.5
    DEL 2
    NEXT k
ENDIF
  DEL 1
RETURN
```

```
!Continuation of
!Executive Script
!Outer members
  ADD 0,-twid/2,thit/2
GOSUB 300 !outer tube
  DEL 1

  ADD 0,twid/2,thit/2
GOSUB 300 !outer tube
  DEL 1

!All the diagonal tubes
FOR n=1 TO tnum
  GOSUB 200 !Longitudinal tubes
  GOSUB 210 !Upper Wing tubes
  GOSUB 220:!Lower Wing tubes
  ADDx tlen
  NEXT n
DEL tnum

END:!------------------
```

The way to get the diagonals done is to start off by getting ONE module right, and the rest will be done with a FOR... NEXT loop.

In reality, you don't have time to experiment, but to show you different ways of solving this, I have shown you two methods, what I call the 'simple' and the 'complex'.

The Simple uses the TUBE command to do ALL the diagonal and wing tubing for each module in one breath. TUBE only requires you to know the XYZ location of the points, which is easy enough.

The Complex does a more traditional craftsmanlike job, working out all the angles and lengths of the diagonals using trigonometry, and then drawing the cylinders. This produces a better looking result (Tube causes some torsional distortion of the rods, a problem that GDL for AC6 may have got rid of.)

The upper wing tubes are done in the same way, using Tube for the easy view and Cylinder subroutines for the complex.

```
200: !Do diagonal tubes
IF simcom=0 THEN!if simple
TUBE 2, 3+2, 63,
     0,0,901,
     t2diam/2,360,4001,

    -tlen/2,0,thit*2,0,
    -tlen/2,0,thit,  0,
     0,0,0,          0,
     tlen/2,0,thit,  0,
     tlen/2,0,thit*2,0
ENDIF

IF simcom THEN !if complex
!Pass parameters
LET clen=dlen: diam=t2diam
  ROTy 90-dtang
GOSUB 260 !tube
  DEL 1
  ROTy -(90-dtang)
GOSUB 260 !tube
  DEL 1
ENDIF
RETURN
```

Note: The TUBE command is done here as an exercise in the use of TUBE, and to show that difficult tasks can be done without the use of any Trigonometry.

Please feel free to leave out the TUBE routines if you are short of time.

```
210:!Upper wing tubes
IF simcom=0 THEN !if simple
TUBE 2, 2+5, 63,
     0,0,901,
     t3diam/2,360,4001,

    -tlen,0,thit,     0,
    -tlen/2,0,thit,   0,
     0, twid/2,thit/2,0,
     tlen/2,0,thit,   0,
     0,-twid/2,thit/2,0,
    -tlen/2,0,thit,   0,
    -tlen,0,thit,     0
ENDIF

IF simcom THEN !if complex
clen=utlen: diam=t3diam
  ADD 0,-twid/2,thit/2 !first
  ROTz ang1
  ROTx 270 + ang2
GOSUB 260 !tube
  DEL 2+1

  ADD 0,-twid/2,thit/2 !second
  ROTz -ang1
  ROTx 270 + ang2
GOSUB 260 !tube
  DEL 2+1

  ADD 0, twid/2,thit/2 !third
  ROTz 180 - ang1
  ROTx 270 + ang2
GOSUB 260 !tube
  DEL 2+1

  ADD 0, twid/2,thit/2 !fourth
  ROTz 180 + ang1
  ROTx 270 + ang2
GOSUB 260 !tube
  DEL 2+1
ENDIF
RETURN


220:! Do Lower Wing tubes
IF simcom=0 THEN !if simple
TUBE 2, 3+2, 63,
     0,0,901,
     t4diam/2,360,4001,

     0,twid/2,thit*2, 0,
     0,twid/2,thit/2, 0,
     0,0,0,           0,
     0,-twid/2,thit/2,0,
     0,-twid/2,thit*2,0
ENDIF

IF simcom THEN !if complex
!Main tube sleeves
  ROTy 90
  ADDz -t1diam*1.5
  CYLIND t1diam*3,t1diam/1.5
  DEL 2

!outrigging tubes
  ROTx 90-ltang
clen=ltlen: diam=t4diam
GOSUB 260: !Cyl lower tube
  DEL 1
  ROTx -90+ltang
GOSUB 260: !Cyl lower tube
  DEL 1
ENDIF
```

The statements

clen=ltlen:

diam=t4diam

is an example of passing parameters. The same routine (260:) will provide a cylinders and end sleeves for many different diameters and lengths.

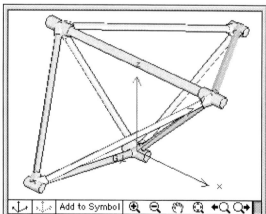

Macros in action: A standard subroutine (260:) has been developed for a Cylinder that has a cone at each end. (This gives the form of the sleeved joints). All you have to do is get the cursor to the right place, point it in the right direction, pass appropriate parameters to the subroutine, and it's done.

```
260: !Cylinder lower tube
  GOSUB 240 !joint
  CYLIND clen,diam/2
    ADDz clen
    MULz -1
  GOSUB 240 !joint
    DEL 2
RETURN


240: !Joint
CONE diam*2,diam,diam/1.5,90,90
RETURN
```

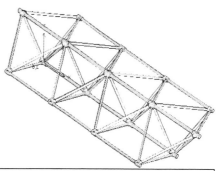

Winged Truss

The joints in this truss look good even at close inspection. Perhaps the cones at the end of each tube could be a bit longer. From this, one can derive the design of cast steel sleeve joints.

One can get the script to write out to disk a list of the data for each tube - see later in this worksheet.

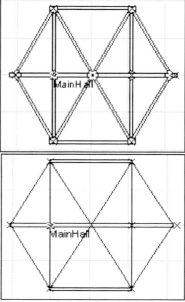

2D Script: Whether you are to use the Truview (using Project2) or a scripted 2-D symbol, you will need Hotspots to pick the truss up with. You also need to write the stretchy hotspots before you draw the truss.

If the user prefers a scripted view (many seconds faster especially if you use the one with complex joints), the the script is below. the sequence is similar to the 3D in that you do a FOR... NEXT loop for the diagonals in each module, and then put in the main longitudinal tubes. As a rule, 2-D scripting is easy if you use a similar structure as for the 3D (loops etc)

As the truss has a name, it is possible to have it display its name in the 2D symbol, using TEXT2. The size of the Text is automatically calculated to be twice the diameter of the main tube.

Autosizing text in 2D

Font size has to be in millimetres. Object is in metres. So multiply the object dimension by 1000. Then divide the resulting size by the Scale of the drawing. This finished size will stick faithfully to the size of the object it relates to, whatever the drawing scale. In this case the font size is twice the tube diameter.

```
fntz=2*t1diam*1000/A_
```

```
!2-D Script for Winged Truss

HOTSPOT2 -tlen/2,0 !Stretchy
HOTSPOT2 A-tlen/2,0 !Hotspots

!Hotspots on each truss element
FOR n=1 to tnum
  ADD2 tlen*(n-1),0
  HOTSPOT2 0,-twid/2
  HOTSPOT2 0, twid/2
  HOTSPOT2 0,0
    DEL 1
    NEXT n

IF shownam THEN          !Annotation
fntz=2*t1diam*1000/A_ !Autosize
DEFINE STYLE 'ttxt' 'Arial',fntz,1,0
SET STYLE 'ttxt'
  TEXT2 0,-t1diam,iden
ENDIF

IF truvu THEN
  PROJECT2 3,270,2
ELSE
  RECT2 -tlen/2,t1diam/2,
    tlen*tnum-tlen/2,-t1diam/2
FOR n=1 to tnum
ADD2 tlen*(n-1),0
  POLY2 6,1,
    0, twid/2,
    tlen/2,0,
    0,-twid/2,
    -tlen/2,0,
    0,twid/2,
    0,-twid/2
  DEL 1
NEXT n

RECT2 0,    twid/2+t2diam/2,
    (tnum-1)*tlen, twid/2-t2diam/2
RECT2 0,   -(twid/2+t2diam/2),
    (tnum-1)*tlen,-twid/2+t2diam/2
ENDIF
```

File Output

IN the previous pages, we mentioned the possibility of outputting to disk a file with the data about the truss. Here it is. You can now add the final parameters.

First, it is important to know WHICH truss it is, as a building project may have several of different lengths.

So we offer the user the chance to name the truss ('iden') and at the same time, we offer them the chance to turn off the feature ('outdat') - we don't want dozens of trusses all simultaneously sending the same data to disk. If the user appoints a truss (the "show-truss") to do the work, the others can remain silent.

By the way, the name 'iden' will determine the name of the file. This file will be placed in the ArchiCAD Data Folder. It takes the name of the truss.

Variable	Type	Name	Value
t2diam	⇄	Diameter Longitudinal tubing	0.070
t3diam	⇄	Diameter Upper wing tubing	0.070
t4diam	⇄	Diameter Lower wing tubing	0.070
truvu	☒	Truview=ON Scripted View=OFF	Off
		Material of Tubing	11
simcom	☒	Simple=OFF Complex=OFF	On
outdat	☒	OutPut DataFile ON / OFF?	On
shownam	☒	Show Name in 2D symbol ON/OFF	On

Add 'outdat' and 'shoname' to the parameters box

```
IF outdat THEN GOSUB 500!File I/O
```

Add this line to the executive script, just above the END statement

Make sure that different trusses have different names, or later trusses will overwrite the file written by one that was processed earlier.

Date and Time

WE want to know the date of the report, in case it was different from the one we wanted. this, along with the name of the truss will appear in the report.

In the date&time script, one uses a REQUEST which investigates a resource in ArchiCAD called 'DateTime' that knows the system time and date. The strings using percent signs can extract the data.

Actually, the whole time and date can be represented in a single string called '%c', but to show you how the strings work, I have joined several ones together - %A gives the day of the week; %d the day number, &B the month; %Y the year and century (millenium bug proof! ha-ha!); %X gives the time in AM or PM.

The rest of the DateTime strings can be found by reading the ReadMe file in the Graphisoft Folder. The whole lot are combined into a text string called 'dstr'.

The Report

FILE INPUT and OUTPUT are not covered in the main GDL manual. But you will find read me files on the ArchiCAD installer disks, and since version 5.0, the File input/output routines have been explained in an appendix to the manual. If you are a Voyager, it's time to read that appendix!

First, the file must be opened and named, a channel defined, and you must set up the way in which the routine will separate data.

The OUTPUT commands then follow; each time you remind it which channel you are writing to (in case you have more than one file open at once - you could be reading from one file, and writing to the other.)

• The report adopts the name put into the 'iden' field in the parameters box.

• The report has TABs ('\t')between fields, so you could copy and paste this to a spreadsheet - or you could reformat it so that it could be read in by Filemaker.

• It's a good idea to have carriage returns to separate groups of data. A report of this kind would be used as a cutting schedule for the tubing and the design of the steel sleeve joints in the truss.

It is not really on to have it report in detail on structural matters, as you would require to ask the user to enter vastly more data, like Live and Dead loads, K-factors, steel grades, joint characteristics etc. However, a report on slenderness ratio is a good example of providing a warning to the designer. This could also flash up in the 2D symbol.

This report does provide the engineer with essential detail like tube lengths, from which calculations would be done - how else could those dimensions be derived, except by the engineer having to calculate them all again?

This is the kind of data that you can get a report to produce. It is much neater and more organised than a Components listing from the Properties scripting, but it is more tiresome for people to have to 'dig around' in the ArchiCAD data folder for the result. If at all possible, I recommend you make a go of Properties scripting.

```
500:!File Output Routine
!Get the Date and Time
x=REQUEST("DateTime","%A %d %B %Y",dstr)
x=REQUEST("DateTime","%X",tstr)
```

REQUEST results in a number (X) which can be discarded, but as a result of making the request, you obtain the value of 'dstr' and 'tstr'.

```
500:!File Output Routine
!Get the Date and Time
x=REQUEST("DateTime","%A %d %B %Y",dstr)
x=REQUEST("DateTime","%X",tstr)

!Write the Report File
ch1=OPEN("TEXT",iden+".txt","SEPARATOR='\t',MODE=WO")
OUTPUT ch1,1,0,"Winged Truss Data:>",iden
OUTPUT ch1,1,0,"Output Date:",dstr
OUTPUT ch1,1,0,"Output Time:",tstr
OUTPUT ch1,1,0,"Cutting Schedule for Tubes in mm."
OUTPUT ch1,1,0," "
  CLOSE ch1
RETURN
```

Channel 1 is opened to allow output to a file, in a Write Only mode (WO)

Winged Truss Data:>	MainHall

Output Date: Sunday 02 January 2000
Output Time: 17:33:04
Cutting Schedule for Tubes in mm.

Upper tubes
  Number :   4
  Length :   2100
  Diameter: 100

Bottom tubes
  Number :   3
  Length :   2100
  Diameter: 100

Diagonal tubes
  Number   : 8
  Length   : 1594.52
  Diameter : 70
  Declination: 48.8141

Upper Wing tubes
  Number   :   8
  Length   : 2168.52
  Diameter :70
  Angle in Plan: 30.2564
  Declination :   16.0625

Lower Wing tubes
  Number   : 4
  Length   : 1897.37
  Diameter : 70
  Declination: 18.4349

Upper Tube Sleeves : 5
Bottom Tube Sleeves: 4
Wing Sleeves LeftH : 4
Wing Sleeves RightH: 4

Slenderness Ratios
Upper   : 1/   21
Lower   : 1/   21
Diagonals: 1/ 23
UpperWing: 1/   31
LowerWing: 1/   27

Do not be dismayed by apparent complexity of this script. Like everything else, type in the first few lines, do a 3D view and see if it works by looking at the Data Folder to see what has landed there. Don't forget that you must include the CLOSE statement or the file cannot be read. As you build up the text, you add in the extra lines.

You need to be pretty precise about the format of the report, so each line is precisely worked out, and appropriate labelling text is put in, always enclosed in quote marks. When you have got the above text working, continue, line by line, until you have completed. You do not need to do all of course - by now, you should have got the idea.

By the way, you notice that it is possible to include algebraic expressions in the OUTPUT statements, such as the ones that calculate Slenderness Ratio. It would be possible to express it as a decimal, but you can see that by playing with the layout, you can get it to lay it out in a more readable form.

In this case, OUTPUT tells it to send, 'ch1' tells it where to send, '1' tells it to start a new line ('0' should append to the most recent line according to the manual) , the final '0' does nothing at all. After all that, you send the data you would like to have in the line, carefully enclosing all text material in quote marks.

Note for Graphisoft: In my humble opinion, the OUTPUT statement is needlessly complicated - why cannot it be as simple as it is in BASIC (a PRINT#1 command)?

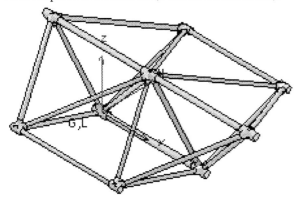

```
500:!File Output Routine
!Get the Date and Time
x=REQUEST("DateTime","%A %d %B %Y",dstr)
x=REQUEST("DateTime","%X",tstr)

!Write the Report File
ch1=OPEN("TEXT",iden+".txt","SEPARATOR='\t',MODE=WO")
OUTPUT ch1,1,0,"Winged Truss Data:>",iden
OUTPUT ch1,1,0,"Output Date:",dstr
OUTPUT ch1,1,0,"Output Time:",tstr
OUTPUT ch1,1,0,"Cutting Schedule for Tubes in mm."
OUTPUT ch1,1,0," "
OUTPUT ch1,1,0,"Upper tubes"
OUTPUT ch1,1,0,"  Number  :",tnum
OUTPUT ch1,1,0,"  Length  :",tlen*1000
OUTPUT ch1,1,0,"  Diameter:",t1diam*1000
OUTPUT ch1,1,0," "
OUTPUT ch1,1,0,"Bottom tubes"
OUTPUT ch1,1,0,"  Number  :",tnum-1
OUTPUT ch1,1,0,"  Length  :",tlen*1000
OUTPUT ch1,1,0,"  Diameter:",t1diam*1000
OUTPUT ch1,1,0," "
OUTPUT ch1,1,0,"Diagonal tubes"
OUTPUT ch1,1,0,"  Number    :",tnum*2
OUTPUT ch1,1,0,"  Length    :",dlen*1000
OUTPUT ch1,1,0,"  Diameter  :",t2diam*1000
OUTPUT ch1,1,0,"  Declination:",dtang
OUTPUT ch1,1,0," "
OUTPUT ch1,1,0,"Upper Wing tubes"
OUTPUT ch1,1,0,"  Number       :",tnum*2
OUTPUT ch1,1,0,"  Length       :",utlen*1000
OUTPUT ch1,1,0,"  Diameter     :",t3diam*1000
OUTPUT ch1,1,0,"  Angle in Plan:",ang1
OUTPUT ch1,1,0,"  Declination  :",ang2
OUTPUT ch1,1,0," "
OUTPUT ch1,1,0,"Lower Wing tubes"
OUTPUT ch1,1,0,"  Number     :",tnum
OUTPUT ch1,1,0,"  Length     :",ltlen*1000
OUTPUT ch1,1,0,"  Diameter   :",t4diam*1000
OUTPUT ch1,1,0,"  Declination:",ltang
OUTPUT ch1,1,0," "
OUTPUT ch1,1,0,"Upper Tube Sleeves :",tnum+1
OUTPUT ch1,1,0,"Bottom Tube Sleeves:",tnum
OUTPUT ch1,1,0,"Wing Sleeves LeftH :",tnum
OUTPUT ch1,1,0,"Wing Sleeves RightH:",tnum
OUTPUT ch1,1,0," "
OUTPUT ch1,1,0,"Slenderness Ratios"
OUTPUT ch1,1,0,"Upper     : 1/",(INT(tlen/t1diam+0.5))
OUTPUT ch1,1,0,"Lower     : 1/",(INT(tlen/t1diam+0.5))
OUTPUT ch1,1,0,"Diagonals: 1/",(INT(dlen/t2diam+0.5))
OUTPUT ch1,1,0,"UpperWing: 1/",(INT(utlen/t3diam+0.5))
OUTPUT ch1,1,0,"LowerWing: 1/",(INT(ltlen/t4diam+0.5))
  CLOSE ch1
RETURN
```

Tips and Tricks

2 ArchiCADs for the price of one!

Mac users – If you only have one ArchiCAD and one dongle – read on. RAM is so cheap now, you can put 256megs of RAM into your machine if it has enough slots.

On your hard disk, make a duplicate of the ArchiCAD directory with just ArchiCAD, Help and Resource files. You don't need to copy the ArchiCAD Library over.

Set both ArchiCAD's memory settings to about just under half of total memory, leaving 16megs for Windows/System.

Open your main file with one AC, and open a copy of the main file or a different file in the other AC. Now you can copy and paste from file to file, or set two different flythroughs rendering overnight!! AC will give priority to the foreground task, but the one behind will chug along in spare moments, and speed up with the foreground AC has finished rendering.

Windows machines manage memory differently and do not 'lock out' the application if it is already running. So the same one can run twice or more. This can lead to crashes and instability.

Syntax errors with CALL and Picture

IN GDL, it is possible to save time by CALLing an object you have already made for example, a Window object can 'call' a Sash, or a Sink unit can 'call' a Tap. These are 'macros'.

However, if the called object is not in a 'loaded library' it will not be found, and you will get error messages.

The same risk applies to Picture Objects which call PICT or TIFF files. You can use the **Load Libraries** command in the File Menu to help your project file find them. On Windows machines, omit the three letter suffix when stating its name in the settings box.

It is most annoying that there is no **pop-up menu** of pictures in the loaded library. You just have to know the name. For a special purpose, such as a human-figures Picture object, you could build a **Values List** of all the known names of PICT/TIFF files and make them easier to select.

Catamaran

T HIS CATAMARAN isn't just here because I like sailing. In fact I have only been on a catamaran once. Modelling one is a way of coming to terms with personal deprivation!(:-) The Cat looks at:

- Using the COONS statement
- Progressively encapsulating components into subroutines
- Using TUBE to form linear elements
- Value Lists
- Defining Materials

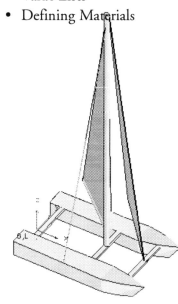

Planning: OK, The catamaran is not totally realistic – it's a simple model to teach some GDL techniques. The main object of the exercise is the contruction of the floats using COONS, and the TUBe for the rigging.

For the float, you could use RULED, and it would perhaps be easier; but the forward end of the bow curves upwards – so the COONS statement is best for a more sculpted 3-D problem.

Variable	Type	Name	Value
A		X Dimension	6.000
B		Y Dimension	3.600
wid		Width of Float	0.800
hit		Height of Float	0.700
fmat		Material of Floats	23
pcol		Pen colour	1

```
!Master Script

len=A: cwid=B

IF catmode='Starboard Tack' THEN tack=-1
IF catmode='Port Tack'       THEN tack=+1
IF sailmode='Reaching/running' THEN tack=tack*2
IF masthit='Mast very high' THEN mhit=len*2.0
IF masthit='Mast medium high' THEN mhit=len*1.8
IF masthit='Mast short'      THEN mhit=len*1.6

mastrad=mhit/150     !Mast Radius
boomlen=len*0.5 !Boom length
boomrad=boomlen/150

DEFINE MATERIAL 'sailcloth' 2, 1.0,1.0,1.0
DEFINE MATERIAL 'rigging'  3, 0.5,0.5,0.5
```

Leave the Value List parsing and Material definitions till later – when they become relevant. First, establish len and cwid.

M aster Script: will grow as the boat grows, but first you establish the roles of A & B. Add the rest in later, when you have written the value lists.

3 D Script: The easiest way to start a COONS is to enter the FOUR corners only, first. Number the corners, as in the diagram below. You get a rectangle. Then, as in the script here, add in the extra points progressively. Remember to increment the number in the first line of the COONS, as you add the extra points.

Technique: Although this is to be a catamaran made of of subroutines, my starting technique is to hammer in some basic code that works. So the early scripts here do not even have line numbers or subroutines.

You only need to build half of one float, as you can mirror this to form one float, and then duplicate the float to make the second float.

```
COONS 2,2,63,!half float
0,0,0,          !Point 1
0,0,hit,        !Point 2

len*0.9,0,0,    !Point 4
len,0,hit*1.1,  !Point 3

0,0,0,          !Point 1
len*0.9,0,0,    !Point 4

0,0,hit,        !Point 2
len,0,hit*1.1   !Point 3
```

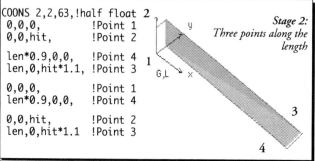

Stage 2: Three points along the length

```
COONS 2,3,63,!half float
0,0,0,              !Point 1
0,0,hit,            !Point 2

len*0.9,0,0,        !Point 4
len,0,hit*1.1,      !Point 3

0,0,0,              !Point 1
0,wid*0.5,0,
len*0.9,0,0,        !Point 4

0,0,hit,            !Point 2
0,wid*0.5,hit,
len,0,hit*1.1       !Point 3
```

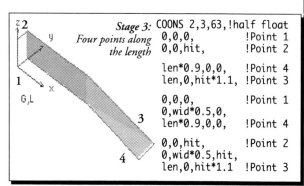

Stage 3: Four points along the length

```
COONS 2,4,63,!half float
0,0,0,              !Point 1
0,0,hit,            !Point 2

len*0.9,0,0,        !Point 4
len,0,hit*1.1,      !Point 3

0,0,0,              !Point 1
0,wid*0.5,0,
len*0.5,wid*0.5,0,
len*0.9,0,0,        !Point 4

0,0,hit,            !Point 2
0,wid*0.5,hit,
len*0.50,wid*0.55,hit,
len,0,hit*1.1       !Point 3
```

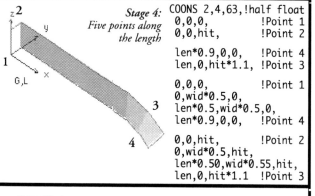

Stage 4: Five points along the length

Points are progressively added along the hull, along the top and waterline. The more points, the smoother the shape. All the locations are based on proportions of width and length.

Elevation of hull, showing rising deck

```
VALUES 'catmode' 'Not Sailing',
   'Starboard Tack','Port Tack'

VALUES 'masthit' 'Mast very high',
 'Mast medium high','Mast short'

VALUES 'sailmode' 'Close hauled','Reaching/running'
```

This is your Value List Script

```
!Catamaran Hull
!for Voyager Course

100: !Half a float
MATERIAL fmat
PEN pcol
COONS 2,6,63,!half float
  0,0,0,           !Point 1
  0,0,hit,         !Point 2

  len*0.9,0,0,     !Point 4
  len,0,hit*1.1,   !Point 3

  0,0,0,           !Point 1
  0,wid*0.5,0,
  len*0.5,wid*0.5,0,
  len*0.7,wid*0.5,0,
  len*0.8,wid*0.32,0,
  len*0.9,0,0,     !Point 4

  0,0,hit,         !Point 2
  0,wid*0.5,hit,
  len*0.50,wid*0.55,hit,
  len*0.70,wid*0.60,hit,
  len*0.85,wid*0.4,hit*1.05,
  len,0,hit*1.1  !Point 3
```

Finished COONS statement with 6 points along its length, & a number allocated to it.

Once the half-float COONS code is working, convert it to a subroutine by putting in an END statement, and putting a number and a RETURN statement either side of the COONS. You still only have half a float!

```
!Catamaran Hull
!for Voyager Course

PEN pcol
RESOL 12

GOSUB 100 !Half Float
END !------------------

100: !Half of a float
MATERIAL fmat
COONS 2,6,63,     !half float
  0,0,0,          !Point 1
  0,0,hit,        !Point 2
  ........
  etc, etc, etc, etc, etc,
  ........
  len,0,hit*1.1  !Point 3
RETURN
```

Left: *The final COONS profile for a half float.*
Above: *The same statement, cocooned into a new subroutine number 100:.*

```
200: !Entire Float
GOSUB 100 !half float
  MULy -1
GOSUB 100 !half float
  DEL 1
RETURN
```

Convert the 3D form to a whole float by repeating subroutine 100, and by using the MULy command for the repeat.

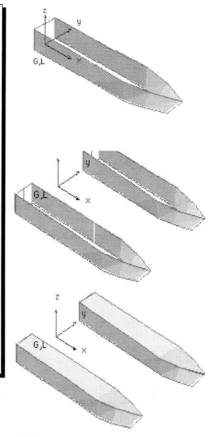

```
!Catamaran Hull
!for Voyager Course

!Floats
  ADDy (cwid-wid)/2
GOSUB 200 !Entire Float
  DEL 1
  ADDy -(cwid-wid)/2
GOSUB 200 !Entire Float
  DEL 1

END !----------------

100: !Half of a float
MATERIAL fmat
COONS 2,6,63,     !half float
  0,0,0,          !Point 1
  0,0,hit,        !Point 2
  ........
  etc, etc, etc, etc, as above
  ........
  len,0,hit*1.1  !Point 3
RETURN

200: !Entire Float
GOSUB 100 !half float
  MULy -1
GOSUB 100 !half float
  DEL 1
GOSUB 110 !Deck
RETURN
```

Both floats now: To get the two floats balanced equally around the centre line, you need to offset the floats – the offset is equal to half the difference of the total width and float width. The routine that makes the float must itself become a subroutine (200). So we have two 'nested' subroutines.

110: The Deck is a COONS that uses the same coordinates as the upper edge points of the hull shape. Copy and paste. Make sure you still follow the procedure of doing the points in the order, 1,2-4,3-1,4-2,3.

Next you need to add the crossbeams that join the floats, and then add in the mast, boom and sail.

```
110: !Deck sloping
COONS 2,5,63,
  0, wid*0.50,hit,    !#1
  0,-wid*0.50,hit,    !#2

  len, 0.0,  hit*1.1,!#4
  len,-0.001,hit*1.1,!#3

  0, wid*0.5,hit,     !#1
  len*0.50,wid*0.55,hit,
  len*0.70,wid*0.60,hit,
  len*0.85,wid*0.4,hit*1.05,
  len,0.0,hit*1.1,    !#4

  0,-wid*0.50,hit,    !#2
  len*0.50,-wid*0.55,hit,
  len*0.70,-wid*0.60,hit,
  len*0.85,-wid*0.4,hit*1.05,
  len,-0.001,hit*1.1 !#3
RETURN

200: !Entire Float
GOSUB 100 !half float
  MULy -1
GOSUB 100 !half float
  DEL 1
GOSUB 110 !Deck
RETURN
```

Tips and Tricks
Objects on Line

THERE is a new resource for ArchiCAD users called **Objects Online**. The site is an online catalog & store for ArchiCAD objects & utilities. It also offers software and training materials for Architects who use Adobe Photoshop. When you have a chance, visit the web site at:

http://www. objectsonline.com

If you get seriously into GDL, **O-O-L** acts as a broker – marketing your GDL objects for you and sending you payments resulting from sales. For more details, contact: David Correia, Objects Online, *david@objectsonline.com*

Writing with Acrobat

Although some applications will 'export to pdf', the best printing quality comes with the official Acrobat authoring tool. Instead of printing to PDFWriter, print in the direction of your normal laserprinter, using Acrobat Distiller as your PPD file, then select 'Save Print File' instead of actually printing. Drag the resulting .PS file onto the icon of Distiller, then select the print quality you need (press or screen). You will get the best result.

300: The cross beams are PRISMs which are better than BLOCKs, since you can generate them from the centre line of the boat.

Make each one, and then DEL back to the origin before making the next one. *Time to add some more parameters! These are Values List ones – use 'abc' as the parameter type and click on the value list button.*

Variable	Type	Name	Value
A	X Dimension	X Dimension	6.000
B	Y Dimension	Y Dimension	3.600
catmode	Abc	Catamaran Sailing Tack	Starboard Tack
sailmode	Abc	Sailing Mode	Reaching/runni...
masthit	Abc	Mast sizing index	Mast very high
wid	↔	Width of Float	0.800
hit	↔	Height of Float	0.700
fmat		Material of Floats	23
pcol		Pen colour	1

```
!Catamaran Hull
!for Voyager Course

PEN pcol
RESOL 12

!Floats
  ADDy (cwid-wid)/2
GOSUB 200 !Entire Float
  DEL 1
  ADDy -(cwid-wid)/2
GOSUB 200 !Entire Float
  DEL 1

!Cross beams
  ADDx len*0.1
  GOSUB 300 !Beam
  DEL 1
  ADDx len*0.55
  GOSUB 300 !Beam
  DEL 1
  ADDx len*0.85
  GOSUB 300 !Beam
  DEL 1

END !-----------------
```

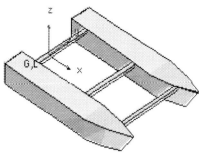

```
300: !cross beam piece
ADDz hit-0.12
PRISM 4,0.1,
  -0.1, (cwid-wid) /2,
  +0.1, (cwid-wid) /2,
  +0.1,-(cwid-wid) /2,
  -0.1,-(cwid-wid) /2
DEL 1
RETURN
```

400: You advance to the base of the mast, and push up a cylinder. To make sure the mast has the oval look of a mast, then you MUL the cylinder in the X direction.

450: At this point, you provide a parametric choice - the boat could be at anchor, or on Port or Starboard tack. It is more manageable to do the boom as a separate subroutine from the mast. The boom is angled at 20 degrees from the axis. If you have written the Value Lists, then you can use 'tack' and the other data from the Master Script to vary the angles of boom and sails. If the boat is not sailing, then the boom is in line with the boat's axis. If it is sailing, it swivels 20 degs for 'Close hauled' and 40 degs for 'Reaching or Running'.

500: In this exercise, the main sail is done as a PLANE, and not as a curved COONS mesh (which would look better), since the original focus of this exercise is on the scripting for the floats.

A small amount of trigonometry is required to make sure that the boom is allowed to slope at 5 degrees. PLANE is the easiest way to make a surface, as you only have to define the X-Y-Z points. It also helps to do the Sail as a separate subroutine, to make debugging easier.

Materials: Note that in the Master Script we defined the Material of 'sailcloth' – as a plastic-like material with an RGB value of 1,1,1 It still looks a bit grey - you need a bit of 'emission' to make it look whiter. At the same time, we can also specify a metallic grey for the rigging.

```
400: !Mast
MATERIAL "Stainless Steel"
  ADD len*0.55,0,hit
  MULx 1.5  !make it oval
  CYLIND mhit,mastrad !mast
  DEL 2
RETURN

450: !Boom
MATERIAL "Stainless Steel"
  ADD len*0.55,0,hit+hit
  ROTz tack*20
  ROTy -90+5
  MULx 1.5     !make it oval
  CYLIND boomlen,mastrad*2/3
  DEL 4
RETURN

500: !Main Sail
MATERIAL 'sailcloth'
  ADD len*0.55,0,hit+hit
  ROTz tack*20
IF tack THEN
  PLANE 3,      !Flat Sail
    -mastrad,0,0,
    -mastrad,0,mhit-hit,
    -boomlen,0,len*0.5*COS(85)
    ENDIF
  DEL 2
RETURN

550: !Jib
!Forestay
MATERIAL 'rigging'
RESOL 3
PUT len*0.85,0,    -1000, 0,
    len*0.85,0,hit,       0,
    len*0.55+0.1,0,mhit+hit,0,
    len*0.55+0.1,0,1000, 0
BODY -1
TUBE 2,NSP/4,63,
  0,0,900,
  0.01,360,4000,
  GET(NSP)
BODY -1

IF tack THEN !Foresail
  MATERIAL 'sailcloth'
  MULy -tack
  PLANE 3,
    len*0.85,0,hit,
    len*0.55+0.1,0, mhit+hit,
    len*0.50, cwid*0.3, hit*2
  DEL 1
ENDIF
RETURN
```

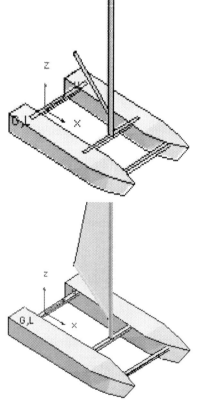

550: Forestay & Jib: Whether you are sailing or at anchor, you need a forestay. This could be done with a CYLIND but would be a difficult piece of Trig. TUBE, in which you only need to know the X-Y-Z locations is far easier, once you get the hang. Do not forget the 'phantom points' with TUBE; in this case, 1000 metres up in the air and down in the deep! Use PUT and GET and BODY -1 to ensure that you have less risk of syntax or unexplained errors. RESOL can be 3, as it is a slender cable, and 3 will suffice.

The jib itself is also a PLANE, swivelled at the same angle as the Mainsail.

600: Rigging: This further demonstrates the use of TUBE to do linear tasks. Instead of a multitude of trig calculations and cylinder commands, one single TUBE moving from XYZ location to the next can do it all in one sequence. A polyline with 900 and 4000 defines the cylindrical section, and RESOL3 makes the cylinder into a triangular section.

```
600:!Rigging
RESOL 3
MATERIAL 'rigging'
PUT  len*0, cwid/2, -1 ,0,
  len*0.40, cwid/2, hit,0,
  len*0.55, 0.08  ,mhit,0,
  len*0.55,-0.08  ,mhit,0,
  len*0.40,-cwid/2, hit,0,
  len*0.00,-cwid/2, -1 ,0
BODY -1
TUBE 2,NSP/4,63,
  0,0,900,
  0.01,360,4000,
   GET(NSP)
BODY -1
RETURN
```

The use of BODY -1 ensures that TUBE works without unexplained errors.

Finishing off

With all these extra subroutines, the executive script now looks like this.

```
!Catamaran Hull
!for Voyager Course

PEN pcol
RESOL 12

!Floats
  ADDy (cwid-wid)/2
GOSUB 200 !Entire Float
  DEL 1
  ADDy -(cwid-wid)/2
GOSUB 200 !Entire Float
  DEL 1

!Cross beams
  ADDx len*0.1
GOSUB 300 !Beam
  DEL 1
  ADDx len*0.55
GOSUB 300 !Beam
  DEL 1
  ADDx len*0.85
GOSUB 300 !Beam
  DEL 1

GOSUB 400: !Mast
GOSUB 450: !Boom
GOSUB 500: !Main Sail
GOSUB 550: !Jib
GOSUB 600: !Rigging
END !-----------------
```

These could also be tidied away into a subroutine

2D Script: Finally, you need to give the Cat a 2 D script for the stretchy hotspots to work, and as it may be difficult to pick up, additional hotspots enabling you to pick it up.

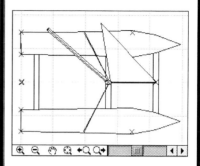

```
!Catamaran
!2D Script
PEN pcol

!Stretchy Hotspots
HOTSPOT2 0,0
HOTSPOT2 A*0.7,-B/2
HOTSPOT2 A*0.7, B/2
HOTSPOT2 0,-B/2
HOTSPOT2 0, B/2

!Pick up Hotspots
HOTSPOT2 0,-B/2+wid
HOTSPOT2 0, B/2-wid
HOTSPOT2 A*0.55,0
HOTSPOT2 A*0.85,0

PROJECT2 3,270,2
```

LOD: At this point, you make decisions on level of detail. If you want a sea scene, this may be good enough, but if you are designing a marina sales area, you may want to add rudders, tiller, netting and more. Level of Detail (L.O.D.) is a constant factor to consider.

Cable Macro

THIS exercise investigates a useful feature of TUBE command, & shows how to make a Macro.

The last digit in the Pathway definition of a TUBE command is a Twist angle. (The best stories always have a twist at the end.) If this angle progressively increases, then the section twists as it moves through space. The first exercise shows simply how this is done. The angle is always absolute, not relative. 10, 10, 10, will go straight, 10, 20, 30 will twist.

MACROS are objects that can be called by other GDL scripts and that behave like a command. For example, the command CYLIND calls up a cylindrical shape with parameters H and R. This one could be called 'TWISTCYL' or 'COILCABL' and only needs the 4 parameters shown on the right.

The 900 and 4000 define a circular section; if these were 901 and 4001, the twisty lines would disappear.

If you have smoothness ON in photorendering this form gets smoothed and the macro is useless – with smoothness OFF, you can clearly see the twists.

Because it will be used as a Macro, it's easier to use single letter variables. It can now be used like CYLIND.

```
!Test TUBE to make coiled cable
!Simple Non parametric demo
RESOL 6
rad=0.5        !Radius
PUT 0,0,-1,0,!twist
    0,0,0,10,
    0,0,1,20,
    0,0,2,30,
    0,0,3,40,
    0,0,4,50,
    0,0,5,60,
    0,0,6,70

MATERIAL 'whitewash'
PEN 1
TUBE 2,NSP/4,63,
    0,0,900,
    rad,360,4000,
    GET(NSP)
```

Variabl	Type	Name	Value
A		X Dimension	1.000
B		Y Dimension	1.000
l		Length of Cable	5.000
d		Diameter of Cable	0.800
n		Number of visible strands 3-12	8
t		Twistiness Index 1 - 10	4

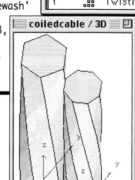

```
!'Coilcabl':GDL Macro

!Error checking
IF n<3  THEN n=3
IF n>12 THEN n=12
IF t<1  THEN t=1
IF t>10 THEN t=10

RESOL n
FOR z=-d TO l+d STEP d
  tw=tw+t^2
  PUT 0,0,z,tw
NEXT z

BODY -1
TUBE 2,NSP/4,63,
    0,0,900,
    d/2,360,4000,
    GET(NSP)
```

```
MATERIAL 'Zinc': PEN 1
CALL coilcabl PARAMETERS l=5,
              d=0.4,n=8,t=6
```
This is how it can be used as a macro

This is a Parametric way of doing the cable so this can be a Macro, used like CYLIND, up the Z-axis

Bendy Bar! Reinforced Concrete assistant

BENDYBAR is an object that can be put to many uses, but its primary use is as reinforcement in concrete. It can be used for drainage and plumbing, or for neon lettering. It consists of a bar that can be bent in six ways, with any degree of curvature, bending angle and twisting angle at each bend.

It is a useful exercise in demonstrating the simple but effective use of ARRAYS, and of making that array visible to the user. It makes what is a complex object vastly more user friendly.

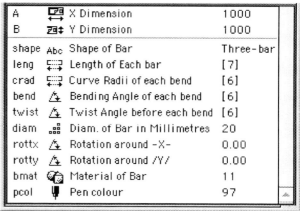

A		X Dimension	1000
B		Y Dimension	1000
shape	Abc	Shape of Bar	Three-bar
leng		Length of Each bar	[7]
crad		Curve Radii of each bend	[6]
bend		Bending Angle of each bend	[6]
twist		Twist Angle before each bend	[6]
diam		Diam. of Bar in Millimetres	20
rottx		Rotation around -X-	0.00
rotty		Rotation around /Y/	0.00
bmat		Material of Bar	11
pcol		Pen colour	97

```
!Bendibar- Reinforcing bars
!Master Script

DIM leng[7],crad[6],twist[6],bend[6]

!This is the long hard
!way to parse a value list
IF shape='1_Single bar' THEN shp=1
IF shape='2_Two-bar'    THEN shp=2
IF shape='3_Three-bar'  THEN shp=3
IF shape='4_Four-bar'   THEN shp=4
IF shape='5_Five-bar'   THEN shp=5
IF shape='6_Six-bar'    THEN shp=6
IF shape='7_Seven-bar'  THEN shp=7
!If all you want is a flag
!then use SPLIT() instead
n=SPLIT(shape,"%n",shp)

!parameter checks
 brad=diam/2000  !Bar radius
 br=brad*1.5
FOR k=1 TO shp-1
IF crad[k]<brad THEN crad[k]=brad
IF bend[k]<0 THEN
    twist[k]=twist[k]+180
    bend[k]=ABS(bend[k])
    ENDIF
IF leng[k]<0 THEN leng[k]=0
  NEXT k
IF leng[shp]<0 THEN leng[6]=0
```

You have to click on this button to make the parameter adopt the form of an Array

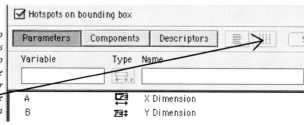

This Routine parses the Value List to work out the user's requirements. These can be converted to a number. You can either use a series of IF statements, or a single SPLIT command can extract the right figures in a single hit.

Look up the SPLIT command – *it's designed to extract a number or a string from a string. By using digits at the start of each configuration description, it only takes a simple "%n" to extract that vital digit.*

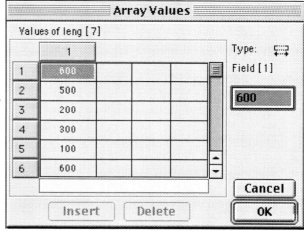

The array is now visible to the user, who can enter data for the bar, such as twist angle, length and sweep with little difficulty.

```
!Bendibar- Reinforcing bars
!3D Script

MATERIAL bmat
PEN pcol
RADIUS brad,brad*2

 ROTx rottx
 ROTy rotty
CYLIND leng[1],brad

FOR k=1 TO shp-1
 ADDz leng[k]
 ROTz twist[k]
 ELBOW crad[k],bend[k],brad
 ADDx crad[k]
 ROTy bend[k]
 ADDx -crad[k]
 CYLIND leng[k+1],brad
 NEXT k
DEL 5*(shp-1)
 DEL 2 !Remove ROTs

END:!------------------------
```

Master Script: The primary job is to parse the Value List. I have shown two methods of doing it. The **parameter checks** build in a number of safeguards, in case of problems such as the curve radius being smaller than the tube radius. I usually write the object first, get it working, then discover the things that can upset it with user-abuse, and write in safeguard routines to catch the snags.

3D Script: Because this uses arrays, the final 3D routine is incredibly short. The FOR... NEXT loop does all the work and the value of 'k' in each run through the loop decides which section of the rod and which bend will be created. I tend to get one run of it working, and then a second. Once that is proven, you can increase the size of the loop. An engineer advised me that 6 or 7 bends in a reinforcing bar would be as many as you could want. But for something like neon lettering, there is a case for making the total number even larger. The routine follows a similar idea to that used in the Handrail in the Discovery course – simple really. The twist added to the bar routine adds 3 dimensional quality to the bar.

2D Script: This tool could be bent into such wierd shapes that it is not practical to work out a 2D script for it. You will have to depend on PROJECT2 for the 2D. However, as a bunch of these bars could get mighty

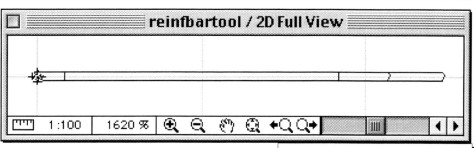

confusing, it helps a great deal to write a script to place cross hairs at the start of the tool, and to a starting Hotspot. It might help to remove Hotspots on the Bounding box, as these could become a dense forest of hotspots when you built a reinforcement cage.

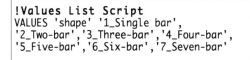

```
!Values List Script
VALUES 'shape' '1_Single bar',
'2_Two-bar','3_Three-bar','4_Four-bar',
'5_Five-bar','6_Six-bar','7_Seven-bar'
```

Value Lists are the way to make objects very user friendly. I use them even when there is a choice of two things that could have been chosen using the 'Booleian choice' parameters.

```
!2D Script
PEN pcol

HOTSPOT2 0,0
PROJECT2 3,270,2

!Cross hair at start
LINE2 br,0,-br,0
LINE2 0,br,0,-br
ARC2 0,0,brad,60,120
ARC2 0,0,brad,150,210
ARC2 0,0,brad,240,300
ARC2 0,0,brad,330,390
```

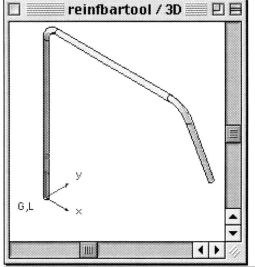

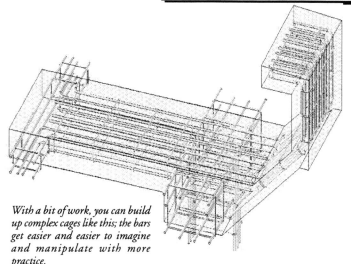

With a bit of work, you can build up complex cages like this; the bars get easier and easier to imagine and manipulate with more practice.

Architects can create Web sites

DOES anyone out there have experience of creating and managing their own web page... >*Neil*

YES, most architects do their own pages themselves nowadays. With the plethora of absurdly easy visual design tools (no html programming required) the idea of a designer paying another designer to put his image out there is not necessary.

Even if you had a graphic designer start it out for you (logos, menus and all) you will definitely want to maintain it yourself and update your samples of work, personnel, skills, and, of course link to your project-specific-web-sites which may be the single most important reason for a project architect to get into web technology.

Over the years I have tried countless web-writer softwares, free and paid for, both Mac and Windows. Though I still use PageMill myself as my primary tool, I would recommend that most people just download the free NetscapeCommunicator4 which includes a very very useful PageComposer. You can leave PageComposer open while viewing with Navigator live and drag and drop images. It will automatically put any graphic files together in any empty folder you pick (to keep a local version on your own hard drive) and automatically Publish the whole site to whichever provider you specify. It even has built in wizards that will design a preliminary page or whole site FOR you. Hard to beat free AND easy AND good.

>*Geoffrey Moore Langdon, AIA*

Deliberate Errors

COMPUTERS work in Machine Code, we work in the world of Applied Maths. We humble earthlings use feet and inches, or millimetres or metres. In between the two, there may be conversion stages like Decimal and Hexadecimal and Binary.

Sometimes when you divide two numbers, or use the INT command, you get tiny errors as a result of this conversion. For example 1/3 produces a recurring number in decimal. INT(9/3) could produce a result of 2 instead of 3 due to tiny conversion errors. FOR k=0 TO 10 STEP 5/2 should produce 4 intervals and 5 locations; but this could result in one of them being lost.

Nobody notices small dimensions like 1/256" or 1 millimetre. So if you write FOR k=0 TO 10+0.001 STEP 2.5, you will eliminate the conversion error, but you will not alter the model at all. I noticed recently that if you divide 6'-0" by 3'-0" you get an error. If you divide by 6'-0" by 2'-11.9999" (yes you can use decimals) you guarantee getting a result of 2. If a piece of GDL simply doesn't work when it should, look for the opportunity to feed in a deliberate error.

Curvy Roof

Object

THIS LOOKS very complex at first sight - but if you are a true Voyager, you will have a go at trying something like it.

The exercise includes:

- **Arrays, to store locations**
- **COONS: form a surface from a profile**
- **TUBE: form a gutter following a complex path**
- **EXTRUDE and POLY from an array**
- **PUT & GET as if it was going out of fashion!**

The first version of this was written by one of my students, Alfred Man in AC 5.1, and was part of a model we did for part of the roof of an office refurbishment scheme in North Notts. I have extensively updated it for AC 6.X. This is a solid that could not be created by any of the solids in the GDL vocabulary – so it must be built from a series of Surfaces for top, sides and bottom, made by GDL. Because they are all repeating the same set of XY locations, use Arrays.

Procedure: First a hand drawn drawing of the required roof was scanned in greyscale - then pulled into ArchiCAD. A Fill is clicked around the outline, making sure the clicks coincide with roofing welts. The Fill is dragged into the 2D script window of a new object, as a POLY2B. The XY list from the fill is dragged into the Master Script (then the rest of the fill thrown away). This seems like a cheat, but it's a very laboursaving way to get XY locations established and more accurately than any other method. If you make the Fill to site on the main origin, then you get a nice clean set of coordinates (without an offset to consider.)

Master Script: The idea is to PUT all the XY points (and the point status code) from the Fill into memory, then to flow them into Arrays for X and for Y, discarding the status codes along the way; then to identify the middle and end points, to help build our COONs and other shapes. Before you build the array, you have to use the DIM command to prepare for the array to be filled – use a number that is Equal to or Larger than the number you intend to put in there. We have 38 points, so a round number of 50 will do for now. Then a For.. Next Loop does the hard work.

Variable	Type	Name	Value
A	⟷	X Dimension	1.000
B	↕	Y Dimension	1.000
hit1		Vertical height at lower eave	0.550
hit2		Vertical height at ridge	1.648
cmat		Material for Ceiling	5
rmat		Material for Roof	2
wmat		Material for Wall	39
gdep		Gutter Section Depth	0.300
ghit		Gutter Section Height	0.200
gthk		Gutter thickness	0.005
gmat		Gutter Material	10
galt		Gutter altitude above base	0.350
shonum	☒	Corner numbers visible ON/OFF	On

```
!Name:Curvy Roof
!Master Script

!Raw Data for points
!Stolen from a POLY2B (Fill)
PUT 0.0,   0.0,      1,  !pt 1
    0.350873, 0.0,      1,
    0.589629, 0.057864, 1,
    0.851114, 0.158436, 1,
    1.092485, 0.299235, 1,
    1.273514, 0.480264, 1,
    1.434428, 0.661292, 1,
    1.555114, 0.822206, 1,
    1.675799, 1.023349, 1,
    1.765522, 1.247996, 1,
    1.778437, 1.421734, 1,
    1.789253, 1.611861, 1,
    1.789253, 1.785883, 1,
    1.789253, 1.991546, 1,
    1.789253, 2.213029, 1,
    1.789253, 2.347501, 1,
    1.789253, 2.529433, 1,
    1.789253, 2.735096, 1,
    1.789253, 3.042829, 1,!pt 2
    5.665204, 3.042829, 1,!pt 3
    5.665204, 2.236759, 1,
    5.665204, 1.690962, 1,
    5.665204, 1.010693, 1,
    5.665204, 0.354154, 1,
    5.665204,-0.262834, 1,
    5.665204,-0.927283, 1,
    5.665204,-1.512631, 1,
    5.665204,-2.153349, 1,
    5.586103,-2.738697, 1,
    5.245969,-3.284494, 1,
    4.668531,-3.648359, 1,
    4.027812,-3.759101, 1,
    3.355453,-3.759101, 1,
    2.714735,-3.759101, 1,
    2.035076,-3.759101, 1,
    1.377927,-3.759101, 1,
    0.737209,-3.759101, 1,
    0.0,     -3.759101, -1  !pt 4

!Defining the array
DIM x[50],y[50]
FOR k = 1 to 38
x[k]=GET(1)
y[k]=GET(1)
nul=GET(1) !throw away all 1's
NEXT k

p1=1    !Array index of Point 1
p2=19   !Array index of Point 2
p3=20   !Array index of Point 3
p4=38   !Array index of Point 4
```

Parameters: The size on plan is determined by the Fill, so A and B are not used, but Heights are parametric, as are the Materials and Gutter details.

3D Script: First the main roof surface roof is to be made with a COONS

2D script: is used here to place Hotspots at all the welt ends, and to illustrate the numbering convention for the COONS that forms the roof surface. Project 2 is used to form the roof because there are only 2 on the building, but for hardened GDL users with more space than I have on the page, it's easy to write a POLY2 routine for the outline and some LINE2 routines for the welts, using the same techniques as in the 3d script.

Comment: Why doesn't this use Subroutines? Well, there are no cursor movements until the Gutter – all commands use precise XYZ locations. Therefore each routine is tidily modular already.

mesh. For this it is important that the number of points along the ridge and the eaves are the same. Then a number of roofing welts are to be drawn that join the eaves to the verge (using TUBE). Then the vertical wall along the ridge, using EXTRUDE. Then, the same technique to do the fascia. Finally, a gutter section (defined by TUBE) must follow the eaves fascia around the curve. Note that TUBE needs phantom points before start and after the end of each section.

```
!Curvy Roof
!first written:AlfMan Sept98
!totally rewritten Jan2000
!by DNC

PEN L_
!Array is in the Master Script

!Drawing the roof
MATERIAL rmat
!Data for Roof Coons
!1 to 2
FOR k = p1 to p2
  PUT x[k],y[k],hit2
NEXT k

!4 to 3
FOR k = p4 to p3 step -1
  PUT x[k],y[k],hit1
NEXT k

!1 to 4
PUT x[p1],y[p1],hit2
PUT x[p4],y[p4],hit1

!2 to 3
PUT x[p2],y[p2],hit2
PUT x[p3],y[p3],hit1

COONS 19,2,63,
  GET(NSP)

!Drawing the end fascia
MATERIAL wmat
PLANE 4,
x[p1],y[p1],0,      !Point 1
x[p1],y[p1],hit2,   !
x[p4],y[p4],hit1,   !
x[p4],y[p4],0       !Point 4

!Drawing the other end fascia
PLANE 4,
x[p2],y[p2],0,      !Point 2
x[p2],y[p2],hit2,   !
x[p3],y[p3],hit1,   !
x[p3],y[p3],0       !Point 3

!Drawing the inside curve
MATERIAL wmat
FOR k=p1 TO p2
  PUT x[k],y[k],1
  NEXT k
EXTRUDE NSP/3,0,0,hit2,0,
  GET(NSP)

!Drawing the outside curve
MATERIAL wmat
FOR k=p3 TO p4
  PUT x[k],y[k],1
  NEXT k
EXTRUDE NSP/3,0,0,hit1,0,
  GET(NSP)

!Drawing the Ceiling
MATERIAL cmat
FOR k=p1 TO p4
  PUT x[k],y[k]
  NEXT k

POLY NSP/2,
  GET(NSP)

!Drawing the roofing welts
MATERIAL rmat
FOR k = p1 to p2
  PUT 0,0,1000,0   !1st Phantom Point
  PUT x[k],y[k],hit2,0
  PUT x[p4+1-k],y[p4+1-k],hit1,0
  PUT 0,0,-1000,0  !last Phantom Pt
NEXT k
```

The 1-2-3-4 numbering convention for the Coons is shown in the 2D display

All of these forms are made by plucking out the appropriate numbers from the Array that was built in the Master Script

```
numb = NSP/16
FOR K=1 TO numb
  TUBE 5,2+2,63,
  -0.03,0.00,0, !Sectionpoints
  -0.03,0.05,0,
   0.03,0.05,0,
   0.03,0.00,0,
  -0.03,0.00,0,
     GET(16)      !Pathpoints
NEXT k

!Drawing the gutter
MATERIAL gmat
!Pathpoints
PUT x[p4]-0.01,y[p4],0,0!1st Phant.Pt
FOR k = p4 to p3 STEP -1
  PUT x[k],y[k],0,0
  NEXT k
PUT x[p3],y[p3]+0.01,0,0!Last Phant.Pt

ADDz galt
BODY -1
TUBE 9,NSP/4,63,
    0,      0,0, !Sectionpoints
    0,   ghit,0,
  -gthk,ghit,0,
  -gthk,gthk,0,
  -gdep+gthk,gthk,0,
  -gdep+gthk,ghit,0,
  -gdep,ghit,0,
  -gdep,0,  0,
    0,  0,  0,
     GET(NSP) !Pathpoints
BODY -1
DEL 1
```

```
!Curvy Roof
!2D Script
HOTSPOT2 0,0
PROJECT2 3,270,2

FOR k=p1 TO p4
HOTSPOT2 x[k],y[k]
  NEXT k

IF shonum THEN
DEFINE STYLE 'CR_txt'
'Arial',
       2*gdep*1000/A_,3,1
SET STYLE 'CR_txt'
TEXT2 x[p1],y[p1],1
TEXT2 x[p2],y[p2],2
TEXT2 x[p3],y[p3],3
TEXT2 x[p4],y[p4],4
ENDIF
```

3D View: Here is the finished solid looking roof, built from 6 surfaces, plus welts and gutter.

```
!Do everything in
!one go! 3DScript
FOR k=p1 TO p2
  PUT x[k],y[k],hit2,15
  NEXT k
FOR k=p3 TO p4
  PUT x[k],y[k],hit1,15
  NEXT k
PUT x[p1],y[p1],hit2,-1

MASS rmat,cmat,wmat,
  NSP/4,0,127,0,
  GET(NSP)
```

Did I hear you ask, Why cannot this all be done with the wonderful MASS command that combines Surface and Solid building so effectively? – well it ALMOST succeeds – except for the flattened areas around the curve.

Arches and Waves!

Object

This exercise is useful for:
- **Building Arches, of course**
- **Using PUT and GET and TUBE**
- **Exploring Mathematics to create more authentic form**

IN THE LONG Handrail exercise, you were shown how to use the TUBE command to follow a long pathway. Circular arcs are very easy anyway once you have cracked it, and if you don't like maths, you can use ELBOW.

However, there is scarcely an arch in real architecture that uses a perfectly round arc, except in the Romanesque style, or in situations where there is some concealed reinforcement to prevent collapse. Round arches are unsafe, and engineering arches, shells and cables are more likely to use the 'funicular line'. The Catalan architect, Antonio Gaudi used hanging chains to calculate the profile of his arches and vaults to ensure that there was axial compression through the arch. For this you need to know how to make a Parabolic arch which follows the funicular line, or a SIN wave which is close to a parabola.

I have worked out my own formulae for deriving Sin wave and Parabolic forms, when you only know the span and height of the arch. To be even more precise, you need to follow the Catenary shape. See the Maths Primer for more detail.

Parameters: This object is stretchy in plan so it uses A. I have used B for height instead of 'zzyzx' here, to allow stretching of the 2D symbol to change height. The cutting styles determine how the legs of the arch will be treated. The number of steps ('nostep') will define the smoothness of curvature of the arc of the arch itself, whereas 'tres' determines the smoothness of the actual tubular surface, if round,

Planning: The Circular arch is to be drawn from a notional centre, using a 'Radial method', whereby the X and Z locations are worked out round that centre. The SIN wave arch is drawn from the left (value 0) to the right (value 180). The Parabolic arch is drawn symmetrically round the centre, from an X-value of -span/2 to +span/2.

A		X Dimension	30.0
B		Y Dimension	14.0
arcshap		Round=0 Sin=1 Parab=2	2
bmat		Bow Arch Material	38
ttyp		Rectang Section=1 Round=0	On
twid		Tube Section Width	0.2
tdep		Tube Section depth	0.3
truvu		Truvu=0 Lay Flat=1	On
nostep		Number of Steps across 4-36	16
cutstyl		Cutting Ends style 0-4	3
tres		Round Tube surface Resolution	6
tiltx		Tilt around X	0.00
tilty		Tilt around Y	0.00
fonthit		Font Height mm (0 for none)	4
pcol		Pen Colour	1

3D Script: Here the script departs from some of the strict rules that have been advocated earlier. If you want the arch to be part of a much larger object, for example Sydney Harbour bridge, or the Golden Gate bridge (in which you invert the arch to make a cable), then you will want to call it as a macro (using CALL). Or, in this case, you can copy and paste the text from here into the larger object as one subroutine. This means it must be written without line numbers, or subroutines – because the whole thing will be a subroutine in the larger object.

The purpose of writing all these parameters into the script is to make the routine portable. If you copied and pasted the script, you would lose the original parameter titles from the arch library object. So, you can manually type in values here before you go to the subroutine.

The CUTPLANE routines are to give you three ways of cutting the feet of the arch to help it fit better into a larger model. This is no problem for waveform arches, but for the circular arch, you have to use some IF-ENDIF logic to avoid cutting if the arch sweeps through more than 180°. Finally one Cutplane action (4) allows you to have only half an arch or a cable.

```
!BOWARCH - Tube Arch Macro

!All done without subroutines to make it portable
!Copy and Paste and update these if using in
!another script, then modify them to suit

!---------- ROUTINE STARTS HERE -----------
!twid  is achieved using the MULy command
!truvu is not used in the 3D
span=A              !A is the span of the ARch
higt=B              !B is the higt of the arch
bmat=bmat           !bmat is Material of the Bowarch
ttyp=ttyp           !ttyp= 1 for square section, 0 for round
twid=twid           !twid is the tube width
tdep=tdep           !tdep is the tube depth
nstep =nostep       !Number of steps in angle/distance
cutstl =cutstyl     !Cutting Style
arcshp =arcshap     !Shape of the Arch
tres   =tres        !Tube Resolution
tiltx  =tiltx       !Leaning angle
tilty  =tilty       !Rotated angle
pcol   =pcol        !Pen colour
GOSUB 2000:!Draw the Arch

END:!-------------------------------------------

2000:!Draw the Arch
  ROTx tiltx: ROTy tilty
IF nstep< 4 THEN nstep=4
IF nstep>36 THEN nstep=36

!For all Arch types (not all data will be used)
  angl =2*(90-ATN((span/2)/higt))!Half angle of bow
  brad =(span/2)/SIN(angl) !Radius of the Bow arch
  stdis=span/nstep          !Stepping distance:SIN
  stangd = 180/nstep        !Stepping angle:Distance
  stangr = (angl*2)/nstep   !Stepping angle:Rotation
```

These parameters are repeated so that you can copy and paste the whole thing to another script

You could now copy 2000: and use it in another program

You need to calculate a number of internal parameters such as sweep angle and radius of the round arch, stepping distances and angles for the wave forms.

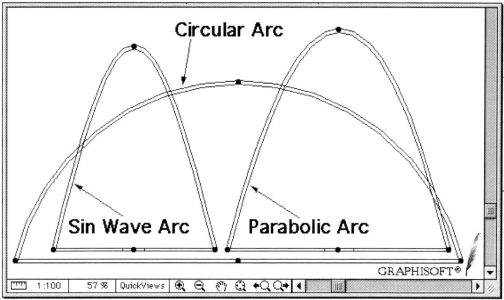

Circular Arc

Sin Wave Arc　　*Parabolic Arc*

GRAPHISOFT®

| 1:100 | 57% | QuickViews |

People think that SIN waves are more curvaceous, but surprisingly, it is more pointy than the pure Parabolic arch form.

If you want a hanging cable - for a bridge - use the arch upside down. Either tilt it round X or Y to make it hang. If it hangs at an angle, then juggle the tilts around X and Y.

```
!Cutplane routine -----------------
!first eliminate large circles from vertical cuts
MATERIAL bmat: PEN pcol !Specify before cutting
IF arcshp=0 AND higt>=span/2 THEN
   IF cutstl=1 OR cutstl=3 THEN
          cutstl=cutstl-1
      ENDIF
      ENDIF


!Vertical Cut
IF cutstl=1 OR cutstl=3 THEN
   ADDx -span/2
   ROTy -90
   CUTPLANE : kut=kut+1
   DEL 2
   ADDx  span/2
   ROTy  90
   CUTPLANE : kut=kut+1
   DEL 2
ENDIF


!Horizontal Cut
IF cutstl=2 OR cutstl=3 THEN
   CUTPLANE 180: kut=kut+1
   ENDIF


!Half Cut
IF cutstl=4 THEN
   ROTy 90
   CUTPLANE: kut=kut+1
   DEL 1
   ENDIF


!Set flag to make arch longer if it's to be cut
ct=1+cutstl
!-------------------------------------
!PUT Sectional Values to Memory
IF ttyp THEN            !Square Section
   PUT tdep/2, tdep/2,0,
       -tdep/2, tdep/2,0,
       -tdep/2,-tdep/2,0,
       tdep/2,-tdep/2,0
   ELSE                  !Round Section
   PUT 0,0,901,
       tdep/2,360,4001
   ENDIF
np=NSP/3               !Number of points
```

kut - This technique of using 'kut' to record the number of cutplanes means that you know how many 'cutend's to do. Material must be specified before you issue Cutplane commands.

Store the outline of the tube section in the memory buffer using PUT, and remember the number or stored points.

*Use **tdep** (depth) to define the depth and the width, and then use MUL later to resize the width.*

```
!BOWARCH - 2Dscript
span=A
bulg=B
 HOTSPOT2   0,0
 HOTSPOT2   span/2,0
 HOTSPOT2  -span/2,0
!PROJECT2 3,270,2
RECT2 -span/2,-twid/2,
span/2, twid/2

IF truvu THEN
   PROJECT2 4,270,1
   HOTSPOT2 0,higt
   LINE2 0,higt-tdep,
         0,higt+tdep
   LINE2 -MIN(1,twid),higt,
         MIN(1,twid),higt
   ENDIF
```

```
!Put all pathway values to memory, RADIAL
!Formula is X=radius*SIN(angle): Z=radius*COS(angle)
IF arcshp=0 THEN
FOR k=-angl-stangr*ct TO angl+stangr*ct+0.1 STEP stangr
   PUT brad*SIN(k),0,brad*COS(k),0
   NEXT k
   ENDIF
```

The Formulae are explained in the Maths Primer

```
!Put all pathway values to memory, SIN wave
IF arcshp=1 THEN
!Formula is y=height*SIN(X*180/span)
FOR k=-stangd*ct TO 180+stangd*ct+0.1 STEP stangd
   PUT span*k/180,0,higt*SIN(k),0
   NEXT k
   ENDIF
```

The 0.1 is a deliberate over-run to ensure that arch doesn't stop short of full length

```
!Put all pathway values to memory, Parabola
IF arcshp=2 THEN
!Formula is y=height - (4*height/(span^2))*X^2
FOR k=-span/2-stdis*ct TO span/2+stdis*ct+0.1 STEP
stdis
   PUT k,0,higt - (4*higt/(span^2))*k^2,0
   NEXT k
   ENDIF
!-------------------------------------------------
!Start building  the actual Arch
RESOL tres
MULy twid/tdep

IF arcshp=0 THEN    !Round
   ADDz -(brad-higt)
   TUBE np,(NSP-np*3)/4,63,
       GET(NSP)
       DEL 1
       ENDIF
IF arcshp=1 THEN    !Sin
   ADDx -span/2
   TUBE np,(NSP-np*3)/4,63,
       GET(NSP)
       DEL 1
       ENDIF
IF arcshp=2 THEN    !Parab
   TUBE np,(NSP-np*3)/4,63,
       GET(NSP)
       ENDIF
DEL 1

IF kut THEN
   FOR k=1 TO kut:CUTEND: NEXT k
   ENDIF

   DEL 2             !Undo Tilts
RETURN
```

We have to work out the X, Y, and Z of each point along the Arch, and 'PUT' them to the memory buffer.
Then, the TUBE command GETS the section and pathway points in one gulp.

For the final construction, I have set out all the IF statements very verbosely so that they can be easily be read and understood by Voyagers

Cutends, this is a useful routine that I use every time I have a number of cutplanes.

2 **D Script**: allowing two views of the object, so it can be stretched.

Multilingual Object

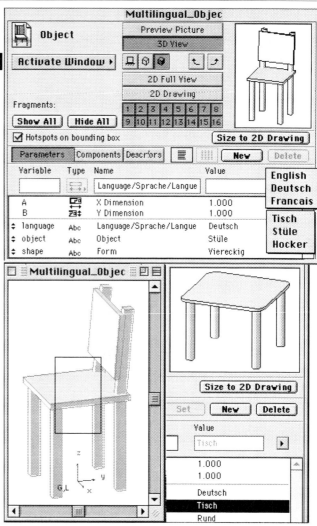

WITH earlier versions of GDL, I long complained that it needed scriptable Pop-Up menus to select options.

I also argued that you needed a way to inform both the 2D and the 3D scripts of commonly used preambles, especially if there are complicated calculation and error checking routines that both must go through.

Well you now have both of these with ArchiCAD 6.x. The key is to Popups is to use the VALUES command, an unexplained and unillustrated part of the GDL manual. The other problem is solved with the 'Master Script' in which you write the common preambles.

This Multilingual object is an illustration of one way to use VALUE lists to cover a variety of languages within the same object. Three objects, in three languages are chosen. The actual Table, Chair and Stool used in the example are extremely simple; the actual form of them is not the issue – the exercise focuses on the **Nesting of IF statements in the Value List Script** to achieve the required result.

Parameters: It is still not possible to script the names and descriptions of the **Parameters**, but in this case, the words **Object** and **Form** are common to English, German and French (with insiginificant spelling variations). The details in each language can be made to popup.

From the **Activate Window** popup, select **Values List**. The actual choices are separated by commas.

```
!Multi-Lingual Object
!Using VALUES List in ArchiCAD 6.0
!Using Parameter Script in ArchiCAD 6.5


VALUES "language" "English",
        "Deutsch", "Francais"

IF language="English" THEN
VALUES "object" "Table","Chair","Stool"
VALUES "shape"  "Round","Rectangular"
ENDIF

IF language="Deutsch" THEN
VALUES "object" "Tisch","Stuhl","Hocker"
VALUES "shape"  "Rund","Viereckig"
ENDIF

IF language="Francais" THEN
VALUES "object" "Table","Chaise","Tabouret"
VALUES "shape"  "Rond","Carré"
ENDIF
```

Surprisingly, the Value List is capable of using IF statements. You use the Master Script to parse the results of the user's choice, and create parameters. In ArchiCAD 6.5, the Value list goes into the Parameter Script.

```
!Multi-Lingual Object
!Master Script

IF language="English"  THEN lingo=1
IF language="Deutsch"  THEN lingo=2
IF language="Francais" THEN lingo=3

IF lingo=1 THEN        !English
   IF object="Table" THEN thing=1
   IF object="Chair" THEN thing=2
   IF object="Stool" THEN thing=3
 IF shape="Round" THEN sqroun=0 ELSE sqroun=1
ENDIF

IF lingo=2 THEN        !Deutsch
   IF object="Tisch"  THEN thing=1
   IF object="Stuhl"  THEN thing=2
   IF object="Hocker" THEN thing=3
 IF shape="Rund" THEN sqroun=0 ELSE sqroun=1
 ENDIF

IF lingo=3 THEN             !Francais
   IF object="Table"         THEN thing=1
   IF object="Chaise"        THEN thing=2
   IF object="Tabouret" THEN thing=3
 IF shape="Rond" THEN sqroun=0 ELSE sqroun=1
 ENDIF

MATERIAL   SYMB_MAT
PEN        SYMB_VIEW_PEN
RESOL      12
```

By the way, you do not need to convert the choices to numbers, but it makes the 2D and 3D scripting tidier.

The students I work with at Nottingham have given me the appropriate words in Swahili, Gujerati, Malay, Portuguese, Arabic, and any number of Nigerian and Chinese Dialects. But lets stick to just three here!!

```
!Multi-LingualObject -3D

!3D form is kept very simple
! - to focus on the purpose
! - the use of
! - branching Value lists.

squilind=400
GOSUB thing


END:!_____

1:!Table,Tisch
!Table Top
 ADDz 0.70
 h=0.03: w=A: d=B:
 GOSUB squilind
DEL 1

!Legs
 FOR k=1 TO 4
  ROTz 90*k
  ADD B/2-0.1,A/2-0.1,0
  h=0.7:w=0.1:d=0.1:r=0.05
  IF sqroun THEN
    GOSUB squilind
    ELSE
    CYLIND h,r
    ENDIF
  DEL 2
  NEXT k
RETURN
```

```
!Multi-Lingual Object
!- 2D Script

PROJECT2 3,270,2
HOTSPOT2 0,0

!I normally script the 2D
!but havent done so to focus
!on the point of the exercise
! - Value lists.
```

```
2:!Chair,Chaise,Stuhl
!Seat
ADDz 0.5
 h=0.03: w=0.45: d=0.45:
 GOSUB squilind
DEL 1

!Legs
 FOR k=1 TO 4
  ROTz 90*k
  ADD 0.18,0.18,0
  h=0.5:w=0.05:d=0.05:r=0.03
  IF sqroun THEN
    GOSUB squilind
    ELSE
    CYLIND h,r
    ENDIF
  DEL 2
  NEXT k

!Back
  ADD -0.18,0.18,0.5
  ROTx -5
  IF sqroun THEN
    GOSUB squilind
    ADDx 0.36
    GOSUB squilind
    ELSE
    CYLIND h,r
    ADDx 0.36
    CYLIND h,r
    ENDIF
    DEL 3

  ADD 0,0.18,0.80
  ROTx 85
  w=0.45:d=0.35:h=0.03
    GOSUB squilind
    DEL 2
RETURN
```

User Interface

This exercise is likely to be the subject of an exploration of the USER INTERFACE Script, with all the parameters in the user's language; owners of this volume are welcome to email me for a free Acrobat based update about the UI.

```
3:!Stool,Tabouret,Hocker
 ADDz 0.4
 w=0.3:d=0.25:h=0.03:r=0.17
 IF sqroun THEN
   GOSUB Squilind
   ELSE
   CONE h,r,r*0.9,90,90
   ENDIF
 DEL 1

!Legs
 CUTPLANE 180
  FOR k=1 TO 4
   ROTz 90*k
   ADD 0.12,0.12,0
   ROT -0.01,-0.01,0.4,180
   h=0.4:w=0.03:d=0.03:r=0.02
   IF sqroun THEN
     GOSUB squilind
     ELSE
     CYLIND h,r
     ENDIF
   DEL 3
   NEXT k
 CUTEND
RETURN

400:!Squilinder
IF sqroun THEN
EXTRUDE 4,0,0,h,63,
  -w/2,-d/2,1,
   w/2,-d/2,1,
   w/2, d/2,1,
  -w/2, d/2,1
ELSE
  EXTRUDE 10,0,0,h,63,
  -w/2,   0,    1,
  -w/2,  d*2/5, 1,
  -w*2/5, d/2,  1001,
   w*2/5, d/2,  1,
   w/2,   d*2/5,1001,
   w/2,  -d*2/5,1,
   w*2/5,-d/2,  1001,
  -w*2/5,-d/2,  1,
  -w/2,  -d*2/5,1001,
  -w/2,   0,    1
  ENDIF
RETURN
```

There are several other things demonstrated here.
• Using variables as names for subroutines ('thing' and 'squilinder'.)
• 'Passing Parameters' to a standardised subroutine; this saves a lot of repetetive typing.
• Using EXTRUDE when PRISM would normally do just as well. This is because, with a fully 2D scripted object it is possible to copy the 3D list of XY locations and paste them into a POLY2_ command.
• The use of the ROT command – whereby you can do a rotation in 3D dimensions in a single line, by stating an X,Y,Z location to define an axis of rotation.

```
!3D Command
  EXTRUDE 10,0,0,h,63,
  -w/2,   0,    1,
  -w/2,  d*2/5, 1,
  -w*2/5, d/2,  1001,
   w*2/5, d/2,  1,
   w/2,   d*2/5,1001,
   w/2,  -d*2/5,1,
   w*2/5,-d/2,  1001,
  -w*2/5,-d/2,  1,
  -w/2,  -d*2/5,1001,
  -w/2,   0,    1
!is easily converted to:-
!2D Command
  POLY2_ 10,1,
  -w/2,   0,    1,
  -w/2,  d*2/5, 1,
  -w*2/5, d/2,  1001,
   w*2/5, d/2,  1,
   w/2,   d*2/5,1001,
   w/2,  -d*2/5,1,
   w*2/5,-d/2,  1001,
  -w*2/5,-d/2,  1,
  -w/2,  -d*2/5,1001,
  -w/2,   0,    1
```

Tips and Tricks
FAQs on the Internet
Many of the problems you have with rendering, plotting, fills, dimensioning etc might be answered in a list of Frequently Asked Questions (FAQ). Go on the Internet to *www.graphisoft.com* and look for the Product Support Page. The answers will walk you step by step to solving your problems.

While you are there take the chance to look at other support systems available on the Web to the ArchiCAD user.

Cellular/Castellated Steel Beam

THIS is a demonstration of the use of CUTPOLY and CUTPOLYA, two of the most useful additions to GDL offered by AC6.x. These act as 'cookie cutters' which will travel through the model until you issue the CUTEND command. The technique of using them is no more complex than that required to make PRISM and PRISM_. Really!

This is a very small subset of an 'intelligent' beam project that I worked on in 1999. This particular beam is only suitable for spacing at centres of 6metres (20 feet) with a floor loading of 5kN/m2 using steel and concrete flooring; and it applies a standard hole size. The intelligent beam will adapt its size automatically (as it is stretched) to fit any beam length and spacing from 3m to 18m, and also does an iterative check that the holespacing will work satisfactorily with the hole diameters (for the hot cutting + welding process) and adjusts either accordingly. This beam can change from Castellated to Cellular, and obeys the general geometric requirements of both types and behaves intelligently within the 6m spacing limit.

The beam-size and hole-shape are dependent on the results of a Values List, so the first script that does any work is really the Master Script (next page). To get the 3D script working you can put the details of a single beam into the Master Script, and when the 3D works, you gradually add more options into the Values List, and into the Master Script, with IF... ENDIF statements to help it read in all the information.

3D Script: In the arched beam in the cookbook, the web of the beam is made from a Prism with holes for the web, and the flanges are made separately with TUBE. In this one the entire beam is one PRISM, stretched along its length, and perforated by a series of CUTPOLYA commands. The placing of these is exactly the same as if you wanted to dump a load of Prisms along the line of the centre of the beam, at a regular holespacing. In order to provide a convincing looking centre weld, and to reduce the amount of points required to define the beam profile, only half the beam is done, and then it is repeated upside down.

It is risky to put an IF statement directly into a FOR next statement, so the subroutine 110: decides whether the section is castellated or round, and stores the appropriate coordinates in the memory buffer.

Do not forget that all CUT statements require a CUTEND to finish; here they are enclosed in a tidy loop.

The PRISM outline is defined first with a sequence of PUT statements. Once you are a Voyager, this is the best way to do ALL but the smallest prisms - simply because you can add, subtract and alter points while you are building it, without syntax errors; and it's tidy – the whole put sequence can be organised in a separate subroutine.

```
!Stretchy Cellular Beam
!3D Script
!Iterative and sizing calculations
!in Master Script

MATERIAL bmat: PEN pcol
RESOL 20 !HiRes for large holes

!Design Holes with Cutpoly
FOR k=1 TO numhol
 ADD holst+holsp*(k-1),0,-bdep/2
 ROTx 90
 ROTz 0
 GOSUB 110:!Put profile - round/hex
 CUTPOLYA NSP/3,1,0,
  GET(NSP)
  DEL 3
NEXT k

!Build Beams
ADDz -bdep/2
GOSUB 100:!Upper Beam Profile
GOSUB 150:!Main Beam
DEL 1

 ADDz -bdep/2
 ROTx 180
GOSUB 100:!Upper Beam Profile
GOSUB 150:!Main Beam
 DEL 2

FOR k=1 TO numhol: CUTEND: NEXT k

END:!-------------------------

100:!UPPER Beam Profile
!Starting with middle as origin
PUT 0,0,13,
-webth/2,        0,15,
-webth/2,        bdep/2-flant-rootr,13,
-webth/2-rootr,bdep/2-flant,    1013,
-bwid/2,        bdep/2-flant,    15,
-bwid/2,        bdep/2,          15,
bwid/2,         bdep/2,          15,
bwid/2,         bdep/2-flant,    15,
webth/2+rootr,bdep/2-flant,     13,
webth/2,      bdep/2-flant-rootr,1013,
webth/2,0,15
RETURN

110:!Profile for CUTting holes
IF rndsq=0 THEN  !Round Hole
 PUT 0,0,913,
   holdm/2,360,4013
 ENDIF
IF rndsq=1 THEN  !Castellated hole
 PUT -holdm/8,holdm/2,15,
     -holwd/2,0,15,
     -holdm/8,-holdm/2,15,
     holdm/8,-holdm/2,15,
     holwd/2,0,15,
     holdm/8,holdm/2,15
 ENDIF
RETURN

150:!Main Beam - half outline
RESOL 12 !for root radius
 ROTz -90
 ROTx 90
 ADDz -blen
PRISM_ NSP/3,blen,
  GET(NSP)
  DEL 3
RETURN
```

Note the use of PRISM_ instead of PRISM. This is to get a realistic curve for the root radius of the beam

Variable	Type	Name	Value
A	⬚↔	X Dimension	5000
B	⬚↕	Y Dimension	1000
holeshape	Abc	Round Holes or Castell	Round Holes
btype	Abc	Beam Size Calculation	1219x305[15]
bmat	🎨	Main beam material	23
pcol	✏	Pen Line	1

Parameters | Components | Descriptors | New | Delete

```
!Stretchy Cellular Beam
!Master Script
!April 1999

!Beam condition
blen=A !Beam length for stretching
IF blen>18 THEN blen=18 !Span limit

!Main Beam Sizes(relate to max span)
IF btype="627x191 [6]"   THEN bcon= 6
IF btype="828x229 [9]"   THEN bcon= 9
IF btype="1078x267[12]"  THEN bcon=12
IF btype="1219x305[15]"  THEN bcon=15
IF btype="1235x305[18]"  THEN bcon=18
IF btype="Automatically sized" THEN
   bcon=3+3*INT((blen*0.99)/3)
   ENDIF !Trick to derive 6/9/12/15/18

!Determine profile of Hole
IF holeshape="Round Holes" THEN rndsq=0
IF holeshape="Castellated" THEN rndsq=1

IF bcon<=18 THEN !------914x305----
bwgt=253    !Weight index
bwid=0.305  !Beam width
bdep=1.235  !Beam depth
webth=0.017 !Beam web
flant=0.028 !Beam flange
rootr=0.019 !Root radius
holdm=0.700 !Hole diameter
holsp=1.000 !Hole spacing
ENDIF

IF bcon<=15 THEN !------914x305-------
bwgt=201    !Weight index
bwid=0.303  !Beam width
bdep=1.219  !Beam depth
webth=0.015 !Beam web
flant=0.020 !Beam flange
rootr=0.019 !Root radius
holdm=0.700 !Hole diam
holsp=1.000 !Hole spacing
ENDIF

IF bcon<=12 THEN !------762x267------
bwgt=173    !Weight index
bwid=0.267  !Beam width
bdep=1.078  !Beam depth
webth=0.014 !Beam web
flant=0.022 !Beam flange
rootr=0.017 !Root radius
holdm=0.700 !Hole diameter
holsp=1.000 !Hole spacing
ENDIF

IF bcon<=9 THEN  !------610x229------
bwgt=125    !Weight index
bwid=0.229  !Beam width
bdep=0.828  !Beam depth
webth=0.012 !Beam web
flant=0.020 !Beam flange
rootr=0.013 !Root radius
holdm=0.500 !Hole diameter
holsp=0.750 !Hole spacing
ENDIF

IF bcon<=6 THEN  !------457x191------
bwgt=67     !Weight index
bwid=0.190  !Beam width
bdep=0.627  !Beam depth
webth=0.009 !Beam web
flant=0.013 !Beam flange
rootr=0.010 !Root radius
holdm=0.400 !Hole diameter
holsp=0.600 !Hole spacing
ENDIF

!continued, right ->
```

The Value list is parsed with a series of IF statements.

A is the means of stretching, but if A is longer than 18 metres, blen sticks at a max of 18m.

✓ Round Holes
Castellated

Automatically sized
✓ 627×191 [6]
828×229 [9]
1078×267[12]
1219×305[15]
1235×305[18]

I hope that all these metre dimensions do not offend the eyes of my U.S. friends, but I do not have a set of U.S. steel tables.

The numbers after the beam name, which are also used as a 'flag' for the beam are the 'recommended maximum span in metres'.

Each beam is thoroughly documented for easy checking.

The author does not accept liability for the structural accuracy of the beams: they are taken from tables.

```
!Stretchy Cellular Beam
!2D Script

HOTSPOT2 0,0
HOTSPOT2 A,0

IF A>blen THEN
HOTSPOT2 18,0
HOTSPOT2 18, bwid/2
HOTSPOT2 18,-bwid/2
ENDIF

!PROJECT2 4,270,1

RECT2 0,-bwid/2,blen,bwid/2
RECT2 0,-webth/2,blen,webth/2

!Put in Holes
IF rndsq=0 THEN holwd=holdm
IF A_<=50 THEN
FOR k=1 TO numhol
  ADD2 holst+holsp*(k-1),0
  RECT2 -holwd/2,-webth/2,holwd/2,webth/2
  DEL 1
NEXT k
ENDIF
```

These are the stretching hotspots: put them in first

These hotspots mark the end of the beam if A>18metres

This can be used as a quick check to make sure the beam looks right in elevation

This is the Beam

2D Script:
If you used PROJECT2, the plan would take too long to redraw/rebuild, so a script built up of RECT2s is the fastest solution.

The final part of the 2D script uses data from the Masterscript to draw the plan of the holes in the web. It could be left out, as it doesn't really show clearly except at large scale. The IF statement means that it is only drawn in 1:50 or 1'=1/4" drawings.

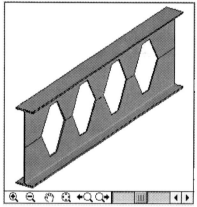

The castellation algorithm follows British Steel guidelines.

```
VALUES "holeshape" "Round Holes","Castellated"
VALUES "btype" "Automatically sized",
       "627x191 [6]","828x229 [9]","1078x267[12]",
       "1219x305[15]","1235x305[18]"
```

Values List: makes the object behave quirkily if there is an error in the GDL, so you often have to be very patient. Put dummy data in the Master Script until everything else is working well.

```
!Master Script Continued
!Procedure for round Holes
IF rndsq=0 THEN
 numhol=INT(blen/holsp) !Number of holes
 holsp=blen/numhol !Final Holespacing
IF numhol=1 THEN holsp=holdm*1.5

!Hole starting position
 holst=(blen-numhol*holsp)/2+holsp/2
ENDIF  !end procedure for Round Holes

!Complex Procedure for Castellated
IF rndsq=1 THEN
 holdm=bdep/1.5    !Hole diameter
 holsp=holdm*1.08
 holwd=holdm*0.83  !Hole width
 numhol=INT(blen/holsp)
!Need to centre the Holes in the beam
 holst=(blen-numhol*holsp)/2+holsp/2
ENDIF
```

Master Script:
This routine checks on the number of holes and hole spacing, and works out how much steel to leave at each end to centre the holes perfectly. In the intelligent beam, the hole diameters are checked and modified.

Arched Cellular Steel Beam

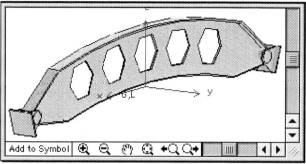

Object

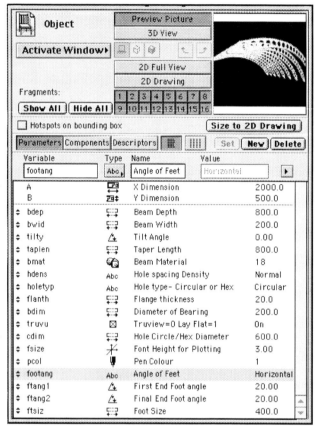

The feet can be swivelled into pre-planned angles, or freely angled. The Hole spacing can be varied.

THIS EXERCISE produces a useful object, but is also a powerful demonstrator of the parametrics of ArchiCAD 6. It has been created especially for Andras Haidekker, the CEO of Graphisoft UK to demonstrate to British Steel an example of parametric component making with GDL.

In particular, it demonstrates:

• **The use of Arrays**. Although it could be done with PUT and GET only, this would require much repetitive typing and time consuming calculation.

• The use of **Value Lists** to make the object friendly.

• The use of **Trigonometry** for forming curves.

• **TUBE** command.

• **2-D Scripting** to enhance the object's usefulness.

• The **Master Script** playing a major part.

You have this on your diskette, and you are very welcome to play with it, but I hope those with a truly *Voyager* level of courage will work through some of the scripts to glean the jewels therein. Although it looks quite polished, it is like most complex things, simple at first, and then added to gradually until it has all the features one wishes for.

Planning: The first thing is to create a PRISM for the Web of the beam. From the start it is best put into an array. The span and curve-line of the beam follows the neutral axis of the beam. Therefore the outline of the upper and lower edges are based on Radius plus or minus half the depth of the beam. The Tapered end is a complication, but this determines the "stepping distance" of each polygonal increment in the beam.

There are a lot of parameters to calculate, and in AC5, these would have to be calculated in the 3D script, and some of them would have to be repeated in the 2D. Now you can put the whole lot into the Master Script.

Variable	Type	Name	Value
footang	Abc	Angle of Feet	Horizontal
A		X Dimension	2000.0
B		Y Dimension	500.0
bdep		Beam Depth	800.0
bwid		Beam Width	200.0
tilty		Tilt Angle	0.00
taplen		Taper Length	800.0
bmat		Beam Material	18
hdens	Abc	Hole spacing Density	Normal
holetyp	Abc	Hole type- Circular or Hex	Circular
flanth		Flange thickness	20.0
bdim		Diameter of Bearing	200.0
truvu		Truview=0 Lay Flat=1	On
cdim		Hole Circle/Hex Diameter	600.0
fsize		Font Height for Plotting	3.00
pcol		Pen Colour	1
footang	Abc	Angle of Feet	Horizontal
ftang1		First End Foot angle	20.00
ftang2		Final End Foot angle	20.00
ftsiz		Foot Size	400.0

Although it enlarges the size of your file, add a Picture into the Preview Window, to make it more user-friendly.

```
! Arcing Beam with Portholes
! Master Script

!Calculate parameters for main beam
   IF nostep<4     THEN nostep=4
   IF nostep>60    THEN nostep=60
   IF taplen<bdep/2 THEN taplen=bdep/2
   IF taplen>bdep*2 THEN taplen=bdep*2
   span=A: higt=B            !DefineStretchyparams
   IF higt<0.02 THEN higt=0.02  !prevent error
   angl =2*(90-ATN((span/2)/higt))!Halfangle of bow
   brad =(span/2)/SIN(angl) !Radius of Bow arch
   circum= 2*PI*brad        !Circumference
   lena = circum*angl*2/360 !Length of Arc
   nostep= INT(lena/taplen+0.5)
   stangr= (angl*2)/nostep  !Step angle:Rotation

!Thrust Bearing and Foot
   IF bdim< bdep/10  THEN bdim=bdep/10
   IF bdim> bdep*0.8 THEN bdim=bdep*0.8
   blen = bwid+flanth*3     !Bearing Length
   ftwid=ftsiz: ftlen=ftsiz
   IF ftwid<blen THEN ftwid=blen
   IF ftlen<bdim+flanth*2 THEN ftwid=bdim+0.04
```

```
!Calculate Circle spacing
   IF hdens="No Holes" OR cdim=0 OR holetyp="None" THEN
      noholes=1
      ELSE
   IF hdens  ="Condensed"  THEN hd=1.2
   IF hdens  ="Normal"     THEN hd=1.4
   IF hdens  ="Extended"   THEN hd=1.8
   IF holetyp="Circular"   THEN ht=0
   IF holetyp="Hexagonal"  THEN ht=1
   IF cdim>bdep*0.9         THEN cdim=bdep*0.9
   crad=   cdim/2            !Circle Radius
   cspa=   cdim*hd           !Circle Spacing
   !Control Number of Circles is adjusted by angle
      numcirc=INT(lena/cspa-2-angl/60)
   cstang =cspa*360/circum  !Stepping angle for Holes
   hangl  =cdim/circum*360  !Sweep angle of one hole
   cangl  =cstang*numcirc   !Sweep angle of holes
   numhole=numcirc-1        !Actual number of holes
   hcrad  =crad*SQR(3)/2    !Radial Height of HexHole
ENDIF
```

Parsing the Value List can be verbose.

```
!Arcing Beam with Portholes
!3D Script

!Array is for
!XY Points on circumf of beam
!and masks
DIM pt[125][3]
  MATERIAL bmat: PEN pcol
  ROTy tilty

!Master Script calculates
!internal parameters

GOSUB 100:!Fill Array with Points
GOSUB 110:!Build Web of Beam
GOSUB 120:!Build Flange of Beam--
GOSUB 150:!Thrust Bearings-------
GOSUB 160:!Feet----------------

   DEL 1 !Undo Tilty
END:!-----------------------
```

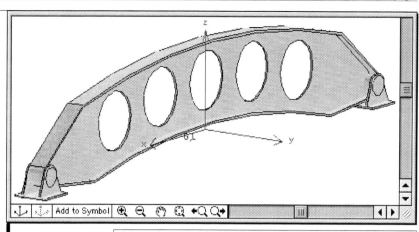

```
100:!Fill Array with Points-------
!First Two Points
   pt[1][1]=(brad+bdim/2)*SIN(-angl)
   pt[1][2]=(brad+bdim/2)*COS(-angl)
   pt[2][1]=(brad-bdim/2)*SIN(-angl)
   pt[2][2]=(brad-bdim/2)*COS(-angl)

!Underside points
   rad=brad-bdep/2:np=2
FOR k=-angl+stangr TO  angl-stangr+0.1 STEP stangr
   np=np+1
   pt[np][1]=rad*SIN(k):pt[np][2]=rad*COS(k)
NEXT k

!End of span
   np=np+1
   pt[np][1]=(brad-bdim/2)*SIN(angl)
   pt[np][2]=(brad-bdim/2)*COS(angl)
   np=np+1
   pt[np][1]=(brad+bdim/2)*SIN(angl)
   pt[np][2]=(brad+bdim/2)*COS(angl)

!Upperside Points
rad=brad+bdep/2
FOR k= angl-stangr TO -angl+stangr-0.1 STEP -stangr
   np=np+1
   pt[np][1]=rad*SIN(k)
   pt[np][2]=rad*COS(k)
NEXT k

!First and Final Point
   np=np+1
   pt[np][1]=(brad+bdim/2)*SIN(-angl)
   pt[np][2]=(brad+bdim/2)*COS(-angl)
```

The diameter of the end bearing determines the shape of the beam end.

SIN and COS are the standard ways of defining cartesian coordinates from Radius and Angle.

The Master script grows from the basic stepping angles and other parameters, to the monster you see here. Value Lists make the object enormously more helpful to the user, but make the scripts more verbose, as you have to parse the value list to extract or convert the results.

Details, such as this section on the feet of the beam do not get added in until they are needed.

```
!Continuing Master Script.......
!Calculate Feet Orientation
IF footang="Horizontal to Span" THEN
   ftang1=0:ftang2=0
   ENDIF
IF footang="Horizontal to Ground" THEN
   ftang1=-tilty:ftang2=tilty
   ENDIF
IF footang="Tangential" THEN
   ftang1=90-angl:ftang2=90-angl
   ENDIF
IF footang="None" THEN nofeet=1
```

```
!Fill Masking Values in Array
FOR k=1 TO np-2
  pt[k][3]=8 !Masking Values
NEXT k
   pt[np-1][3]=13 !Last but one Point
   pt[np  ][3]=-1 !Last Point
   !0.1 deliberate error
RETURN:!-----------------------

110:!Build Web of Beam------------
!Put all points from array to Buffer
FOR k=1 TO np
   PUT pt[k][1],pt[k][2],pt[k][3]
   NEXT k

!Drill Holes, unless "No Holes"
IF NOT(noholes) THEN
   RESOL 16
   FOR k=-cangl/2 TO cangl/2+0.1 STEP cstang
     GOSUB 200+ht:!Circular or Hex
     NEXT k
ENDIF

!Now Build it!
   ROTx 90
   ADDY -brad+higt
   ADDz -0.01
PRISM_ NSP/3,0.02,
   GET(NSP)
   DEL 3
RETURN:!-----------------------

120:!Build Flange of Beam-------------
   IF flanth<0.01   THEN flanth=0.01
   IF flanth>bdep/8 THEN flanth=bdep/10
!PUT Sectional outline
   PUT -bwid/2, 0,      0,
       -bwid/2,-flanth,0,
        bwid/2,-flanth,0,
        bwid/2, 0,      0

!Put Pathway points for Tube
   PUT pt[np][1],0,pt[np][2],0 !1st Phantom pt
   FOR k=1 TO np
     PUT pt[k][1],0,pt[k][2],0
     NEXT k
```
continued overleaf....

```
!Arching Beam with holes drilled
!Value List

!Hole Density
VALUES "hdens"     "Condensed","Normal",
                   "Extended","No Holes"
!Hole Type
VALUES "holetyp" "Circular","Hexagonal",
                 "None"

!Foot Orientation
VALUES "footang" "Free Angle","None",
                 "Horizontal to Span",
                 "Horizontal to Ground",
                 "Tangential"
```

```
    PUT pt[2][1],0,pt[2][2],0 !Lst Phantom pt

    ADDz -brad+higt
 TUBE 4,np+2,63, !Flange
    GET(NSP)
    DEL 1
RETURN:!------------------------------
```

```
150:!Thrust Bearings------
    ADDx -A/2
    ROTx 90
    ADDz -blen/2
 CYLIND blen,bdim/2
    ADDx A
 CYLIND blen,bdim/2
    DEL 4
RETURN:!------------------------------
```

When you have the array correctly organised, it is as easy and quick as this!

```
160:!Feet----------------------
 IF NOT(nofeet) THEN
    ADDx -A/2
    ROTy ftang1
    GOSUB 170:!Foot
    DEL 2
     ADDx A/2
     ROTy -ftang2
    GOSUB 170:!Foot
    DEL 2
    ENDIF
 RETURN
```

*Note the use of a Booleian NOT( ) command to decide if the feet should be drawn. Note that I have used the flange thickness **flanth** as an all purpose definer of thickness for the feet modules.*

```
170:!Foot
ADDz -bdim
PRISM 4,flanth,
 ftlen/2, ftwid/2,
 ftlen/2,-ftwid/2,
-ftlen/2,-ftwid/2,
-ftlen/2, ftwid/2

 ROTx 90
 ADDz bwid/2
GOSUB 175:!flange in foot
 ADDz -bwid-flanth
GOSUB 175:!flange in foot
 DEL 4
RETURN
```

```
175:!flange in foot
PRISM_ 7,flanth,
 -ftlen/2,0,15,
 -bdim/2-flanth,bdim,15,
 0,bdim,915,
 0,bdim*3/2+flanth,3015,
 bdim/2+flanth,bdim,3015,
 ftlen/2,0,8,
 -ftlen/2,0,15
RETURN
```

```
200:!Circular Hole definition-------
 PUT brad*SIN(k),brad*COS(k),913,
     crad,360,4013
RETURN
```

```
201:!Hexagonal definition-----------
 PUT (brad)*SIN(k-hangl/2),        (brad)*COS(k-hangl/2),        15,
     (brad+hcrad)*SIN(k-hangl/4),(brad+hcrad)*COS(k-hangl/4),15,
     (brad+hcrad)*SIN(k+hangl/4),(brad+hcrad)*COS(k+hangl/4),15,
     (brad)*SIN(k+hangl/2),        (brad)*COS(k+hangl/2),        15,
     (brad-hcrad)*SIN(k+hangl/4),(brad-hcrad)*COS(k+hangl/4),15,
     (brad-hcrad)*SIN(k-hangl/4),(brad-hcrad)*COS(k-hangl/4),15,
     (brad)*SIN(k-hangl/2),        (brad)*COS(k-hangl/2),        -1
RETURN
```

!Arcing Beam with Portholes
!2D Script

Use PROJECT2 while you are doing this, until you get the script working. This object requires some Trig, as it can be tilted.

```
 PEN pcol
```

```
!Main Outline
 HOTSPOT2 0,0
 HOTSPOT2  (A/2)*COS(tilty),0
 HOTSPOT2 (-A/2)*COS(tilty),0
 RECT2 -A/2*COS(tilty),-bwid/2,
       A/2*COS(tilty), bwid/2
```

```
!Centreline
 LINE2 B*SIN(tilty), bwid,
       B*SIN(tilty),-bwid
 HOTSPOT2 B*SIN(tilty), 0
```

It is useful to know the centre of the beam

```
!Points for stretching
 HOTSPOT2 -A/2,0
 HOTSPOT2  A/2,0
```

Whenever you have to repeat some typing, use a subroutine.

truvu draws an elevation of the truss, super-imposed over the plan view, with additional Hotspots and Text display. Essential for 'docking' it to the building accurately.

```
!Thrust Bearing
  ADD2 -A/2*COS(tilty),0
  GOSUB 100:!Bearing
  ADD2 A*COS(tilty),0
  GOSUB 100:!Bearing
  DEL 2

 IF truvu THEN
  PROJECT2 4,270,2
  HOTSPOT2 0,B
  HOTSPOT2  B*SIN(tilty),    B*COS(tilty)
  HOTSPOT2 -A/2*COS(tilty), A/2*SIN(tilty)
  HOTSPOT2  A/2*COS(tilty),-A/2*SIN(tilty)
    GOSUB 200:!Text Display
  ENDIF

 END:!-------------------------------------
```

```
100:!Bearing
  RECT2 -bdim/2,-blen/2,
         bdim/2, blen/2
  LINE2 0,bwid,0,-bwid
RETURN
```

*When your **text string** is more complicated than a single quotation, build it up using the PLUS symbol. Mathematical quantities have to be converted with the STR function.*

```
200:!Text Display
DEFINE STYLE "btext" Arial,fsize,1,0
 SET STYLE "btext"
 btstr="Arc'd beam, Rad="+ STR(brad,5,2)+",
               Span="+STR(span,5,2)
  TEXT2 -A/2,bwid*3,btstr
RETURN
```

Use Arial font to be sure of being usable on PC and Mac

I apologise that this exercise is not enormously annotated, but the script contains plenty of comments, and has a logical structure. If you are a true Voyager, it will be interesting to analyse how it's done from the object in the Cookbook library.

I realise that traditional steel castellation is not done to a curved beam, but I have seen photographs of curved castellated beams – presumably cut out after curving. It's fun working out the algorithm for rotated hexagonal holes!

Artlantis no parallel views?

I am often asked why Artlantis does not cater for parallel (axonometric) views. Artlantis is a ray tracer, which means that each ray of light is followed from its source to the eye of the viewer. With parallel projection, there is no one eye point to trace the light back to.

If you want parallel views, position the camera 1000 metres, or even 10000 metres away from the model, zoom into the model and you will have the nearest thing that it can provide to a parallel view. If that's not parallel enough, make the camera more distant.

Tips and Tricks
ArchiCAD-Talk on the Internet

A most excellent source of information and expertise is available to ArchiCAD users through the Internet. Graphisoft US very kindly host a 'listserver' conference called ArchiCAD-talk. If you have email access, make a new message, address it to **"archicad-talk@graphisoft.com'** and make the subject of the message **'subscribe'**. Leave the message blank.

You will now get about 25 messages a day from users all over the world, debating GDL, rendering, plotting, and all manner of useful things. You may be astonished at the quality of the messages. You will also be able to post questions and answers on the conference.

If the quantity is so great that you are crushed by it (turn it off when you go on holiday!), then send another blank message using the words **'subscribe digest'**. This turns off the main flow of messages and sends you one big one only, every day. Send the word **'unsubscribe'** and you will be able to stop both messages and digests.

Most of the Tips and Tricks in the GDL Cookbook have evolved from ArchiCAD-Talk, and I am grateful to all the contributors.

Use Acrobat!

A CROBAT is one of the most helpful software innovations of the decade. As a totally cross platform format, independent of applications, it can be used for drawings and books with the original quality retained, for viewing and printing. Acrobat is a PostScript display to screen & printer, somewhat like a "Print Preview".

Buy the Acrobat authoring module to convert any file, including ArchiCAD drawings, into a readable format. Everybody buying a computer or software now has Acrobat Reader. This can do for ArchiCAD what .DWF files do for AutoCAD. Send drawings to Clients, Building Inspectors or Contractors.

With AC6, you can place an acrobat file into the Documentation folder, for reading with the HELP menu. This could be a drawing reference list, the GDL Cookbook, an instruction manual for special GDL objects, phone numbers of your team or anything else useful.

You can set flags to make Acrobat files safe against being changed or printed if you wish to – as I do with the Cookbook version on PDF.

MASS – terrain modelling

THE GDL MASS command which creates a terrain or membrane was a welcome addition to AC6.0, but is painful to write from scratch. But if you use the Mesh tool in ArchiCAD to create the outline, and some of the points, you can export it as an object, open it in GDL. Or you can just drag it from the Project window into the 3D Script. It has now been saved as a MASS command. You can now change bottom and side attributes, modify some of the existing points, add more points and change material.

Putting Roads into the Mesh tool

Ricardo Borges wrote:
Is there a way to make cuts with 90 degrees on the mesh; and make "roads" that follow the differents heights of the mesh to show on the rendering?
From: Duane Valencia VFrontiers@aol.com
YES, you can cut holes in your mesh and create roads of a different material. I use the following procedure....
1. Create complete mesh
2. Duplicate mesh a known distance from the original (so you can move it back later)
3. Draw your road using lines / arcs
4. Add nodes at each topo intersection of the new road outline
(IMPORTANT!.. If you don't, the hole will force the topos back to the nearest node leaving a little gap in your mesh)
5. Use the lines to cut the mesh, leaving only the road.
6. Adjust this mesh up a short (minute) distance and give it a new material.
You can also use the road geometry to CUT a hole into the mesh if you want. I find this unnecessary if your road is slightly above the land mesh.

Server advice

Gerald Abrams wrote:

I have three mac work stations am in the process of upgrading my equipment. I would like to know more about the advantage, expense and special features of using a Server for AC. Also is there anything that I can read that can overview servers in general.

Ralph Wessel, Walker Co-partnership Architects
Basically a dedicated server is much less likely to crash in a teamwork situation. It can keep the same software open and running continuously, unlike the average user who is constantly opening and closing apps and documents. Memory allocation is more predictable and caching becomes more effective. I don't think working on a machine that's serving files is much fun either.

Moreover, you'll get much better performance if you run 'real' file sharing software like AppleShare IP rather than the peer-to-peer sharing built in to the basic OS. Refer to:
<http://www.apple.com/appleshareip/>

I wouldn't consider NT for serving files to Macs – for whatever reason, it delivers data much slower to Macs than to PC's. AppleShare IP delivers information to Mac clients at about 3 times the rate of NT.

However, if you don't need to make a quick decision, take a look at Mac OS X Server:
<http://www.apple.com/macosx/server/>

Mac OS X will provide excellent server performance, and has some unique characteristics. If your client machines are recent models (G3/iMac) you can boot and run them entirely from the server, which makes software updates and coordination an easy task.

Tips and Tricks

Battered Walls

From: Rex A. Maximilian rex@envision-ats.com May 1999

ANSWERING the question: "Just curious if there is a way to make non-vertical walls in AC 6.0. Has anyone run into this situation?"

Here's the best work around we've come up with for making battered walls. Try this exercise, and then apply it appropriately for your needs. The key factor is that it remains a wall, and accepts windows and doors!

--- EXAMPLE ---

1) Draw a 1'-6" thick wall at 90 degrees (up direction), with the reference line to the RIGHT. Set the height of the wall VERY high (around 20' or so.) Set the bottom of the wall to ZERO.

2) Create a new layer called "Battered Wall Cutter." ...Or if you are using our Envision templates "Walls (Battered Cutter)," will work with our system.

3) Set the pitched roof settings with a ZERO thickness and set it to the layer mentioned in step #2. Make sure that the plate line height is set the same as the bottom of the wall (ZERO). Set your roof pitch to your desired battered angle.

4) Draw the plate line on the LEFT edge of the wall, or on the OPPOSITE side of the walls reference line and click the pitch direction to the right, or towards the wall. Draw the polygon shape of the roof to match the shape of the wall.

5) Select the roof and wall together and go under the EDIT menu and choose "Trim to Roof." Then choose the "Trim Top" button.

6) Select the wall afterwards, and reset the height of the wall to your desired height... Let's choose 6'-0".

If you look at the 3D view of the wall, you will see that it is battered. Not only is it battered, but it also remains a wall. You can add windows and doors to it, stretch it, and other wall functions. Try doing that to a roof, mesh or a GDL that you created for your battered wall... YOU CAN'T !!!

Other tips for battered walls:

1) Group the wall and wall cutter roof together. When you do 3D views, simply turn off the "Walls (Battered Cutter)" layer off. When they are grouped, you can be sure that if you move or delete them, they act together.

2) You can also select all the roofs, or some roofs as the case may be, and reset their slope. Select the walls and "Undo Trim," raise their heights again, and recut to the adjusted slope!

3) You can copy this wall to the side of your model. Then, drag copies into place all over your project and stretch the walls to create all of your battered walls so you don't have to repeat the battering steps above. Remember to copy and stretch the "cutter roof" as well incase you need to adjust the slope in the future.

Let me know if anyone encounters any problems with this method. It's all relatively simple!

Good Luck, Rex A. Maximilian, Envision ATS, LLC

Walls in conversion work

AC 6.0 allows dotted or other linetypes for the outline of walls, windows, doors and library parts – great for those doing conversion work, to indicate walls to be taken out. If you don't want the wall to show in 3D, just 'explode' it to 2D!

Use ArchiGuide!

From: Peter <bennison@club-internet.fr

I cannot seem to do a simple count of objects (spots on a lighting layout) with the new super sophisticated calculate function – frustrating when it is something that could be done with great ease and speed in Archicad5.0 and previous versions.

Bradley Skaggs replies:

You may want to check out ArchiGuide Online. Issue 18 dealt exclusively with the new super sophisticated calculate menu. There is an example as well that shows you how to do a simple object count.

bradley skaggs, skaggs|design, san francisco, CA, usa author of ArchiGuide Online:

 http://www.archiguide.com

[**Editors Note**: this is just one example of the many reasons why the really committed ArchiCAD user and Cookbook reader should also checkout the information available at ArchiGuide Online and ArchiCAD-Talk!]

Digital Cameras and Kodak CD

...are wonderfully useful to the ArchiCAD user. Enjoy instant results for catching textures of brickwork, shop windows, grass, paving etc. Instant access to Picture objects for people, plants and building facades. No waiting for the chemist to develop the photos and then find a scanner. The quality is not as good as a 'real' camera, but for AC use the quality is adequate, and the speed is significant. Budget at least £350. Try... Fuji, Canon, Sony, Kodak, Casio.

If you must use traditional camera film, consider asking your developer to put it onto Kodak CD. Saves all the work of scanning and provides a permanent archive of site and texture photos.

Using Comments

VERY few people use **Project Comments**, but it really is useful for making notes – a small text editor at your fingertips. It is also good for leaving notes for colleagues to read if you are collaborating. Each note is automatically date and time recorded.

Another text editor is the **Library Comment** window. Use it as means of providing a small piece of Documentation for your object - for example style settings for door or furniture. Under ArchiCAD 6.5, you will also be able to provide extended information for the user in the USER INTERFACE.

Quicker Section Elevations

HERE is a great trick to open all elevations and sections at once:

Go to the plan view, select all section/elevation. Then with right mouse click(PC) or control mouse click, open section/elevation, then click OK to open all of the selections.

Now while it is regenerating go get a soda and come back and there they are, ready to view.

John Mulcahy Rockefeller/Hricak Architects, Venice, CA

Hyperbolic Paraboloid

THIS OBJECT was written as a result of visiting the gas station in Palm Springs by Albert Frey in April 1999 with architectural students. It used to greet visitors come to Palm Springs from LA. It was due for demolition, but was saved by architectural conservationists. It has now been converted into a garden sculpture gallery and sales area.

COONS is difficult enough to write in any circumstances, but if you can devise a maths routine that will calculate all the points along the side, then it is considerably easier. First, analyse the shape – a Hyperbolic Paraboloid is distinguished by the fact that all the members connecting the sides are perfectly straight, but when used in combination, they produce an elegant saddle shaped curve.

Parameters: You have to decide how the user will 'describe' this in the parameter box. Wherever possible, make use of the A and B, to make it stretchy, and to reduce the number of options in the remainder of the dialog box. Because the 'hyparb' is assymmetrical, you can base it on A and B with an offset to define the centre location. Once the basic structure is working, add in the Materials and get the Value lists working.

Project planning: The strategy is to get all the work done by a sequence of PUT statements, and then (if these are all arranged correctly), you throw the whole lot at the COONS in the form of a GET(NSP) statement.

If you first create an array holding the XYZ locations of each corner, you only need to derive the XYZ of all the points along the straight lines joining them to describe the COONS.

If the 2D was to be based on PROJECT2, you could do the whole thing in the 3D script, but as this object is 2D scripted, you must start with the Master Script.

Master Script: Although the parsing of the Value List appears first, it is best to fit that in later, and just get the surface working. You can still write the Value List out, and think out the range of options you will offer the user.

3 D Script: Has been annotated section by section on the next page. Notice how small the executive script is, because this is a difficult one and is best subdivided into modular tasks.

```
VALUES 'edgt' "Square","Round"
VALUES 'tubecon' "Surface, No tubes",
               "Edge Tubes+Surface",
               "Surface Tubes+Surface",
               "All Tubes+Surface",
               "All Tubes, No Surface"
```

Values List: you can write this later when you have got the basic surface working correctly

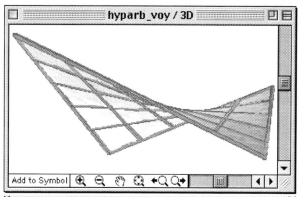

hyparb_voy / 3D

Add to Symbol

Variable	Type	Name	Value
A		X Dimension	6.000
B		Y Dimension	3.000
tubecon	Abc	Tubes condition	Surface Tubes +...
ofst		Off centre dimension	1.000
numsub		Number of Beam Subdivisions	5
hita		Height of point 'A'	1.000
hitb		Height of Point 'B'	2.000
dimt		Section size of edge tube	0.100
edgt	Abc	Tubes Profile	Square
sftbpc		Relative Size % of SurfTubes	50
hpmat		Material for HyParb	39
frmat		Frame Tubing Material	3
smoo		Smoothness of Surface (2-36)	12
slif		Raise Surface ON/OFF	Off

```
!Hyperbolic Paraboloid - Master Script

!Parse Value List
IF tubecon="Surface, No tubes"       THEN tcon=0
IF tubecon="Edge Tubes+Surface"      THEN tcon=1
IF tubecon="Surface Tubes+Surface"   THEN tcon=2
IF tubecon="All Tubes+Surface"       THEN tcon=3
IF tubecon="All Tubes, No Surface"   THEN tcon=4

!State Arrays
DIM pnt[3][10]
x=1: y=2: z=3

!Build Array: main points
!Point West
PUT -A/2+ofst,0,hita
!Point North
PUT  0,B/2,0
!Point East
PUT A/2+ofst,0,hitb
!Point South
PUT 0,-B/2,0

FOR k=1 TO 4 !Main array
 pnt[x][k]=GET(1)!X value
 pnt[y][k]=GET(1)!Y value
 pnt[z][k]=GET(1)!Z value
NEXT k

FOR k=5 TO 7 !Extend array by 3
 pnt[x][k]=pnt[x][k-4]!X value
 pnt[y][k]=pnt[y][k-4]!Y value
 pnt[z][k]=pnt[z][k-4]!Z value
NEXT k

!Correct User Errors
IF smoo<2 THEN smoo=2
IF smoo>36 THEN smoo=36
IF numsub<1 THEN numsub=1
IF smoo<numsub THEN smoo=numsub
```

!State Arrays It makes it easier to manage if the arrays are always referred to by letters x, y, and z, even though numerically, they are 1, 2, and 3.

The easiest way to fill an array is to use a series of PUT statements to build the numbers, then use GET to fill the array. The array needs to be 7, not 4, so that when you use a TUBE command for the edge beams, you will be able to do the 'phantom points'.

Because the sides of the hyparb will be subdivided by beams, you might like a denser degree of subdivison for the surface than for the beams. So the error correction routine ensures that the surface is never coarser than the beam layout.

```
!Hyperbolic Parabaloid
!3D Script
!Voyager Course, Cookbook
!Main parameters set up in Master Script

!Build Surface
IF tcon<=3 THEN GOSUB 100:!Surface

!Build Edgetubes
IF tcon>=1 THEN
GOSUB 130:!Edgetube
ENDIF

!Do Surface tubes
IF tcon>=2 THEN
 GOSUB 150:!Surface tubes routine
  MULy -1
 GOSUB 150:!Surface tubes routine
  DEL 1
ENDIF

END:!_____
```

```
100:!Build Surface
!Feed COONS points to memory
p1=1:p2=2 !1 to 2
   GOSUB 110
p1=4:p2=3 !4 to 3
   GOSUB 110
p1=1:p2=4 !1 to 4
   GOSUB 110
p1=2:p2=3 !2 to 3
   GOSUB 110
```

The surface building exercise follows the technique outlines earlier in the book, for COONS commands. 1 to 2, 4 to 3, 1 to 4 and 2 to 3. The corners of the hyparb have been numbered in the order West, North, East, South.

```
!Build it
ADDz slif*dimt*sftbpc/150
MATERIAL hpmat
COONS NSP/12,NSP/12,63,
     GET(NSP)
     DEL 1
RETURN
```

The COONS, when it comes, is short and decisive. You can later apply a lift command (ADDz) if the user wants it raised above the surface beams.

```
110:!Subroutine: workout XYZ
     !Increments
xinc=(pnt[x][p2]-pnt[x][p1])/smoo
yinc=(pnt[y][p2]-pnt[y][p1])/smoo
zinc=(pnt[z][p2]-pnt[z][p1])/smoo

FOR k=1 TO smoo+1
PUT pnt[x][p1]+xinc*(k-1)
PUT pnt[y][p1]+yinc*(k-1)
PUT pnt[z][p1]+zinc*(k-1)
NEXT k
RETURN
```

This subroutine does the real work of calculating the XYZ locations of the side points. For each side, the increments in X, Y, and Z are calculated (xinc, yinc and zinc) and applied in a For.. Next loop to build the list. 'smoo' is the number of points along the surface edge.

```
120:!Define Section Profile
IF edgt="Square" THEN
  PUT  w, w,0
  PUT -w, w,0
  PUT -w,-w,0
  PUT  w,-w,0
ELSE
  PUT 0,0,901,
   w,360,4001
ENDIF
 sp=NSP/3 !Section points
RETURN
```

This routine draws out the beam sections, based on the user's preferences in the Value List.

```
130:!Build Edge Tubes
w=dimt/2 !Section Radius
IF tcon=2 THEN w=dimt*sftbpc/200
GOSUB 120:!Define profile

!Define edge pathway
 FOR k=1 TO 7
 PUT pnt[x][k],pnt[y][k],pnt[z][k],0
 NEXT k

!Build tube all in one
RESOL 8
MATERIAL frmat
 TUBE sp,7,63,
    GET(NSP)
RETURN
```

This is the easiest part of the whole script. Joining up the points on the array.

Build the tube pathway in a Loop containing PUT statements

The tricky IF statement above is to convert the edge beamroutine to build the same size as the surface beams if the real edge beams are required to be omitted. Using GET, the final TUBE command is simple.

```
150:!Surface tubes routine
!Increments for first line
xinc1=(pnt[x][2]-pnt[x][1])/numsub
yinc1=(pnt[y][2]-pnt[y][1])/numsub
zinc1=(pnt[3][2]-pnt[3][1])/numsub

!Increments for second line
xinc2=(pnt[x][3]-pnt[x][4])/numsub
yinc2=(pnt[y][3]-pnt[y][4])/numsub
zinc2=(pnt[z][3]-pnt[z][4])/numsub
```

Two lots of increments need to be worked out, for the points at each end of the beam.

```
!Points for start+end of surface tubes
FOR k=1 TO numsub-1
x1=pnt[x][1]+xinc1*k
x2=pnt[x][4]+xinc2*k
y1=pnt[y][1]+yinc1*k
y2=pnt[y][4]+yinc2*k
z1=pnt[z][1]+zinc1*k
z2=pnt[z][4]+zinc2*k
```

I am surprised at how difficult this was. It turns out to be easier to do just one set of beams, on the north side, and then repeat the whole lot, using a MULy -1 command in the executive script.

```
!Define Phantom Points
x0=x1+(x1-x2)
x3=x2-(x1-x2)
y0=y1+(y1-y2)
y3=y2-(y1-y2)
z0=z1+(z1-z2)
z3=z2-(z1-z2)

w=dimt*sftbpc/200 !Profile section
GOSUB 120:!Define profile
```

This is a fiendishly useful piece of script for ensuring that TUBEs have butt ends. I use it frequently. I feel almost reluctant to give it away.

```
!Draw it
MATERIAL frmat
  TUBE sp,4,63,
     GET(NSP),
     x0,y0,z0,0,
     x1,y1,z1,0,
     x2,y2,z2,0,
     x3,y3,z3,0
NEXT k
RETURN
```

As the distribution of edge points for the beam is different to that for the surface, it's not worth filling an array. As the beams are all one piece, it's not worth using PUT. Generate the XYZ locations on the fly and just throw them at the TUBE command.

Tips and Tricks

Artlantis Export

EXPORTING an ArchiCAD model to Artlantis must be done from a camera perspective view. A plain Artlantis save does not export ALL textures; the resulting file is manageable but may need you to feed textures to the surfaces. Exporting to full Artlantis 3 format can create a database file of textures and everything, and beware, this could be 20 or 30 megabytes in size. If any one material in the ArchiCAD model has more than 65000 polygons, your export may fail, or Artlantis may be unable to open the file. If you have a lot of trees or tubes, make a duplicate of the Leaf material or of Stainless Steel.

Artlantis - Losing VR cameras on Resave

From: Bruce Haniel

I was doing a multicamera VR in Artlantis 3.5. Went back to Archicad to amend the model, saved over the original Artlantis file and nominated the original as the 'model'. And the 'model' cameras were to be used in the dialogue window.

From: Michael Hohmann

Don't save over the original file but use a new file name and use the previous Artlantis file as the template file. Set textures, cameras lights and sun to be used from the template file. works for me....

```
!Hyperbolic Parabaloid - 2D Script
!May 1999: David NicholsonCole
!Main parameters set up in Master Script

HOTSPOT2 -A/2+ofst,0
HOTSPOT2 A/2+ofst,0
HOTSPOT2 0,B/2
HOTSPOT2 0,-B/2
HOTSPOT2 0,0

!PROJECT2 3,270,2

FOR k=1 TO 5
PUT pnt[x][k],pnt[y][k]
NEXT k

POLY2 5,1,
  GET(NSP)

!Surface Tube lines
IF tcon>=2 THEN
GOSUB 150:!Surface tubes routine
  MUL2 1,-1
GOSUB 150:!Surface tubes routine
  DEL 1
  ENDIF

END:!---------------------
```

If you are in a hurry, the Project2 and the Hotspots are all you need

The POLY2 routine is simply a re-hash of the routine which draws the edgebeam tubes, except that you do not bother with height (z), and POLY2 does not require phantom points.

2D Script: The PROJECT2 command is used until you are sure that your 2D script is working. The first five active lines are all you need, if you are in a hurry, and would make my pagination a lot easier – I could fit this all on 2 pages. But this is an impressive demonstration of how easy 2D scripting can be once you have conquered a very difficult routine in 3D. Just omit the height factor, and replace 3D entities with their 2D equivalent. The Loops are virtually the same.

```
150:!Surface tubes lines
!Increments for first line
  xinc1=(pnt[x][2]-pnt[x][1])/numsub
  yinc1=(pnt[y][2]-pnt[y][1])/numsub

!Increments for second line
  xinc2=(pnt[x][3]-pnt[x][4])/numsub
  yinc2=(pnt[y][3]-pnt[y][4])/numsub

!Points for start+end of surface tubes
FOR k=1 TO numsub-1
  x1=pnt[x][1]+xinc1*k
  x2=pnt[x][4]+xinc2*k
  y1=pnt[y][1]+yinc1*k
  y2=pnt[y][4]+yinc2*k

!Draw it
  LINE2 x1,y1,x2,y2
  HOTSPOT2 x1,y1
  HOTSPOT2 x2,y2
NEXT k
RETURN
```

The surface beam line routines are a simple re-hash of the same thing in the 3D script, omitting height (z), and using LINE2 instead of TUBE to draw the beam lines. It is good to add in the Hotspots at ends, as the object can more easily be picked up.

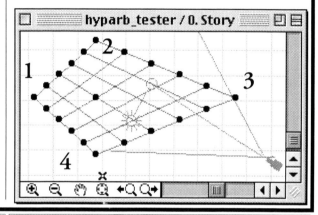

Reasons to use ArchiCAD-Talk: No. 1

Gyuri Juhasz   computerhumaninteractions
gjuhasz@graphisoft.hu   Graphisoft R&D Rt
phone 361 437 3121   fax 361 437 3099

TO all who recently questioned whether GraphiSoft reads at all your input: YES.

Many GS people in the US and in Hungary watch the maillist, including programmers, designers, techsup staff. We have no strict policy on how we respond. Access to ArchiCAD-TALK is free and we would like to participate in this list on the same non-compulsory basis as you.

We do not want to answer each and every problem mentioned here. We read the digest version with a long delay and in most cases the AC-Talker community responds faster than we do.

Suggestions for product improvements are always welcome. In many cases we do not talk just listen, archive, analyze and think. All problems and wishes are entered in our databases which are the foundation of future ArchiCAD releases. And we spend so much time with our computers that progress, simply statistically, is unavoidable :)

And please do not forget: we are no maillist police, you bash our product and company as you wish. However we are just humans and in many cases, we prefer stay silent if a posting just hurts.

peace, gyuri

[**Editors Note:** see elsewhere in the Cookbook how to connect to ArchiCAD-Talk[

Hide window symbol?

YOU may want to place a window above a door, or place a minor window above a major window, but want to be able to decide which one will show. This depends on whether you created the window, or if it is a Graphisoft library window. (One is reluctant to alter them so perhaps you should do this to copies.)

Laszlo Nagy (lnagy@graphisoft.hu) *offers:*

Add a new parameter 'show2d' /Booleian type/"Show 2D symbol ON/OFF?". In the 2D script, insert this line at the top: **IF NOT(show2d) THEN 1000**

Place the window, then use the settings box to switch 2D off. This will have the effect of leaving the window existing in 3D but invisible in the plan. If show2d=1 it means there is a 2D Symbol. In this case the normal Script is executed. If it is zero it will go to 1000 where the following lines are:

```
END:!this stops the existing script running into this one
1000:!Place this script at the END of the existing script
ADD2 0, WIDO_SILL
IF WIDO_REVEAL_SIDE=1 THEN
ADD2 0,WALL_THICKNESS-2*WIDO_SILL-WIDO_FRAME_THICKNESS
ENDIF
PEN WALL_FILL_PEN
FILL WALL_FILL
POLY2_B 4,6,WALL_FILL_PEN,WALL_FBGD_PEN,
- -A/2,-C_,0,A/2,-C_,0,A/2,0,0,-A/2,0,0
PEN WALL_SECT_PEN
LINE_TYPE WALL_LINETYPE
LINE2 -A/2,-C_,A/2,-C_
LINE2 -A/2,0,A/2,0
END
```

This will basically draw a fill and lines which get their types from the Wall's global variables. It works even if you flip the window (a tough task to do). *Regards, Laszlo Nagy, Graphisoft Budapest*

API

NOW that ArchiCAD 6.x has settled into use, and arrays in GDL are more commonly used, GDL can develop into something smarter and more powerful. The remainder of the CAD industry need be envious that only ArchiCAD gives its users the ability to create parametric smart objects.

The rival product AutoCAD has a huge sub-industry of add-ons which do heating engineering, lighting, solar heating, chemical engineering, structural calculations, membranes. Because GDL didn't support arrays, the GDL developer couldn't begin to do most of these things. Unless you have the resources of Abvent or other developers associated with Graphisoft, normal users have been deprived of the tools for small scale development – which could have turned into major products if they showed promise.

An exciting development offered by ArchiCAD 6.x is API, an 'advanced programming interface' that goes well beyond GDL. API allows developers to build higher level Add-ons to ArchiCAD; these can be added to the main menus of ArchiCAD. GDL is limited in that it only participates in the form of library objects. GDL can only read information about the environment through Global Variables, but API routines can exist in the whole environment of ArchiCAD – they can interact with live elements of the main project like walls, slabs and fills. The Add-ons are analogous to the plug ins you can get for Netscape, Photoshop, Quark and Pagemaker, appearing in the menus or tool pallettes, and radically extending the usefulness of the parent application.

Unfortunately, to develop APIs, you have to spend a lot of money on C++ and more money on the interface information from Graphisoft, and spent several years becoming a programmer, instead of an Architect or Designer. There won't be a Cookbook on API, not from this author, anyway! You have to buy the API kit, so you need to be sure you will make it pay. Would you have bought GDL if it was a separate application and you had to pay over £1000 for it?

Add-ons promised by Graphisoft include such things as a timber roof wizard, drainage and tubing wizard, extrusion (profiler) and lathing wizard. Several of these have already appeared on the Graphisoft website. One very useful add-on is the one that checks for duplicates – objects that are the same and that exist in precisely the same 3D or 2D space.

ArchiCAD 6.5 Update

The addition of the User Interface capability in the GDL of ArchiCAD 6.5 brings GDL a happy step closer to API. Although API retains the ultimate ability to read a wide range of data in the project file, the UI allows GDL programmers to build user friendly dialog boxes with editing fields, images, thus leaping far beyond the confines of the normal parameter settings box.

The following is quoted directly from Graphisoft's own overview on the API

Add-On types

ADD-ONS are small pieces of software that add functionality to ArchiCAD. By developing an add-on, you have the possibility to extend the following menus and popups of ArchiCAD:

1.1 General API
Import/Export filters that allow you to open and save ArchiCAD data in different foreign file formats. Installed Add-Ons may appear in the Open, Merge, Open Library Part and Save as dialog boxes, which are invoked from the File menu.

Tools-type Add-Ons add editing possibilities. Their commands appear at the bottom of the Tools menu of ArchiCAD. They are allowed to perform any legal operation on the ArchiCAD database like creating, deleting and modifying either elements, attributes, or library parts.

Listing-type Add-Ons add listing possibilities. Their commands appear at the bottom of the Calculate menu of ArchiCAD. They are allowed to process the ArchiCAD database and create listings which fit to any special needs. These kinds of Add-Ons also can assign custom properties to each element type through the listing page of the tool settings dialogs.

1.2 Rendering API
Rendering type Add-Ons add new rendering engines to ArchiCAD. They appear in the Rendering Settings dialog box, like the Z-Buffer Rendering Engine.

1.3 GDL API
You can also extend the file I/O operations via GDL scripts. By developing a GDL add-on you can write GDL scripts which are able to connect to, read from, and write to external databases.

1.4 Custom Object API
Custom object editors, like StairMaker or ArchiSite, can extend the standard toolbar of ArchiCAD. They are able to mount a new icon into the toolbar, and build custom library parts.

All developer kits assume that you are a programmer who is familiar with the C language. With the exception of the Rendering API they also require considerable knowledge of GDL programming.

Look at the APIs

GRAPHISOFT have now released several API created Add-Ons, some of which are available on the Web for free download.

The most interesting from the 3D point of view is the **Profiler**, in which you click-draw an outline. When you double click or close the profile, the next clicks you do will describe a pathway. An example of the use is for skirtings and covings around rooms, for architraves and trims. This example using the Tubular object profiler is to show you how it is done; Cookbook readers may be keen to analyse the script produced as a result.

Variable	Type	Name	Value
A		X Dimension	5.795
B		Y Dimension	7.265
mat		Material	0
fll		Fill on Plan	65
dir	☒	Change direction	Off
closed	☒	Closed	On
zzyzx		Height	1.081

These are the parameters created by Profiler. 'closed' is used by the revolution surface routine, not by the tubular object profiler.

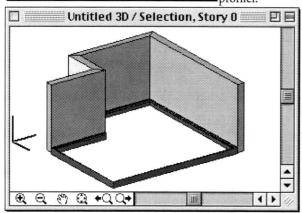

The tubular object profiler always seems to close up the pathway, but if you can get into the 3D script, you can forcibly shorten it to allow doorways.

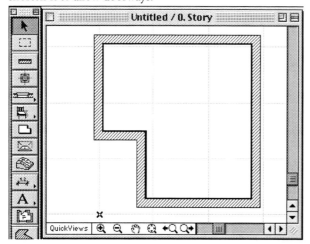

The tubular object part of Profiler is a good way to prototype shapes: with some intelligent tweaking by a GDL savvy user, the results can be far more 3-dimensional.

Master Script
```
! Created by TubeAPI
IF dir THEN dir=-1 ELSE dir=1
```
This controls the user's choice to 'mirror' the profile – used by both 2D and 3D scripts.

3D Script
```
MUL a/5.496027, b/5.576086, zzyzx/0.257124
RESOL 36
MATERIAL mat
mask=16
begx=1.587353
begy=0.000000
endx=-0.001344
endy=3.174706
TUBE 9, 9, mask,
    0.000000*dir, 0.251494, 2,
    0.000000*dir, 0.000000, 2,
    -0.041290*dir, 0.000000, 2,
    -0.041290*dir, 0.163283, 2,
    -0.033783*dir, 0.170791, 2,
    -0.033783*dir, 0.225218, 2,
    -0.041290*dir, 0.230849, 2,
    -0.016891*dir, 0.257124, 2,
    0.000000*dir, 0.251494, -1,
    begx, begy, 0, 0,
    0.000000, 0.000000, 0, 0,
    -0.001344, 3.174706, 0, 0,
    5.494683, 3.174706, 0, 0,
    5.494683, -2.401380, 0, 0,
    1.587353, -2.401380, 0, 0,
    1.587353, 0.000000, 0, 0,
    0.000000, 0.000000, 0, 0,
    endx, endy, 0, 0
```
The usual MUL commands allow the total object to be stretchy; but stretching using MUL will distort the profile.

The begx and begy and endx and endy are the location of Phantom points. The Profiler usually takes the second and the penultimate points as the phantom points.

Status codes are not documented for TUBE, but a value of 2 tells the photorenderers to put a clear break at the joints.

There is no twist, and no 'Z' value in the profiler. But you can use profiler to generate a first script which you can then change to suit your needs. Add a twist!

2D Script
```
PROJECT2 3, 270, 2
FILL fll
MUL2 a/5.496027, b/5.576086
HOTSPOT2 5.494683, 3.174706
HOTSPOT2 5.494683, -2.401380
HOTSPOT2 -0.001344, 3.174706
HOTSPOT2 -0.001344, -2.401380
HOTSPOT2 2.746669, 0.386663
HOTSPOT2 0.000000+dir*(0.041273), 0.000000+dir*(0.041290)
HOTSPOT2 0.000000+dir*(0.000000), 0.000000+dir*(0.000000)
HOTSPOT2 -0.001344+dir*(0.041308), 3.174706+dir*(-0.041290)
HOTSPOT2 -0.001344+dir*(0.000000), 3.174706+dir*(0.000000)
HOTSPOT2 5.494683+dir*(-0.041290), 3.174706+dir*(-0.041290)
HOTSPOT2 5.494683+dir*(0.000000), 3.174706+dir*(0.000000)
HOTSPOT2 5.494683+dir*(-0.041290), -2.401380+dir*(0.041290)
HOTSPOT2 5.494683+dir*(0.000000), -2.401380+dir*(0.000000)
HOTSPOT2 1.587353+dir*(0.041290), -2.401380+dir*(0.041290)
HOTSPOT2 1.587353+dir*(0.000000), -2.401380+dir*(0.000000)
HOTSPOT2 1.587353+dir*(0.041290), 0.000000+dir*(0.041290)
HOTSPOT2 1.587353+dir*(0.000000), 0.000000+dir*(0.000000)
HOTSPOT2 0.000000+dir*(0.041273), 0.000000+dir*(0.041290)
HOTSPOT2 0.000000+dir*(0.000000), 0.000000+dir*(0.000000)
POLY2 14, 6,
    0.000000+dir*(0.041273), 0.000000+dir*(0.041290),
    -0.001344+dir*(0.041308), 3.174706+dir*(-0.041290),
    5.494683+dir*(-0.041290), 3.174706+dir*(-0.041290),
    5.494683+dir*(-0.041290), -2.401380+dir*(0.041290),
    1.587353+dir*(0.041290), -2.401380+dir*(0.041290),
    1.587353+dir*(0.041290), 0.000000+dir*(0.041290),
    0.000000+dir*(0.041273), 0.000000+dir*(0.041290),
    0.000000+dir*(0.000000), 0.000000+dir*(0.000000),
    1.587353+dir*(0.000000), 0.000000+dir*(0.000000),
    1.587353+dir*(0.000000), -2.401380+dir*(0.000000),
    5.494683+dir*(0.000000), -2.401380+dir*(0.000000),
    5.494683+dir*(0.000000), 3.174706+dir*(0.000000),
    -0.001344+dir*(0.000000), 3.174706+dir*(0.000000),
    0.000000+dir*(0.000000), 0.000000+dir*(0.000000)
```
The plan view of the skirting is shown. the Profiler then describes all the hotspots that follow the skirting, and provides a POLY2 which can provide a fill pattern that covered the skirting if the detail is to be omitted.

The 'dir' value is used to mirror the section, if required. If you were to change the 3D script significantly, you would have to reduce the 2D Script to an essential minimum - removing the POLY2.

I have only been able to get the Revolution Surface function of Profiler to work once correctly, but keep trying! It works with REVOLVE, and can equally well be tweaked by crafty GDL-smiths.

The 6.5 User Interface – part 2

Theory Object

ANYBODY who has used the Graphisoft doors in **Archi-CAD 6.5** will recognise that a profound improvement has occurred to the user interface, the most noticeable being the arrival of the **Pictorial Value list**. The fact that the GDL-writer can create a whole series of custom designed dialog boxes offers a wealth of opportunities. Let's look at how to do this, and make some Golden Rules to ensure success.

Open and examine the object called **UI_Tester.gsm**. You may want to examine the 3D script in your own time for examples of PUT and GET, Cutpoly, Revolve, and Polylines, but for this exercise, it isn't annotated with comments.

Parameters: The parameter box is made as below, and of course, the user who like the traditional parameter box can still enjoy some new features such as hierarchically grouped parameters. The Object is defined with the use of a Value List, placed in the Parameter Script.

Leaf styles

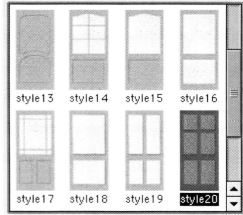

Anyone using ArchiCAD 6.5 must be delighted at the addition of Pictorial Valuelists. But the manual does not really explain clearly how this is done. Let's try and do the same with the list of simplified objects below.

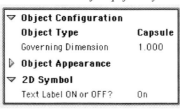

The procedure for producing 'rocking button' hierarchical parameter boxes is discussed in the Discovery section.

3D Script: This contains a dozen primary object shapes, and a conventional Values List is used to enable these to be selected from the normal parameters box. The script is printed overleaf.

```
VALUES 'objtyp' 'Cube','Cylinder',
   'Sphere','Capsule','Dome','Pyramid',
   'Cone','Torus','Tincan','Big_Ell',
   'Dish','Handle'
```

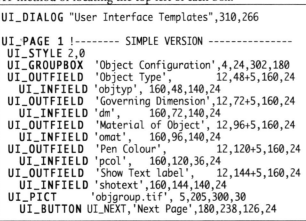

User Interface Dialog – the straightforward approach

HERE is a typical page containing a number of parameter names and Edit boxes and Popup menus, using a simple XY method of locating the top left of each box.

```
UI_DIALOG "User Interface Templates",310,266

UI_PAGE 1 !-------- SIMPLE VERSION --------------
 UI_STYLE 2,0
 UI_GROUPBOX  'Object Configuration',4,24,302,180
 UI_OUTFIELD  'Object Type',        12,48+5,160,24
   UI_INFIELD 'objtyp', 160,48,140,24
 UI_OUTFIELD  'Governing Dimension',12,72+5,160,24
   UI_INFIELD 'dm',     160,72,140,24
 UI_OUTFIELD  'Material of Object', 12,96+5,160,24
   UI_INFIELD 'omat',   160,96,140,24
 UI_OUTFIELD  'Pen Colour',         12,120+5,160,24
   UI_INFIELD 'pcol',   160,120,36,24
 UI_OUTFIELD  'Show Text label',    12,144+5,160,24
   UI_INFIELD 'shotext',160,144,140,24
 UI_PICT       'objgroup.tif', 5,205,300,30
   UI_BUTTON UI_NEXT,'Next Page',180,238,126,24
```

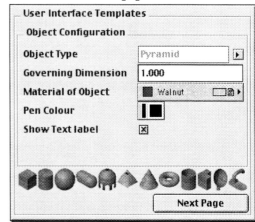

This is Page 1 of the object called UI_Tester.gsm (on your Cookbook CD). The first page of an object's UI should contain the primary user information such as shape and size. Note that OUTfields have to be 4-5 pixels higher than an INfield if the text is to line up.

If the User Interface Script has any working commands in it, the user will see an extra button in the settings box, like this. If your UI dialog has everything needed for the user, then you can hit the 'Set as Default' button to force it to come up when the library part is first opened.

Command Statements in the User Interface (UI)

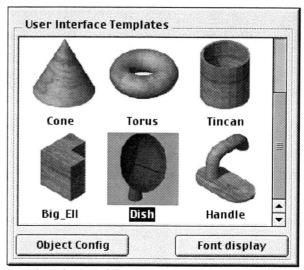

IN case you have no Manual to hand, let's re mind you of the commands in the UI.

For all of these:

• **X and Y** are the location of the **Top Left** point of the box or button.

• **Width and Height** are the relative dimensions of the box or button from that top left corner to the **Bottom Right** corner.

• All dimensions are in screen pixels.

• **Text expressions** are either in quotes or can be a variable that contains a string of text.

Ha! The Holy Grail of the User Interface – Page 2 demonstrates the Pictorial ValueList. In this, the display is arranged in little tiled images of the contents of the Value List, 3 across, in 4 rows. This is done with the UI_OUTFIELD command, fully explained in the next few pages.

• UI_DIALOG title [, sizex, sizey]

This starts off all UI scripts, stating that you want a UI, and defining its size. In Object building this is fixed permanently at 310x266, but shows that Graphisoft are leaving it open for the design of future interfaces of a different size – no longer having to fit into the existing objects dialog box.

• UI_PAGE pagenum

You can have many pages in the UI, so they should be clearly numbered, starting from '1'. Everything after this command is on the page referred to until the next UI_PAGE statement. You can move between pages by making buttons for Next or Previous Page. Unfortunately, you cannot make buttons for all pages – you must move page by page.

The GDL writer should write pages in the order of significance – 'Main configuration' first page, perhaps 'Colours and materials' after that, and perhaps '2D symbol and display' finally – unless you want to add a last page with 'User instructions and information'.

• UI_BUTTON type,text, x,y, width,height

You can make buttons to go to the Next Page or the Previous Page. (I hope that buttons will be available in future versions to do more.)

type: UI_PREV: goto the previous page
UI_NEXT: go to the next page

• UI_GROUPBOX text, x,y, width,height

Groupbox gives you a rectangular box around a group of smaller items, and it can be titled, as in the example here, 'Object Configuration'. The words sit at the top of the Groupbox, and break the top line. If the text is '' (nothing) the Groupbox is drawn cleanly without text.

• UI_SEPARATOR x1,y1, x2,y2

A Separator is just a LINE that can be drawn in the box. The manual says that lines can ONLY be Horizontal or Vertical, but if you disobey this and define 2 XY locations with a diagonal relationship (as in RECT2) you get a GroupBox that does not print a title.

x1, y1: starting point coordinates
x2, y2: endpoint coordinates

• UI_PICT expression, x,y [,width,height]

You can bring a jpg or tif file from a loaded library and display it as a Picture element in the dialog box.

expression: File name or index number of the picture, with its name in full, including 3-letter suffix. If you use an index number of zero (0), it will display the Preview picture of the library part, the advantage being that it doesn't need to be in the loaded libraries.

width, height: Width and height in pixels; the picture's original width and height values will be used if you leave this blank. If you specify width and height, GDL will squeeze the picture to fit. It is best to make your picture the right number of pixels to save it the trouble.

• UI_STYLE fontsize,facecode

This gives you the choice of **three** font type/sizes and several styles. It uses existing **system fonts**, and you do not define an actual font by name – it would cause chaos in UI design if you could because the end user might not have that font. Using system fonts you can be sure it will work for the user.

Fontsize: On the Mac, **fontsize 0** (normal) uses 10-point Geneva, **fontsize 1** (small) uses 9-point Geneva and **fontsize 2** (large) uses 12-point Chicago. PC users will have fonts of similar sizes like Arial. ~~fontsize: one of the following values:~~

Facecode: similar to the STYLE definition in the GDL Manual, but the values cannot be used in combination. For this, 0=Normal, 1=Bold, 2=Italic, 4=Underline, 8=Outline, 16=Shadow.

• UI_OUTFIELD text, x,y, width,height

This allows you to write some text in the UI dialog, for example the description of a parameter, or some instruction to the user. We have all been frustrated by lack of space to describe parameters in the old box. Now you have the space to help your user. Maximum length of the text is 550 letters, so you can write a reasonable description. You can also write an IF statement that changes the text according to the answer. For example, the text could be displayed in English, French or whatever, and in my example (page 3), the text knows if the object selected is a Cube, a Cylinder or whatever, and tells the user how the object is made.

- **UI_INFIELD "name", x,y, width,height [,
versionFlag, pictName, nrImages, nrRows,
cellX, cellY, imageX, imageY,
imageExp1, text1,**

...,

imageExpn, textn]

This is where the real power of the UI is to be found! The UI_INFIELD can accept user data for Dimension, Text, Value Lists, Pen colour and all the usual things either in Edit fields or in Popup menus; but it can also display a Pictorial Value List (containing thumbnail images of your doors, windows or objects), making it **vastly more user friendly.** UI_INFIELD knows whether to show an Edit field or a Menu because you have created the parameters and defined their type in the main parameter box. If you are using the UI exclusively, then you could **hide** the parameters from the parameter box so that they are **only** visible in the UI. The example on the previous page shows a variety of UI_INFIELDs including Value list (text), Dimension, Material, Pen and Booleian. If as a result of your choice, other things change (e.g if user selects a circular object, you need to ask the user questions about diameter, and if user selects a polygonal one, you need to ask about sides) then the Interface script is re-read and the current page is rebuilt – it causes a slightly annoying delay, but when you know why it is doing it, you can live with it.

name: Parameter name (defined in the parameter settings)

x, y: The position of the edit text, popup or control

width, height: width and height in pixels

That is all you need for normal Edit field or Pop down INFIELDs.

If you wish for a Pictorial ValueList, you need to have defined the ValueList first, and then you need the following:

versionFlag: Reserved, so for now, always put 1 in there.

pictName: Name of the image file (jpg or tif) containing a gridded arrangement (matrix) of images (as described earlier), in the order in which you want them to be seen.

nrImages: Total number of images in the matrix

nrRows: Number of rows of the matrix

From 'nrImages' and 'nrRows', GDL works out the arrangement and will cut the image of the matrix up into equal tiles and use them in order from top left to bottom right.

cellX, cellY: Width and height of a cell as you wish them to be seen within the Pictorial ValueList field, including the image – and the text which must fit the space, of course.

imageX, imageY: Width and height of the image tile that is to be fitted into the Cell – this must be smaller than the CellX and CellY or there will not be space for the text.

Now you follow with a list of the index numbers and names of each image tile, in the same order – from top left to bottom right.

imageExpi: index number of the i-th image tile in the matrix, starting with 1.

texti: text name in the i-th cell.

For example:- 1,'Cube',2,'Cylinder',3,'Sphere' and so on.

Well that sort-of explains it (in slightly more words than in the manual) but here follows a detailed description of the process, and of course you have UI_Tester.gsm to play with and examine until you get the hang of it.

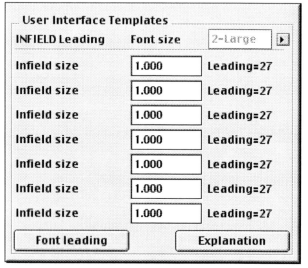

Fonts Display and IF statement: Page 3 shows the variety of Fonts and Styles available. Use the font size selector to change the block of text (about Programming) to see how the font size changes and affects the appearance of the page. If text flows out beyond the limits defined by Width and Height, it simply gets lost.

IN_FIELD Leading (vertical space between lines) – Page 4 of the UI_tester demonstrates this effectively. You can change the fontsize and the whole page is reformatted with a different value for Leading.

Write a User's Manual! – Page 5 demonstrates how you could use the UI to write a user's manual for your object, or insert a copyright notice or manufacturer's address and email. Remember that the maximum letters in one OUTfield is 550.

```
!User Interface demo
!GDL Cookbook
!3D Script

IF objtyp='Cube'      THEN ot=1
IF objtyp='Cylinder'  THEN ot=2
IF objtyp='Sphere'    THEN ot=3
IF objtyp='Capsule'   THEN ot=4
IF objtyp='Dome'      THEN ot=5
IF objtyp='Pyramid'   THEN ot=6
IF objtyp='Cone'      THEN ot=7
IF objtyp='Torus'     THEN ot=8
IF objtyp='Tincan'    THEN ot=9
IF objtyp='Big_Ell'   THEN ot=10
IF objtyp='Dish'      THEN ot=11
IF objtyp='Handle'    THEN ot=12

d2=dm/2 !Half size
 MATERIAL omat
 PEN pcol
 RESOL 20
GOSUB 100+ot


END:!----------------

101:!Cube
d2=dm/2
PRISM 5,dm,
    d2,  d2,
   -d2,  d2,
   -d2, -d2,
    d2, -d2,
    d2,  d2
RETURN


102:!Cylinder
CYLIND dm,d2
RETURN


103:!Sphere
SPHERE d2
RETURN


104:!Capsule
  ADDz d2
  ROTy 90
  ADDz -d2
CYLIND dm,d2
  MULz -1
ELLIPS d2,d2
  DEL 2
  ADDz d2
ELLIPS d2,d2
  DEL 3
RETURN
```

```
105:!Dome
ROTy -90
FOR k=1 TO 8
ROTx k*45
PUT 0,d2/5,13,
    d2/2,d2/5,13,
    d2/2,-d2/5,1013,
    0,-d2/5,15,
    0,d2/5,15
CUTPOLYA NSP/3,1,0,
    GET(NSP)
DEL 1
NEXT k

PUT 0,d2,1,
    d2,d2,1,
    d2,0,901,
    d2,-80,4001,
    d2-dm/10,80,4001,
    d2,d2,1,
    0,d2-dm/9,1,
    0,d2,1
REVOLVE NSP/3,360,0,
    GET(NSP)
    DEL 1
FOR k=1 TO 8
    CUTEND
    NEXT k
RETURN

106:!Pyramid$
MATERIAL 0
ADDz dm*2/3
CUTPLANE
DEL 1
MATERIAL omat
PYRAMID 5,dm,63,
    d2,  d2,1,
   -d2,  d2,1,
   -d2, -d2,1,
    d2, -d2,1,
    d2,  d2,1
CUTEND
ADDz dm*3/4
CUTPLANE 180
DEL 1
PYRAMID 5,dm,63,
    d2,  d2,1,
   -d2,  d2,1,
   -d2, -d2,1,
    d2, -d2,1,
    d2,  d2,1
CUTEND
RETURN
```

```
107:!Cone
  CONE dm,d2,0.001,90,90
RETURN

108:!Torus
ROTy -90
PUT 0,d2/2,901,
    d2/4,360,4001
REVOLVE NSP/3,360,63,
    GET(NSP)
DEL 1
RETURN

109:!TinCan
PUT 0,0,913,
    d2,360,4013,
    d2*9/10,360,4013
PRISM_ NSP/3,dm,
    GET(NSP)
CYLIND d2/10,d2*9/10
RETURN

110:!Big_Ell
PUT -d2,0,
    -d2,dm,
    0,dm,
    0,d2,
    d2,d2,
    d2,0,
    -d2,0
PRISM NSP/2,dm,
    GET(NSP)
RETURN

111:!Dish
  ROTz 180
CONE d2,d2/6,d2/16,90,30
  DEL 1
  ADDz d2
  ROTy -30
PUT 0, 0.001,1,
    d2,0.001,901,
    d2,-45,4001
REVOLVE NSP/3,
        360,0,
    GET(NSP)
  ROTy 90
CONE d2,d2/50,
    0.001,90,90
  DEL 3
RETURN
```

```
112:!Door Handle
!Escutcheon
PUT 0,0,913,
    0,-d2/2,13,
    d2/2,-180,4013,
    d2,d2/2,13,
    d2,0,913,
    d2/2,-180,4013,
    0,-d2/2,-1,
!Keyhole
    d2,      d2/20,15,
    d2/1.5, d2/20,13,
    d2/1.5,-d2/20,1013,
    d2,    -d2/20,15,
    d2,     d2/20,-1
PRISM_ NSP/3,d2/10,
    GET(NSP)

!Handle
 ROTz 90
CYLIND d2/2,d2/5
 ADDz d2/2
ELBOW d2/3,90,d2/5
 ADD d2/3,0,d2/3
 ROTy 90
CYLIND d2/2,d2/5
 ADDz d2/2
ELBOW d2/3,90,d2/5
 DEL 5
RETURN
```

```
!User Interface Demo
!2D Script

PEN pcol
PROJECT2 3,270,2
HOTSPOT2 0,0

IF shotext THEN
DEFINE STYLE 'otxt' 'Arial',
       (dm/6)*1000/A_,5,0
SET STYLE 'otxt'
TEXT2 0,0,objtyp
ENDIF
```

You want a Pictorial Value List?

THE first step to making a user interface that incorporates a Pictorial Values List is to generate all the 3D or Rendered views of your object/s, put them into Photoshop (or similar) and arrange them in an orderly grid. The graphic matrix in this example is 270x360 pixels so that the objects are perfectly arranged in 4 rows across of 3 across, with 90x90 pixels each. Set your ArchiCAD rendering window to 90x90 and patiently produce, then copy and paste each image into one file. The grid does not have to be in the same arrangement as it will be seen in the dialog box, but it helps enormously in composition if you arrange it as you wish the user to see it. Although I originally worked out that the images would best be 90x90, I found that they fitted better if I got GDL to squeeze the images down to 80x80.

• UI_INFIELD "name", x,y, width,height [,
versionFlag, pictName, nrImages, nrRows,
cellX, cellY, imageX, imageY,
imageExp1, text1,
...,
imageExpn, textn]

See the next pages for a working example of the Pictorial Value List and design guidelines.

UI Design Guide: Some golden rules, warnings, advice and notes.

Theory

- **Preview** – As you build the Interface script, you can keep clicking on the **Preview** button to see how it is going. If you have made a mistake, you usually get a blank grey UI dialog box. Do not panic, check through your script for errors.

- **UI_Box size** – because the box has a surround line, the realistic design size is 308x264 pixels, not 310x266.

- **Long texts** – in the UI_OUTfield, text blocks work out their own wordwrap on a Lefthand justified basis and if the text (with your choice of font and style) exceeds the box size, it just gets lost. The text all has to be written on one line in the GDL Interface script window (which is difficult), and has an absolute limit of 550 letters (or bytes).

- **Leading** – (the distance between lines of text) is very important, as it has to work with the INfield boxes which have their own leading. If you do not get Leading right, your UI dialogs will look untidy, and you will have to use trial and error. I have done research into leadings for OUTfields and INfields, to save you hours of guesswork.

  For OUTfields, the inbuilt leading of a continuous flow of text is 13 pixels for fontsize 0, 12 pixels for fontsize 1 and 16 pixels for fontsize 2.

  For INfields, the edit boxes set themselves, and seem have a default height of 20 pixels high for size 0, 15 high for fontsize 1, and 23 pixels high for fontsize 2, regardless of what you set height to. My recommended minimum Leading for INfield boxes is 4 pixels more than the height, i.e. 24 for f'size 0, 19 for f'size 1, and 27 for f'size 2.

  INfield boxes have shadows round them, to simulate a hole for Edit fields and a button for Popup menu fields (which are included in the Leading figures given here). For this reason, Popups look 2 pixels longer than Edit fields of identical size, so you could artificially shorten them.

  INfield boxes do very wierd things if you do not get leading and height right according to the numbers above. If you set the Height to less than the above figures for whichever font, they have their own mind. The rule they follow is: Go to the XY location required; Measure downwards the silly height that in in the script; then measure UPwards the height that the INfield box ought to be. Result is that they appear higher than you wanted.

- **Lining up Fields** – INfield boxes place the text in the centre of the box vertically and left justified horizontally, whereas text in an OUTfield sits lower in its rectangle. Therefore, if you wish the text of an OUTfield box to line up with text in an INfield, then the XY start of the OUTfield has to be 4-5 pixels higher than the INfield.(I say '4-5' not '4 or 5' because it is inconsistent)

- **Hide Parameters?** – if you depend entirely on the UI, then you still need to make the parameters in the parameter settings box, but you may (as in my example) have a parameter that only has relevance to the UI dialogs; so for that one, you need to click on the 'Hide Parameter' button so that the user does not get confused.

- **Lock Parameters** – some parameters only refer to certain conditions – for example if the object is circular, then there are questions about diameter and surface smoothness. If the

object is polygonal, there are questions about edges – so the smoothness questions should be locked. You cannot dynamically **Hide** a parameter, so the next best thing is to **Lock** it. You can use the LOCK command (in the Parameter Script) to lock out parameters that are not relevant to the user's choice. In the UI, you can have alternative Pages (using a long IF statement) depending on the user's choice of object.

- **Indents** – (X value in boxes and fields) should be 12 if you want it to line up with the Title of the dialog box; if you use a Groupbox, the relative indent will still be 12. So you should indent OUTfields to 12+the indent of the Groupbox, and the texts will line up with the Groupbox title.

- **PEN** – Best width for a PEN INfield is 36 – this will give you a nice square pallette box.

- **Buttons** – (for Next and Previous pages) are always in fontsize 2 (large) so you need to allow for this. Minimum height for a button is 20 high, 24-26 is safe and good looking. The button should float about 2 pixels clear of the boundary at the bottom, so I recommend a maximum Y value of 238 for buttons 24 high. Instead of writing Next and Previous, you can write the titles or descriptions of the next or previous pages.

- **Bugs!** – I have had a few problems on the first release of AC-6.5 when building UI scripts (crashes, self destruction or erasure of parameters), so I recommend you save frequently and change the file name regularly as you develop – then save under its final name when all is well.

- **Bugs!** – The Booleian INfield does not work correctly in the first release of AC-6.5, you need to go back to normal params box. It's a case of click click many times, and sometimes it works, sometimes not.

Pictorial Value list guidelines

- **Field sizing** – When you have a Picture list that contains more images that can fit in the window at once, a scroll bar will appear at the right hand side. The practical usable area with a scroll bar has a maximum width of 279 which allows five cells of 55 each, four cells of 69 each, three cells of 93 each, or two of 139 each. The Pictorial Value lists in GS's single leaf doors use 4 cells of 65 width each. Practical field height is 210, so a cell should be 102-105 for the images to appear cleanly. Try to make your Photoshop file the same width as the field of cells, otherwise GDL has to stretch or squeeze the image tiles to fit the space allotted – and this can result in distortions or unexpected aliasing.

- **File format** – Although TIFs always work well, you can safely use TIFs with LZW compression, or JPEGs.

- **Cell sizes** – The Cell height MUST be at least 22 pixels higher than the Imagetile or the text will be omitted. Cell size must be bigger than the Imagetile.

- **Complete the list** – If the item in the Value list is omitted from the list in the UI_OUTFIELD command, the item will be omitted from the Pictorial Value list.

User Interface – bells and whistles

```
UI_DIALOG "User Interface Templates",310,266


UI_PAGE 1 !------------------------------------------------
 UI_STYLE 2,0
 led=24     !Leading of Infield Boxes
 dy =0      !Distance downwards in Y
dy=dy+led
 UI_GROUPBOX 'Object Configuration',4,dy,302,led*7.5
dy=dy+led
 UI_OUTFIELD 'Object Type',12,dy+5,160,24
   UI_INFIELD 'objtyp',160,dy,140,24
dy=dy+led
 UI_OUTFIELD 'Governing Dimension',12,dy+5,160,24
   UI_INFIELD 'dm',160,dy,140,24
dy=dy+led
 UI_OUTFIELD 'Material of Object',12,dy+5,160,24
   UI_INFIELD 'omat',160,dy,140,24
dy=dy+led
 UI_OUTFIELD 'Pen Colour',12,dy+5,160,24
   UI_INFIELD 'pcol',160,dy,36,24
dy=dy+led
 UI_OUTFIELD 'Show Text label',12,dy+5,160,24
   UI_INFIELD 'shotext',160,dy,140,24
dy=dy+led
 UI_STYLE 1,0
 UI_OUTFIELD 'Page 1:Object config; Page 2:Pictorial Values list;',          12,dy,  290,16
 UI_OUTFIELD 'Page 3:Fonts display; Page 4:Infield leading; Page 5:Explanation',12,dy+16,290,16

 UI_PICT 'objgroup.tif',5,205,300,30
 UI_BUTTON UI_NEXT,'Pictorial Selector',180,238,126,24


UI_PAGE 2 !------------------------------------------------
UI_STYLE 2,0
UI_OUTFIELD 'Pictorial Selector',10,25,200,25
UI_INFIELD 'objtyp',4,20,300,210,
           1,'objselector.jpg',12,4,
               92,102,         80,80,
               1,'Cube',       2,'Cylinder',
               3,'Sphere',     4,'Capsule',
               5,'Dome',       6,'Pyramid',
               7,'Cone',       8,'Torus',
               9,'Tincan',    10,'Big_Ell',
              11,'Dish',      12,'Handle'

 UI_BUTTON UI_NEXT,'Font display', 180,238,126,24
 UI_BUTTON UI_PREV,'Object Config', 3,238,126,24

UI_PAGE 3 !------------------------------------------------
IF objtyp='Cube'      THEN odstr='Use a cubic PRISM'
IF objtyp='Cylinder'  THEN odstr='Make with CYLIND'
IF objtyp='Sphere'    THEN odstr='Make it with SPHERE'
IF objtyp='Capsule'   THEN odstr='Use CYLIND + ELLIPS'
IF objtyp='Dome'      THEN odstr='Use REVOLVE+CUTPOLYA'
IF objtyp='Pyramid'   THEN odstr='Easy! Use PYRAMID!'
IF objtyp='Cone'      THEN odstr='Easy! Make with CONE'
IF objtyp='Torus'     THEN odstr='REVOLVE a circle'
IF objtyp='Tincan'    THEN odstr='Circular hollow PRISM'
IF objtyp='Big_Ell'   THEN odstr='Make it with a PRISM'
IF objtyp='Dish'      THEN odstr='Use CONE and REVOLVE'
IF objtyp='Handle'    THEN odstr='Use PRISM, CYLIND, ELBOW'

spa=16             !Pixels per line for text
textstring1='Your object is a '+objtyp
UI_STYLE 2,0    !title of page
UI_OUTFIELD 'Font display',4,16+5,150,24
UI_SEPARATOR 4,38,300,38

!Display of random sizes + styles
FOR k=44 TO 210 STEP spa*2
   UI_STYLE    INT(RND(3)),INT(RND(5))
   UI_OUTFIELD textstring1,4,k,156,spa
   UI_STYLE    INT(RND(3)),INT(RND(5))
   UI_OUTFIELD odstr,4,k+spa,156,spa
   NEXT k
```

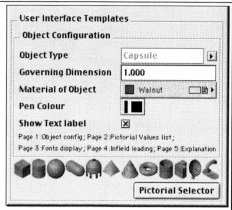

1 Here, I have used variables called 'led' and 'dy' so that I can experiment with different Leadings. As there are 5 pages, an OUTfield in small font tells the user what the other pages contain. The UI_PICT will squash down to the specified size 300x30, but if you make it that size first, there is less distortion and quicker display.

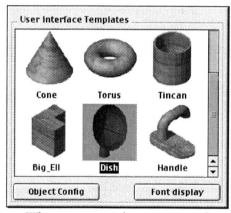

2 When you get it right, it is amazing how short the script needs to be! See next page for additional guidelines on making Pictorial Valuelists.

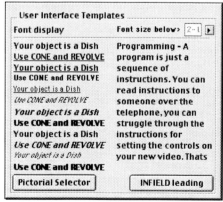

3 This page displays a variety of font sizes and styles (using random numbers) and shows how an IF statement can be used to change the contents of the dialog box. As 'fontui' for the font size is only used in the UI boxes, it remains hidden in the parameter box.

```
!Long Text block with Font selection
UI_STYLE 0,1   !select font size for text
UI_OUTFIELD 'Font size below>',160,16+5,99,20
UI_INFIELD  'fontui',260,16,46,20
x=SPLIT(fontui,'%n',fntui)
UI_STYLE fntui,0
UI_OUTFIELD 'Programming - A program is just a sequence of
instructions. You can read instructions to someone over the
telephone, you can struggle through the instructions for setting
the controls on your new video. Thats a program!',160,44,148,180
  UI_BUTTON UI_NEXT, 'INFIELD leading',180,238,126,24
  UI_BUTTON UI_PREV, 'Pictorial Selector',  3,238,126,24

UI_PAGE 4 !----------------------------------------------
  UI_STYLE 2,0    !Title of page
UI_OUTFIELD 'INFIELD Leading',4,16+5,150,22
UI_OUTFIELD 'Font size below>',130,16+5,99,22
UI_INFIELD  'fontui',215,16,90,24
x=SPLIT(fontui,'%n',fntui)
  UI_STYLE fntui,0
IF fntui=0 THEN spa=24  !Pixels per line for INFIELD
IF fntui=1 THEN spa=19  !Pixels per line for INFIELD
IF fntui=2 THEN spa=27  !Pixels per line for INFIELD
leding="Leading="+STR(spa,2,0) !print string in box
UI_SEPARATOR 4,40,300,40

FOR k=45 TO 210 STEP spa
  UI_OUTFIELD 'Infield size',4,k+5,124,spa
  UI_OUTFIELD leding,215,k+5,90,spa
  UI_INFIELD  'dm',130,k,80,spa
  NEXT k
  UI_BUTTON UI_NEXT, 'Explanation',180,238,126,24
  UI_BUTTON UI_PREV, 'Font leading',3,238,126,24

UI_PAGE 5 !----------------------------------------------
  UI_STYLE 2,0
UI_OUTFIELD 'Explanation of the UI_exercise', 12,20,290,24
UI_STYLE 0,0
UI_OUTFIELD 'The first page was a typical page that you might
use to replace the normal parameters box.', 12,36,290,28
UI_OUTFIELD 'The second page was a demonstration of a Pictorial
Values List, e.g. for a Door library.', 12,68,290,28
UI_OUTFIELD 'The third page was a demonstration of ways of
defining fonts and styles. Try changing the font. It also demon-
strates IF statements in the User interface', 12,100,290,42
UI_OUTFIELD 'The fourth page demonstrated the different leadings
of INFIELD boxes for different fonts. Leading is the space between
successive lines of type.', 12,146,290,42
UI_OUTFIELD 'The fifth page demonstrated how you can use a page
of the User Interface to provide a detailed users manual.',
12,192,290,28
  UI_STYLE 0,1
UI_OUTFIELD 'Good luck with your attempts to build the User
Interface!',160,220,140,42
  UI_BUTTON UI_PREV,"INFIELD leading",3,238,126,24
```

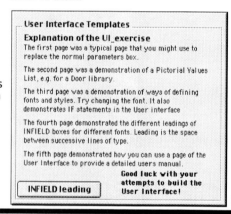

4 Note that by using the SPLIT command, one can avoid several lines of IF statements to parse Value list of font sizes. When you change the font size, the box is reformatted to demonstrate the importance of Leading. Long texts have to be written till they hit the extreme right hand end of the script window – maximum 550 letters!

5 Getting started with the User Interface is a bit painful, but in some ways, it's just another form of 2D scripting, and gets easier as you do more of it. You also find that your vocabulary of things-you-can-do-with-UI gets more sophisticated as you do more of them.

Right: The new look of User Interface enabled Library objects

Mental Health Warning!

ALTHOUGH I have used IF-statements (and so do Graphisoft in the manual), **DO NOT USE IF-statements in the UI script unless strictly to do with UI matters.** IF-statements regarding parameters can result in a crash in which half or more of the parameters delete themselves, and the ones which are left change to values of zero or near-infinity. Parameter changes and error checks can be made in the PARAMETERS script.

Although the guidelines here are meant to make it easier, you still need a paper and pen and a lot of trial and error to get the UI just right. Build ALL the parameters you are going to want first before you design or build the UI; adding latecomers to the UI is a painful nuisance. And after you have saved graphics for use in the UI, don't forget to load libraries.

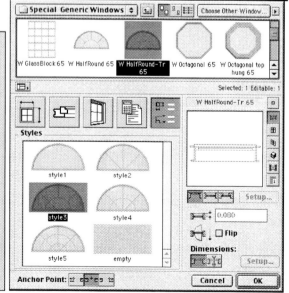

GDL Cookbook: User's Logbook

Your Name:

Support address of the Cookbook author:
davidnc@innotts.co.uk / david@the-object-factory.com

Exercises tackled (in depth) in the Cookbook with dates:

Date started GDL:

Date started with the GDL Cookbook:

Objects created off user's own initiative, with dates:

Note of bugs, errors or omissions in the GDL Cookbook
Please send these to David NC when you have accumulated enough: your report may be influential in later editions.